Space

D1235656

OXFORD **PHILOSOPHICAL** CONCEPTS

OXFORD **PHILOSOPHICAL** CONCEPTS

Space

A HISTORY

Edited by Andrew Janiak

OXFORD
UNIVERSITY PRESS

OXFORD
UNIVERSITY PRESS

Oxford University Press is a department of the University of Oxford. It furthers
the University's objective of excellence in research, scholarship, and education
by publishing worldwide. Oxford is a registered trade mark of Oxford University
Press in the UK and certain other countries.

Published in the United States of America by Oxford University Press
198 Madison Avenue, New York, NY 10016, United States of America.

CIP data is on file at the Library of Congress
ISBN 978-0-19-991412-8 (pbk.)
ISBN 978-0-19-991410-4 (hbk.)

1 3 5 7 9 8 6 4 2

Paperback printed by Marquis, Canada
Hardback printed by Bridgeport National Bindery, Inc., United States of America

Contents

Series Editor's Foreword

Oxford Philosophical Concepts (OPC) offers an innovative approach to philosophy's past and its relation to other disciplines. As a series, it is unique in exploring the transformations of central philosophical concepts from their ancient sources to their modern use.

OPC has several goals: to make it easier for historians to contextualize key concepts in the history of philosophy, to render that history accessible to a wide audience, and to enliven contemporary discussions by displaying the rich and varied sources of philosophical concepts still in use today. The means to these goals are simple enough: eminent scholars come together to rethink a central concept in philosophy's past. The point of this rethinking is not to offer a broad overview but to identify problems the concept was originally supposed to solve and investigate how approaches to them shifted over time, sometimes radically.

Recent scholarship has made evident the benefits of reexamining the standard narratives about western philosophy. OPC's editors look beyond the canon and explore their concepts over a wide philosophical landscape. Each volume traces a notion from its inception as a solution to specific problems through its historical transformations to its modern use, all the while acknowledging its historical context. Each OPC volume is a history of its concept in that it tells a story about changing solutions to its well-defined problem. Many editors have found it appropriate to include long-ignored writings drawn from the Islamic and Jewish traditions and the philosophical contributions of women. Volumes also explore ideas drawn from Buddhist, Chinese, Indian, and other philosophical cultures when doing so adds an especially helpful new perspective. By combining scholarly innovation with focused and astute analysis, OPC encourages a deeper understanding of our philosophical past and present.

One of the most innovative features of Oxford Philosophical Concepts is its recognition that philosophy bears a rich relation to art, music, literature, religion, science, and other cultural practices. The series speaks to the need for informed interdisciplinary exchanges. Its editors assume that the most difficult and profound philosophical ideas can be made comprehensible to a large audience and that materials not strictly philosophical often bear a significant relevance to philosophy. To this end, each OPC volume includes Reflections. These are short stand-alone essays written by specialists in art, music, literature, theology, science, or cultural studies that reflect on the concept from their own disciplinary perspectives. The goal of these essays is to enliven, enrich, and exemplify the volume's concept and reconsider the boundary between philosophical and extraphilosophical materials. OPC's Reflections display the benefits of using philosophical concepts and distinctions in areas that are not strictly philosophical and encourage philosophers to move beyond the borders of their discipline as presently conceived.

The volumes of OPC arrive at an auspicious moment. Many philosophers are keen to invigorate the discipline. OPC aims to provoke philosophical imaginations by uncovering the brilliant twists and unforeseen turns of philosophy's past.

Christia Mercer
Gustave M. Berne Professor of Philosophy
Columbia University in the City of New York

Abbreviations and References

Ancient Works

DK = *Fragmente der Vorsokratiker*. Edited by H. Diels and W. Kranz. Berlin, 1951.

Aristotle

References to works by Aristotle use so-called Bekker numbers, which correspond to the pagination and line numbers of Bekker's 1830 edition of the text. These will be found in the margins of any reliable edition or translation.

Descartes

AT = *Oeuvres de Descartes*. Edited by Charles Adam and Paul Tannery. Paris: Vrin, 1996.

H = *Treatise of Man*. Edited and translated by Thomas Steele Hall. Cambrdige, MA: Harvard University Press, 1972. The title of this work is more usually translated as *Treatise on Man*, and that form is used herein.

O = *Discourse on Method, Optics, Geometry and Meteorology*. Translated by Paul J. Olscamp. New York: Bobbs-Merrill, 1965. The title of Descartes's *Dioptrique* is translated herein as *Dioptrics* (as opposed to *Optics*).

Kant

A/B: A = corresponds to the first-edition pagination of Kant, *Critique of Pure Reason* (1781); B = corresponds to the second-edition pagination of the *Critique* (1787).

References to all other texts in Kant's corpus are to the volume and page numbers in the Akademie edition, *Kants gesammelte Schriften* (Berlin, 1902–).

Plato

References to works by Plato use so-called Stephanus numbers, which correspond to the pagination and line numbers of a famous Renaissance edition of Plato's texts that appeared in the late sixteenth century. That edition used the letters a–e to split up sections of the text. Any reliable edition or translation will include these numbers in the margins.

Contributors

MICHAEL FRIEDMAN is Suppes Professor of Philosophy of Science at Stanford University and works on the history and philosophy of science from the sixteenth through the twentieth centuries. The author or editor of eleven books and numerous articles, Friedman is a leading figure in philosophy of science, in the study of Kant's thought, and in the interpretation of logical positivism and its aftermath. His books include *Foundations of Space-Time Theories* (Princeton, 1983), *Kant and the Exact Sciences* (Harvard, 1992), and *Kant's Construction of Nature* (Cambridge, 2012).

BANU GÖKARIKSEL is Professor of Geography and the Royster Distinguished Professor for Graduate Education at the University of North Carolina, Chapel Hill. The author of numerous articles concerning women and society in the Islamic world, Gökariksel's research has been funded by the National Science Foundation and has been covered widely in the international press, including by NPR and *Le Monde*.

JEREMY GRAY is Emeritus Professor of Mathematics at the Open University in England. A leading figure in the history of modern mathematics, he is the author of numerous papers and many books, including *Henri Poincaré: A Scientific Biography* (Princeton, 2012), *The Hilbert Challenge* (Oxford, 2000), and *Ideas of Space: Euclidean, Non-Euclidean and Relativistic* (Oxford, 1989).

JENNIFER GROH is a professor of psychology and neuroscience and of neurobiology at Duke University. Groh's lab is funded by the National Institutes of Health and the National Science Foundation. She is the author of numerous scientific papers and of *Making Space: How the Brain Knows Where Things Are* (Harvard, 2014).

MARI YOKO HARA is a Mellon Postdoctoral Fellow in art history at Columbia University. The author of several papers on Renaissance art history, she is currently writing a book about Baldassare Peruzzi and the art of painter-architects in sixteenth-century Italy.

GEORGE HART taught engineering and computer science for many years at Columbia University and Stony Brook University. He is now a freelance mathematical sculptor, with sculptures currently on display at universities around the United States. He is also the author of many papers and of *Multidimensional Analysis: Algebras and Systems for Science and Engineering* (Springer, 1995).

GARY HATFIELD is the Adam Seybert Professor in Intellectual and Moral Philosophy at the University of Pennsylvania. The author or editor of eight books on modern science and philosophy, Hatfield is a leading figure in history and philosophy of science, with a focus on the history of natural philosophy, theories of perception, and the philosophy of psychology. His books include *The Natural and the Normative: Theories of Spatial Perception from Kant to Helmholtz* (MIT, 1990) and *Perception and Cognition: Essays in the Philosophy of Psychology* (Oxford, 2009).

NICOLE HELLER is a museum fellow and the curator of the Anthropocene at the Carnegie Museum of Natural History in Pittsburgh. Heller holds a PhD in biological sciences from Stanford University and was previously a Google fellow for science communication.

ANDREW JANIAK is Professor and Chair of philosophy at Duke University, where he is also a Bass fellow. Janiak is the author or editor of four books about Isaac Newton and modern philosophy, including *Newton as Philosopher* (Cambridge, 2008) and *Newton* (Wiley-Blackwell, 2015). He is also the co-leader of Project Vox, a digital humanities endeavor designed to promote teaching and research of neglected philosophical work by early modern women.

MI GYUNG KIM is a professor of history at North Carolina State University. A leading historian of chemistry, she is the author of many papers concerning the history of chemistry and the place of science in the French enlightenment.

She is also the author of *Affinity, That Elusive Dream: A Genealogy of the Chemical Revolution* (MIT Press, 2003) and *The Imagined Empire: Balloon Enlightenments in Revolutionary Europe* (Pittsburgh, 2016).

MARIJE MARTIJN is the C. J. de Vogel Professor of Ancient and Patristic Philosophy at Vrije Universiteit Amsterdam. The author of numerous papers on ancient mathematics, science, and philosophy, Martijn is also the author of *Proclus on Nature* (Brill, 2010).

BARBARA M. SATTLER is a senior lecturer in philosophy at the University of St. Andrews in Scotland, having previously taught at Yale University and the University of Illinois at Urbana-Champaign. She is the author of numerous articles concerning science and philosophy in antiquity, including papers on Aristotle, Plato, Parmenides, and Zeno. She is also the author of *The Concept of Motion in Ancient Greek Thought: foundations in logic, method and mathematics* (Cambridge, 2020).

EDITH DUDLEY SYLLA is Professor Emerita of History at North Carolina State University, where she taught history of science for many years. The author of numerous articles and the editor of several books, Sylla is one of the world's leading historians focusing on medieval science. She has written on a wide range of topics stretching from the thirteenth to the eighteenth century and has discussed the thought of many prominent historical figures, including Jacob Bernoulli, John Buridan, William of Ockham, and Nicole Oresme.

Introduction

Andrew Janiak

Space is ubiquitous. So are spatial concepts. Scholars in architecture, art history, mathematics, cosmology, ecology, neuroscience, sculpture, chemistry, and geography employ concepts of space and articulate concepts with spatial components. It would be hopeless to list them all, and equally fruitless to search for patterns among them, or for their common node. One needs a specific focal point. In our case, the history of philosophy—and the ways in which philosophers in different eras have pondered space—is our focus. We will also consider some of the myriad intersections between philosophical discussions of space and treatments in other disciplines and enterprises. Some of these intersections are obvious: philosophers and scientists in the nineteenth century were deeply influenced by and played important roles in articulating the new non-Euclidean geometry developed by mathematicians like Bolyai and Lobachevsky. The intertwining of

Andrew Janiak, *Introduction* In: *Space*. Edited by: Andrew Janiak, Oxford University Press (2020). © Oxford University Press.

DOI: 10.1093/oso/9780199914104.003.0001

the history of geometry with the history of philosophical treatments of space is intimate and obvious. Other intersections are less obvious: Were early modern philosophers influenced by the development of Renaissance perspective? How did the emergence of microscopy affect philosophical conceptions of space? We will emphasize some of these connections through the essays on philosophers' views in various eras and through our short essays, or "Reflections," interspersed throughout the volume.

Since our volume is organized historically, our first task is to avoid a harmfully anachronistic presupposition in approaching space. We do not presuppose that each era broached in this book—from early antiquity to modernity—involved philosophers who thought about what *we* now call *space*. Nor do we assume that there is a *single* concept of space whose history we can trace. There may very well be concepts with an unambiguous history that can be traced through time, but SPACE is not one of them.[1] Instead, we have jointly adopted several guiding questions, including the following: Did philosophers in previous eras think about something called space? Did they have a concept of space at all? Or were they primarily thinking about concepts with spatial significance, such as the concept of an object, a person, a city, or a place? Just as important, did they regard space as a significant topic of philosophical reflection, analysis, and debate? If they did, was that due to reasons internal to philosophy or ones arising from theology, mathematics, natural science, or elsewhere? In this sense, although our official title is *Space: A History*, we might also embrace the alternative, *Space: The Emergence of a Concept*. Unsurprisingly, it took centuries for our modern SPACE to emerge, or perhaps for a single concept to emerge. Tracing that emergence is our joint task in this volume.

Another potential anachronism, and attendant confusion, arises from the insistence on a historical perspective for philosophy, coupled

---

1 Following convention, the concept is hereafter denoted SPACE, thereby distinguishing it from both space itself and the word "space."

with the failure to apply the same wise rule to other disciplines. For instance, we may insist that philosophers in the first half of the seventeenth century treated space differently from those in the second half, and then forget to treat accompanying developments in, say, experimental technology with the same historical care. Perhaps for obvious reasons, it is especially important for our approach to recognize historically shifting conceptions of geometry during the epochs under study in this volume. To a contemporary reader, geometry is important in this context because it just is the science of space. Concomitantly, it may seem obvious that the approach outlined in Euclid's *Elements* was the first systematic attempt to understand the nature of space. But in earlier historical periods, philosophers and mathematicians did not necessarily regard Euclid as providing a doctrine or treatment of something called space or as a description of what we would call physical space (as Jeremy Gray discusses in his Reflection). That may sound odd to modern ears, but caution in this area seems to be warranted by the ancient and medieval evidence. Indeed, some influential scholarship suggests that in previous periods in history, Euclid was sometimes regarded as discussing not space (or SPACE) but the construction of figures and their various properties. A fully historical approach, then, will provide not only a historically precise conception of philosophy but an equally precise, historically rich conception of the various disciplines with which philosophers engaged in dialogue throughout the ages.

The Oxford Philosophical Concepts series includes a novel element mentioned earlier: it enriches the chapters written on different eras in philosophical history with short essays called "Reflections" that tackle related developments in myriad other fields. The Reflections in this volume fall into two broad categories. First, some of them are easily paired with closely related philosophical essays. Because Gary Hatfield's chapter concerns philosophical theories of vision and optics from the Middle Ages to modernity, it is nicely paired both with Mari Hara's essay on the use of perspective in Renaissance painting and with

Jennifer Groh's contribution on the understanding of visual space in contemporary neuroscience. The art historian Hara documents the ways in which Italian Renaissance artists famously and influentially employed their knowledge of geometry and optics to introduce linear perspective into their painting and architecture, thereby bridging the expected gap between art and science. Groh's essay, written from the perspective of a neuroscientist, shows the ways in which populations of neurons form a map that mirrors the perceived topography of some region in the world. The historian of science Mi Gyung Kim's Reflection on early modern laboratory spaces, which discusses figures such as Boyle and Newton, is easily paired with Andrew Janiak's chapter on early modern conceptions of space. Kim shows that the early modern chemical laboratory contained equipment—such as Boyle's air pump— designed to operationalize the notion of empty space, but also served to represent an ideal social order. In another case, two Reflections intersect nicely with one another. Jeremy Gray concisely characterizes the fascinating and complex story of how mathematicians came to regard Euclidean geometry as merely one among a set of possible geometries, some of which involved a different notion of lines than is contained in the famous parallel postulate. The veritable explosion of philosophical ideas that accompanied this story—from the development of conventionalism to the rethinking of a priori knowledge—is well known. The Reflection by the mathematical sculptor George Hart brings Gray's discussion into dialogue with contemporary artistry by showing how one can sculpt objects to express intriguing features both of Euclidean and of non-Euclidean spaces. The remarkable images of Hart's sculptures in this volume will assist readers in imagining a wide array of spaces.

The Reflections in the second broad category are not paired one-to-one with our philosophical chapters or with other Reflections. They approach space from the perspective of other disciplines—especially cultural geography and ecology—that raise intriguing questions, ones that philosophers may have overlooked. These Reflections help to enrich our overall treatment of space and its concepts over the centuries. The Reflection by the cultural geographer Banu Gökariksel discusses public spaces in Istanbul from a sociopolitical perspective, indicating (e.g.) that a particular place within a global city can be gendered in various ways that are rendered legible primarily through detailed scholarship on the group. Philosophers and mathematicians have often noted that a space might be *occupied* or *empty, curved* or *flat*; it expands their imaginations to show how a space might be *gendered*. The Reflection by the biologist Nicole Heller, which concerns the methods used in ecology to infer evolutionary facts from the patterns of organisms in space, serves to challenge philosophical assumptions about what counts as an object or a body occupying space. When the object in question is an ant colony—it is the entity falling under selection pressure rather than the individual organism—we encounter intriguing questions about the sense in which it behaves both like a single object occupying some large space and like a series of autonomous entities, each moving through space independently of the others. Clearly, ant colonies pose tough questions for the metaphysically minded.

When we jointly conceived of this volume's contents, it was initially tempting to include only Reflections that would pair neatly with our philosophical essays. But we resisted the temptation. Just as the first set of Reflections may enrich the way in which philosophers think about their own history, the second set of Reflections may prod philosophers to think about space from a novel perspective. After all, philosophers may not ordinarily think that a space can be gendered and that a location can help to constitute one's gender identity. So we include these disciplinarily varied and highly creative Reflections to avoid the attractive, but ultimately unwise, plan of neatly matching the contents of each chapter with a specific and clearly related Reflection. It might make sense to approach certain concepts, especially concepts that are primarily or solely philosophical in character, in that way—one thinks of consequentialism or idealism—but philosophers do not hold exclusive, or even primary, sway over the concept of space. They never have.

Indeed, philosophers have thought about space in considerable depth over the centuries, but so have architects and geographers, biologists and geometers, artists and physicists. Our Reflections do not *comprehensively* represent these various disciplinary approaches to space, which may be an impossible task, but they do provide an entrée into a wider world, enriching the set of possible ideas about space a philosopher might have in her scholarly repertoire.

Even a causal reader will notice that our treatment of SPACE ends in the high Enlightenment with the work of Immanuel Kant. We have chosen not to bring the discussion up to the present. This choice is not intended to signify that philosophers and their compatriots simply stopped thinking about space after Kant. In a way, it is meant to signify, or to admit, something like the very opposite! Space became more important after Kant, not less. First of all, as is evident already in the "Transcendental Aesthetic," the first main section of the *Critique of Pure Reason* (first edition, 1781), Kant placed the discussion of space at the very heart of his philosophical revolution. His treatment of the representation of space—contending that it is a pure intuition rather than an empirical representation of any kind, or a concept (*Begriff*) of any kind—is already understood to undergird transcendental idealism in some significant ways. Second, this emphasis on space and its representation was prescient: philosophical developments (following Kant's work) conspired with parallel developments in natural science and mathematics to ensure that space would remain a major topic of consideration throughout the nineteenth and twentieth centuries. As Gray chronicles in his Reflection, the nineteenth century saw the rise of non-Euclidean geometry, a revolutionary development involving the work of Bolyai, Lobachevsky, and Gauss. This striking change in mathematics was perhaps overshadowed by the even more impressive beginning of the new century: by 1905 Einstein's first revolutionary ideas, contained in the *special* theory of relativity, taught the world to speak of "space-time" rather than space and time separately. A mere decade later, Einstein's second burst of revolutionary ideas, expressed in his *general* theory, meant that space would forever be thought of as exhibiting non-Euclidean features (such as variable curvature) based on the distribution of mass-energy. These developments were not merely revolutionary in the sense that they overturned centuries of assumptions in mathematics, philosophy, and science—they went so far as to trespass the bounds of what had been assumed to be possible at all. It's shocking enough to hear that Euclid did not have the final word on geometry after roughly two thousand years; it's another thing entirely to learn that the real world is non-Euclidean and that space itself interacts causally with material objects on a vast, cosmological scale. These are ideas that Isaac Newton would not have dreamed of on his wildest day.

Given all the excitement concerning space in the nineteenth and twentieth centuries, the reader may wonder why this volume ends just before these developments took shape. Intriguingly, these developments are not merely exciting per se; they are intimately connected—one might say, internally related—to the development of analytic philosophy itself. As is well known, analytic philosophy emerged in the early twentieth century in part through the influence of logical positivism on the pragmatism-infused thought of Americans like W. V. O. Quine and many others. And for its part, logical positivism was centrally concerned with the revolutionary developments in mathematics and science during its own heyday, developments in which SPACE played a leading role. It is no coincidence, for instance, that Moritz Schlick, a founding member of the Vienna Circle, published one of the very first books concerned with the general theory of relativity (in 1917), with Hans Reichenbach publishing a distinctive treatment of relativity just three years later.[2] Similarly, Rudolf Carnap's most important early

---

2 Moritz Schlick's *Raum und Zeit in der gegenwärtigen Physik* (Springer, 1917) went into several editions; by 1920 it was already on its third edition and was translated into English that same year by Henry Brose of Christ Church, Oxford, as *Space and Time in Contemporary Physics* (reprinted by Dover in 1963). Schlick's account was certainly tracking "contemporary physics": the edition of 1920 had to be changed to reflect the remarkable confirmation of Einstein's general theory of relativity the year before! See also Hans Reichenbach, *Relativitätstheorie und Erkenntnis apriori*

publication, which involved the intersection of philosophy, physics, and mathematics, was entitled *Der Raum* (Space) and appeared just a few years after Schlick's work.[3] By the end of the 1920s, Reichenbach had already contributed another major work on space and time.[4] Since the discussion of space and time was central to science and mathematics during the Vienna Circle, they were central to the newly emerging philosophy of that time. In tandem, since philosophy of science was central to the development of analytic philosophy in the English-speaking world in the previous century, and space and time, in turn, have always been central topics within philosophy of science, the literature within analytic philosophy on space and time is vast.[5]

These facts about the twentieth century mean that recent developments concerning space have received the lion's share of the attention in the past few decades. The interested reader will have no trouble finding philosophical accounts of space and time from just about any moment in the past century or more. However, scholarly treatments of space and of SPACE in antiquity, the medieval period, the Renaissance, and the early modern period are much less common. In this way, our volume can serve as a kind of supplement to the existing

(Berlin: Springer, 1920), which was translated by Maria Reichenbach in 1960 as *The Theory of Relativity and a priori Knowledge* (Berkeley: University of California Press).

3 Rudolf Carnap, *Der Raum: Ein Beitrag zur Wissenschaftslehre*, Kant-Studien Ergänzungshefte 56 (Berlin: Reuther and Reichard, 1922).

4 Hans Reichenbach, *Philosophie der Raum-Zeit-Lehre* (Berlin: De Gruyter, 1928), translated in 1957 by Maria Reichenbach and J. Freund as *The Philosophy of Space and Time* (New York: Dover).

5 In addition to the translations of important publications by members of the Vienna Circle (see, e.g., notes 2 and 4 above), major works in English-speaking philosophy dealing with space and time published over the past fifty years include the following: Adolf Grünbaum, *Philosophical Problems of Space and Time* (New York: Knopf, 1963); Howard Stein, "Newtonian Space-time," *Texas Quarterly* 10 (1967): 174–200; Bas van Fraassen, *An Introduction to the Philosophy of Time and Space* (New York: Random House, 1970); Larry Sklar, *Space, Time and Spacetime* (Berkeley: University of California Press, 1974); Jill Van Buroker, *Space and Incongruence* (Dordrecht: Reidel, 1981); Michael Friedman, *Foundations of Space-time Theories* (Princeton, NJ: Princeton University Press, 1983); John Earman, *World Enough and Spacetime* (Cambridge, MA: MIT Press, 1989); Robert DiSalle, *Understanding Spacetime* (Cambridge, UK: Cambridge University Press, 2006). The literature is simply too vast to do it justice here.

philosophical scholarship.[6] The monumental importance of the twentieth century for thinking about space cannot be denied. But perhaps we can supplement our knowledge of that time by producing a volume in which we give pride of place to figures whose ideas about space are less well known. Hence in this volume, in lieu of discussing Riemann and Einstein, Poincaré and Minkowski, we emphasize the likes of Aristotle and Proclus, Hobbes and Kant, Ibn al-Haytham and Leibniz.

One happy consequence of our approach is that our volume exhibits a kind of intellectual unity. For all of the figures in this volume, geometry was Euclidean, space and time were separate things, and both geometrical space and the physical space in which we live could be fundamentally understood through the kinds of reasoning already codified in antiquity. Naturally, the figures discussed in this volume engaged in vociferous disputes on a wide range of topics: the finitude of the world, space's basic relation to matter, the possibility of the vacuum, God's relation to space and the world, and so on. But all of these disputes occurred within certain basic intellectual confines. Obviously, Euclid and Aristotle lived in a fundamentally different world than Kant, but in this respect their intellectual horizons were remarkably and profoundly aligned. For this reason, the Reflections by Gray and Hart, which concern the emergence of non-Euclidean geometry in history and the possibility of its representation through mathematically sophisticated sculpture, serve to form a kind of intellectual boundary for our volume. Since they discuss the developments in mathematics that would help to usher in a new world, the world that we now occupy,

---

6 Even the very best works, ones with the most sophisticated historical accounts of the development of physics and concomitant ideas about space and time, will tend to give pride of place to the nineteenth and twentieth centuries, even while acknowledging the significance of earlier ideas and figures. Although they occupy decidedly distinct philosophical perspectives, Cushing and Torretti both illustrate this broad point in their works from the very late twentieth century. See James Cushing, *Philosophical Concepts in Physics* (Cambridge, UK: Cambridge University Press, 1998), and Roberto Torretti, *The Philosophy of Physics* (Cambridge, UK: Cambridge University Press, 1999), both of which begin with antiquity (Aristotle, Ptolemy, etc.) but move quickly on to Newton and then beyond.

they are profoundly important. But from the perspective of the historical figures that appear throughout our volume, these developments were not far off on the horizon—they were beyond the horizon. Lying beyond the limits of what was considered possible, they occupied an intellectual space exceeding the limits of the human imagination. This volume tries to capture a bit of what it was like to live in that world, which is now long passed.

CHAPTER ONE

Space in Ancient Times

FROM THE BEGINNING TO ARISTOTLE

Barbara Sattler

1. INTRODUCTION

In the roughly four hundred years from the earliest Greek texts to
Aristotle, many of the most basic questions about space were raised
for the first time in western thought and answered in a great variety of
ways. These are questions such as What is the task of space—is it to answer the question where some body is situated and where it is moving,
or is it rather to delimit one thing from another and thus to be a condition for plurality? Does it have an internal structure? If so, what is
its internal structure like? Is space itself some kind of a bodily entity,
or is it nonbodily, as, for example, a vacuum? And what do the answers
to these questions tell us about its ontological status? Is it of the same
status as the bodily things? Is it something more fundamental, given
that everything seems to need to be somewhere in order to exist? Or

Barbara Sattler, *Space in Ancient Times* In: *Space*. Edited by: Andrew Janiak, Oxford University Press
(2020). © Oxford University Press.
DOI: 10.1093/oso/9780199914104.003.0002

is it just a feature of bodily things and as such ontologically dependent on bodies?

While most of these questions will at least be touched upon, I will concentrate here on one important stream in the development of spatial thinking during the early ancient period: the establishment of space as a magnitude independent of time that can nevertheless be combined with time. If we look at prephilosophical or the earliest philosophical accounts of space, for example, at Hesiod's and Anaximander's, we see that time and space (and sometimes also matter) are often not clearly distinguished: something is described as far off, where this might be meant either temporally or spatially or both. And Anaximander's *apeiron* seems to be the basic ground out of which everything develops, materially, temporally, as well as spatially. This lack of a clear distinction between time and space leads to problems when we try to give an account of motion, as motion requires an understanding of the relationship between time and space. With the atomists Leucippus and Democritus we will see a first attempt to develop a clear notion of space in contrast to matter. But the atomists are completely silent on the notion of time. And simply omitting one of the two magnitudes, time or space, when accounting for motion leads to another kind of problem, as Zeno's paradoxes will show.

The next steps in this development can be seen with Plato's *Timaeus*: drawing on atomistic as well as Pythagorean ideas concerning space, it posits time and space as two completely independent magnitudes. Time is created and introduced in order to make the universe more intelligible, while space—Plato's receptacle, which some scholars have also understood as exhibiting features of matter—is uncreated and an essential part of what Plato's "creator" god starts out with and has to put into order. In fact, time and space are so different that it is unclear how they could be combined at all for the purposes of giving an account of motion.

This task, central for any natural philosophy, is finally tackled in Aristotle's *Physics*. Aristotle's conception of *topos* as the first immobile limit of an object's surrounding is often understood as a mere notion of a vessel. As such it seems not only to be too narrow to be of any use for understanding motion but also to be merely an account of place, not of space. I will show, however, that Aristotle in fact provides us with an understanding of *topos* that prepares the notion of a general frame of reference, which allows for locating things in the world as well as for an account of motion. What enables Aristotle to combine space with time in his account of motion and to reply to Zeno's paradoxes of motion is his understanding of both time and space as continua.

But before we jump into the unfolding of this story, let us start with a few general methodological considerations.

1.1. Methodological Prelude: Problems and Possible Criteria for Space

The period dealt with in this chapter raises at least two serious problems for an investigation of space:

1. Several of the thinkers we will consider do not have an explicit account, notion, or concept of space; explicit discussion of how to understand space only starts with Plato and Aristotle. I hope to show that it is nevertheless fruitful to look at the way pre-Platonic thinkers deal with what we consider to be spatial ideas or notions. But in order to understand how far implicit accounts of space can be found in these thinkers, we ourselves will have to think about possible criteria for space that allow us to identify such spatial notions.

2. Some of the most important spatial terms in Greek in this period—*chôra, topos, diastêma*, and *kenon*—do not necessarily match one to one with our spatial vocabulary.

Let us look at both points in somewhat more detail.

I.I.I. POSSIBLE CRITERIA FOR SPACE

What we understand by space depends, among other things, on how it is related to bodies: Is it itself a body like other physical bodies in the world (presumably just somewhat bigger), as, for example, a container? Or is it genuinely different from ordinary bodies? If the latter, is space just the relation of bodies or its own entity?

Furthermore, we will have to look at the question of whether it has an internal structure and, if so, whether it is orientable, bounded, or infinite, or its opposite. Is it everywhere homogeneous or not, isotropic or anisotropic, continuous or discrete?[1] Does space possess a particular dimension? Is it metrizable?[2] And what are the consequences of assuming space to have a certain structure? For example, if we assume our space to be finite and bounded, it seems that a linear motion will have to stop at a certain point.

The most important point for an understanding of space, however, seems to be the question of what we take its function to be: Is space that in which something can be situated, that in and through which something can move, or that which separates or delimits one thing from another? What we take the main task of space to be will also depend on whether we think of it as physical or mathematical space. As physical space, it should explain at least one decisive aspect of the objects of our experience: either the possibility of their motions or their separateness or (at least in part) their shape. As a mathematical space, on the other hand, one of its main virtues should be that it allows for all possible mathematical constructions in such a way that for whatever construction we perform, we will never run out of space.

However, while *we* take the distinction between mathematical and physical space to be vital, we will have to investigate whether it is at all

---

1 By "isotropy" we normally understand that something exhibits equal properties in all directions, while "homogeneity" means that something is uniform throughout.

2 Some of these features we are more used to from mathematical spaces (e.g., orientability), some from physical ones.

important for the ancients. At least within the Pythagorean tradition this distinction does not seem to be crucial, as one and the same spatial notion, the void, is used to separate mathematical entities as well as sensible things.[3] So we should leave it open as a possibility that our distinction between physical and geometrical space may not be a distinction the ancients would draw.

It might seem that they are compelled to make such a distinction given that the prevailing notions of the universe as the most comprehensive physical space assume it to be finite and bounded, whereas (Euclidean) mathematical space is infinite. However, while this sounds like a screaming tension to us, there does not seem to be an explicit discussion of it in preclassical and classical ancient times; spatial notions are just used by mathematicians as well as by natural philosophers. And while we find an explicit discussion of physical space in Aristotle, we do not have any evidence of a discussion of space by the mathematicians during these times.[4]

1.2. A Brief Look at Some of the Main Spatial Terms

1.2.1. TO KENON

Kenos is normally translated as "empty" or "void," the nominalization of this adjective, *to kenon*, as "the void."[5] In common language only the adjective is used, while the substantive expression is tied to philosophical contexts. In its first philosophically interesting use, with Melissus

---

3 DK 58 B 30.

4 As Max Jammer, *Concepts of Space: The History of Theories of Space in Physics* (Chelmsford, MA: Courier, 2013) points out, also the anisotropy of space with Aristotle and the inhomogeneity of space with Plato seem to make physical space incompatible with the geometrical space used in Greek mathematics (if we can take Euclid's *Elements* as evidence). Aristotle does of course distinguish between physical and mathematical things, but since mathematica are abstractions from physical things, mathematical space is not a separate space over and above the physical one. And for him mathematical space is in fact not infinite but just as big as we need, so he does not face a discrepancy between a finite physical world and an infinite mathematical space.

5 For the discussion of *to kenon*, *chôra*, and *topos* I am especially indebted to Keimpe Algra's *Concepts of Space in Greek Thought* (Leiden: Brill, 1994), chapter 2.

and the atomists, *to kenon* is a physical interpretation of the Eleatic notion of nonbeing, what is not. In accordance with the multifaceted use of nonbeing, *to kenon* gets used in different ways by the atomists, and Aristotle takes up these different notions in his refutation of the void in the *Physics*, where he also points out potential conflicts between them.[6]

In general, *to kenon* means "emptiness"; as such it can refer either to (1) empty extension or space or to (2) a specific empty thing or part of a thing (like an empty vessel).[7] But it can also refer to (3) space or place as such.[8]

1.2.2. *CHÔRA* AND *TOPOS*

Chôra is a two- or three-dimensional extension, which can be occupied. The basic meaning of *chôra* is "land," "region," "ground"; when it is applied to a smaller extension it can also mean "stretch," "field," or "place"—it points out the place where one is or should be. *Topos* is largely used synonymously with *chôra*. But while *chôra* already appears in Homer, *topos* cannot be found before Aeschylus.[9]

As for the relationship of *chôra* and *topos*, people like to translate *chôra* as "space" and *topos* as "place." However, there is no one-to-one match between *topos* and place and *chôra* and space; the adequate translation depends very much on the context.[10] When both are used

---

6 For example, when he uses the notion of a void as an occupier of space against the notion of the void as itself space in 217a4 ff. Aristotle, *Aristotle's Physics: A Revised Text*, ed. W. D. Ross (Oxford: Clarendon Press, 1936).

7 In the first sense it is independent of any possible thing that may be in it; in the second sense, by contrast, it is dependent on the thing that is empty (e.g., on the vessel).

8 Cf., for example, Aristotle's report on such a usage in *Physics*, 214a14.

9 For *chôra* cf., for example, Homer, *Iliad* XXIII, 521, or *Odyssey* VIII, 573; for *topos*, Aeschylus, *The Persians*, 769.

10 In *Timaeus* 19a, for example, Plato talks about the *chôra* of a person in a class society dependent on his ability; we would probably translate it as the "place" (rather than "space") that the less deserving should change with the more deserving. For the relation between *chôra* and *topos* see especially Algra, *Space*, 33–38; also Benjamin Morison, *On Location: Aristotle's Concept of Place* (Oxford: Oxford University Press, 2002), 23, 121–32.

together, *topos* may denote a part of *chôra*. But in contrast to *chôra*, *topos* can also be used to denote relative location or position in relation to a surrounding. And *topos* is often understood to be fully occupied place, while *chôra* as only partly occupied. *Topos* can also denote the underlying extension not of individual things but of the whole universe and is thus used for indicating what we would call "space."

With the Hellenistic schools, the Epicureans and the early Stoics, *chôra*, *topos*, and *kenon* become technical terms. *Topos* refers to the space that is occupied by a body and *kenon* to the space that is not occupied by a body. For the Epicureans *chôra* indicates the space a body is moving through,[11] while for the Stoics *chôra* is an interval partly occupied by a body and partly unoccupied.[12] But the time we are looking at, which is before the early Stoics and Epicureans, does not use these terms in a fixed, technical way.

1.2.3. *DIASTÊMA*

Diastêma basically means "distance." It can refer to distance in general or to a specific distance, as, for example, the distance and hence interval between notes in music or the distance between the center of a circle and any point on its circumference, hence the radius. These distances need not be spatial; for example, the *diastêma* between two numbers such as 1 and 2 is what we would understand as the interval between the two numbers.[13] But it is prominently used also for spatial extension, such as the spatial extension between bodies, and also covers what we would call spatial dimensions: length, breadth, and depth.[14]

---

11 In this way the Middle Ages also employed the distinction between place, which refers to location, and space, which is employed in contexts of motion.

12 Cf., for example, Sextus Empiricus, *Adversus mathematicos* 10.2–4, in *Sexti Empirici Opera* (Teubner: Leipzig, 1914–61); Richard Bett, ed. and trans., *Sextus Empiricus: Against the Logicians* (Cambridge, UK: Cambridge University Press, 2005).

13 See, for example, Aristotle, *Physics* 202a18.

14 See, for example, Aristotle, *Physics*, 209a4.

Looking at some of the main spatial terms used by the Greeks up to
Aristotle, we see that the following spatial ideas are of importance: the
term *diastêma* expresses the idea of a distance; *chôra* and *topos* refer to
the notion of a certain extended area, but also to a specific point or section within such an area; and the term *kenos* conveys the idea that there
needs to be something that allows for motion and separation.

2. THE VERY BEGINNING: SPACE IS NOT CLEARLY DISTINGUISHED FROM OTHER MAGNITUDES
2.1. Hesiod

In Hesiod we find the first significant image of space in Greek literature: chasm. But we are also confronted with several passages that do
not clearly distinguish between space and time. Right from the very
beginning of Hesiod's *Theogony*—his cosmogony and genealogy of the
gods—temporal and spatial notions are closely intertwined:

> In truth, first of all Chasm came to be, and then broad-breasted
> Earth, the ever immovable seat of all the immortals who possess
> snowy Olympus's peak and murky Tartarus in the depth of the
> broad-breasted earth, and Eros. . . .
>   From Chasm Erebos and black Night came to be; and then Aether
> and Day came forth from Night, who conceived and bore them after
> mingling in love with Erebos. Earth first of all bore starry Sky, equal
> to herself, to cover her on every side, so that she would be the ever im-
> movable seat for the blessed gods. (lines 116–27, Most's translation)

First of all Chasm came to be. A chasm (Greek, χάος) usually is some
gap within a (or between two) spatially extended things.[15] Hesiod
does not determine the chasm in any way further, but it seems to

---

15 The Greek term χάος is often translated as "chaos." However, in his translation of the *Theogony*
   Most rightly points out that this misleadingly suggests a jumble of disordered matter. By contrast,

be something we would characterize as spatial. Also Aristotle in his *Physics* understands it as a first notion, or proto-notion, of space, since it shows that we need something *where* all other things can then come into being. This fits also with the next thing that comes into being, Gaia, "broad-breasted earth." Thus we start out with the spatial dimensions of depth (chasm) and breadth (broad-breasted). Presumably, if earth has breadth, she also has length, so that we have all three spatial dimensions (or, as is more common in ancient times, all six spatial extensions, since each of our three dimensions has a to and fro).[16] In addition, earth also possesses the height of Mount Olympus, which makes her "the ever immovable seat of all the immortals"; she provides *location* for the gods. Thus also the gods are given a space, snowy Olympus, before they come into being.

Earth is the main spatial reference point: it is from earth that we can say Tartarus is below and, later on, that Ouranos is above. However, while earth is seen as something clearly limited,[17] in contrast to the indeterminate Tartarus, we are not given any clear shape and size of Gaia;[18] all we hear is that Gaia is encircled by Oceanus.

While it seems we get only a spatial setup of the universe in the beginning, it is actually from the very first spatial notion, chasm, that we get the first temporal notion: from chasm *night* came into being. And from night and darkness (Erebos)[19] day is generated, so something else that we would characterize as temporal. There is no indication in the

---

Hesiod's term indicates a gap or opening; cf. also Geoffrey Stephen Kirk, John Earle Raven, and Malcolm Schofield, eds., *The Presocratic Philosophers: A Critical History with a Selection of Texts* (Cambridge, UK: Cambridge University Press, 1983), 37 (hereafter KRS), who point out that the term "chaos" comes from the root *cha*, which means "gape," "gap," or "yawn."

16 Cf., for example, Aristotle's *Physics*, which talks about three dimensions (*Physics* 209a4–6) or six extensions (*Physics* 208b12–14). The dimension of depth has the up and the down, etc.

17 She is limited above by Ouranos, and for her below, we are told in lines 621–22 that Obriareus, Cottos, and Gyges have to dwell under the earth, at the edge or limits of the earth. By contrast, Pontos (sea) is explicitly called boundless (*apeiron*) in line 678.

18 Gaia is on the one hand treated as a person, on the other hand as a place, in which, for example, Zeus can be hidden as in a container (lines 479–83).

19 Erebos is also seen as a *place*; see line 669 and Homer, *Odyssey* X, 528 and XII, 81.

text that now the dimension we are looking at is changing; rather, in the same genealogical way as one spatial notion comes to be from another (e.g., Ouranos from Gaia, heaven from earth), so a temporal notion like night comes to be from the spatial chasm.

That time and space are not strictly distinguished is also clear from other passages in Hesiod. For example, in *Theogony* 721–25 we read:

> For so far is it from earth to murky Tartarus. For a brazen anvil falling down from heaven nine nights and days would reach the earth upon the tenth: and again, a brazen anvil falling from earth nine nights and days would reach Tartarus upon the tenth. Round it runs a fence of bronze, and night spreads in triple line all about it like a neck-circlet, while above grow the roots of the earth and unfruitful sea. (Hugh G. Evelyn-White's translation with alterations)

Tartarus is described as being encircled by a fence—"round it runs a fence of bronze"—which seems normal for something spatial. But then we hear that "night spreads in triple line all about it like a neck-circlet." Thus something that is usually seen as a temporal unit, night, is here treated as something spatial.

Furthermore, the way in which spatial distances between heaven and earth and between earth and Tartarus are determined is in terms of time, namely in terms of anvil days: ten anvil days from sky to earth and ten more from there to Tartarus. An anvil day presumably is the distance an anvil will fall in a day.

You might think that "day" here is a spatial unit, since we are talking about a day in the sense of how much space an anvil covers in a day. Thus a day seems to be a way to determine a unit of space. After all, this is before the time of having an Ur-meter in Paris, with the help of which at least all scientific measurements are done. So perhaps this is a way for Hesiod to indicate for people in Boeotia, as well as in Athens, in Asia Minor, and on the Peloponnese how long this distance is: it is

awfully long.[20] Of course, nobody knew how far an anvil would fall in
a day. (How would they have found out?) So this is not really an easier
way to determine a certain spatial extension. And even if we treat it as
straightforwardly a unit of space, it would still originally be some temporal unit that was then turned into a spatial one.

Summing up, we can say that there are three main spatial notions in
Hesiod:

1. With chasm we get the idea of a *where* in which things can
   come into being. But it is a mere opening that is in no way
   further determined and thus does not provide any further
   spatial orientation.
2. With Tartarus and Ouranus we are given a basic below and
   above and can determine a motion's up and down.
3. With earth all three dimensions are fully unfolded. It is
   extension that is in the foreground and the *possibility* of
   location, not so much actually tracing down a specific spot
   where something is situated.

In spite of these spatial notions, we saw that Hesiod does not strictly
distinguish between spatial and temporal notions, as becomes especially clear when we are dealing with limits. That a clear-cut distinction
between time and space might not be something regarded as a matter
of fact or even desirable we also see in Anaximander.

2.2. Anaximander and the Early Cosmologists

Cosmology can be seen as a, if not the, starting point of philosophy.
Thales, the first philosopher, allegedly predicted a solar eclipse, and

---

20 It is not uncommon also in later times to use the time a normal journey would take in order to indicate a distance; cf., for example, Herodotus II, 5, where he indicates the part above Lake Moeris
that has been gained from the river as "up to a three-day sail."

an important part of what we know about the Ionian thinkers is how they thought the universe was set up. Cosmology naturally not only includes some thinking about space, the spatial arrangement of the world, but it also brings spatial and temporal phenomena together: the locomotion of heavenly bodies and thus a process in space is used to determine temporal units and to calculate time.

Many cosmologies work with the idea of a clear center of the universe, usually the earth. This center may be loaded with a special value, as we see, for example, with the Pythagoreans;[21] it is usually defined not in relation to something else but as an absolute center. But already in Anaximander—and later on also in the atomists—we seem to encounter the idea of infinitely many worlds;[22] in this case we can talk about a center only relative to our world, not of the universe as such.

Thales not only gives an account of the position of the earth in the universe—it is floating on water, that is why it is not "falling down"—but he also seems to have raised an important question for many philosophers to come, namely whether there is one basic entity, principle, or element that can help explain the plurality of phenomena in our world. Thales thinks that there is such a principle and that it is water, which can then turn into the other elements.

To judge from Aristotle's testimony (*Physics* 204b22–29), Anaximander seems to have reacted to this basic question of Thales by criticizing Thales's attempt to establish water as this basic principle: water cannot be a suitable first principle since it is one specific element and thus does not qualify to give rise also to the other elements. If water itself is seen to be cold and wet, for example, it is unclear how its opposite, the dry and warm stuff, can come out

---

21 However, since the center in the universe is the most valuable place, it cannot be occupied by earth for the Pythagoreans, but has to be occupied by what itself is most valuable: by fire.

22 Though there is some dispute among scholars whether Anaximander did indeed assume infinitely many worlds and whether, if he did so, these infinitely many worlds are coexistent or successive; cf. KRS 124ff.

of it. Instead, we need something that itself is not one of the four elements and thus can give rise to all four equally.[23] Anaximander's first principle, the *apeiron*—the Greek term literally means "unlimited," "infinite," or "indeterminate"—can guarantee this by being itself indeterminate and unlimited. By being indeterminate and unlimited the *apeiron* can be the source for the abundant array of phenomena and the incessant process of their coming into being and passing away. It allows for unlimited processes in what we today would see as three different ways, as a material, spatial, and temporal ground of things:[24] "Anaximander . . . said that the source and element of existing things was a certain nature of the *apeiron*, from which come into being the heavens and the world in them. This is *eternal and unageing*, and it also *surrounds all the worlds*" (DK 12 A 11, B2 Hippolytus *Ref.* I, 6, 1–2, my italics).

1. The *apeiron* is that from which (*ex hês*) the heavens and the worlds come into being. Thus it seems to be some matter-like stuff out of which everything can come into being.[25] The generation of everything out of it is possible, since it itself is not determined and limited in the way some particular piece of matter or material thing is.

2. The *apeiron* is "eternal and unageing"[26] and thus temporally infinite. The infinite duration is a necessary condition for the unceasing processes of the phenomenal world.

---

23 We get a reflection of this thought later on, in Plato's account of the receptacle in the *Timaeus*: there all elements come into being in the receptacle, and the receptacle is prepared for this by being itself free of any of the features the elements possess.

24 See DK 12 A 9–11.

25 KRS translate *archê* even as "material principle."

26 For *apeiron* used in a temporal sense, see also fragment DK 12 B3, where it is claimed that the *apeiron* is "immortal . . . and indestructible," and Simplicius in *Phys.* 1121.5 (fr. 113 in KRS), where we hear that infinitely many worlds come to be and pass away *ad infinitum* (*ep' apeiron*).

3. The *apeiron* surrounds all the worlds and thus is the most embracing space.[27] It allows all motions and changes to take place in it.[28]

We see that Anaximander's *apeiron* has spatial, temporal, as well as material connotations. Anaximander himself does not specify whether he takes it to be a material, temporal, or spatial principle. Indeed it seems the *apeiron* can explain the rich plurality of phenomena and their generation exactly by possessing features of all three.

There are of course other spatial notions to be found with the early Presocratics. There is, for example, the Pythagorean notion of the void as a separator: void is understood as a *limit* between numbers[29] and thus as what we would think of as an unphysical notion of space, but it is subsequently also seen as delimiting bodies. Accordingly, there does not seem to be a systematic difference between mathematical and physical space for the Pythagoreans. And there is Parmenides's powerful analogy of a sphere for giving an account of the complete homogeneity of what truly is. However, the next account of a spatial notion I will concentrate on is the one by Parmenides's most important student, Zeno.

---

27 The spatial characteristic of the *apeiron* is stressed by KRS, since they think that the term *apeiron* is used only as indicating spatial infinity before Anaximander. However, KRS themselves suggest that one understanding is to take it as unlimited in extent and *duration*. And Aristotle understands Anaximander's *apeiron* also as material when in *Physics* 203a16ff. and 204b22ff. he understands the *apeiron* as something beyond or besides the elements which are opposed to each other. Also Charles Kahn, *Anaximander and the Origins of Greek Cosmology* (New York: Columbia University Press, 1960), 233 understands the *apeiron* as combining the idea of space with the "the material which fills it."

28 That Anaximander is interested in spatial notions can be seen not only in his interest in cosmology but also in the fact that he is the first thinker reported to conceptualize a map of the area around the Mediterranean Sea in the Greek world; see DK 12 A 1.

29 We usually tend to think that numbers are naturally discrete, so they would not need anything to "separate" them. However, with Philolaos, who is the first Pythagorean of whom we have trustworthy fragments, discreteness seems to be grounded by the void. See C. A. Huffmann, *Philolaus of Croton: Pythagorean and Presocratic. A Commentary on the Fragments and Testimonia with Interpretive Essays* (Cambridge, UK: Cambridge University Press, 1993). Void is seen as granting separation and location (DK 58 B 30) but not yet as a basis for motion.

2.3. Zeno's Paradoxes of Topos and Motion

While with Hesiod and Anaximander we saw that time and space are not clearly distinguished, with Zeno we find the consistency of the notion of motion and of the central spatial notion of *topos* put into question. In his paradox of *topos* Zeno poses the problem of whether place does indeed exist. His paradoxes of motion point out some possible problems with the internal structure of motion and space as well as problems that arise if we give an account of motion solely in terms of the space a motion covers without taking into account the time this motion takes.

2.3.1. ZENO'S PARADOX OF *TOPOS*

We find the earliest explicit formulation of Zeno's *topos* paradox in Aristotle's *Physics* 209a23–25:[30] "Zeno's difficulty demands some explanation: for if everything that exists has a place, it is obvious that also place will have a place, and this will go on *ad infinitum*."

This paradox claims that if everything that exists is in a place and place itself exists, then place will be in a place, *ad infinitum*. Or, in somewhat more detail:

1. Whatever exists is in something.
2. Whatever is in something is in a place.
3. If place is something that exists, it has to be in something and thus in a place.
4. But then place would be in a place, which again would have to be in a place *ad infinitum*.

    And the implicit conclusion to be drawn from this is that place does not exist,[31] because if there were an infinite series,

---

30 For a more detailed discussion of this paradox and another paradox of Zeno connecting *topos* and motion (DK 29 B4), see my paper "Space and Place in Zeno."

31 For filling in yet more details, such as that nothing is in itself and that there are no circular chains of places, see Morison, *On Place*, who devotes his chapter 3 to this paradox. See also Aristotle, *Aristotle's Physics, Books III and IV*, ed. Edward Hussey (Oxford: Oxford University Press, 1983), 110; Jonathan Barnes, *The Presocratic Philosophers* (London: Routledge, 1982), 256–58.

we would not be able to give a genuine answer to the question
where something is.[32]

We can find an implicit variation of this paradox in Plato's *Timaeus*,
when it is claimed in 52b that everything that exists must be in a place
and occupy some space, while what does not do so cannot exist. But in
the *Timaeus* we are told this is a claim in a dreamlike state, since what
truly is—for Plato, the Forms—is not in anything.[33] This variation
in the *Timaeus* attacks the truth of the first premise, that everything
there is has to be in something. Aristotle will block the conclusion by
demonstrating the second premise to be false; in his *Physics* he points
out that things can be *in* something in eight different ways. So while
being in something in the sense of location is a prominent sense, it is
by no means the only one, and place can thus be in something in some
other sense. But Zeno's paradox does raise the question what kind of
existence place has, and we will see the atomists, Plato, and Aristotle
analyzing this problem further.

2.3.2. ZENO'S RUNNER PARADOX

While the paradox of place raises problems we get into if we think
of place or space as being itself a body, Zeno's runner paradox raises
problems if we think of space simply as an extension. It points out the
problematic part-whole relation that an extended spatial magnitude
seems to display, and it shows the problems we get into if in our account of motion we concentrate only on space and leave out time completely. The basic setup of the paradox is as follows.[34]

---

32 Cf. Morison, *On Place,* 92–95.

33 One may object that the Forms could be said to be in the individual things which participate in
them; at least the language of the "presence" of the Forms in the middle Plato might seem to suggest that (as, for example, the *Phaedo*). However, we are also told that the Forms are independent
of this relationship. So while usually they will be present in some individual sensible thing or other,
their existence is in no way dependent on these sensible things. And the sense of "in" in which the
Forms are in a sensible thing is not the local one employed in the second premise.

34 See Aristotle, *Physics* 233a21–26, 239b11–14, and 263a4–11.

If something moves over a certain spatial distance, for instance, a runner wants to cover a certain finite race course, he first has to cover half of this distance. Of the second half, the runner again has to cover the first half, and then again the first half of the still remaining distance, etc. So he will have to pass an infinite number of spatial pieces before reaching the end of the finite distance, and he will have to pass these infinitely many spatial pieces in a finite time. I will not deal with the first point here, how a finite spatial extension can contain infinitely many parts; instead I will briefly talk about the second point, that the runner seemingly has to cover an *infinite* number of *spatial pieces* in a *finite time*. With Zeno's paradoxes we are thus facing the problem that of the two magnitudes which are necessary to determine movement, namely time and space, the latter is thought to be infinite and the former finite.

Aristotle—our source for this paradox—reacts to this problem by pointing out that if the spatial magnitude covered in a motion is continuous and infinite, so (and in the very same way) is the time taken, and vice versa. What leads to the problem under consideration here is thus the fact that Zeno does not take time into account sufficiently. For, although time is explicitly mentioned in the paradox when asking for the possibility of covering the infinitely many parts in a *finite time*, it is ignored in the process of division. Otherwise, if Zeno had considered time as well as space and as a magnitude like space,[35] he would have put the division roughly like this: First the runner has to cover half the racing course in half the time. Of the remaining half-course, he then has to cover another half in half of the half time, and so on *ad infinitum*. If Zeno had really considered the correlation of time and space,

---

35 The problem is not only to take time into account at all—Zeno might have said that what is moving is *first* here, *later* there, and *before* that at another place without this changing the paradox at all—but to take it into account as something which can be divided in exactly the same way as space can and which has to be divided whenever the distance of a movement is divided. However, this presupposes a basic similarity in the structure of time and space, which we find only in book 6 of Aristotle's *Physics*.

each marking off of a spatial part would have led to a marking off of the corresponding temporal part (see Figure 1.1).

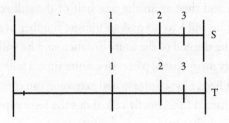

Figure 1.1 Zeno's runner paradox—division of time and space.

With Zeno, we see the beginning of a clear distinction between time and space—though only by neglecting time.[36] In the following we will see the beginning of a clear distinction between matter and space with the atomists.

2.4. The Atomists and the Notion of the Void

The notion of a void is one of the first spatial notions that can allow for an account of locomotion. Putting it in abstract terms, we can frame the basic problem motion raises as follows: In order for x to move, there has to be some y in which or into which x can move. But y cannot be the very same kind of thing as x, for then x could not move in or into y without there being two things of the same kind in the same spot, which would lead to collocation. It is this problem that the introduction of the void into the philosophical discussion seems to react to.

In fragment 7 Melissus[37] understands what is, Being, as what is full. What is full can move only into what is not full, into what is empty,

36 For a more thorough discussion of this paradox, see my article "Aristotle's Measurement Dilemma," *Oxford Studies in Ancient Philosophy* 52 (2017): 257–301, and especially my unpublished book manuscript "Natural Philosophy in Ancient Greece: Logical, Methodological, and Mathematical Foundations for the Theory of Motion," chapter 3.

37 There is a dispute among scholars who introduced the notion of a void first into the philosophical discussion of the time, the atomists or Melissus (leaving out potentially earlier claims about the void by the Pythagoreans because of unclear sources).

the void.[38] Thus void seems to be a necessary condition for motion. Melissus claims that there is no void and that Being, what is full, is accordingly unmoved and unlimited.

The atomists take up the strict division between what is and what is not from the Eleatics in the physical interpretation it is given by Melissus. But they understand Nonbeing qua void as a basic concept *on a par* with Being and thus turn the ontological distinction between what is and what is not into what today we would understand as a clear distinction between a spatial and a material notion: what is, Being, are the atoms; what is not, Nonbeing, is the void. The atoms are eternal and indivisible bodies, and all the phenomena we experience in the world come to be out of an arrangement of these atoms. Being that *out of* which all the phenomena come to be, the atoms can be seen as predecessors of a notion of matter. When the atoms get attached to each other, these phenomena come to be *in* the void. The void can thus be seen as a basic notion of space that is a condition for what we experience as "generation" and for the locomotions of the atoms which underlie this "generation."

The atomistic distinction between atoms and the void also allows for avoiding Zeno's paradox of *topos*. We saw that this paradox claims that if everything that exists is in a place and place itself exists, then place will be in a place, *ad infinitum*. The atomistic position allows us to block this regress by understanding void in such a way that it itself does not exist in the same sense in which the bodily things exist that are in a place. While void in some sense exists, it is not a Being, not an atom.

With the void of Leucippus and Democritus, we get not only some spatial notion but something that can be seen at least as a basis for a full notion of space. The void is, on the one hand, introduced as separating what is, atoms. It thus guarantees their plurality. On the

---

38 Here we also seem to get a prefiguration of the distinction between space and matter.

other hand, it is that *in* which the full atoms can move and thus allows
for motion.[39] And by being that in which the atoms are, it allows for
location in the sense that everything is in it, everything can be placed
in it. But since the void is completely without internal structure,
it itself does not help us to define the particular position a body is
occupying; the only way we can determine its particular place is in
relation to other bodies.

As that *in* which the atoms move, the void seems to be mere extension, without exerting any force or power upon the atoms; the void
thus has no influence on the motions of the bodies. And there seems
to be no friction involved; accordingly, the atomists do not show any
need to account for the continuation of motion—as we would think
it to be the case in a frictionless Newtonian universe. They explain
changes only in the directions of motion. Such changes are accounted
for by the basic setup of the atoms and their motions in the void: the
atoms move continuously with extreme rapidity and bump into each
other; these collisions then lead to new paths for the atoms involved.[40]
Changes of direction are thus the product of interactions between
different atoms.

The idea of space manifest in the atomistic void seems to be an
early and rough predecessor to an infinite, homogeneous, and isotropic space.[41] But the later atomists, the Epicureans, felt obliged to
assume an anisotropic space[42] in order to answer a criticism that had

---

39 Cf., e.g., DK 68 A37, line 29: the atoms "travel in the void." Aristotle and Simplicius repeatedly
provide testimony of the atomists' claim that the atoms move in the void; Simplicius even explicitly identifies *topos* with the void. Cf. Simplicius's commentary on *De Caelo* 294.33ff.

40 See Ps-Plutarch, *Epitome* I.4, in C. C. W. Taylor, *The Atomists: Leucippus and Democritus.
Fragments: A Text and Translation with a Commentary* (Toronto: University of Toronto Press,
1999), testimonium 79a. If their shape allows, the atoms can also stay together after a collision,
until some other collision separates them.

41 Any further structure, any anisotropy comes in only with the whirls when a world comes into
existence.

42 While Jammer, *Concepts*, 11–13 thinks that "the idea of a continuous homogeneous and isotropic
space," which seems to be introduced with the atomistic notion of the void, "seems to have been
too abstract even for the theoretically minded atomists," he nevertheless points out how via
Epicurus and Lucretius we get to exactly such an idea, though then space is taken to be anisotropic.

been prominently raised by Aristotle in his *Metaphysics*. Aristotle there complains that the atomists had not explained why the atoms move in the first place rather than stand still.[43] Epicurus answers this by claiming that the atoms naturally move downward due to their weight.[44] While Epicurus understands space still as homogeneous, it is not isotropic any longer; it has the same structure everywhere and is not curved, but it does not display the same characteristics in all directions because the downward direction is distinguished vis-à-vis the other directions: it is the preferred direction for the motions of the atoms. This anisotropy of space, however, raises the problem that now there is no reason left why atoms should bump against each other rather than just all fall down in straight lines. The introduction of the swerve is meant to ensure that the atoms still bump into each other and the phenomenal universe remains in motion.[45]

It seems that Leucippus's and Democritus's notion of the void is indeed a very fruitful, even if not fully developed, notion of space.[46] And it allows the atomist to distinguish clearly the void qua the empty from the full qua atoms, and thus to pave the way for distinguishing matter and space. In the next section we will see that Plato prepares the ground for distinguishing time and space not simply by neglecting time, as we saw Zeno do, but by giving both, time and space, their own ontological status.

---

43 "The question of the origin and nature of motion in things they [the atomists] too ignored, just as blithely as the others" (*Metaphysics* 985b, lines 19–20).

44 We have conflicting reports for the Presocratic atomists' assumption of weight: Aetius seems to claim that it is only Epicurus who introduces weight as a characteristic of the atoms, while Aristotle and his commentators ascribe weight to Presocratic atoms. But in any case, the pre-Epicurean atomists do not seem to employ weight in order to account for the motions of the atoms.

45 Cf. Lucretius, *De rerum natura* 2.225–50.

46 For a discussion of why Aristotle does not consider the Presocratic atomists to be predecessors for his investigation of space and David Sedley's claim that we should not understand their void as a notion of space, see my unpublished book manuscript "Ancient Notions of Space," chapter 3.

3. THE SECOND STAGE: TIME AND SPACE AS TWO
COMPLETELY INDEPENDENT MAGNITUDES
3.1 Plato's Timaeus

In order to fully understand our sensible world, the late Plato of the *Timaeus* claims, we need to introduce a third metaphysical principle, in addition to Being and Becoming (52a) known from earlier Platonic texts, what he calls the receptacle. From the time of Plato's Academy onward, there have been debates whether the receptacle should be understood as space or as matter or as showing features of both. In the twentieth and twenty-first century space has been the preferred option, even if it is usually not clarified what is actually understood by space. Nevertheless, understanding the receptacle as some kind of space seems a secure interpretation given that in 52a Plato explicitly calls the receptacle *chôra*. While a notion of time can be introduced within the metaphysical framework we are used to from the middle Plato, a notion of space, the receptacle, requires a development of the whole metaphysical basis.

But why is the receptacle so fundamental for the structure of the world? According to Plato's *Timaeus*, the sensible things are copies or images of intelligible Forms. But as images they need something *in which* they can appear, and this is the receptacle.[47] Furthermore, the world is moving and changing and the receptacle helps to explain the initiation of these processes. Finally, in spite of all the processes taking place, there is also some stability within this sensible world, which allows us to understand the world, and the receptacle is also involved in this task. Let me briefly explain how the receptacle is meant to fulfill each of these three tasks.

---

47 The *Timaeus* calls the sensible things images (*eikôn*, 52c2), appearances (*phantasma*, 52c3), or copies (*mimêmata*, 50c5) of the Forms. And in 52c4 Plato makes it clear that the images and appearances need something *in which* to appear.

1. That in which a sensible thing as an image of a Form appears can neither be the image itself, nor the intelligible paradigm. It has to be something over and above the Form and the thing that has come into being, a third kind: the receptacle. The Form guarantees that a sensible thing is the particular thing it is, for example, fire, because it is an image of the Form of fire. But the receptacle is responsible for the thing to be a *sensible* thing, since it is once the image of the Form appears in the receptacle that it is the sensible thing we perceive.

2. According to the *Timaeus*, the cosmos is set up by a divine craftsman: in the beginning there are traces of the four elements, fire, air, water and earth, that appear in the receptacle and move in a disorderly way; the demiurge bestows order onto these traces, shapes them into geometrically structured elements and all there is into the dodecahedron of the world-body, and forms the well-ordered cosmos in such a way that it itself is an image of the eternal paradigm.

   The receptacle fulfills crucial functions both before and after this "creation" of the cosmos. Before the creation, it is centrally involved in the initial motion of the elemental traces. The initial motion in the physical world is caused by the uneven powers of the traces in the receptacle: because of their unevenness the traces move the receptacle and are moved by it in turn; thus the receptacle is itself moved and causes motion (52e–53a).

   Furthermore, while the initial motion of the traces and the receptacle is chaotic, it leads, nevertheless, to some sorting. This is why Plato compares it to the motions of a winnowing basket: shaking the traces, we get the heavy and dense parts on one side and the light and rare ones on another side. The immediate effect is a first spatial order: fire traces come to be here, water traces there.

3. While the elements constantly change into each other, that in
   which they appear, the receptacle, stays stable. In this way the
   receptacle ensures some stability. It is a stable "this," as Plato calls
   it, by being that *in which* something moves and in which the
   elements change into each other (49e7–50a2) and by ensuring
   the continuous possibility for these processes to take place.[48]

What allows the receptacle to fulfill these different functions is a
rather peculiar combination of features:

1. The receptacle is free of all those shapes that the things
   appearing in it possess; it is amorphous. This allows it to
   receive all elements equally well; we saw that to be all-receiving
   (*pandeches*, 51a8) is one of its core functions.[49]
2. The receptacle is itself not visible (*anoraton*, 51a7) and indeed in
   no way perceptible (52b2). This is important, because otherwise
   it would itself be a sensible thing, and hence possess a certain
   form, while what the receptacle is meant to be is rather the *basis*
   in which the sensible things come into being and which thus
   enables them to be perceptible.[50]
3. However, the receptacle seems to be treated as something
   physical and sensible to some degree, since it is itself moved. We
   saw that this is necessary in order to explain the initial motion.
   Furthermore, this seems to be how it can allow the Form-copies

---

48 For a fuller discussion of these three points, see my paper "A Likely Account of Necessity: Plato's
   Receptacle as a Physical and Metaphysical Basis of Space," *Journal of the History of Philosophy* 50
   (2012): 159–95.

49 We saw with Anaximander that we need something that itself is not one of the four elements and
   thus can give rise to all four elements equally. This idea seems to be in the background also with
   Plato's account of the receptacle, since we are told that in order for the receptacle to allow for all
   elements to come into being and to be in it, the receptacle itself cannot have any of the features of
   the elements.

50 We can say that phenomenologically the receptacle is nothing but what appears in it; ontologically, however, the receptacle is also a necessary condition for the existence of the sensible world.

to become sensible things: the receptacle guarantees their physical existence by being itself physical to some degree.

4. Finally, while the receptacle is also treated as something physical, it is, first and foremost, a metaphysical genus and as such eternal.

In order to understand the spatial characteristics that this entity and its content provide us with in the *Timaeus*, we should take into account that this part of the *Timaeus* is not concerned with any old sensible thing but actually with the *elements* of these sensible things. For Plato the four elements of the philosophical tradition, earth, water, air, and fire, are constituted by geometrical bodies; they are tetrahedra (fire), octahedra (air), icosahedra (water), and cubes (earth). We see how the physical and the geometrical world are closely linked. Each of the geometrical bodies is made up of one of two basic kinds of triangles. Thus for Plato three-dimensional bodies are composed out of two-dimensional surfaces by moving the surfaces and changing the angles between them. An image of fire, for example, can appear in the receptacle because (1) there are basic triangles in the receptacle, and (2) they can be arranged so as to form an image of the Form of fire.

If we now look at the spatial features we find in the *Timaeus*, we see that in fact most of them do not come from the receptacle but rather from its content, the elements and their traces. The latter present us with three spatial aspects: (1) regionalization, (2) distance, and (3) extension, which implies a certain dimensionality. It is only (4) continuity that is actually provided by the receptacle. Let us look at each of these features in turn.

1. As the shaking motion of the receptacle leads to a basic order of the traces like to like, we also find a regionalization based on the distribution of the elements (53a). Basic regions are established as the traces of fire gather together here, those of earth there.

2. The traces and elements also allow for introducing a notion of distance. We may say, for example, that the fire traces gather together near the traces of air and further away from the traces of water. A rough way to determine such distances would be with the help of the amount of the traces: two traces are close to each other if only a few are in between, and they are far away if they are separated by a lot of traces. With the traces we can determine only degrees of nearness, not the exact quantity of the distances between the traces, because they are of irregular shape. However, after creation, when the elements possess their full geometrical structure, they could be used for measuring distances in the universe: one triangle could in principle be taken as a basic unit to measure out whatever distance needs to be determined.

3. As for dimensionality, Plato considers the elements and their traces as bodies and explicitly claims they possess three dimensions,[51] made up, however, of two-dimensional triangles. By contrast, the receptacle on its own is amorphous; it does not possess any *determined* form that it would keep permanently. But it receives either three-dimensional elements and traces or two-dimensional triangles. Accordingly, it must have the potentiality for dimensionality, but this potentiality needs to be actualized by its content.

4. The spatial feature that we can claim as specific for the receptacle is the continuity it guarantees between different surfaces and bodies; so there are no gaps between, say, a body here and a body there.

Given these features, should we understand the receptacle as space, either geometrical or physical space? Probably not. The receptacle on its own cannot be a geometrical space, as it misses one of the most

---

51 53c. As a consequence, the receptacle has to allow for at least three dimensions.

basic features of any space, dimensionality, which it inherits from the things in it. And the idea of a metric cannot be based on the receptacle considered on its own, as we saw. Any further spatial structure is also derived from its content.

But why, then, does Plato call it space (*chôra*)? The reason for this seems to be that the receptacle is the continuous and constant "this" *in which* everything in the sensible world comes to be, exists, and can move and change.[52] Accordingly, we can say that on its own the receptacle provides the *basis for space* by granting this continuity, while all further spatial aspects come in through the traces of the elements.

However, we get a fully fledged notion of space in the *Timaeus* if we consider not only the receptacle but also the world-body in the form of a dodecahedron that the demiurge forms, and the content of the receptacle together. The universe, as made up of these three ingredients, introduces a full geometrical space: it has three dimensions, is fully compressed and connected—there are no disjoint patches—and also closed and bounded.[53] The continuity between the elements is secured by the receptacle, and the basic triangles allow for the possibility of determining the distances between elements, and thus for a basic metric.

Accordingly, we can say that we do find what *we* would call a geometrical space in Plato.[54] It is a space that is not independent of the bodily elements but also not simply reducible to them and their relations. And this geometrical space is also open to a physical interpretation: the geometrical structure of the elements explains how the elements can be transformed and where they move to, and in this way explains the changes and locomotions of the elements.

---

52 In addition, we might count as spatial features of the receptacle before creation the fact that, as we have seen, it is itself movable and can in turn move—features of interest for a possible physical space.

53 We could even claim that it is orientable with respect to the basic elements as they can have an orientation (e.g., they can be right-handed) once the order of the universe is given.

54 More specifically, it is what we would call a Euclidean space, since the difference between the sizes of the triangles matters, as does the difference between the two basic triangles.

How does this notion of space now relate to Plato's notion of time? In the *Timaeus*, the receptacle, as the basis for space, and time are completely separate entities: the receptacle is uncreated and essentially connected with the chaotic motions before creation, while time is created by the demiurge so as to bestow rational order onto the world. Time and space are thus situated on two completely different ontological levels. And this gap cannot be bridged with the help of the fact that both are connected in some sense with mathematics. For time is connected with arithmetic and proportion theory, while, as we saw, the receptacle is connected with geometry. It remains unclear in the *Timaeus* how the two could possibly be connected, for example, when we want to give an account of speed.

4. THE THIRD STAGE: THE COMBINATION OF TIME AND SPACE AS TWO INDEPENDENT MAGNITUDES
4.1 Aristotle

So far we have seen time and space treated either as not clearly distinct or as separate to such a degree that they possess an entirely different ontological status and that it is unclear how they may be connected at all. Before we examine how far Aristotle succeeds in bringing these two magnitudes together for an account of motion with the help of his notion of the continuum, we will first look at his notion of space in some detail.

4.1.1 THE TASK OF ARISTOTLE'S NOTION OF *TOPOS*
That spatial notions play an important role for Aristotle already becomes clear from his *Categories*, which names "where" as one of the ten categories. The category of "where," however, like some others, is mentioned only briefly and exemplified solely by reference to the location of something ("in the marketplace," "in the Lyceum"). Later on we find *topos* among the continuous quantities; it is continuous since the

parts of the body that occupy it are continuous.[55] But in the *Categories*, we get no indication which role *topos* plays for an account of motion, since motion is obviously not a focus in this work. But motion is, as we will see, the crucial focus for the discussion of space in the *Physics*, where Aristotle gives his fullest discussion of spatial notions. Aristotle usually uses the word *topos* in this discussion, which some people took as an indication that he is not talking about space but only about place. However, we saw earlier that the word in itself does not necessarily indicate that. So let us look at the main tasks that *topos* is meant to fulfill in the *Physics*:

1. *Topos* is a necessary condition for locomotion to take place and for our understanding of locomotion: there needs to be a "where,"[56] or a "where from" and a "where to," in order for a body to change its position, for mutual replacement to take place, and for us to be able to account for such a locomotion.[57]

2. Furthermore, *topos* is connected to some form of power, as each of the elements has its specific place to which it naturally moves, for example, fire in its natural motion always moves up, earth always down.[58]

3. Finally, the continuity of space is meant to guarantee the continuity of locomotion and time: at least in the order of understanding, the continuity of motion and time rests on the continuity of space.[59]

---

55 Interestingly, this order is inverse to the order we will find in *Physics* book 6. Cf. Henry Mendell, "Topoi on Topos: The Development of Aristotle's Concept of Place," *Phronesis* 32 (1987): 206–31 for the idea of a clear development in Aristotle's spatial account from the *Categories* to the *Physics*. The fact that *topos* is discussed under the category of quantity rather than of "where" raises the question of how *topos* is related to the idea of location in the *Categories*; cf. also Algra, *Space*, 124ff.

56 In fact, we need a "where" also when an object is at rest, that is, without reference to a direction.

57 See 208b1–8. Space thus serves as a metaphysical and epistemological basis.

58 These powers have been interpreted differently in the tradition: according to some accounts, *topos* itself is seen as possessing some power to attract, while according to others, the power rests in the elements.

59 See *Physics* 219a10–19 and book 6.

These tasks show that the main focus of Aristotle's investigation is—as we should expect from his very project in the *Physics*[60]—locomotion. We would not ask what *topos* is if there were no locomotion, according to Aristotle. Thus, what Aristotle is interested in is clearly what we would think of as physical, not as mathematical space.

4.1.2 DEVELOPMENT OF ARISTOTLE'S ACCOUNT

According to Aristotle, the three tasks space fulfills mean that *topos* is (1) not itself a body, but that (2) space is also not completely separate from bodies in the way a void is, and that (3) the relationship between a body and its place/space is not a part-whole relation.

1. Aristotle shows that while *topos* has the same dimensions as a body, it is not a body: if *topos* were a body, there would be two bodies in the same spot, *topos* and the body that is in this *topos*. Furthermore, *topos* can also not be the form or matter of a body, since matter and form cannot be separated from the body to which they belong. But it is essential that *topos* is separate from particular bodies, since in order to account for re-placement, one particular body has to hold a place now that previously another one held, or another one will hold in the future.[61] Similar problems would arise if we assumed *topos* to be an independently existing interval between the extremities of a container, what Aristotle calls a *diastēma* (209b14ff.).

---

60 In the *Physics*, Aristotle wants to investigate *physis*, "nature," in the sense of that which has a principle of motion and rest in itself; see the beginning of book 2.

61 *Topos* possesses two essential features that show it to be neither form nor matter: (1) it is that which surrounds something and thus is a kind of limit; (2) it can also be independent of that which it surrounds. While the form of a body may be thought of as "surrounding" or "limiting" the body in some sense, the form cannot be independent of the body in the sense that it can also limit or surround some other body, as *topos* can. Matter, on the other hand, cannot be thought as surrounding or limiting a body; rather, it is itself limited. In arguing against *topos* being matter, Aristotle understands he is also arguing against Plato's conception of the receptacle in the *Timaeus* (209b11–13). Cf. my article "A Likely Account of Necessity" for a discussion of the degree to which Aristotle's *topos* and Plato's receptacle share basic functions and why, nevertheless, Plato does not mistake space for matter.

2. While Aristotle argues against *topos* being thought of as a
   body or a feature of the body it contains, he also wants to
   argue that it cannot be completely independent of bodies. For
   then it could be the case that there is no body in it, and this
   would make it unavoidable to think of it as a kind of void. The
   assumption of a void, which Aristotle understands as totally
   undifferentiated nonbeing (215a11), would threaten the core
   of his theory of *kinêsis*, the concept of a continuum. This
   threat has a logical and a dynamical side: from a mere logical
   point of view, the assumption of a void would mean that gaps
   within the universe would be possible, and thus the continuous
   connection of the different parts of the universe would not be
   ensured any longer,[62] on which Aristotle's own physics clearly
   depends. As far as dynamics is concerned, the assumption
   of a void would make it inexplicable how an impulse can be
   passed on within the Aristotelian framework, if there is no
   surrounding body that takes over the impulse in the void, and
   how bodies can keep a certain direction in their motion.[63]
   And given that the void is completely undifferentiated so that
   we do not have any resources to distinguish different places,
   there could then be no natural motion. For natural motions are
   motions to a specific place, as, for example, the motion of earth
   to the center of the world.[64]

3. Finally, Aristotle quite in detail marks off the relation between
   a body and its place from the relation of a part to its whole.
   With both relations one relatum seems to be *in* the other, the
   part in the whole, the body in its place. However, as Aristotle
   points out, a part always moves *with* a body, while a body
   moves *in* a place (211a29–b5). The place is independent from

---

62 See 213a33–34.
63 See 215a23–24.
64 See 215a9–14.

the body which is in it.[65] The notion of "in" at play here is not the one in which the part is contained in the whole or in which the whole consists in its parts. Rather, the "in" referring to the relation of a body to its *topos* is the same "in" we use when we say "something is *in* a vessel."[66]

This understanding of "in" is the right notion for the relationship between a body and its *topos*. It is, however, as Aristotle spells out in detail, not the only one, and so Zeno's paradox of *topos* does not work, since *topos* itself can be "in something" in one of the other senses of "in" without thus creating an infinite regress. Aristotle thinks that we would get into a paradox only if "in" could merely be used in one, the spatial sense, because only then would it be true that it's a mark of the existence of everything, even of place, to be in a place. Thus Aristotle rejects Zeno's second premise in his paradox of *topos*, that "whatever is in something is in a place."

4.1.3 DEFINITION OF *TOPOS* AND ITS TRADITIONAL UNDERSTANDING

After carefully ruling out that *topos* could be understood as matter, form, or an extension (*diastêma*) between the boundaries of the thing which surrounds,[67] the following definition remains for Aristotle as the only possibility:

---

65 If that which is contained is immediately continuous with its container, it is a part, while if it is only in contact with the container, it is a body in a place; cf. Ross, *Aristotle's Physics*. For a part of a continuum to move *in* its whole, it would need to be actualized, and there are infinitely many parts that could be actualized.

66 But once an element is in its natural place, it behaves like a part that is separable behaves to its whole. (On the notion of a natural place, see later discussion.)

67 See 211b5–212a2. For an explanation of why it is exactly these three possibilities which arise as possible candidates for place and have to be ruled out, see Mendell, *Topoi*, 219ff. Aristotle's rejection of understanding *topos* as *diastêma* can in part be seen as an attack on atomistic assumptions of a void.

τὸ τοῦ περιέχοντος πέρας ἀκίνητον πρῶτον, τοῦτ᾽ ἔστιν ὁ τόπος
The first/immediate unmoved limit of that which surrounds—that
is *topos*. (212a20–21)

The three pieces of definition of place, (1) "limit of that which surrounds,"
(2) "first" or "immediate," and (3) "unmoved," Aristotle elucidates immediately before this definition. By claiming *topos* to be like "a vessel
which cannot be moved around" in 212a15–16, Aristotle makes it obvious how to understand "the limit of that which surrounds": in the
same way as the (inner) edge of a vessel forms the boundary of what
it contains, *topos* has to be thought of as a surrounding limit or frame.
And as the vessel is able to take up anything (bodily) whatsoever, there
can be anything whatsoever in a place. *Topos* is the limit not of the
body that is surrounded, but of the body which surrounds.

Topos being a limit has two attributes: it is to be unmoved and it is
prôton, "first/immediate." The last is usually taken to mean something
like "being directly adjacent to." This attribute seems to guarantee the
continuity in the universe and to prevent any assumption of a void between a body and its place. In addition, *topos* has to be unmoved. This
requirement seems to be necessary for two reasons: first, if a body is in
place *A* which is itself moving in place *B*, then we will only be able to
locate the body if we refer to *B*, but not if we refer to *A*. Second, if *topos*
itself was moved, we would have to state where this place moves and
thus would get into a Zeno-like paradox of *topos*,[68] according to which
each place has to have a place itself, which again will have a place, *ad
infinitum*.

Traditionally the definition of *topos* has been interpreted in such
a way that *topos* is understood as an unmoved *vessel*. Since Aristotle
talks about a *prôton* limit, the focus has been on a vessel that contains
nothing but the single body assumed to be in the *topos*. Although many

---

68 Aristotle refers to this paradox in 209a23–25.

scholars of Aristotle's *Physics* take it that in the course of his treatise on place there is a shift to a more static definition than the image of a vessel allows for, this does not prevent them from assuming that Aristotle's notion of *topos* should be understood as the container of a body, and more precisely the container which is of the very same extension as the body in it.[69]

This understanding has two problematic consequences, which Aristotle, it is usually claimed, does not deal with sufficiently: first, such an account provides us only with a theory of place but not with one of space—a shortcoming that seems to be already obvious from Aristotle's choice of words when he uses *topos* instead of *chôra* to refer to the object of his investigation. Second, it is problematic how such a definition of place can be reconciled with Aristotle's focus on *kinêsis*, because a vessel of exactly the same size as the thing contained will not allow for any motion. So has Aristotle given up on the initial idea that his account of *topos* should help to explain motion? I do not think so. In contrast to the traditional understanding of Aristotle and its problematic consequences, I want to show in the following that his definition of *topos* fits his conception of *kinêsis,* since he does not conceive *topos* as being an unmoved vessel, but rather as what we could call a frame of reference. As a consequence, we will see that his theory of *topos* is not only a theory of place but also of space.

The secondary literature has been worried about what happens if the *surrounded* body moves, since it is not clear how it can do that in a vessel of exactly its own size. By contrast, what Aristotle worries about in his investigation is what happens if the *surrounding* body is moving. Looking at this case in the following section will make it clear what the core of Aristotle's notion of *topos* in fact is.

---

69 Cf., e.g., Myles Burnyeat, "The Sceptic in His Place and Time," in *Philosophy in History*, ed. Richard Rorty, Jerome Schneewind, and Quentin Skinner (Cambridge, UK: Cambridge University Press, 1984), 232n15: "The refinement [i.e., that Aristotle is now taking the surrounding body to be static] does not threaten the condition that the place of X is equal to X (211a28–9) and contains nothing but X."

4.1.4 REVISED UNDERSTANDING WITH THE HELP OF THE RIVER EXAMPLE

Let us first have a closer look at Aristotle's definition of *topos*.[70] We have seen that *topos* as the limit of that which surrounds has two attributes: it is to be "unmoved" and it is *prôton*, "first/immediate." We saw that the last is usually taken to mean something like being "directly adjacent to." Taking it like that, "unmoved" and "first/immediate" exclude each other if the thing which is immediately surrounding is itself moved.[71] For then the thing which is directly adjoining is not unmoved, and what is unmoved is not directly adjoining.

To understand these two pieces of the definition better, let us have a look at how Aristotle continues immediately after his reference to the vessel in 212a16–20: "So when something moves inside something which is moving and the thing inside moves about, as a boat on a river, the surrounding thing functions for it as a vessel rather than as a place; place is meant to be motionless so that it is rather the whole river that is *topos*, because as a whole it is motionless." In this example of a boat on a river the two features "unmoved" and "immediate" seem to exclude each other. So what does Aristotle do? He uses this example to point out that the place of a body need not be immediately adjacent in the way the side of a wall of a container directly touches the contained thing. Place rather is the limit of the *first* thing that is unmoved. (We can think of it as an adjacent limit insofar as it is not separated by any discontinuous gap from the thing moved.) Thus, place is not (necessarily) something which directly touches the thing moved, but rather the *nearest thing resting*, as the river is in its (more or less) unchanging extension. Place is the *prôton* limit of what surrounds a body, not in the sense of immediate but in the sense of the *first* thing that is unmoved. We are in fact not dealing with two different features, unmoved and

---

70 This section is heavily influenced by Ulrich Bergmann, *Unveröffentlichte Studie zum Aristotelischen Ort* (Fassung Minden 2004).

71 Cf., e.g., Ross, *Aristotle's Physics*, 575f.

first, but with the feature "the first unmoved" limit. Accordingly *topos* should not be thought of as an unmoved *vessel*; this is just a first pass of Aristotle when he develops his notion of *topos* in the *Physics*, and the passage just quoted clearly contrasts vessel and *topos*. Rather, *topos* is a resting limit—a frame of reference—within which the body is situated and which, under certain, but not all, circumstances, can be made so precise as to contain only the one body in question. The interpretation of *topos* as such a frame of reference also explains why Aristotle at the end of his treatise on *topos* can suddenly say that *topos* can be a kind of surface (212a28). For in order to locate something or the motion of something, it is enough, under normal circumstances, to refer to two dimensions. ("Where is he sailing today?" "In the Nile delta." This answer need not refer to depth; it would also be understandable if we lived in a two-dimensional world.)

Place is this resting thing not insofar as it is itself a certain body,[72] for example, the river, but rather insofar as it forms the boundary of a certain area in which the movement takes place. Thus the resting thing forms the limit in the sense of delimiting a certain area. In this way Aristotle conceives of *topos* as the nearest resting frame of reference. But in contrast to modern frames, as, for example, the Cartesian co-ordinate system, which are purely logical, place as a frame of reference with Aristotle is always thought to be physical, i.e., as given by the bodies of this world. The reason for this restriction is that for Aristotle space is, ontologically speaking, nothing over and above bodies.[73]

Aristotle's definition of *topos* presupposes the physical continuity of the universe, since without this continuity the frame of reference and the thing moved in this frame could not be directly connected.

---

72 As there are no further spatial entities with Aristotle over and above bodies, place has to be a body surrounding the moving body. Nevertheless, its being a body is not what is important for its being *topos*.

73 For a reply to the objection that the passages in the *Physics* which take place to be the same size as the surrounded thing seem to make the interpretation of place as such a frame of reference impossible, see my book manuscript "Ancient Notions of Space," chapter 5.

As place is taken to be the area *in* which something moves and not as a point *to which* movement takes place, *topos* itself can in turn ensure the continuity of the movement.

But why, then, does Aristotle choose the term *topos* for such a frame of reference? We saw earlier that in contrast to *chôra*, *topos* can also be used to denote relative location or position in relation to a surrounding. Given that for Aristotle the *topos* of a body always positions this body in relation to another body, to the surrounding body, this term seems to have been appropriately chosen.[74]

The focus on the image of a vessel seems to have led to the opinion shared by most Aristotle scholars that Aristotle's *Physics* develops only a theory of place but not of space. Accordingly, it is claimed that Aristotle's theory lacks the possibility of accounting for directions, for the relations of positions, and so on.[75] However, Aristotle's example of the ship shows that all these determinations can be derived from his conception of *topos* as the nearest resting system of reference: *location* is possible with the help of the nearest resting thing, and, if appropriate, it allows for a further tightening of the frame. For example, a ship is on the river, near Cairo, where there is the landing stage, and so on. (Going further in that way we will be able to distinguish the location of a boat on the river from the location of any other boat nearby.) The *relation of positions* can be established, for example, by the relation of two boats on the river. *Directions* can be defined with the help of the relation of the place of a body to another place, for example, the ship

---

74 When Aristotle gives his own view concerning place as the location of a body relative to the immediate surrounding, he uses the term *topos*; he uses *chôra* and *topos* interchangeably in places where he talks about opponents.

75 To take just one example, Wagner in his commentary on the *Physics, Aristoteles, Physikvorlesung* (Akademie Verlag, 1995) thinks that with Aristotle the principles which are essential for a theory of space are missing: "Größe" (size), "Richtung" (direction), "Lage" (position), "Lageverhältnisse" (relations of positions), and "Ortsbestimmung" (location) of spatial things. Jammer, *Concepts*, 19 claims that Aristotle only develops a theory of position in space. Cf. also Ross, *Aristotle's Physics*, 54, and Hussey, *Aristotle's Physics III and IV*, xxviii, for the claim that Aristotle does not have a notion of space.

may be on the river at Cairo and from there moves toward the mouth of the river. Thus, the example of the ship and Aristotle's thoughts about a *topos koinos*—the common *topos* different things share—make it obvious that his theory of *topos* is also a theory of space.[76]

4.1.5. NATURAL PLACES AND THE UNIVERSE

But what about the world as a whole? Can it, according to Aristotle's account of *topos*, itself be in a place or space? No. For Aristotle only that which is surrounded by a body is in a *topos* (212a31–32). But then the universe as a whole can itself not be in a place or space since there is no further body that could surround the world as a whole. Aristotle is explicit about this: "But, as has been said, the heavens as a whole [i.e., the universe] is not somewhere or in a *topos*, since there is no body that surrounds them" (212b8–10).[77] In the philosophical tradition this claim has led to confusions and heavy attacks against Aristotle's account, perhaps most vividly expressed by the question "But what happens if I stretch out my arm at the edge of the universe? Either I cannot do so, which means that there must be something there to prevent me from doing this, or I can, in which case my arm has to be somewhere and thus in a place."[78] However, this question mixes up different notions of space: it confuses Aristotle's notion of the limit of a surrounding body with a notion of space as an independent entity that is a necessary condition for anything being extended or moving. It is as if we employed a Cartesian coordinate system in order to locate something and then somebody asked, "Where in your coordinate system is the coordinate system situated?"

---

76 This interpretation is also supported by Aristotle's claim in 212b23–24 that his account of *topos* ensures that *topos* does not have to grow if the thing in it grows, which would not be possible on the traditional interpretation, where *topos* has to be in contact everywhere with the thing in it.

77 Cf. also *De Caelo* 279a, where we are told that beyond the world body there can be neither *topos* nor time or void, since they all depend on bodies.

78 Cf., for example, Lucretius, *De rerum natura*, I 963–83, where the question is framed as whether we can throw a spear at the (alleged) edge of the universe.

So far we have dealt with *topos* as a freely eligible, although body-bound, frame of reference in which a body can move in any direction. By contrast, what has come to be called "natural places"[79] are fixedly given destinations of a movement. They are the places which the four elements will move to and rest if not hindered by some external force, and they thus determine the direction the motion of the elements will take. All elements, all simple bodies, have the potentiality to perform a natural motion, i.e., a motion that is not caused by something external, and their natural motion will be to their natural place: earth will move to the center of the universe, fire will move up to the circumference, and so on.

This idea of natural places goes hand in hand with the idea of a fixed matrix of the universe; there is an objective above and below. For us human beings what is above, below, etc. depends on how we position ourselves. But in the universe above is where fire will move to naturally, below where earth moves to, and so on.[80] Accordingly, the universe as a whole can be described in its setup as follows: In the middle there is a sphere of earth; this is surrounded by a water sphere, then a sphere of air, and a sphere of fire. Beyond the sphere of fire, and that means beyond the moon, there is a sphere of aether, out of which the stars are formed.

This idea of fixed natural places not only introduces what we may call anisotropy into Aristotle's notion of *topos*; it also gives an objective orientation in the universe and thus enhances the knowability of the spatial structure of the world.

---

79 Aristotle himself only talks about the *idios* or *oikeios* place—the place belonging to some element, or that in which the elements rest naturally (276a24), or about "its place (*autou topos*) to which it moves if nothing hinders it" (208b11).

80 See *Physics* 208b14–22 and *De Caelo* II, 2. These directions are objectively given for Aristotle. By contrast, in Plato's *Timaeus* above, below, right, left, back, and front are always relative to a certain perspective—either our own or one of the elements, so that for, let us say, fire to move down will always be to move to wherever there is lots of fire, but the place where there is lots of fire could vary. See *Timaeus* 63e.

4.1.6 COMBINING SPATIAL AND TEMPORAL MAGNITUDES

For Aristotle, time and space are clearly distinguished magnitudes; space is important only for locomotion, while time is connected with all kinds of processes (also, for example, alteration and generation). However, if we want to give an account of motion, we also need to bring these two different magnitudes, time and space, together; we want to be able to claim that a certain body covers a certain amount of space in a certain time, or that another body was faster than this first body because it covered the same space in less time or it covered more space in the same time. We see that in order to account for motion and its speed, we need to be able to bring time and space in a certain relation to each other and to divide time and space with respect to each other.

The way Aristotle can explain this connection of time and space is by showing that whatever else we can say about time and space, their basic structure as magnitudes is the same: both can be understood as continua; i.e., both are magnitudes that are always further divisible. Aristotle spends most of book 6 of his *Physics* showing that time, space, and motion are continua and how we can understand such continua: they are wholes that are prior to their parts so that (potential) parts are acquired only by dividing the whole; they possess potentially infinitely many parts, not all of which can be actualized at the same time; and their limits are such that we have to distinguish between division points or inner limits, which mark off potential parts, and outer limits, which mark off one continuous thing from another.[81]

This understanding of time and space guarantees that we can measure motion in terms of time and space, as we see it done in Aristotle's comparisons of two locomotions of different speed. It also allows Aristotle to respond to Zeno's runner paradoxes: it explains how a finite whole can contain infinitely many parts and how an

---

81 For a detailed discussion of Aristotle's account of continuity, cf. my book The Concept of Motion in Ancient Greek Thought: foundations in logic, method, and mathematics (Cambridge, UK: Cambridge University Press, 2020)

infinite number of *spatial* pieces can be covered in a finite *time*. And while both time and space share the structure of continua, this does not mean that space does not also possess its own, specific features; while time and space can be combined, they are also magnitudes independent of each other.

Reflection

BODY SPACE/CITY SPACE

Veiling as an Embodied Spatial Practice

Banu Gökarıksel

What would a spatial approach to veiling reveal about this practice?
How does veiling create the body as a space and produce a new
space that the veiled women traverse? I explore these questions
by drawing upon the recent scholarship in geography and related
disciplines about space as a relation of bodies and as produced by
bodily experiential practices. I approach Muslim women's veiling as
an embodied spatial practice that participates in the production of
the body space and shapes the experiences of women as they move
across the city. My empirical focus is on Istanbul, Turkey. In Turkey,
veiling has turned into quite a significant divisive political issue,
especially in the 1990s, and it was actively regulated by the state. It
has recently become relatively more accepted (e.g., the headscarf
ban is no longer enforced at universities and for state employees),
but veiling remains a contentious practice.

Space, Body, and Religion

Recent theorizations have rejected the treatment of space as a fixed
entity with clear and stable boundaries, as simply a metaphor, and

Banu Gökarıksel, *Body Space/City Space* In: *Space*. Edited by: Andrew Janiak, Oxford University Press
(2020). © Oxford University Press.
DOI: 10.1093/oso/9780199914104.003.0003

as merely a stage or a container where things happen. Instead, geographers today commonly understand space as an active agent in social, economic, cultural, and political phenomena. At the same time, they emphasize its constant production through practices and thereby its incompleteness and fluidity. Doreen Massey, for example, theorizes space as an ongoing process, always in the making, and inevitably plural. She proposes that we imagine space "as a simultaneity of stories-so-far." Her approach emphasizes the volatility of space rather than its fixity; the boundaries of space are not rigid (despite political actions to impose rigidity by, for example, building up and militarizing borders) but changing and porous, and the relations that produce or are produced by space stretch out geographically and temporally.[1]

Feminist geographers have taken this view of space to destabilize the binaries that dominate geographical thinking, such as place versus space, private versus public, and local versus global. In such binary constructions, place, private, and the local are rendered feminine and particular and studied mainly by those interested in grounded and situated research. In contrast, the approach to space, public, and the global continue the tradition of disembodied, supposedly rational, and inherently masculinist views of the world and their claims to universality. Sallie Marston and others have added a problematization of the concept of scale to this body of work, calling into question the treatment of scale (from body to global) as given and not as a social construction.[2] Woodward, Jones, and Marston extend this criticism of scale to challenge the eagle's point of view of the world, instead advocating for the fly's.[3] Instead of space or place, they propose

1 Doreen Massey, *For Space* (London: Sage, 2005), 9; Doreen Massey, *Space, Place, and Gender* (London: John Wiley & Sons, 2013).

2 Sallie A. Marston, "The Social Construction of Scale," *Progress in Human Geography* 24, no. 2 (2000): 219–42; Sallie A. Marston, John Paul Jones, and Keith Woodward, "Human Geography without Scale," *Transactions of the Institute of British Geographers* 30, no. 4 (2005): 416–32.

3 Keith Woodward, John Paul Jones, and Sallie A. Marston, "Of Eagles and Flies: Orientations toward the Site," *Area* 42, no. 3 (2010): 271–80.

using the concept of site, which they argue better captures the actual
materialities and situated experiences that are often rendered invisible
by dominant ideologies. My approach shares this emphasis on the
material and the experiential dimensions of space.

As part of this critical rethinking of the key concepts of geography
there is also a recent interest in studying the body as space.
Described as the most intimate geography, or the geography closest
in, the body is not only the site where social, cultural, political,
and economic processes are experienced but also where they are
materialized.[4] Humanistic geographers are often credited for
putting the body into geography as they explore phenomenological
understandings of places. For example, Tuan writes, "Body
implicates space; space co-exists with the sentient body."[5] In
geographies of religion, the significance of the body is recognized
and emphasis has shifted to understanding how embodied acts
and bodily practices produce religious geographies.[6] From this
perspective, the body is not "a mere receptacle or 'inscriptive surface'
for the work of representation-cum-discourse" of religion, but "the
body and bodily practices are central to the enactment of sacred
space."[7] Thus, the body can no longer be taken as a given, and the
question of how it is produced as a space comes to the fore. Here
I examine this question with regard to the practice of veiling.

4 See Gillian Rose, "Geography and Gender, Cartographies and Corporealities," *Progress in Human
   Geography* 19, no. 4 (1995): 544–48; Felicity J. Callard, "The Body in Theory," *Environment and
   Planning D: Society and Space* 16, no. 4 (1998): 387–400; Robyn Longhurst, "The Body and
   Geography," *Gender, Place & Culture* 2, no. 1 (1995): 97–106, Robyn Longhurst, "(Dis)embodied
   Geographies," *Progress in Human Geography* 21, no. 4 (1997): 486–501; Robyn Longhurst,
   Bodies: Exploring Fluid Boundaries (London: Routledge, 2001).

5 Yi-Fu Tuan, "Humanistic Geography," *Annals of the Association of American Geographers* 66, no. 2
   (1976): 266–276, cited in Longhurst, *Bodies*, 15.

6 Julian Holloway and Oliver Valins, "Placing Religion and Spirituality in Geography," *Social &
   Cultural Geography* 3, no. 1 (2002): 5–9.

7 Julian Holloway, "Make-believe: Spiritual Practice, Embodiment, and Sacred Space," *Environment
   and Planning A* 35, no. 11 (2003): 1961–74.

Veiling and the Body

Some Muslims accept veiling as a religious requirement. This practice is often seen as an important component of the Islamic code of modesty for women. Writing about other religions, a volume that examines clothing, the body, and religion mostly frames the relations among these three areas in terms of social control: clothing becomes the means of regulating and disciplining the body.[8] In western Orientalist works on Islam and the Middle East and North Africa, this aspect of veiling has dominated the way this practice has been simplistically (mis)understood historically. In western and secular modernist eyes, the veil hides women's bodies or makes them invisible in public spaces. This invisibility is seen as a sign of Muslim women's repression within a modern secular understanding of freedom that values visibility.[9] In an attempt to counter such views, Lila Abu-Lughod proposes that we view the veil as enclosing a private space akin to the private space of the home for women.[10] She takes Papanek's study of the veil as "portable seclusion" to develop the view of the veil as a "mobile home."[11] The veil as a mobile home aptly demonstrates how the practice of veiling actively creates space.

From this perspective, the creation of a secluded private space inside the veil does not so much restrict women's spatial mobility, and hence freedom (from a western liberal point of view). On the contrary, veiling enables women's movement across the city. Yet this reframing of the veil as mobile home does not challenge the assumption about the veil as enclosing a space within (as if other

---

8 Linda B. Arthur, *Religion, Dress and the Body* (Oxford: Berg, 1999).

9 Malek Alloula, *The Colonial Harem* (Minneapolis: University of Minnesota Press, 1986).

10 Lila Abu-Lughod, "Do Muslim Women Really Need Saving? Anthropological Reflections on Cultural Relativism and Its Others," *American Anthropologist* 104, no. 3 (2002): 783–90.

11 Abu-Lughod, "Do Muslim Women," 785. Also see Hanna Papanek, "Purdah in Pakistan: Seclusion and Modern Occupations for Women," in *Separate Worlds,* ed. Hanna Papanek and Gail Minault (Columbus, OH: South Asia Books, 1982), 190–216.

kinds of clothing do not do the same) and creating an interior invisible to the onlooker, just like the walls of a house. Further, there is little room for thinking about how veiling creates the space of the body from this perspective. I argue that veiling does create the body as a space but one that is relational and not discrete or stable. Veiling, instead, delineates a porous boundary between the interior and the exterior, the private and the public. The veil is also visible and participates in the visual economy of public spaces.[12] Just like any other boundary, the veil does not completely close off an interior or private space that is removed from social and political processes. Instead it acts upon the body, becomes part of a process that produces the body in relation to gender ideology, social norms, class expectations, moral conduct, and religious practice. It becomes the means through which the body, its physicality, as well as emotions are assembled and regulated, certain desires and habits are cultivated, and certain others avoided or eliminated. Approaching veiling as an embodied spatial practice brings into focus how it participates in the production of the body, bodily behaviors, and emotions.[13] Viewing veiling as an embodied spatial practice allows the examination of the spatial experiences of and through the veiled body. The bodywork of veiling includes the cultivation of piety and modesty through everyday practices. Through veiling belief is formed, enacted, and embodied.

The case of one of my research participants in Istanbul, whom I will call Neriman, demonstrates the need for viewing veiling in

12 See Banu Gökarıksel and Anna Secor, "'Even I Was Tempted': The Moral Ambivalence and Ethical Practice of Veiling-Fashion in Turkey," *Annals of the Association of American Geographers* 102, no. 4 (2012): 847–62; Banu Gökarıksel and Anna Secor, "The Veil, Desire, and the Gaze: Turning the Inside Out," *Signs: Journal of Women in Culture and Society* 40, no. 1 (2014): 177–200.

13 Banu Gökarıksel, "Beyond the Officially Sacred: Religion, Secularism and the Body in the Production of Subjectivity," *Social and Cultural Geography* 10, no. 6 (2009): 657–74; Banu Gökarıksel, "The Intimate Politics of Secularism and the Headscarf: The Mall, the Neighborhood, and the Public Square in Istanbul," *Gender, Place, and Culture* 19, no. 1 (2012): 1–20.

such terms that emphasize embodiment and spatiality.[14] I met
Neriman in 2004. She explained to me that she grew up as a
nonpracticing, secular Muslim. When she decided in college
to begin wearing a headscarf and modest clothing as part of her
newfound Islamic commitment, many things changed in her life.
She became subject to the headscarf ban that was enforced at her
university at the time. Her family disowned her. And her relation
to her own body completely shifted. She understood her body as
not accepting her new mode of being. The most poignant sign
of this rejection was her shedding of lots of hair. She re-created
her body space by starting to shave her head (which she saw as
a disciplining tool), trying to learn how to walk and sit in skirts
(she was used to pants), and watching her body constantly for any
unwanted exposure, even of her wrists. Thus Neriman had to work
on her body and produce it anew. Her example shows that the veil
is much more than a mobile home or portable seclusion. It does
not simply enclose a space within. It certainly is not merely a shell,
not only because it affects the experience and presentation of the
self but also because it transforms that embodied self physically and
emotionally.

VEILING AND CITY SPACE

Veiling emerges as a productive lens through which to understand
space not only because of its significance for the creation of the
body. Veiling deeply affects the way veiled women can and do
move across, experience, and participate in the (re)production
of different city spaces. Writing about the experiences of veiled
women in Istanbul, Anna Secor argues that, rather than a single and

---

14 See also Gökarıksel, "Beyond the Officially Sacred."

uniform city space, when we approach the city of Istanbul through
the lens of veiling, we find multiple "regimes of veiling/unveiling"
that govern this urban space.[15] Secor's analysis shows that the
meanings and experience of veiling/nonveiling varies across urban
space; in one district nonveiling may be the norm, while in another
veiling may be the common and expected practice. I will use three
city sites to examine the embodied experiences of veiled women
in contemporary Istanbul: the upscale Akmerkez shopping mall,
the main street and mosque complex of the religiously and socially
conservative Fatih neighborhood, and the Beyazıt Square, where
many protests over the headscarf ban and other political issues take
place.[16]

Akmerkez opened in 1993 at the intersection of three upper-
middle-class neighborhoods of Istanbul. I conducted interviews
at this shopping mall in 1996 and 2000–2001. My research
demonstrated the construction of Akmerkez as a secular modern
space due to its management and the daily practices of mall patrons.
Akmerkez's advertisements and management contribute to the
construction of the mall as secular by displaying Ataturk's pictures
and speeches and, by doing so, visibly aligning itself with secular
modernity. One of the main components of the secularity of mall
space was the rendering of the veil as backward, lower class, and not
modern, and therefore out of place in the mall. Veiled women were
often made to feel that they do not belong in Akmerkez, and they
expressed their discomfort in Akmerkez and similar spaces in the
mid-1990s.

Yet this was not a secularity that went uncontested. The visibility
of religion in shopping malls gained more prominence especially
in the 1990s with the rise of a conservative Muslim elite. Shopping

15 Anna Secor, "The Veil and Urban Space in Istanbul: Women's Dress, Mobility and Islamic
Knowledge," *Gender, Place and Culture: A Journal of Feminist Geography* 9, no. 1 (2002): 5–22.
16 For a more detailed discussion, see Gökarıksel, "The Intimate Politics."

malls have become more smoothly incorporated into daily urban life and have become the popular destination of a new Islamic bourgeoisie and an aspiring Islamic middle class. Those who are part of the Islamic bourgeoisie assert themselves as deserving and legitimate members of the consumerist public constituted by the shopping mall. Today it is common to see fashionably dressed headscarf-wearing women in almost all shopping malls (perhaps still with the exception of Akmerkez). The prime minister's wife, Emine Erdoğan (who wears a headscarf and whose dress style is frequently discussed in the media), closed down the expensive British-based Harvey Nichols store in the fancy Kanyon mall (opened in 2006) for a shopping spree one Saturday in 2007.

In contrast to the contested secularity of mall space, we find a simultaneous plurality of styles, sartorial practices, and ideologies on the streets of the conservative Fatih district. Fatih, taking its name after the Ottoman conqueror of the city, is the paradigmatic Muslim *mahalle* (neighborhood) in its spatial organization and historical demographics. At the center of this area is the large and beautiful mosque complex, completed in 1471 as the first monumental project of Ottoman imperial Istanbul. Today most of these structures have disappeared, but the mosque remains very popular. The square surrounding the mosque serves as a playground, a picnic area, and a social space of a very different nature than that of the privately owned, closely monitored, and meticulously orchestrated spaces of shopping malls.

On Fatih's main street, Fevzi Paşa Boulevard, is a concentration of Islamic financial institutions interspersed with other banks, foreign exchange bureaus, clothing stores, tourism and *hajj* (Islamic pilgrimage) agencies, restaurants, and cafés. The main street of this area is lined with stores that feature a mix of styles, including the latest fashions for veiled women. Women on the streets are dressed in an amazing range of sartorial styles, including a diversity of veiling styles, from the completely enveloping black *çarşaf* to

little colorful headscarves worn over close-fitting shirts and jeans.
They walk around, work, meet friends at cafés, get money from
the bank, take their kids to the park, and go shopping. The veil is
very much "in" place in the streets of Fatih. Rather than feelings
of discomfort that dominate the discussions of veiled women on
Akmerkez, women speak about how comfortable they feel in Fatih.
They define this area as "their" Istanbul. Since veiling is generally
accepted (and no one is refused service at a café or a store because
of the headscarf), the differences between various styles of veiling
and the crafting of an individual style come to the fore in veiled
women's discussions about Fatih.

Just a short walk away from Fatih is Beyazıt Square. This public
city square dates back to Byzantine times but is constantly being
remade. It is delineated by Istanbul University's monumental main
entrance, the Beyazıt Mosque, street vendors that carry old books,
an Islamic calligraphy museum, and a few coffeehouses frequented
by activists. All of these places have been central to political
mobilization against the state and secularism in different ways and
in different eras. Istanbul University, the first modern university of
the Ottoman Empire, has been one of the strictest and consistently
forceful implementers of the headscarf ban, especially following the
1997 coup. The imposing historical gate of the university became
one of the central sites of numerous demonstrations and clashes
between students and the guards and police in the 1980s and 1990s.
Many women have had encounters with the entity called "the state"
at this gate, embodied by security guards who asked them to take
off their headscarves.

Across from this gate stands the highly ornate Beyazıt Mosque,
dating to the early sixteenth century. In front of the mosque there is
a protest almost every week, often following Friday prayers. Crowds
spill out of the mosque after the *cuma*, joining others (mostly
women) who have been waiting for the demonstration. The issues
vary in scope, from the headscarf ban in Turkey to supporting the

wave of protests in the Middle East. These protests have made this square famous not only as the hotbed of Islamist activism but also for the escalated police presence and violence with which the state has tried to suppress such activity.

In the summer of 2004, as I was returning from a day of research in Fatih, I had my first encounter with a Friday protest in Beyazıt Square. The topic was not the headscarf ban; the demonstration was organized to oppose U.S. president George W. Bush's arrival in Istanbul for a NATO summit. First I noticed the police and panzers lined up on the far side of the square. Then I heard *Allahuekber*s (lit. "God is Great") coming from inside the mosque. Demonstrators started to pour out from the mosque. Others joined this crowd, carrying posters that pictured Bush, British prime minister Tony Blair, and Israel's prime minister Ariel Sharon side by side. Women, dressed in different veiling styles, participated in this demonstration. They wore scarves on their heads and draped *kaffiyeh*s around their shoulders as a sign of solidarity with Palestinians. They were clustered on one side of the crowd, following impromptu gender segregation rules. That day I witnessed only one of many instances of an expanding field of women's activism—in this case, grappling with regional and global politics. There are many more protests that similarly find and formulate connections between women's day-to-day lives and events in Egypt, the Israeli occupation of Palestinian territories, or U.S. Middle East policy. Beyazıt Square becomes the place where transnational imaginaries of being Muslim are formed through collective action, and veiled women take center stage in these formations.

CONCLUSION

A spatial approach to veiling shows how this practice transforms even the most intimate and smallest of spaces: the body. Veiling participates in the production of the body as a space by organizing this space emotionally as well as materially. Body space is produced not in isolation but relationally: other bodies, objects, emotions, political motivations, and spaces all come into play in the production of body space through veiling practices. Complex political, social, and cultural processes and spatial relations shape the meaning of veiling and the veiled body. In Turkey, class relations, contested practices of secularism, Islamist politics, a growing consumer society, and a concern for lived Islam are among the factors that impact the encounters of the veil and the veiled body. A veiled woman experiences different city spaces quite differently, as this Reflection's journey from Akmerkez to Fatih to Beyazıt Square shows. However, veiled women rarely simply encounter these spaces; their very presence also participates in the remaking of these spaces. Approaching veiling as an embodied spatial practice thus opens up new questions to explore how veiling is productive of spaces and participates in the continuous process of space-making. This discussion shows that spaces are continuously made and remade through daily practices, and no boundary goes unchallenged nor remains permanent.

CHAPTER TWO

Imagine a Place

GEOMETRICAL AND PHYSICAL SPACE IN PROCLUS

Marije Martijn

1. INTRODUCTION

Contrary to what one might expect, among the Platonists of late antiquity we find a rich and varied collection of conceptions of space or place,[1] due not just to their inherently rich ontology but also because of their dialectic interaction with predecessors.[2] Questions raised by or in response to Plato and Aristotle, concerning the relation between space and place, matter, bodies, motion, vacuum, divisibility, and the category place belongs to, led to a plethora of answers.[3] The metaphysical

---

1   I discuss the terminology later.

2   For surveys of ancient concepts of space see Keimpe Algra, "Concepts of Space in Classical and Hellenistic Greek Philosophy," PhD dissertation, University of Utrecht, 1988; for Late Neoplatonism, see S. Sambursky, "Place and Space in Late Neoplatonism," *Studies in History and Philosophy of Science* 8 (1977): 173–87; S. Sambursky, *The Concept of Place in Late Neoplatonism* (Jerusalem: Israel Academy, 1982); Richard Sorabji, *The Philosophy of the Commentators 200–600 AD: A Sourcebook, Volume 2: Physics* (London: Duckworth, 2004).

3   The most influential passages in this context are Plato, *Timaeus,* and Aristotle, *Physics* IV 1–5.

Marije Martijn, *Imagine a Place* In: *Space.* Edited by: Andrew Janiak, Oxford University Press (2020). © Oxford University Press.
DOI: 10.1093/oso/9780199914104.003.0004

presuppositions of Neoplatonism, furthermore, led to an elaboration of the notions of place on three ontological levels: at the level of the physical realm, at that of the soul, and at that of the transcendent intellect. Our main ancient source on this topic is Simplicius, who left us a fascinating critical overview of Greek theories of place and space.[4]

At the level of physical bodies, we find place as a kind of container, or containing cause (cf. Plato's *chôra*), a mold or measure, a power which sorts the elements (Simplicius's and Damascius's views), or even a kind of body. This last and, according to Simplicius, "innovative" theory, which holds that place is a kind of light, is that of Proclus.[5] We will return to this notion in section 3. If we go one level up the Neoplatonic ontological ladder, from bodies to souls, we find the influential notion of space as the so-called intelligible matter of incorporeal extension or the place of mathematical objects (*phantasia*, Syrianus, Proclus, cf. Plotinus). This notion is discussed in section 2. Finally, at the level of the transcendent intellect, we find intelligible space, as the source and cause, the Form, so to speak, of lower kinds of space, analogous to eternity as the cause of time. This intelligible space is also the *locus*, to put it vaguely, of Intellect. Varieties of this kind of space are found in Iamblichus, Damascius, and Plotinus but *not* in Proclus, who instead criticizes it.[6]

This chapter will discuss Proclus's understanding of the "place of ideas" (*dA* III.4): imagination. We will focus especially on a problem of its use in geometry: When we imagine a three-dimensional object or an object in motion, what do we do? Where does this take place? My proposal is that these questions, which concern the possibility of

---

4 Simplicius presents his overview in the Corollary on Space, *In Phys.* 601–44, at 601.13ff. See Simplicius, *Corollaries on Place and Time*, trans. J. O. Urmson, Ancient Commentators on Aristotle (London: Duckworth, 1992), 3. A useful summary is to be found in Sorabji's introduction to the volume.

5 Proclus's view on space as a body is further elaborated at Simplicius, *In Phys.* 611.10–614.8, and critically investigated at 618.7ff. See section 3.

6 For Simplicius's overview, and Proclus's criticism of Plotinus's intelligible *matter*, see later discussion.

mental space, can be solved on the basis of the correspondence and relation between physical space and imagination, which is actually a kind of space.[7]

Phantasia, or imagination, is the capacity of the soul used in figurative thought such as in geometrical constructions. Discursive reasoning (*dianoia*) and imagination together reason about figures by "projecting" or "unfolding" *logoi* and performing operations on them. It is not entirely clear, either in Proclus or in the scholarly literature, what kind of extension imagination uses. Most scholars assume that it uses a two-dimensional screen, but we will defend the thesis that it is instead three-dimensional space.[8] The question concerning the nature of imagination is interesting for those who wish to understand Proclus, but it is also relevant in light of, on the one hand, the claim that Proclus's geometrical imagination was the precursor of the Kantian notion of space and, on the other hand, current theories of picture perception.

Help in understanding imagination may be found in Proclus's "innovative" notion of physical space, which has been considered a precursor of other later views (e.g., the medieval theory of the empyrean as the place of the bodies in the universe).[9] Proclus, as mentioned, argues that space has to be a kind of light, corporeal but immaterial, consisting of very fine matter, and that it is established by the World Soul as the place of the world.[10] Close parallels between our soul and the World Soul suggest that it too has recourse to something like imagination.

7 This is not a revolutionary proposal; see, e.g., D. G. MacIsaac, "Phantasia between Soul and Body in Proclus' Euclid Commentary," *Dionysius* 19 (2001): 125–36, who shows quite clearly why imagination has to be a kind of space but glosses over some differences we will address later.

8 Cf. D. Rabouin, "Proclus' Conception of Geometric Space and Its Actuality," in *Mathematizing Space: The Objects of Geometry from Antiquity to the Early Modern Age*, ed. Vincenzo De Risi (Basel: Birkhäuser, 2015), 105–42.

9 P. Duhem, *Le système du monde: Histoire des doctrines cosmologiques de Platon à Copernic*, vol. 1 (Paris: Hermann, 1959).

10 M. Griffin, 2012. "Proclus on Place as the Luminous Vehicle of the Soul," *Dionysius* 30 (2012): 161–86.

The evidence for this suggestion is thin, however. Divine Intellect, World Soul, and Nature collaborate in shaping the cosmos by infusing it with rational creative principles (*logoi*), which are characterized by Proclus as "projected." It is therefore tempting to assume that the role of the World Soul is comparable to that of the human soul and that some kind of imagination is in play.

In the following, I will show to what extent imagination and space are indeed analogous and in which sense they are not. The *tertium comparationis* will be the so-called vehicle of the soul.[11]

Section 2 presents the notion of imagination and its relation to matter and extension. Section 3 discusses the World Soul and physical space and the parallels between it and imagination. And section 4 contains a short conclusion with some considerations for further research.

Before we get on our way, a remark on terminology: the main Greek terms referring to space, place, and extension are *chôra, topos,* and *diastêma,* respectively, but these are not the only terms used, and, more important, they are often not used systematically and univocally, so their precise meaning has to be derived from the context.[12]

---

11 A. Lernould, "Imagination and Psychic Body: Apparitions of the Divine and Geometric Imagination according to Proclus," in *Gnosticism, Platonism and the Late Ancient World: Essays in Honour of John D. Turner,* ed. Kevin Corrigan et al. (Leiden: Brill, 2013), 595–607.

12 For a wonderful overview of ancient terminology and concepts related to space and place, especially in the context of geometry, see Henry Mendell, "What's Location Got to Do with It? Place, Space, and the Infinite in Classical Greek Mathematics," in *Mathematizing Space: The Objects of Geometry from Antiquity to the Early Modern Age,* ed. Vincenzo De Risi (Basel: Birkhäuser, 2015), 15–63. For terminology in Proclus, see also L.P. Schrenk, "Proclus on Space as Light," *Ancient Philosophy* 9, no. 1 (1989): 87–94. *Chôra* does not occur as related to space or place in geometrical works between Plato and Proclus, according to Mendell. In Proclus's case, this may be because he reserves the term for the first substrate, i.e., physical necessity. See G. Van Riel, "Proclus on Matter and Physical Necessity," in *Physics and Philosophy of Nature in Greek Neoplatonism,* ed. R. Chiaradonna and F. Trabattoni (Leiden: Brill, 2009), 231–57.

2. *PHANTASIA* AND INTELLIGIBLE MATTER: ARGUING FOR SPACE

For Proclus, geometrical proofs require the use of both discursive reasoning and imagination.[13] In his commentary on Euclid's plane geometry, he describes imagination in terms that suggest a two-dimensional screen. However, besides the obvious fact that stereometry requires three dimensions (and that the ultimate aim of Euclid's *Elements*, or so Proclus states, is to construct the Platonic solids), even in plane geometry three dimensions are needed; according to Proclus, real scientific proofs in plane geometry use motion of the plane figures. Other examples are the use of points outside the plane (e.g., for solid perpendiculars)[14] and the use of infinite lines.[15] These demands suggest instead that imagination itself is three-dimensional space. We will start by clarifying Proclus's views of what he thinks are properly scientific proofs in plane geometry: kinematic constructions. Subsequently we will discuss the role and nature of imagination and so-called intelligible matter and indications, besides the requirements of geometrical proofs, that geometry as Proclus sees it indeed uses a three-dimensional space.

2.1. Constructing a Helix: Kinematic Constructions

What is a helix? And how do we construct it? One way to find out is to put a squirrel at the foot of a tree and point it to a nut way up and at the back. The path it will follow up the tree is a helix. But that is a perceptible, sloppy helix. To obtain proper knowledge of the helix, we need a universal definition, as well as a universally valid method

---

13 For a recent overview of the history of this notion in ancient thought, see A. Sheppard, *The Poetics of Phantasia: Imagination in Ancient Aesthetics* (London: Bloomsbury Academic, 2014).

14 *In Eucl.* 283.13–19.

15 A related issue which is also addressed in contemporary philosophy of mathematics (Andrew Arana and Paolo Mancosu, "On the Relationship between Plane and Solid Geometry," *Review of Symbolic Logic* 5 (2012): 294–353), but which we will not go into here: using three-dimensionality in plane geometry means, for Proclus, proving the (ontologically or logically) prior from the posterior, which does not render the proof scientific or explanatory.

of constructing it. Proclus's first introduction of the construction of a cylindrical helix is that it is "traced by a point moving uniformly along a straight line that is moving around the surface of a cylinder. This moving point generates a helix any part of which coincides homoeomerously with any other."[16] He then rephrases the method in slightly but saliently different wording, namely that "the very mode of generating the cylindrical helix shows that it is a mixture of simple lines, for it is produced by the movement of a straight line about the axis of a cylinder and by the movement of a point along this line."[17] Besides the emphasis on the cylindrical helix being homoeomerous, which is not relevant to our purposes,[18] we see a shift here from a passive to an active formulation. Whereas in the first passage we read that the helix is traced (*grafomenên*) and generated (*ginetai*), in the second passage instead we read about its generation (*genesis*) and begetting (*gennatai*).

With this shift to slightly stronger terminology Proclus in fact introduces an improvement on Euclidean proofs. A description or a diagram of the construction of a helix would be deficient. To construct a helix, we need a cylinder, a line on the cylinder, a point on the line, and (uniform) *motion*. In other words, we need a *kinematic construction*. And for this construction, we need three dimensions.

As Orna Harari has convincingly argued, Proclus sometimes presents kinematic constructions as alternatives to Euclid's constructions, because of Neoplatonic metaphysics and epistemology: we need to find

---

16 *In Eucl.* 105.1–5, trans. Morrow: τὴν περὶ τὸν κύλινδρον ἕλικα γραφομένην, ὅταν εὐθείας κινουμένης περὶ τὴν ἐπιφάνειαν τοῦ κυλίνδρου σημείου ὁμοταχῶς ἐπ' αὐτῆς κινῆται. γίνεται γὰρ ἕλιξ, ἧς ὁμοιομερῶς πάντα τὰ μέρη πᾶσιν ἐφαρμόζει.

17 *In Eucl.* 105.18–22: δηλοῦν δὲ τῆς κυλινδρικῆς ἕλικος τὴν μίξιν τὴν ἐκ τῶν ἁπλῶν καὶ αὐτὴν τὴν γένεσιν. γεννᾶται γὰρ τῆς μὲν εὐθείας κύκλῳ κινουμένης περὶ τὸν ἄξονα τοῦ κυλίνδρου, τοῦ δὲ σημείου φερομένου ἐπὶ τῆς εὐθείας.

18 Proclus in the broader context defends the position that a geometrical object may be homoeomerous without being simple. The cylindrical helix is introduced as an example. It is homoeomerous because every part of it can be superimposed on every other part. But it is not simple. There are three types of lines: straight, curved, and mixed. And the helix is the prime example of a mixed line.

the simple causes which generated the complex world we live in.[19] Likewise, it is in the generation "before our eyes" of a mathematical object from simpler mathematical objects (a complex line from a simple one, a triangle from lines) that we understand what its true causes are.[20] Harari's example is the kinematic construction of an equilateral triangle.[21] Proclus there identifies "the motion of the straight lines, the one moving towards the side where it makes the interior angle, the other moving away from the side where it makes the exterior angle," as the *cause* of the generation of increase in the exterior angle and of decrease in the interior angle, respectively. And from this, he says, "you can infer how the generation of things brings before our eyes the true causes of what is sought."[22] As Harari says, "Through the kinematic construction, Proclus does not merely show that certain attributes hold for a triangle, he also shows that these attributes are derived from the triangle's being. . . . The kinematic construction accords with this metaphysical conception; it grounds the triangle's attributes in its mode of generation."[23]

So the kinematic construction, according to Proclus, provides us with perfect and scientific proof, as opposed to proof from nonnecessary attributes.[24] In the example, the auxiliary line used in the Euclidean proof of prop. I 16 is not essentially related to the geometrical object in question. Therefore, although that proof gives us a true conclusion,

---

19 O. Harari, "Methexis and Geometrical Reasoning in Proclus' Commentary on Euclid's Elements," *Oxford Studies in Ancient Philosophy* 30 (2006): 361–89.

20 For physical generation, see section 3.

21 Proclus provides this construction as proof of prop. 16, that in any triangle, if one side is produced (using an auxiliary line), the resulting exterior angle is greater than either of the interior and opposite angles.

22 *In Eucl.* 310.3–8, modified by Morrow: αἰτία δὲ τούτων ἡ κίνησις τῶν εὐθειῶν, τῆς μὲν ἐφ' ἃ ποιεῖ τὴν ἐντὸς γωνίαν κινουμένης ἐπὶ ταῦτα, τῆς δὲ ἐφ' ἃ ποιεῖ τὴν ἐκτὸς γωνίαν ἀπὸ τούτων φερομένης. καὶ ἔχεις ἐκ τούτων συλλογίζεσθαι, πῶς αἱ γενέσεις τῶν πραγμάτων ὑπ' ὄψιν ἡμῖν τὰς ἀληθινὰς ἄγουσι τῶν ζητουμένων αἰτίας.

23 Harari, "Methexis," 385–86.

24 *In Eucl.* 206.12–26.

it does not give us any information regarding the cause of that conclusion or of the object.

An important question, then, is where, and what, is "before our eyes"? And, equally important for our purposes, who is doing the moving in the kinematic construction? Proclus does not have in mind construction in sand or in wax. And it is not so much the point or line itself that moves; it is us. For example, the construction of the cone is formulated as follows: "*If we think* (*noesantes*) of a circle lying in a plane with a point above it and from the point project a straight line to the circumference of the circle and *set the line in revolution, we shall produce* (*poiêsomen*) a conical surface, which is mixed."[25] So a kinematic construction is performed "before our eyes" in the sense of "in thought." "We think" of a circle. And we are the movers and the creators: in thought, *we project* a line and set it in *motion* and thereby *produce* a cone.[26]

2.2. Discursive Thought, Imagination, and Projection

The thinking involved in geometrical constructions is not, of course, purely performed by discursive thought (*dianoia*).[27] We can reason and talk about universal essences and essential properties of geometrical entities,[28] but we cannot perform any operations on them. For that, we need particular images. Not necessarily physical ones, however, as we can use "imaged" (to avoid "imagined" or "imaginary") ones: projections of the principles in imagination (*phantasia*).[29] Our

---

25 *In Eucl.* 118.10–14. The surface of the cone is mixed, because it is both a triangle and a circle.
νοήσαντες γὰρ κύκλον ἐν τῷ ὑποκειμένῳ ἐπιπέδῳ καὶ σημεῖον μετέωρον καὶ ἀπὸ τοῦ σημείου προσεκβάλλοντες εὐθεῖαν τῇ τοῦ κύκλου περιφερείᾳ καὶ περιελίξαντες αὐτὴν ποιήσομεν κωνικὴν ἐπιφάνειαν μικτὴν οὖσαν.

26 We will return to the ontological status of the resulting product later. (Is it imaginary? Real?)

27 The question is not "What are mental images of perceptible qualities?" For this see Marmodoro 2014.

28 The Greek here is *logoi*, which is often translated as "creative reason principles" because they are the rational structures derived from the transcendent Forms, which create entities on lower levels of the ontological hierarchy.

29 For discussions of imagination from Aristotle to Proclus, see Sheppard, *Poetics*.

understanding or discursive thought contains the principles of geometrical entities, as lower Platonic forms, but cannot see them "wrapped up" in a kind of unitary vision. Instead, it "unfolds and exposes them and presents them to the imagination sitting in the vestibule." It then explicates its knowledge "in imagination or with its aid" and can hence study them in separation from sensible things, because imagination provides a "matter apt for receiving its forms."[30]

This description of imagination, which "sits in the vestibule" (i.e., just outside) of discursive reasoning, shows what are the attributes making it a suitable—and even indispensable—assistant to the geometer's discursive thought: it is separated from the perceptible; it offers a receptacle (*hypodochê*),[31] a special kind of matter for the unfolded geometrical entities,[32] as well as a tool for unfolding them. A tool, because it has a productive and "formative activity," and a special kind of matter, because it exists "in and with the body," and hence it "always produces individual pictures that have divisible extension and shape."[33]

---

30 *In Eucl.* 54.27–55.6, trans. Morrow. The "vestibule" is an allusion to Plato, *Phil.* 64c, and is used as a metaphor for a transitional space between inside and out. (In ancient Greece, it was the place where young men were allowed to court maidens.) ἔχουσα γὰρ ἡ διάνοια τοὺς λόγους, ἀσθενοῦσα δὲ συνεπτυγμένως ἰδεῖν ἀναπλοῖ τε αὐτοὺς καὶ ὑπεκτίθεται καὶ εἰς τὴν φαντασίαν ἐν προθύροις κειμένην προάγει καὶ ἐν ἐκείνῃ ἢ καὶ μετ' ἐκείνης ἀνελίττει τὴν γνῶσιν αὐτῶν, ἀγαπήσασα μὲν τὸν ἀπὸ τῶν αἰσθητῶν χωρισμόν, τὴν δὲ φανταστὴν ὕλην εὐτρεπῆ πρὸς ὑποδοχὴν εὑροῦσα τῶν ἑαυτῆς εἰδῶν.

31 As has been pointed out by scholars, there are remarkable parallels between Proclus's imagination and Plato's receptacle (*hypodochê*) as presented in the *Timaeus*; see C. Bouriau, "L'imagination Productrice: Descartes entre Proclus et Kant," *Littératures Classiques* 45 (2002), "L'imagination au XVIIe siècle," 48–49; G. Claessens, "Proclus: Imagination as a Symptom," *Ancient Philosophy* 32, no. 2 (2012): 402–4. Cf. L. P Schrenk, "Proclus on Corporeal Space," *Archiv Für Geschichte Der Philosophie* 76 (1994): 151–67. Claessens argues Proclus would have had two reasons to draw a parallel with the receptacle. First of all, the fact that imagination is a kind of matter, as is the receptacle. And second, there is a necessity of an intermediate category, connecting Being to Becoming, both in Plato's universe and in Proclus's mathematics. As Proclus, however, follows Aristotle in equating matter and the receptacle (*In Tim.* II 10.4–9), with Proclus, *Commentary on Plato's Timaeus, Volume III—Book 3, Part 1: Proclus on the World's Body*, ed. and trans. D. Baltzly (Cambridge, UK: Cambridge University Press, 2007) we will not treat these parallels separately.

32 On the relevance of the receptacle from Plato's *Timaeus*, see later discussion.

33 *In Eucl.* 51.20–52.3: καὶ γὰρ ἡ φαντασία διά τε τὴν μορφωτικὴν κίνησιν καὶ τὸ μετὰ σώματος καὶ ἐν σώματι τὴν ὑπόστασιν ἔχειν μεριστῶν ἀεὶ καὶ διῃρημένων ἐστὶν καὶ ἐσχηματισμένων τύπων οἰστική, καὶ πᾶν ὃ γιγνώσκει τοιαύτην ἔλαχεν ὕπαρξιν.

The imagination used in geometry is not what became of it in modern times: it does not produce fiction, because it receives its contents from a higher source.[34] Imagination, as intermediary between perception and intellect, is not "moved" from outside the body, as is perception, but receives knowledge from intellect. Since it is bound to the body, however (more on which later), it "draws its knowledge out of the undivided center and into the medium of division, extension, and figure."

For this reason everything that it thinks is a picture or a shape of its thought. It thinks the circle as extended, and although this circle is free of external matter, it possesses an intelligible matter provided by the imagination itself. This is why there is more than one circle in the imagination, as there is more than one circle in the sense world; for with extension there appear also differences in size and number among circles and triangles.[35]

The essence of the circle is not extended, but in the geometer's imagination it gains extension. Moreover, although the circle is not a corporeal entity, the extension is accompanied by a special kind of matter, "intelligible matter." That is why geometry can work with, e.g., a plurality of circles, and of different sizes, even if there is a unique essence of circle, without magnitude.

To sum up, imagination is a creator of cognitive entities; it has a productive motion of its own, with which it brings the undivided universal

---

34 Note, however, that as Sheppard, *Poetics*, has shown, this same imagination or (in Iamblichus) a second type of imagination may also be used for imagining nonexistent entities, by "looking down," rather than up.

35 *In Eucl.* 52.20–53.5: ἡ δ' αὖ φαντασία τὸ μέσον κέντρον κατέχουσα τῶν γνώσεων ἀνεγείρεται μὲν ἀφ' ἑαυτῆς καὶ προβάλλει τὸ γνωστόν, ἅτε δὲ οὐκ ἔξω σώματος οὖσα ἐκ τοῦ ἀμεροῦς τῆς ζωῆς εἰς μερισμὸν καὶ διάστασιν καὶ σχῆμα προάγει τὰ γνωστὰ αὐτῆς, καὶ διὰ τοῦτο πᾶν, ὅπερ ἂν νοῇ, τύπος ἐστὶ καὶ μορφὴ νοήματος, καὶ τόν τε κύκλον διαστατῶς νοεῖ τῆς μὲν ἐκτὸς ὕλης καθαρεύοντα νοητὴν δὲ ὕλην ἔχοντα τὴν ἐν αὐτῇ, καὶ διὰ τοῦτο οὐχ εἷς ἐν αὐτῇ κύκλος, ὥσπερ οὐδὲ ἐν τοῖς αἰσθητοῖς. ἅμα γὰρ διάστασις ἀναφαίνεται καὶ τὸ μεῖζον καὶ τὸ ἔλασσον καὶ τὸ πλῆθος τῶν τε κύκλων καὶ τῶν τριγώνων.

knowledge of intellect into extension, division, plurality, and shape; it is in the body; and it makes pictures in and with intelligible matter.[36] The presence of extension, shape, and intelligible matter has led scholars of modern philosophy to see Proclus as the forerunner of notions of absolute space.[37] In this context it is interesting to compare the tentative proposal of Mendell, in his discussion of the different uses of the term τόπος in Proclus: "τόπος is a region (dare I say space) where a construction is to take place."[38]

2.3. Matter (Intelligible) and Dimensionality

As we will see, however, the standard interpretation of the material side of imagination is that it is a screen onto which figures are projected; in one case the relation between rational principle and image is described as that between a novel and its film.[39] We will first elaborate this view, and then show it to be unnecessary and untenable.

---

36 D. Nikulin, *Matter, Imagination and Geometry: Ontology, Natural Philosophy and Mathematics in Plotinus, Proclus and Descartes* (Ashgate, 2002), speaks of "visualizable extension" and "quasi-extension" and of geometrical figures as "appearing" to be extended. I agree, as long as we maintain that the extension, although visualized, is nonetheless real.

37 See, e.g., M. Domski, "Newton and Proclus: Geometry, Imagination, and Knowing Space," *Southern Journal of Philosophy* 50, no. 3 (2012): 389–413.

38 Mendell, "What's Location?"

39 See MacIsaac, "Phantasia"; Richard Sorabji, *Matter, Space and Motion* (London: Duckworth, 1988). Cf. Christoph Helmig, "Aristotle's Notion of Intelligible Matter," *Quaestio* 7 (2007): 53–78. "These objects are not abstracted from sensibles, as Aristotle would hold, but projected into *phantasia* by discursive reason (*dianoia*). Hence, *phantasia* figures as a projection screen for *dianoia*." Cf. D. Nikulin, "Imagination and Mathematics in Proclus," *Ancient Philosophy* 28, no. 1 (2008): 153–72: "This act or process of picture-like 'visualization' of a non-extended and indivisible mathematical object, or λόγος, as a geometrically extended and divisible figure or φαντασόν may be compared to a novel on film" (166). See also O. Harari, "Proclus' Account of Explanatory Demonstrations in Mathematics and Its Context," *Archiv für Geschichte der Philosophie* 90, no. 2 (2008): 137–64. Cf. Morrow: "and that onto which it is projected is the so-called 'passive intellect' (τὸ δὲ ἐν ᾧ τὸ προβαλλόμενον παθητικὸς οὗτος καλούμενος νοῦς, *In Eucl.* 56.15–18; cf. 17.4–6)"; P. Lautner, "The Distinction between Phantasia and Doxa in Proclus' *In Timaeum*," *Classical Quarterly* 52 (2002): 257–69. R. Chlup, *Proclus: An Introduction* (Cambridge, UK: Cambridge University Press, 2012), and Nikulin, "Imagination," have both "in/into" and "on/onto." Rabouin ("Proclus' Conception") in his article on Proclus's conception of geometric space does not seem to think there is a tension between screen and space. (See later discussion.) So far, I have found only one scholar who consistently speaks of projection *in* or *into* imagination: D. J. O'Meara, *Pythagoras Revived* (Oxford: Clarendon Press, 1989).

Intelligible matter is like perceptible matter in that it is suitable to the reception of universals and their multiplication into individuals, but unlike it in the sense that it receives imaged (imagined or imaginary) objects rather than perceptible ones.[40] This is and is not intelligible matter as we know it from Aristotle.[41] In the *Metaphysics*, Aristotle introduces the distinction between sensible and intelligible matter: "One type of matter is intelligible, one sensible, and in a definition one part is always matter, the other actuality, e.g., the circle is a plane figure" (*Met.* H 6, 1045a33–35).[42] The parallel with "a round bronze" (1045a26–27), where "round" is the form and "bronze" the matter, suggests that in the definition of the circle, "plane" or "plane figure" is the intelligible matter. Elsewhere, Aristotle describes intelligible matter as the nonsensible substrate of (otherwise sensible) things, such as mathematicals.[43] As Helmig emphasizes, the link between this notion of intelligible matter and imagination seems to be in the background already in Aristotle, who states that thinking is impossible without images, which implies that it requires imagination, and without a continuum, which in turn implies that it requires something similar to intelligible matter.[44]

Proclus, however, criticizes the Aristotelian notion of intelligible matter because he takes it to be passive,[45] although, considering the

---

40 *In Eucl.* 51.9–20.

41 For Aristotle's notion of intelligible matter, see Helmig, "Aristotle's Notion," with references in n1. Helmig argues for a unitary notion of intelligible matter in Aristotle. See also T. K. Johansen, *The Intellect and the Limits of Naturalism* (Oxford: Oxford University Press, 2012).

42 Aristotle introduces the notion of intelligible matter in this context to solve a particular problem, namely how to maintain the unity of a substance in spite of its definition containing two elements. By identifying the two as form and (intelligible) matter (rather than, e.g., two ontologically equal components, such as Platonic Forms), this aporia is solved.

43 The essence of the hemicircle exists, not because it is part of the essence of the circle but because of the nonsensible substrate of a circle, which can be cut in half. *Met.* Z 10 1036a9–12 and 1036b33–1037a6. See also *Met.* K, 1, 1059b15–16.

44 Helmig, "Aristotle's Notion," with ref. to *dM* 449b31–450a2 and 450a7–8, cf. *dA* III 4, 429b18–22.

45 *In Eucl.* 52.3. The passage inspiring the equation of intelligible matter with passive intellect is probably *dA* 430a17–19, with a24. Cf. also *In Tim.* I 244.20–22 and III 158.5–10, where Proclus refers to imagination as the "last echo" of intellect.

fact that discursive thought works without shape also according to Aristotle, we need an active, shaping matter; this matter should even have a certain form of "knowledge," i.e., be capable of somehow contributing to the knowledge of the geometer.[46] Plotinus too has a notion of intelligible matter, which Proclus also criticized, mainly because he suggests the presence of a shapeless, formless, and indeterminate substrate of the Forms, the *locus* of the intellect. This Space (capital *S*) would have to be the source and cause of lower kinds of space, analogous to Eternity as the cause of time. However, at the level of the Intellect, says Proclus, indeterminacy is present as the power of the determinate (the Forms), not as their substrate.[47] Proclus does use the same Platonic expressions as Plotinus, e.g., τόπος νοητός (*Resp.* 509d2, 517b5) and τόπος ὑπερουράνιος (*Phdr.* 247c3, discussed extensively by Proclus at *TP* IV 22–23), but explains them as metaphors.[48]

But Proclus's own description is problematic as well:

> Soul, exercising her capacity to know, *projects on* the imagination, as on a *mirror*, the ideas of the figures; and the imagination, receiving in *image* form these *reflections* of what is within, by their means affords the soul an opportunity to turn inward from the images and attend to herself. It is as if a man looking at himself in a mirror and

---

46 This criticism is due to the equation of intelligible matter with passive intellect.

47 At *TP* III 9 39.15–40.8 we read that the Plotinian hylomorphic description of Being would be correct in Proclus's view only if "form" refers to the unity and existence of Being and "matter" corresponds to (is the ἀνάλογον of) its power (δύναμις). Plotinians misunderstand Plato if they posit a shapeless, formless, and indeterminate nature at the level of intelligible being. Limit and unlimited are present there, but relate to one another not as matter and form but as existence and power.

48 The expression *topos ideôn* (cf. Arist. *dA* III.4) should not be taken to refer to a ἕδρα, "seat" (*In Parm.* 930.10–20). Cf. *In Tim.* I 385.30–386.2, where the Orphic reference to a "gulf" (χάσμα) is likewise interpreted as the Forms' place or space (ὡς χώρα τῶν εἰδῶν καὶ τόπος) without place (ἕδρα). There is another, more interesting kind of absolute space, referred to by Proclus as ὁ ἀληθῶς τόπος (*In Tim.* I 161.5ff.). More on this later. For a general remark on Greek terminology of space and place see earlier discussion.

marveling at the power of nature and at his own appearance should wish to look upon himself directly.[49]

The image of the mirror, which reflects projected images, suggests that intelligible matter is flat—which would be a problem for kinematic constructions. Other passages seem to confirm this:

> Our geometer [i.e., Euclid] has chosen one of [the different kinds of surfaces], the plane, ... for his inquiry can proceed more easily with this than with any other surface.... For this reason also he gives his work the subtitle "plane geometry." And thus we must think of the plane as *projected* and *lying before our eyes* and the understanding as writing everything upon it, the imagination becoming something like a plane mirror to which the ideas of the understanding send down impressions of themselves.[50]

This passage and others like it are full of references to Proclus's predecessors. "Before our eyes" echoes Aristotle's *On the Soul* (427b18–22), and the reflection in a mirror is a well-known Platonic image. It is not the treacherous use of the mirror that is echoed here,[51] however, but a more positive Platonic example: the liver in the *Timaeus* (70e ff.),

---

49 Proclus, *In Eucl.* 141.4–12, trans. Morrow, modified by O'Meara, *Pythagoras Revived*. οὕτως ἡ ψυχὴ κατὰ τὸ γνωστικὸν ἐνεργοῦσα προβάλλει περὶ τὴν φαντασίαν ὥσπερ εἰς κάτοπτρον τοὺς τῶν σχημάτων λόγους, ἡ δ' ἐν εἰδώλοις αὐτὰ δεχομένη καὶ ἐμφάσεις ἔχουσα τῶν ἔνδον ὄντων διὰ τούτων τῇ ψυχῇ παρέχεται τὴν εἰς τὸ εἴσω στροφὴν καὶ πρὸς ἑαυτὴν τὴν ἀπὸ τῶν εἰδώλων ἐνέργειαν· οἷον εἴ τις ἑαυτὸν ὁρῶν ἐν κατόπτρῳ καὶ θαυμάσας τὴν τῆς φύσεως δύναμιν καὶ τὴν ἑαυτοῦ μορφὴν ἑαυτὸν ἰδεῖν θελήσειεν καὶ λάβοι δύναμιν τοιαύτην, ὥστε ὅλως ὁρῶν καὶ ὁρατὸν ἀποτελεσθῆναι.

50 *In Eucl.* 120.13–121.7, trans. Morrow. ὧν μίαν ὁ γεωμέτρης ἐκλεξάμενος, τὴν ἐπίπεδον ... καὶ γὰρ εὐπορώτερος ὁ λόγος αὐτῷ γίνεται μᾶλλον ἢ ἐπ' ἄλλης ἐπιφανείας. ... καὶ γὰρ τὴν πραγματείαν ἐντεῦθεν ἐπίπεδον προσείρηκεν καὶ οὕτω δεῖ νοεῖν τὸ μὲν ἐπίπεδον οἷον προβεβλημένον καὶ πρὸ ὀμμάτων κείμενον, πάντα δὲ ὡς ἐπὶ τούτῳ τὴν διάνοιαν γράφουσαν, τῆς μὲν φαντασίας οἷον ἐπιπέδῳ κατόπτρῳ προσεικασμένης, τῶν δὲ ἐν διανοίᾳ λόγων τὰς ἑαυτῶν ἐμφάσεις εἰς ἐκεῖνο καταπεμπόντων.

51 For this image, known from *Republic* and *Sophist*, see D. De Smet, M. Sebti, and G. De Callataÿ, *Miroir et Savoir: La Transmission D'un Thème Platonicien, Des Alexandrins À La Philosophie Arabo-Musulmane. Actes Du Colloque International Tenu À Leuven et Louvain-La-Neuve, Les 17 et 18 November 2005*, vol. 38 (Leuven: Leuven University Press, 2008).

which is like a mirror in that it receives images from the rational soul—and through which the rational soul can study itself.[52] Such loyalty to Plato is perhaps not a very satisfactory answer to the question why imagination is portrayed as two-dimensional, as it does not explain why Proclus now emphasizes the planeness of the mirror. Two further reasons may be that, in the second passage quoted Proclus explains the subtitle of Euclid's work and its focus on plane geometry, and that in general the *flatness* refers to the reliability of the images. The actual mirrors of Proclus's day and age were probably not very smooth, which would allow reflections, but not perfect ones; as Nikulin in "Imagination and Mathematics in Proclus" rightly emphasizes, by likening imagination to a kind of "*smooth* surface," Proclus points out that it is unlike "the mirror of bodily matter, which distorts the projections of discursive reason."

The downside of this analogy as a whole, of course, is that we are left with very flat figures, which does not combine very well with the three-dimensionality of stereometrical figures or, for that matter, to some of the kinematic constructions Proclus finds in plane geometry.[53]

The same seems to be true for Proclus's description of the product of *phantasia* as *typoi*,[54] imprints or pictures. This notion echoes both *Tim.* 70e, mentioned just now, and *Tim.* 50c, where the natural world is compared to the result of a signet ring pressing its imprints into wax. Now although the imprints in wax are not entirely flat, the picture is

52 Cf. Christoph Helmig, *Forms and Concepts. Concept Formation in the Platonic Tradition* (Berlin: De Gruyter, 2012); A. Sheppard, "The Mirror of Imagination: The Influence of Timaeus 70e ff.," in *Ancient Approaches to Plato's Timaeus*, ed. R. W. Sharples and A. Sheppard (London: Institute of Classical Studies, 2001), 203–12; R. Arnzen, "Wie Mißt Man den Göttlichen Kreis? Phantasievermögen, Raumvorstellung und Geometrischer Gegenstand in Den Mathematischen Theorien Proclus', Al-Fārābīs und Ibn Al-Haythams," in *Imagination—Fiktion—Kreation: Das Kulturschaffende Vermögen Der Phantasie* (Munich: Saur Verlag, 2003), 115–40.

53 Cf. Claessens, "Proclus," 4n10.

54 "Imagination, both by virtue of its formative activity and because it has existence with and in the body, always produces individual pictures (*typoi*) that have divisible extension and shape, and everything that it knows has this kind of existence" (*In Eucl.* 51.20–52.3). Cf. *In Tim.* I 343.9–10: δόξα δὲ φαντασίαν, διότι μετὰ τύπου καὶ μορφῆς, ὧν αὐτὴ κρείττων· Doxa is better than *phantasia*, because the latter works with *typos* and *morphe*.

still that of forms printed *onto* something. From this perspective, the mirror is a more successful image, to the extent that we at least have the perspective of the three dimensions projected on the plane.

And again, Proclus at times describes the activities of geometers with flat Platonic images as being analogous to those of a painter, i.e., drawing figures (*schêmata*), but in thought,[55] or of imagination as being a painter, while common perception (*koinê aisthêsis*) is a clerk.[56] Finally, there is the familiar terminology, used primarily for the activity of discursive thought but also for its acting upon and with imagination: unfolding, developing, unrolling—imagination as scroll.[57]

How does the need for three dimensions square with these two-dimensional metaphors? Many of the expressions used, which ultimately go back to Plato, are also used in contexts which actually concern shaping in three dimensions: for example, the demiurge is also a painter, and in shaping the universe he unfolds the Forms.[58] And although a *typos* is the imprint of a seal, it is also a mold, a figure in relief, a lifelike image. (Children are *typoi* of their parents.)

So the analogies used in describing imagination need not imply that the *tertium comparationis* includes the number of dimensions involved, and there is no need in this respect to speak of projection of *pictures onto* imagination or intelligible matter.[59]

Part of the difficulty in understanding the kind of extensionality figuring in Proclus's theory is the fact that it is unclear what *probolê*,

55 *Euthyd.* 290b–c; cf. *Meno* 73e. Cf. Nikulin, "Imagination," 165.

56 Plato, *Philebus* 39b. Cf. Proclus, *In Remp.* I 233.8–16: οὐ μὴν ἀλλ' ὅ γε ἐν τῷ <Φιλήβῳ> [p. 39b] Σωκράτης τὸν ζωγράφον ἐν ἡμῖν ἕτερον λέγων εἶναι τοῦ γραμματέως τοῦ διὰ τῶν αἰσθήσεων γράφοντος ἐν τῇ ψυχῇ μιμήματα τῶν παθημάτων, ὧν αἱ αἰσθήσεις ἀπαγγέλλουσιν, οὐκέτι τοῦτον ἐνεργοῦντα μετὰ τῆς αἰσθήσεως, ἀλλ' αὐτὸν καθ' αὑτὸν ἀνακινοῦντα τοὺς ἀπ' ἐκείνων τύπους ἐνδείκνυται τὸν ζωγράφον κατὰ τὸ φανταστικὸν τάττων, τὸν δὲ γραμματιστὴν κατὰ τὴν κοινὴν αἴσθησιν, ἕτερα εἶναι ταῦτα κατ' οὐσίαν ἀλλήλων.

57 *In Eucl.* 62.11–12: κατὰ δὲ τὰς μέσας γνώσεις ἀνελίττει τοὺς διανοητικοὺς λόγους καὶ ἐξαπλοῖ. Cf. also 54.27–55.18 (O'Meara, *Pythagoras Revived*, 166).

58 For the demiurge as painter, see, e.g., *In Tim.* II 281.21, inspired by *Tim.* 55c; for his unfolding the Forms, see *In Crat.* 101.4.

59 Helmig, *Forms and Concepts*, 213.

projection, really means. As a description of an action (of projecting, throwing, or thrusting forward) the expression is quite clear. The range of objects that may be projected—e.g., a spear, a shield, a tongue of land, a jutting rock, and an elephant's trunk[60]—is not very informative with regard to the nature of that in which what is projected ends up. The combination of the image of the flat mirror with *probolē* as putting forward a weapon or shield in defense brings to mind the image of a flat screen, especially to us who are so used to flat screens. However, the examples show that other options are not excluded.

Helmig argues that the main point made by the word *probolē* in the specific context of Proclus's epistemology is that of the external presentation of our innate *logoi*, i.e., the forms as they are present in our intellect. Recollection (*anamnēsis*) for Proclus consists in unfolding the *logoi* and presenting them, holding them out, to oneself.[61] Helmig also shows that, in general, in the context of recollection, translating *probolē* as "projection" is misleading, as it supposes a receptacle of some sort. The exception, he concludes, is geometry, where we do find such a receptacle, namely the intelligible matter of *phantasia*.

Instead, I would like to propose that, for all instances of *probolē*, we could use the sense of "projection" or "holding out" if the receptacle in question is a type of empty space—primarily to allow us to put some distance between us and that which is projected. The obvious benefit in general would be a univocal notion, and more specifically, it would fit our understanding of intelligible matter. Of at least twenty-five instances of *probolē* and cognate terms in the *Euclid Commentary*, only five have a prepositional attribute informing us regarding that onto/into which the soul projects the *logoi*. In those five cases, it is the context which determines the preposition: "in (*en*) passive intellect,"

---

60 Liddel and Scott, s.v.

61 Helmig, *Forms and Concepts*.

"about (*peri*) imagination," and even "as if in (*eis*) a mirror."[62] Only in the explanation of the "plane" of plane geometry, with the combined metaphors of a mirror and drawing, do we end up with projection "onto" (*epi*): "We must think of *this plane* [of plane geometry; my emphasis] as projected and lying before the eyes, discursive thinking as if writing all things onto it, and imagination as likened to a plane mirror."[63] So it is the Platonic images used that determine the terminology and the appeal of the images that give imagination its reputation as a screen,[64] but all we need is, strictly speaking, some form of distance between us and the object of projection.

Corroboration for the suggestion that in Proclus's geometrical imagination the objects are furthermore projected in three-dimensional space[65] can be found in the work of his teacher, who was a major source of inspiration.

Syrianus offers an enlightening presentation of mathematical objects and their places. His focus is different from that of Proclus, as he is commenting on Aristotle, specifically on his criticism of a Platonic notion of the place of mathematicals as generated simultaneously with the mathematicals (*Met.* N 1092a17–21). Interestingly, however, Syrianus does not follow Aristotle's lead by defending a Platonic proper place of *particulars*,[66] but instead replies by pointing to the specific location of geometrical solids as opposed to physical bodies on the one hand and

---

62 *In Eucl.* 56.16–18: τὸ δὲ ἐν ᾧ τὸ προβαλλόμενον παθητικὸς οὗτος καλούμενος νοῦς; 57.7–8: αὐτὰ δὲ ἕκαστα τὰ διαιρούμενα καὶ συντιθέμενα σχήματα περὶ τὴν φαντασίαν προβέβληται; 141.5–6: προβάλλει περὶ τὴν φαντασίαν ὥσπερ εἰς κάτοπτρον τοὺς τῶν σχημάτων λόγους; cf. 137.6–7.

63 *In Eucl.* 121.2–6: δεῖ νοεῖν τὸ μὲν ἐπίπεδον οἷον προβεβλημένον καὶ πρὸ ὀμμάτων κείμενον, πάντα δὲ ὡς ἐπὶ τούτῳ τὴν διάνοιαν γράφουσαν, τῆς μὲν φαντασίας οἷον ἐπιπέδῳ κατόπτρῳ προσεικασμένης.

64 Cf. the emphasis of Helmig, *Forms and Concepts*, 297, inspired by Mueller's tracing of Proclus's position to Iamblichus. Interestingly, however, in Iamblichus we find an image that is missing from Proclus, namely of mathematical objects as shadows falling on the ground: *dCMS* 8.47–52 (trans. Sheppard and Martijn), cf. *dCMS* 34.4–8. Iamblichus's primary interest is the ontological dependence of mathematical entities (the first appearance), but he is certainly also discussing the place of appearance of mathematical objects in the soul (the second appearance).

65 We will return to the equation of intelligible matter with space in section 3.

66 Allowing for their separation, *Met.* N 1092a19–20.

forms on the other:[67] he holds that our imagination is the *place* (*topos*) of mathematical bodies, just as matter is the place of enmattered forms. Physical matter receives enmattered forms from nature but is entirely passive and irrational and cannot really possess the forms, whereas the imagination "receives [i.e., is a receptacle for] mathematical body from the higher soul" and "both knows it and is able to preserve it to the extent that it is <in> it." Syrianus then presents a short hierarchy of four kinds of places (*topoi*), namely the place of physical bodies, the place of enmattered forms, the place of mathematical bodies, and the place of immaterial reason principles.[68] Syrianus's discussion of kinds of place is interesting in a number of ways. First is his broad use of *topos*, rather in the way we might use *locus*; this is unfortunate, one might say, as it suggests a certain semantic looseness, which makes the passage less informative. That said, however, it looks like Syrianus is taking place here as a material receptacle of sorts, or perhaps a natural place, with properties appropriate to the ontological level in question. Note, however, that Syrianus's distinction of imagination as the place of mathematical bodies, and physical matter as the place of enmattered forms is confusing as it apparently puts imagination on a par with matter and mathematical bodies with forms; the later distinction of four levels is clearer, despite the fact that Syrianus is not very explicit about which four places he is referring to. The confusion may be resolved by appealing to the third factor Syrianus introduces, besides what we may call matter and form, namely the source of the forms (nature and the higher soul, respectively). In that

---

67 Note that geometry uses superimposition of figures.

68 Syrianus *in Met.* 186.16–28: οὐδ' ἂν ἡμεῖς ἀστοχόν τι λέγοιμεν περὶ τοῦ θείου Πλάτωνος φήσαντες αὐτὸν τοῖς μαθηματικοῖς σώμασι τὴν φαντασίαν ἡμῶν τόπον ποιεῖν, ὥσπερ τοῖς ἐνύλοις εἴδεσι τὴν ὕλην, διαφέρειν δὲ τοσοῦτον ὅτι παρὰ μὲν τῆς φύσεως ἡ ὕλη τὸ ἔνυλον εἶδος ὑποδεχομένη οὔτε οἶδεν ὃ δέχεται οὔτε διακατέχειν αὐτὸ δύναται, παρὰ δὲ τῆς ἄνω ψυχῆς ἡ φαντασία τὸ μαθηματικὸν σῶμα δεξαμένη καὶ θεωρεῖ αὐτὸ καὶ διαφυλάττειν ἐφ' ὅσον ἐστιν <ἐν> αὐτῇ δύναται· ἄλλος οὖν τόπος σωμάτων φυσικῶν, ἄλλος ἐνύλων εἰδῶν, ἄλλος μαθηματικῶν σωμάτων, ἄλλος ἀύλων λόγων. There is a textual problem here (the subclause ἐφ' ὅσον ἔστιν αὐτῇ, where the subject of ἔστιν is missing). We follow Kroll and Mueller by adding ἐν. On Syrianus's notion of imagination, see also G. Watson, *Phantasia in Classical Thought* (Galway: Galway University Press, 1988).

case, the four "places" Syrianus distinguishes are, I propose, physical matter as the place for natural bodies (as the compound of matter and form), nature as the proper place for enmattered forms, mathematical matter (i.e., imagination, as a whole or in its receiving aspect) as the place for mathematical bodies, and discursive thought (the "higher" soul) as the place of the immaterial reason principles. This reading also renders imagination parallel to the place of natural bodies, i.e., a kind of matter, but mathematical bodies parallel to natural bodies rather than to enmattered forms—which makes more sense, because mathematical objects are here investigated *as bodies*. We will return to Syrianus later.

First, however, let us turn to a rather poetic and, at first sight, mystifying variety of Syrianus's hierarchy in Proclus's own work. In his thirteenth essay on Plato's *Republic*, on the speech of the Muses (*Republic* 8), Proclus describes a genealogy of five "motions," or cognitive activities of the soul, presenting their shared origin, their relative subject matters or methods of operation, their relative position on the epistemological ladder, and the correlative levels on the ontological ladder, in three phases or "dimensions." First, soul is "above" and directed to intellect. This is called its "first dimension" (*to prôton . . . diastêma*), a line—the straight line of emanation, but also the circular line of reversion.[69] Second, when the soul "goes into herself," she develops a second dimension and "becomes plane," "squaring herself" by thought. She "moves" in a rectangular square when she is using discursive (scientific) thought, but in an oblong when she mixes thought with opinion, unequal cognitive capacities being paralleled by unequal sides. Next comes the third dimension, which is where imagination comes in:

Inclining towards the things that come after her, [soul] deepens the planes, making a cube out of the square life, and begetting

---

69 Emanation is the metaphysical process of generation from a higher cause; reversion is the process of the resulting product perfecting itself by imitating its origin.

imagination (for imagination, too, is a kind of passive intellect, which wants to be active inwards, but is weak through the fall into the solid), and [making] the oblong according to the analogous procession, by sinking into dissimilar solids [i.e., with unequal sides—MM] and begetting perception, which is knowledge from dissimilars, the bodily and the incorporeal.[70]

This passage does not offer a clear indication of where direct description ends and metaphor begins, but it is safe to say the following: Proclus presents a hierarchy of types of cognition that is parallel to a hierarchy of types of mathematical entities or dimensions.[71] Intellectual activity is compared to a (straight and circular) line, discursive thought and opinion to square and rectangular planes, and imagination and perception to solids, a cube, and an oblong, respectively. Whatever that means, the close relation between the place of physical and mathematical bodies in Syrianus, and between the three-dimensionality of perception and imagination as "sunk" or "fallen into the solid" in Proclus is suggestive.

2.4. Impossible and Infinite Space

So far we have been investigating the three-dimensionality of imagination. Before we move on to a further study of intelligible matter, a brief aside on the difference between three-dimensional extension and space.

---

70 Proclus *In Remp.* II 52.4–11, my trans. ἄνω μὲν γὰρ οὖσα καὶ πρὸς νοῦν τεταμένη μετὰ τὴν ἀμέρειαν τὴν νοερὰν τὸ πρῶτόν ἐστι διάστημα καὶ ἔστιν εὐθεῖα μὲν διὰ τὴν πρόοδον, κύκλος δὲ καὶ οὗτος ὡς γραμμὴ κυκλιζομένη διὰ τὴν ἐπιστροφήν· εἰσιοῦσα δὲ εἰς ἑαυτὴν ἐπιπεδοῦται, καὶ μέχρι μὲν διανοίας ἱσταμένη τετραγωνίζει ἑαυτήν, τὸ ταὐτὸν καὶ ὅμοιον ἐν τῇ διανοητικῇ κινήσει τῷ διάνοια εἶναι πρὸς διάνοιαν κινουμένη ἔτι σώζουσα, δόξαν δὲ μετὰ διανοίας συμμίξασα κινεῖται κίνησιν ἐπίπεδον μὲν ὡς ἐκ δυεῖν γενομένην δυνάμεων ἀλλήλαις συμμιγνυμένων, ἀνίσων δὲ οὐσῶν ἐκείνων προμηκίζει αὐτὴν ἀφ' ἑαυτῆς· εἰς δὲ τὰ μετ' αὐτὴν ῥέπουσα βαθύνει τὰ ἐπίπεδα, τὴν μὲν τετραγωνικὴν ζωὴν κυβίζουσα καὶ φαντασίαν γεννῶσα (καὶ γὰρ ἡ φαντασία νοῦς τίς ἐστιν παθητικὸς ἔνδον μὲν ἐνεργεῖ ἐθέλων, ἀσθενῶν δὲ διὰ τὴν εἰς τὸ στερεὸν πτῶσιν), τὴν δὲ προμήκη κατὰ τὴν ἀνάλογον πρόοδον εἰς τοὺς ἀνομοίους ὑφιζάνουσα στερεοὺς καὶ τὴν αἴσθησιν γεννῶσα, γνῶσιν οὖσαν ἐξ ἀνομοίων, σώματος καὶ ἀσωμάτου, καὶ ἑαυτῆς εἶναι μὴ δυναμένην.

71 This hierarchy may be inspired by the Pythagorean tetraktys.

For imagination to be a kind of (imaged) space, we need more than the dimensions of, or the spatial receptacle coinciding with, the figures construed—we need the dimensions as such, possibly boundless. As Rabouin has convincingly shown, that is precisely what is presupposed in some geometrical constructions: constructions requiring infinite lines, such as prop. 12, or constructions of the impossible, need actual infinite space which also allows for actual impossibilities.[72] This infinite space cannot itself be the object of study because only the limited can be known.[73] The infinite is thus inferior to the limited. Rabouin shows that the autonomy of imagination, and thereby its inferiority and difference from discursive thought, accounts for the possibility of constructions using infinite lines. Using the analogy of the eye recognizing darkness without seeing it, Rabouin paints a picture of the imagination picturing that which escapes thought, infinite lines and other impossibilities, in the "opacity of space."[74]

2.5. The Vehicle of Imagination

Further evidence in support of understanding the "material" component of imagination as a kind of space is to be found in the parallel between human imagination as it operates in geometry and the forming activity of the World Soul, and between intelligible matter and a certain type of physical matter, which is in fact space.[75] To best approach this parallel, we will briefly turn to the relation between imagination and the so-called vehicle of the soul: that which connects soul with body. Then we will move on to the universal counterpart of the human soul, the World Soul, to find out whether it has something like imagination

---

72 Rabouin, "Proclus' Conception," cf. *In Eucl.* 284.21.
73 Rabouin, "Proclus' Conception," re *In Eucl.* 285, 5–17, cf. Proclus *In Eucl.* 291. See also *In Eucl.* 86.7–23.
74 Cf. *In Eucl.* 286.9–12: εἶναι τὸ ἄπειρον ὑποτίθεται τῇ τῆς φαντασίας ἀοριστίᾳ τῆς τοῦ ἀπείρου γενέσεως ὑποβάθρᾳ χρωμένη.
75 See Riel, "Proclus."

as well and to evaluate the candidates for a cosmic counterpart of intelligible matter. The basic underlying assumption of these sections, that whatever we find at the human level, we find, *mutatis mutandis*, at the cosmic level, is derived primarily from Proclus's metaphysics of the soul as set out in his *Elements of Theology* (esp. §§184–211).[76]

For Proclus, imagination (including intelligible matter) as used in geometry is a function of the so-called pneumatic vehicle of the soul. The notion of the soul's vehicle (*ochêma*), or the "subtle body," as that which connects the incorporeal soul with a physical body, is best known from Iamblichus but is to be found also in Porphyry. The vehicle, for which Platonists found inspiration both in Plato (*Tim.* 41e and *Phdr.* 247b) and in Aristotle (*Gen. An.* 736b), is taken either to be created at once by the demiurge (Iamblichus) or bit by bit by the soul itself in its descent (Porphyry). It is considered a lower and mortal kind of soul, or the organ of the lower, more corporeal functions of the soul, on the one hand, and, after purification, that which facilitates the soul's ascent.[77] Proclus distinguishes two vehicles, one mortal, pneumatic vehicle and one immortal, luminous vehicle. The latter is the eternal means of transport of the rational soul; the former consists in layers of accretions the soul needs in order to obtain a position in the sensible world.[78]

Imagination is described by Proclus as an internal, and hence pure and immaterial, type of perception, which takes place within the pneumatic vehicle: "The imagination remains internal and contemplates the shapes and the figures in the *pneuma*" (as opposed to perception,

---

76 See also Helmig, *Forms and Concepts*; J. Opsomer, "The Integration of Aristotelian Physics in a Neoplatonic Context: Proclus on Movers and Indivisibility," in *Physics and Philosophy of Nature in Greek Neoplatonism*, ed. Riccardo Chiaradonna and Franco Trabattoni (Leiden: Brill, 2009), 189–229.

77 H. Dörrie and M. Baltes, *Der Platonismus in Der Antike: Grundlagen—System—Entwicklung. Band VIa Die Philosophische Lehre Des Platonismus: Von Der "Seele" Als Der Ursache Aller Sinvollen Abläufe*, vol. 6.1 (Stuttgart: Frommann-Holzboog, 2002); J. F. Finamore, *Iamblichus and the Theory of the Vehicle of the Soul* (Chico, CA: Scholar's Press, 1985).

78 *In Tim.* III 236.31–36; *In Remp.* II 107,14ff. Cf. Watson, *Phantasia*.

which contemplates the external).[79] This pneuma, or the pneumatic
vehicle, consists of a kind of air and fire.

3. THE CASE OF NATURE AND THE WORLD SOUL

In the previous sections, we have ignored the distinction between
space and matter in explaining the three-dimensionality of intelligible
matter. The fact of the matter is, of course, that Proclus speaks of intelligible *matter* rather than space. In the following, I will compare the
activities of the human soul to those of nature and the World Soul and
argue that for Proclus, space is a kind of matter. Subsequently, I will
argue that intelligible matter is likewise a kind of space.

We saw that Proclus himself draws a parallel between the "matter
of things tied to sensation and the matter of imagined objects." The
matter underlying sensible forms—physical, corporeal, tangible—is
the matter of things "moulded by nature" (*In Eucl.* 7). Neoplatonic
hylomorphism has objects consisting of a universal reason principle
and matter—intelligible or perceptible matter, each with the apposite
type of reason principle; these principles are descendants of the *logos*
in discursive thought and nature, respectively.[80] So the parallel invoked
here, between physical and geometrical objects, is analyzed into that
between intelligible matter and physical matter, on the one hand, and
the *logoi* or reason principles deriving from discursive thought and nature, on the other.[81] It is worth our while to pay closer attention to that
parallel.

---

79 *In Tim.* III 286.26–29: ἔνδον δὲ μένουσα καὶ ἐν τῷ πνεύματι θεωροῦσα τὰς μορφὰς καὶ τὰ σχήματα
φαντασία.

80 *In Eucl.* 54.18–25: διττὸν οὖν σοι νοείσθω τὸ καθόλου τὸ ἐν τοῖς πολλοῖς, τὸ μὲν ἐν τοῖς αἰσθητοῖς, τὸ δὲ
ἐν τοῖς φανταστοῖς. καὶ ὁ κυκλικὸς λόγος διττὸς καὶ ὁ τριγωνικὸς καὶ αὐτὸς ὁ τοῦ σχήματος, ὁ μὲν ἐπὶ
τῆς νοητῆς ὕλης, ὁ δὲ ἐπὶ τῆς αἰσθητῆς. πρὸ δὲ τούτων ἦν ὅ τε ἐν διανοίᾳ λόγος καὶ ὁ ἐν τῇ φύσει, ὁ μὲν
τῶν φανταστῶν κύκλων ὑποστάτης καὶ τοῦ ἐν αὐτοῖς ἑνὸς εἴδους, ὁ δὲ τῶν αἰσθητῶν. Cf. 86.13–14.

81 Considering the Aristotelian context of the discussion concerning geometrical universals, and
the contrast between natural and "psychic" objects, nature here may be used in the broad sense
of "the rational and causal factors in the natural world." It may also be, however, nature as the
near-irrational quasi-hypostasis below soul. This is how Lernould, "Imagination," reads it. On this

Imagination is a cognitive capacity of the soul, which cooperates with discursive reasoning. In the commentary on Euclid, the relevant context is the *human* soul and its capacities. As such, however, all souls have the same capacities, albeit *mutatis mutandis*. So these same capacities also occur at the level of the World Soul.

Plato describes Soul—that is, the World Soul—as being inserted into the center of the cosmos, permeating it all the way through and covering it on the outside (*Tim.* 34b). Proclus, in his commentary to the *Timaeus*, explains this World Soul as an entity intermediate between the transcendent and the immanent; it is both indivisible (in its hypercosmic aspect) and divisible (in its encosmic powers). Present everywhere in the body of the cosmos but ontologically superior. It has been suggested that Proclus sees the World Soul as ordering the cosmos mathematically by her imagination.[82] This suggestion is based primarily on the fact that Proclus describes the World Soul as "unrolling" and projecting reason principles.[83] The mention of projection as such is not decisive, however, as Proclus at times uses it merely as a synonym of procession or emanation, and in many different contexts.[84] It has also been argued that the World Soul does not require imagination, among other reasons because it is not irrational, whereas imagination is a capacity of the irrational soul.[85]

Nature, see also M. Martijn, *Proclus on Nature: Philosophy of Nature and Its Methods in Proclus' Commentary on Plato's Timaeus* (Leiden: Brill, 2010); Opsomer, "Integration."

82 J. F. Finamore and E. Kutash, "Proclus on the Psychè: World Soul and the Individual Soul," in *All from One: A Guide to Proclus*, ed. Pieter d'Hoine and Marije Martijn (Oxford: Oxford University Press, 2016), 122–38.

83 *In Tim.* II 124.16–20, possibly with I 79: τοιαύτη γὰρ καὶ ἡ ψυχή, τὴν ὅλην ἀπειρίαν τοῦ ὄντος ἅμα μὴ δυναμένη δέξασθαι· δηλοῖ γοῦν ζῷσα κατὰ μετάβασιν καὶ προβολὴν ἄλλων λόγων καὶ ἄλλων, οὐκ ἔχουσα τὴν ἄπειρον ζωὴν ἅμα πᾶσαν παροῦσαν. ἀεὶ οὖν ἀνελίττουσα τὴν ἑαυτῆς ζωήν. For Plotinus's view of this process, see Dillon 2013.

84 For example, applied to Zeus in *In Crat.* 104. Cf. *In Tim.* II 208, the World Soul's activity as projecting divine activity in time. Cf. III 307.30–31, souls projecting the *logos* of humans. *In Parm.* 896: Thinking is called the projection of *logoi* by the soul. *In Tim.* I 79: Cognitive perfection of the soul by the projection of *logoi*, i.e. delivery of speeches through Hermes (trans. Tarrant misses the subtleties, but cf. trans. at 148).

85 See MacIsaac, "Phantasia"; Helmig, *Forms and Concepts*. The irrational world soul is a gnostic notion, which Proclus does not adopt.

In the following, we will investigate whether the description of the nature of the World Soul and its projection of reason principles gives us any information as to the receptacle, the matter or space, of that which is projected. What, in turn, can we conclude on the basis of that with regard to the imagination?

3.1. The World Soul's Projection

Like the human soul, the World Soul possesses the reason principles, *logoi*, prior to their "unrolling" into, in this case, sensible objects. This possessing is cognitive: although the World Soul does not perceive the sensibles as such (it is not affected by ontologically lower entities), nor have knowledge of them "after the fact," so to speak, it does know the sensibles because they are "causally included" in it.[86]

The World Soul, we read, "has the logoi of the sensibles, projected from itself" (προβεβλημένους ἔχει τοὺς λόγους τῶν αἰσθητῶν ἀφ' ἑαυτῆς, predicative participle).[87] What is this projecting by the World Soul? Baltzly may be right that this notion of projecting has its origin in theories of perception (and perhaps in theories of visual rays?), but the working of projection in Proclus's epistemology is broader. In Iamblichus's theory of perception, for example, as described by

---

86 *In Tim.* II 311.16–25. This fits the Iamblichean theory that the gods know the sensible realm "in the appropriate manner," i.e., not as sensible but as fitting their own essence and cognitive capacities, unitarily, undividedly, eternally, etc. On the soul's knowledge, see also *El.Th.* §195: "Every soul is all things. . . . Now those things whereof it is the pre-existent cause it pre-embraces in the exemplary mode. . . . Accordingly it pre-embraces all sensible things after the manner of a cause, possessing the rational notions of material things immaterially, of bodily things incorporeally, of extended things without extension." Πᾶσα ψυχὴ πάντα ἐστὶ τὰ πράγματα. . . . ὧν μὲν οὖν αἰτία προϋπάρχει, ταῦτα προείληφε παραδειγματικῶς. . . . τὰ μὲν ἄρα αἰσθητὰ πάντα κατ' αἰτίαν προείληφε, καὶ τοὺς λόγους τῶν ἐνύλων ἀύλως καὶ τῶν σωματικῶν ἀσωμάτως καὶ τῶν διαστατῶν ἀδιαστάτως ἔχει. Proclus, *Commentary on Plato's Timaeus, Volume IV—Book 3, Part 2: Proclus on the World Soul*, trans. D. Baltzly (Cambridge, UK: Cambridge University Press, 2009), refers in this context to the *atoma eidē*, the lowest universal, just above individuals (cf. *In Parm* 970.23–24). On the World Soul's perception, see also Helmig, *Forms and Concepts*, 226, 237.

87 Baltzly translates as "possesses the projected rational-forming principles of sensibles on its own," but considering the position of *probeblēmenous* I prefer my translation—and, to be honest, also because it fits my aims better.

Simplicius, the soul projects *logoi* onto the sensory organ to match the sense impression. A fit results in recognition of an object. This is not what Proclus is thinking of in this context, of course, as the World Soul has no sensory organs. But perhaps the parallel is geometry: the World Soul, like the human *phantasia*, projects rational principles in a move that is not primarily cognitive but creative—and importantly, creative of space.[88]

Nature is without reason *or imagination (aphantastos)*[89] and just puts the *logoi* into action: "If, then, it is Nature that changes the reason-principles of the sperm from potentiality to the fully formed actuality, it is Nature that has the reason-principles in actuality; therefore, although without reason or imagination, it is nevertheless the cause of the reason-principles in natural things."[90] Before Nature does its work, however, the World Soul prepares the grounds. The "daimonic place" (*topos daimonios*) mentioned in book 10 of the Republic (614c1), Proclus tells us, is extension, i.e., place in the genuine sense (*hôs alêthôs topos*).[91] The World Soul,

> which has the formal principles of all things divine and which depends on what comes before itself, imposes upon different parts of space a special affinity with different powers and certain symbols of the various orders among the gods. For this space is suspended immediately after her, and functions as her connate instrument. So

---

88 And like the human soul, it has a strong connection with mathematics, a bit more on which later.

89 *In Parm* 902: Nature is not just unintelligent but also irrational and unimaginative (οὐ γὰρ μόνον ἀνόητος, ἀλλὰ καὶ ἄλογος ἡ φύσις καὶ ἀφάνταστος). Cf. *In Parm* 955 and *Dec Dub* 45.4. It seems Proclus has copied the term *aphantastos* from Syrianus but modified its meaning. Where Syrianus uses it in a positive sense, for pure, unimaged forms, Proclus devaluates it as referring to what comes below *phantasia*.

90 *In Parm*. 792.20–25, trans. Morrow: Εἰ τοίνυν ἡ φύσις ἐκ τοῦ δυνάμει μεταβάλλει τοὺς λόγους τοῦ σπέρματος εἰς τὴν κατ᾽ ἐνέργειαν διάπλασιν, αὕτη ἂν ἔχοι κατ᾽ ἐνέργειαν τοὺς λόγους· διὸ καὶ ἄλογος οὖσα καὶ ἀφάνταστος ὅμως ἐστὶ λόγων αἰτία φυσικῶν.

91 See next note. We will ignore the context of the afterlife.

she, being a rational and psychical cosmos, brings this too to be a perfect cosmos of space and life through the divine tokens.[92]

As this extension is immobile, "the unmoved extension that is ever illuminated by the gods," one could call it space; it does not move or change, but it does always participate in rational principles, as opposed to the extension of material objects, which do move and change and are at times illuminated, i.e., participating, and at times not.[93]

The generation of this space is concomitant with the generation of the different types of souls, as we find in Proclus's reading of the construction of lower types of souls by the demiurge from the remainder of the mixture of the indivisible and the divisible (*Tim.* 41d). The transition from the indivisible (intellect) to the divisible (physical) requires the intermediate of soul. But within the realm of soul, a distinction can be made, following the development of mathematical ratios from the unit, between a hypercosmic type of soul, which requires only one dimension (linear numbers) and is hence not involved in the corporeal, and hypercosmic-encosmic souls, requiring two dimensions (plane numbers).[94] The construction of souls, in other words, is at the same

92 *In Tim.* I 161.5–12, trans. Tarrant, slightly modified: τίς δὲ ὁ τόπος οὗτος, εἴρηται μὲν ἔμπροσθεν (138, 21ff., 139, 9ff.), ὅτι τὸ διάστημα καὶ ὁ ὡς ἀληθῶς τόπος· κατὰ γὰρ τοῦτον αἱ διαιρέσεις τῶν θείων κλήρων, ἵν' ἀεὶ ὡσαύτως ἐστηκότες ὦσι πρὸ τῶν κατὰ χρόνον ὑφισταμένων. προσθετέον δὲ καὶ νῦν, ὡς ἡ τοῦ παντὸς ψυχὴ λόγους ἔχουσα τῶν θείων ἀπάντων καὶ ἐξηρτημένη τῶν πρὸ αὐτῆς ἄλλοις τοῦ διὰ στήματος μορίοις πρὸς ἄλλας δυνάμεις ἐντίθησιν οἰκειότητα καὶ σύμβολα ἄττα τῶν διαφόρων ἐν θεοῖς τάξεων· προσεχῶς γὰρ αὐτῆς ἀπαιωρεῖται τοῦτο τὸ διάστημα καὶ ἔστιν ὄργανον αὐτῇ συμφυές. κόσμος οὖν οὖσα αὕτη λογικὸς καὶ ψυχικὸς ἀποτελεῖ καὶ τοῦτον τὸν κόσμον διαστατὸν καὶ ζωτικὸν διὰ τῶν θείων συνθημάτων. The divine tokens are the *logoi*, which function not only as principles of rational formation but also as aids in reversion, as they are always connected and hence provide access to the divine realm they originate in. It seems that MacIsaac, "Phantasia," is suggesting that the extension of human phantasia is the paradigm or cause of physical space. This makes no sense, as the individual soul is inferior to the World Soul and hence to physical space.

93 *In Tim.* I 162.4–10: καὶ δὴ καὶ τὸν τόπον οὐ τὴν γῆν οὐδὲ τὸν ἀέρα τοῦτον ἀκουστέον, ἀλλὰ πρὸ τούτων τὸ διάστημα τὸ ἀκίνητον καὶ ἀεὶ ὡσαύτως ὑπὸ τῶν θεῶν προσλαμπόμενον καὶ τοῖς τῆς Δίκης κλήροις ὃ ιηρημένον· τὰ γὰρ ἔνυλα ταῦτα ποτὲ μὲν ἐπιτήδεια πρὸς μετοχὴν ἐστι θεῶν, ποτὲ δὲ ἀνεπιτήδεια, καὶ δεῖ πρὸ τῶν ποτὲ μετεχόντων εἶναι τὰ ἀεὶ ὡσαύτως ἐξηρτημένα τῶν θεῶν. Cf. *In Tim.* I 138.22.

94 *In Tim.* III 251.29–255.2, esp. 252.21–31, with R. P. Winnington-Ingram, "Note Du Professeur Winnington-Ingram Sûr 251.29 Ss," In *Proclus Commentaire Sûr Le Timée*, vol. 5 (Paris: Vrin, 1968), 125–28.

time the generation of dimensionality, with the World Soul, which has a hypercosmic element and an encosmic one, forming the transition from one to three dimensions.

An interesting possibility, which we will not investigate further here, is that by space as the "connate instrument," Proclus actually means Nature, which is also the instrument of the World Soul.[95] That would make Nature the counterpart of intelligible matter, and the World Soul the counterpart of dianoetic thought. Together, they would be the cosmic counterpart of imagination. We will briefly consider another option, the luminous vehicle, further on.

3.2. Space

The extension (*diastema*) which is the connate instrument of the World Soul is the complete extension of the cosmos and could be called space.[96] Proclus's work *On Space* is not extant, but Simplicius reports on his views extensively in the *Corollary on Space*.[97] Proclus is the only philosopher, Simplicius tells us, to maintain the innovative position that place (three-dimensional extension) has to be a body, albeit an immaterial one.[98] Or as Siorvanes phrases it, "Corporeal light begins with body in its pure state, place."[99] Proclus's main argument, which he presents within the Aristotelian framework of the distinction between shape, matter, and extension between extremities, is that

---

95 On this see Martijn, *Proclus*.

96 Cf. L. Siorvanes, *Proclus: Neo-Platonic Philosophy and Science* (Edinburgh: Edinburgh University Press, 1996).

97 For further evidence from Proclus's own works, see later discussion.

98 Simplicius, *In Phys.* 611.10–13. Proclus's position and arguments are presented by Simplicius at *Corollary* 611.10–614.8; Simplicius critically discusses the arguments given at 614.8–618.7. For a good summary see Griffin, "Proclus." On Proclus's notion of space, see Griffin, "Proclus"; Sorabji, *Matter, Space and Motion*; Schrenk, "Proclus on Space as Light"; Schrenk, "Proclus on Corporeal Space"; Siorvanes, *Proclus*. On differences between Plotinus and Proclus on this topic, see C. Russi, "Causality and Sensible Objects: A Comparison between Plotinus and Proclus," in *Physics and Philosophy of Nature in Greek Neoplatonism*, ed. R. Chiaradonna and F. Trabattoni (Leiden: Brill, 2009), 145–71, who, however, overemphasizes the opposition.

99 Cf. Siorvanes, *Proclus*, 242.

of the necessity of equality between a body and its place. The only thing quantitatively equal to a solid, Proclus argues, is another solid.[100] To prevent having to postulate interpenetration of material bodies, he assumes an immaterial body, which is a special kind of light.[101]

Moreover, because it has to be superior to the living beings inside it and serve as intermediary between the World Soul, which is motionlessly alive, and the bodies, whose life consists of motion, space also has to be alive, yet immobile[102]—the perfect intermediary between the spiritual and the physical. These properties are the counterparts of the active aspect of intelligible matter and its allowance of interpenetration.

In his *Commentary on the Republic*, Proclus himself elaborates on the nature of the light in question, albeit in a specific exegetical context: Plato's mention of a light seen by the souls of the deceased (Myth of Er, *Republic* X 616B).[103]

This light, "stretching from above throughout all of heaven and earth, like a pillar, very similar to the rainbow, but more luminous and more pure," Plato calls "the bond of heaven."[104] Proclus follows Porphyry in identifying it as the first vehicle (*ochêma*) of the world soul and the cosmic counterpart of the luminous vehicle of human souls,[105]

100 Simplicius, *In Phys.* 611.36–612.1.

101 Simplicius, *In Phys.* 612.16 ff. On immaterial bodies passing through material ones, cf. *In Remp.* II 162.24–163.1. See also J. F. Finamore, "Iamblichus on Light and the Transparent," in *The Divine Iamblichus: Philosopher and Man of Gods*, ed. Hans Blumenthal and E. G. Clark (Bristol, UK: Bristol Classical Press, 1993), 55–64.

102 Simplicius, *In Phys.* 613.10–15. Cf. Duhem, *Le système*, 1:340. On spiritual motion in Proclus, see Opsomer, "Integration."

103 *In Remp.* II 193.21–202.2. As Siorvanes, *Proclus*, points out, this passage is important but was often overlooked. It may even be one of the main sources of Proclus's theory. For Proclus's ideas on light as emanation from the One and existing at all lower levels of the metaphysical hierarchy, in ever increasing degrees of materiality or corporeality, and the possibility that Iamblichus held the same views, while harmonizing Aristotle and Plato on this matter, see Finamore, "Iamblichus."

104 Plato, *Resp.* 616b4–c2:ἄνωθεν διὰ παντὸς τοῦ οὐρανοῦ καὶ γῆς τεταμένον φῶς εὐθύ, οἷον κίονα, μάλιστα τῇ Ἴριδι προσφερῆ, λαμπρότερον δὲ καὶ καθαρώτερον . . . εἶναι γὰρ τοῦτο τὸ φῶς σύνδεσμον τοῦ οὐρανοῦ.

105 *In Remp.* II 196.25–29, 197.13–14. We will not go into the puzzling suggestion raised by "first vehicle," that the World Soul might have a pneumatic vehicle as well.

a vehicle which the World Soul brings forth itself, together with the demiurge, as its "home."[106] It is superior to heaven and earth, as it holds them together, and it is visible, but only to our luminous vehicle, not to the physical eye.[107] This cosmic vehicle depends on the World Soul,[108] is immobile and indivisible and the seat (*hedra*) or place (*topos*) of stationary and moving things.[109] True space, then, is the vehicle of the World Soul and an intermediary between soul and body.[110]

Proclus (*apud* Simplicius) opposes the unity of the vehicle to the multiplicity of the bodies in it (τὴν μὲν φωτὸς ἑνός, τὴν δὲ ἐκ πολλῶν σωμάτων; Simplicius, *Corollary* 612.30–31). In other words, the luminous vehicle is coextensive with the whole, whereas the World Soul projects its *logoi* into parts of it. On the basis of the analogies between the World Soul and the human soul, between sensible and mathematical objects, we may be tempted to conclude that the intelligible matter used by the human soul in geometry is the spatial aspect of the vehicle of the human soul.[111] Interestingly, there is an important potential source of inspiration for this view in Aristotle, who uses an analogy of light to describe the passive or potential intellect: "There is another (intellect) which is what it is by virtue of making all things: this is

106 *In Tim.* II 281.12–14: ἀλλ' αὐτὴ προελθοῦσα συμπαράγει τῷ πατρὶ τὸν ἑαυτῆς οἶκον, μᾶλλον δὲ τὸ ὄχημα ἑαυτῆς.
107 *In Remp.* II 195.1–11, 199.18–21.
108 *In Remp.* II 196.29, 197.14.
109 *In Remp.* II 197.21–198.2. See also the summary at *In Remp.* II 198.26–29.
110 *In Crat.* 31.12–13 and Simplicius, *In Phys.* 613.7–10; 613.27–29, with Siorvanes, *Proclus*, 255–56. See also Siorvanes, *Proclus*, 256, on the ways in which space is intermediary between soul and body.
111 Siorvanes, *Proclus*, 253–54, is right to point to the many points of convergence between Philoponus's and Proclus's notions of space, but as he also indicates (255–56), there is an important difference: Proclus's space as light is an active entity, not a void (which has only the "empty force" of pulling something in). On Philoponus's notion of space in response to Proclus, see F. A. J. De Haas, *John Philoponus' New Definition of Prime Matter: Aspects of Its Background in Neoplatonism and the Ancient Commentary Tradition* (Leiden: Brill, 1997), 69; P. Mueller-Jourdan, *Gloses et Commentaire Du Livre XI Du Contra Proclum de Jean Philopon: Autour de La Matière Première Du Monde*, Philosophia Antiqua 125 (Leiden: Brill, 2011).

a sort of positive state like light; for in a sense light makes potential colours into actual colours."[112]

Some support for our interpretation may be found in Syrianus's response to Aristotle's criticism of mathematical Platonism. Syrianus offers a rather enlightening general discussion of place and space, which must be behind Proclus's theory. Aristotle's claim that two solids cannot occupy the same place at the same time is countered by Syrianus by referring to "certain philosophers" who posit that "extension pervades the whole universe."[113] As we will see, this is a (purposely vague?) reference to the Platonist view of the vehicle of the world soul.[114]

Syrianus goes on to refer to this "place and extension," which is not a mathematical body but is a solid (in the sense of three-dimensional) and is similar to the mathematical in being intangible, immobile, and immaterial, free from resistance and of any passibility, and hence not subject to Aristotle's criticism of interpenetration.[115] He then presents an important analogy between the existence of that "place and extension" and a mathematical body, which is both helpful and not when compared to Proclus's views:

> Even as the mathematical body comes to be, when the reason-principle (*logos*) is put forth (*problêthentos*), in discursive intellection (*dianoia*) in virtue of the vital spirit (*pneuma*) and the imaging faculty (*phantasia*) inherent in the spirit (for at one and the same time the reason-principle of a sphere, for instance, comes into

---

112 *dA* 430a14–16: ὁ δὲ τῷ πάντα ποιεῖν, ὡς ἕξις τις, οἷον τὸ φῶς· τρόπον γάρ τινα καὶ τὸ φῶς ποιεῖ τὰ δυνάμει ὄντα χρώματα ἐνεργείᾳ χρώματα.

113 *In Met.* 84.31–32. See *Met.* Δ 998a7–15, *N* 1076a38–b13; Syrianus, *In Metaph.* 84.27–86.7. See also the discussion at Siorvanes, *Proclus,* 254, and Proclus's arguments for the necessity of, on the one hand, an eternal and immaterial "first body" or vehicle for each participated soul (*ET* §196) and, on the other, a mortal vehicle, which is "more material" (§§205–10).

114 Possibly more specifically to Porphyry; see earlier discussion of *In Remp.* II 196.22–27. See the references in Dillon and O'Meara 191n39.

115 *In Met.* 84.20–86.37. Simplicius on Syrianus: *In Phys.* 618.25–619.2.

consciousness, and the imaging faculty beholds a mathematical sphere, endowed with immaterial bulk [*onkos*]), just so this spherical extension in the universe possesses its substance in co-operation with the will and vision of Intellect, while through its contemplation of all the Forms it makes it capable of embracing all bodies, both each individually and the totality of them as one.[116]

Syrianus sees a clear parallel between the existence of the complete and spheric extension of the cosmos and the generation of a mathematical body: both have their origin in a form of thought (discursive thought and Intellect, respectively). Two problematic aspects of this text are that Syrianus compares the cosmic sphere with *a* mathematical body, not with a space in which that body is constructed, and that there is no explicit mention, at the cosmic level, of projection, vehicle, and imagination.[117]

4. CONCLUSION

Let us sum up our main findings. Human imagination as used in geometry consists in two elements: discursive thought projecting *logoi* and intelligible matter actively receiving them; intelligible matter is not two- but three-dimensional; imagination originates in the pneumatic vehicle of the soul; the World Soul, on the other hand, projects her version of the same *logoi*, generating three-dimensional space in the

---

116 *In Met.* 85.4–15.

117 Elsewhere Syrianus mentions a difference between our luminous vehicle, which he describes as having three-dimensional extension, and a mathematical body, as it moves, and mathematical entities do not. For us, this passage is less relevant, as it starts from the Aristotelian notion of a geometrical body, which does not fit Proclus's view (of kinematic construction, e.g.): τό τε αὐγοειδὲς ἐν ἡμῖν ὄχημα τριχῇ διαστατὸν εἴ τις ἀπεφήνατο εἶναι καὶ οὐκ ἀντίτυπον, οὐ γεωμετρούμενον ἀντικρυς εἶναι σῶμα τοῦτο διισχυρίζεται· πῶς γὰρ τό γε ζωῆς καὶ κινήσεως πλῆρες καὶ πάντων <ἐν> ἡμῖν εὐκινητότατον κατὰ τὴν συνεγνωσμένην Ἀριστοτέλει κίνησιν ὡς ἀκίνητον ἄν τις ἐν τοῖς γεωμετρουμένοις κατατάξειεν; *In Met.* 86.2–7.

process; Nature then activates the *logoi*; and the space created by the World Soul is its luminous vehicle.

There are many remaining questions. For one thing, a problem for identifying human imagination with the World Soul's projection into and of space, of course, is that the luminous vehicle, as one may recall, was the higher, immortal vehicle. Human imagination instead works with the lower vehicle, the pneumatic one. Moreover, we saw that the space of the World Soul is immobile, whereas geometrical constructions require motion (which would mean that intelligible matter itself needed another, immobile space to be in).[118] For this problem there may be two solutions: one, that here we simply see which *mutanda* are *mutata*—in which respects, in other words, the human soul is inferior to the World Soul. Here we may recall also the infinity necessary in geometry but impossible in the physical world. The second solution would be to relegate imagination, as suggested earlier, to the level of Nature, which one could then perhaps even consider calling the pneumatic vehicle of the World Soul, and compare intelligible matter to the level of the so-called enmattered forms. We will leave these matters undecided.

Finally, two brief thoughts on the relevance of Proclus's views to later thought. It has been suggested that Proclus's view of imagination seems to "anticipate the Kantian doctrine of the schematism of the understanding (*Verstand*), which links the pure concepts of the understanding with pure intuition of space and time and according to which images are generated by rules or schemata which correspond to the geometrical concepts."[119] Morrow, in his introduction to Proclus's Euclid Commentary, even presents this as evident.[120] Schmitz, however, has

---

118 I thank one of the participants in Oslo for pointing this out to me.

119 A. Powell, "Review of Markus Schmitz, *Euklids Geometrie Und Ihre Mathematiktheoretische Grundlegung in Der Neuplatonischen Philosophie Des Proklos*, Würzburg: Konighausen & Neumann, 1997," Philosophia Mathematica 8 (2000): 339–45.

120 G. R. Morrow, *Proclus: A Commentary on the First Book of Euclid's Elements, Translated with Introduction and Notes*, 2nd ed. (Princeton, NJ: Princeton University Press, 1992), lix.

argued against this parallel, pointing out that Proclus does not have the concept of pure intuition and that the two thinkers have different notions of producing the image of an idea. The parallel, he says, goes no deeper than the fact that the imagination plays an important role in Proclus's philosophy of geometry.[121]

Deciding on this issue goes beyond the scope of this chapter, of course.

A second point to be made here is the relevance Proclus's views may have to cognitive scientists or philosophers of mathematics—and, vice versa, the help we may find in understanding Proclus, not by reading more Proclus but by turning to contemporary work. What is this non-physical extension the soul uses in doing geometry? In philosophy of mathematics, as mentioned, many puzzles remain to be answered regarding the mathematical practice, epistemology, semantics, ontology, methodology, logic, psychology, and pedagogy of using three dimensions (including stereometry) in geometry.[122] In cognitive science, we may think of questions regarding, e.g., mental rotation: What does an architect do when she imagines rotating a building?[123] And is it even possible to imagine manipulating an image, which is what geometers do, considering the supposed separation of picture perception from the perception of visually guided motor interaction?[124] But for now, these questions merely serve to open up new vistas in our imagination.[125]

---

121 Schmitz, 197, 215, 214–15. Schmitz argues that in Proclus the idea of a geometrical figure exists beforehand as a simple undivided existent which is projected onto extended and divisible matter in terms of images. Kant, on the other hand, has the notion of a construction of a geometrical concept which defines the concept itself in pure spatial intuition (see Kant's *Critique of Pure Reason* A713/B741 [1929]). On the comparison, see also Arnzen, "Wie Mißt," 132.

122 Arana and Mancosu, "On the Relationship," n15.

123 B. Mitrović, "Leon Battista Alberti, Mental Rotation, and the Origins of Three-Dimensional Computer Modeling," *Journal of the Society of Architectural Historians* 74, no. 3 (2015): 312–22.

124 As proposed by Gabriel Ferretti, "Pictures, Action Properties and Motor Related Effects," *Synthese* 193, no. 12 (2016): 3787–817.

125 I thank the other contributors to the volume and audiences in Lisbon, Amsterdam, Utrecht, Munich, and Oslo, where I presented different parts and versions of this paper. I would specifically like to thank Peter Lautner for his suggestions.

Reflection

ANTS IN SPACE

Nicole E. Heller

The possibility of inferring ecological and evolutionary processes from the patterns of organisms in space is a central insight of ecological science. Charles Darwin's theory of evolution stemmed from observations of finches in the Galapagos Islands. Different finch species coexisting on the same island were divergent in beak size. Finch species on different islands overlapped in beak size. Beak size affects what seeds a bird can eat. Darwin reasoned that over time individual birds on the same island would be in competition for limited seed resources and that this pressure had acted on coexisting populations such that character traits diverged. The pattern of birds on the landscape revealed the history of past evolution.

Darwin's work taught that ecology and evolution play out in a spatial arena where organisms interact. How organisms position themselves in space allows inferences about how they live their lives and their relationships with each other. To make good inferences we must view patterns at the appropriate scale. Most ecological work is done in areas with messy or unclear boundaries, where researchers must make arbitrary decisions about where to draw the box within which observations will be made. Researchers struggle

Nicole E. Heller, *Ants in Space* In: *Space*. Edited by: Andrew Janiak, Oxford University Press (2020).
© Oxford University Press.
DOI: 10.1093/oso/9780199914104.003.0005

to know whether the spatial area examined and the patterns observed within that area are meaningful relative to the scale at which processes are occurring.

Too often we measure the lives of other organisms ~~by~~ using our own human scale of experience. As John Wiens wrote in 1989, "Ecologists deal with phenomena that are intuitively familiar, and we are therefore more likely to perceive and study such phenomena on anthropocentric scales that accord with our own experiences."[1] This tendency may be more or less correct depending on whether we are studying a mouse or a moose. The scale problem is particularly acute as our sense of space changes in our daily lives through technological innovations. As we move around larger spatial arenas with greater ease and share information more freely at global scales, we may have the tendency to examine the lives of organisms at larger scales as well.

In the remainder of this short Reflection, I discuss how this general bias toward studying phenomena at the anthropocentric scale can lead to bizarre ideas about organisms. Specifically, I discuss the case of the ant colony and how the methods developed to reveal the ant colony, which were initially applied at the spatial scale of ant movement, have now swelled to the scale of global human movement, leading to new, problematic concepts and theories. I argue this enlarged sense of space has disconnected the spatial pattern of the ant's behavior from the ecological and evolutionary processes ecologists seek to infer.

Ant Colonies

The ant colony is a superorganism. The activities of a single ant are rather meaningless unless understood as a function of the survival

---

1 John A. Wiens, "Spatial Scaling in Ecology," *Functional Ecology* 3, no. 4 (1989): 385–97.

of the colony. The colony is the unit under selective pressure. We can think of the queen as the ovary and the workers as the soma. The colony occupies a physical space the same way a human or a plant body occupies a physical space. But because the ant colony is also a collectivity—a group of distinct ant bodies spread out in space—the colony can be distributed in a variety of ways at any time. If we were to map every ant associated with an individual colony, and then draw a line around the area that contained that set of ants, this could be considered the colony space in time.

Researchers therefore study ant populations by mapping colonies, not individual ants. Because ant colonies are underground, we can observe only a fraction of colony activity from above. When there are multiple holes near each other on the ground surface, with ants of the same species coming and going, a first step is to determine if those holes are part of the same colony. A common method to detect colony membership is to introduce the ants to each other and see how they react, called an aggression test. This can be done easily by taking, on the tip of a pencil, an ant from one nest and dropping it near the entrance of another nest, or by bringing ants from separate nests together in a vial. If workers ignore each other, they are considered part of the same colony. If they react in alarm, for example quickly backing away or lunging in attack, the ants are treated as separate. Early work, conducted largely in England and the United States in the nineteenth and early twentieth centuries, described standard ant colonies as a queen and her closely related daughters living together, sharing work and reproduction, in one nest. Colony space as a single sessile nest could be relatively easily delimited in space and time.

Over time, as more species of ants have been studied in more varied locations, new colony formations have been discovered, including large, diffuse, sprawling colonies, in which ants are socially connected across many spatially distinct nests, sometimes over hundreds of meters. These colonies defy standard assumptions about eusocialty—social organization in which individuals forgo their own reproduction and aid in the reproduction of others— because they are not ideal-typic family units: a queen and her daughters, who gain inclusive fitness benefits due to shared genetic material. Rather, these sprawling nest aggregations are more like communes. Nests contain many multiple mated queens all living together and being cared for by unrelated workers. When a colony appears to be highly diffuse and shows a lack of aggression between ants from separate nests, it is said to be unicolonial.

The ant I studied most extensively, the Argentine ant, is a model unicolonial species. It is also considered a "tramp species" because it has been spread worldwide through human commerce. The first unicolonial populations were documented in bounded locales, such as a large football field or upland meadow. Recently, through the application of vial tests across oceans, it has been discovered that Argentine ants are nonaggressive over more than half their global range. This observation has led to the widely popular idea of a global, "single mega colony that has taken over the world."[2]

Yet this global megacolony is not socially linked, a key attribute of a colony. Thus we see that, as vial tests have been conducted at ever larger spatial scales, the relationship between space and the individual colony has become disassociated. The ant colony has morphed from a delimited spatial entity—a bounded group of workers cooperating in reproduction and growth—to an abstract spatial entity: the global, unbounded group of workers that do not fight *if* introduced.

Information about ant colonies that is based on aggression tests among ants living in spatial proximity helps us to understand the ant colony. It matters because those ants are in contact in their daily lives; they are bounded in a network of interactions.[3] Their

2 For instance, Matt Walker, "Earth News: Ant Mega-Colony Takes Over World," BBC Earth News, July 1, 2009, http://news.bbc.co.uk/earth/hi/earth_news/newsid_8127000/8127519.stm.
3 See Deborah M. Gordon, *Ant Encounters: Interaction Networks and Colony Behavior* (Princeton, NJ: Princeton University Press, 2010), for an elegant description of interaction networks in ants.

interactions influence their collective fitness in a significant way, either negatively or positively, and thus may provide fodder upon which natural selection can act. The colony space in this local scenario emerges from the relative position of cooperative nests at the scale of ant movement.

This same relationship between space and the individual does not emerge from testing what happens when two ants from holes spaced thousands of kilometers apart are put in a vial. This is because the relative position of cooperative nests that will never interact, either directly or indirectly, shouldn't matter to the ant, or her colony. This vial test then appears to define a relationship between nests that is virtual rather than material. These ants are linked *by the possibility of merging or the possibility of cooperation*, but not because they are in fact merging or cooperating. This colony space, then, defined by the set of nests that do not fight when sampled across the globe, emerges at the geographic scale of human experience, not ant experience.

The information inferred from the spatial ecology of vial tests at the global scale, rather, tells us about the network of human trade in the twentieth century, as these ants were carried around with commerce. And the pattern of aggression raises fascinating questions about how ants recognize other ants and how recognition is related to genetic and environmental cues, as well as questions about the evolution and stability of eusociality. But it is not evident that these global-scale vial tests tell us much about the ant colony. Rather this global, single megacolony exists virtually, in the ether of human imagination. Perhaps it is not surprising that the virtual global colony should emerge at the same time as human movement, capital, and information flows have taken on a great globalizing scope in the late twentieth century.

I am guessing such scaling problems may be rather general phenomena. To venture to know something about another being, it is essential as researchers that we commit ourselves to the embodied experience of that being. When we measure patterns at different spatial scales, we cease to describe the same thing. The burden of the biologist is to determine what processes and relationships emerge at which scale—to identify the extent of the spatial arena at which the dramas of an organism's life unfold.

CHAPTER THREE

Concepts of Space in the Fourteenth Century

WORKS OF NICOLE ORESME AND SELECTED

EARLIER WORK FOR COMPARISON

Edith Dudley Sylla

I. INTRODUCTION

According to a document describing the planned series Oxford Philosophical Concepts, the editors were asked to "think of a volume as describing the prominent events in the life of the concept." Using the metaphor of "life," perhaps one should say that in the Middle Ages the modern concept of "space" had not yet been born. In the fourteenth century, Aristotelian natural philosophy and Aristotelian science were one and the same, and the two were linked to theology by use of similar methods or analytical tools. In Aristotelian natural philosophy the concept most closely related to "space" was "place" (*locus* in Latin), where place was taken to be the closest unmoving surface surrounding a body in place, as Aristotle defined it in book IV of his *Physics*. During

Edith Dudley Sylla, *Concepts of Space in the Fourteenth Century* In: *Space*. Edited by: Andrew Janiak, Oxford University Press (2020). © Oxford University Press.
DOI: 10.1093/oso/9780199914104.003.0006

the fourteenth century another definition of place, which Aristotle had considered but rejected, came to find some support. That was the definition of place as the space (*spatium* in Latin) intercepted between the sides of the container that would be void if there were nothing located there. The Latin word *spatium*, however, already meant colloquially a place within which it was easy to move. Then, during the fourteenth century in technical contexts *spatium* took on not the meaning of Newtonian absolute space or three-dimensional extension, but the new scientific meaning of "distance" or "interval" in one or two dimensions—this as part of the development of mixed mathematical sciences of motion. This was the most significant fourteenth-century achievement linked to the Latin *spatium*. Consequently, what was done in the area of a mixed mathematical science of motion will be discussed here as well as consideration of the possibility of empty space inside or outside of the cosmos. The multiple lives of space in the fourteenth century will be examined within the works of the outstanding fourteenth-century Parisian author Nicole Oresme.

There are many ways in which the topic "concepts of space in the later Middle Ages" might have been understood. The initial interpretation might be to suppose that the word "space" refers roughly to a concept close to Newton's absolute space, so that the topic of this chapter would be what inklings people in the later Middle Ages had of what Newton later called absolute space. In *From the Closed World to the Infinite Universe*, Alexandre Koyré traced such a concept back to the Cambridge Platonists. In developing the concept of the Scientific Revolution of the Seventeenth Century, Koyré wrote:

> This scientific and philosophical revolution . . . can be described roughly as bringing forth the destruction of the Cosmos, that is, the disappearance, from philosophically and scientifically valid concepts, of the conception of the world as a finite, closed, and

hierarchically ordered whole . . . and its replacement by an indefinite and even infinite universe which is bound together by the identity of its fundamental components and laws, and in which all these
components are placed on the same level of being.[1]

. . . Absolute space, with its physico-metaphysical implications . . . is
indeed the necessary and inevitable consequence of the "bursting of
the sphere," the "breaking of the circle," the geometrization of space,
[and]of the discovery or assertion of the law of inertia as the first
and foremost law or axiom of motion.[2]

To consider medieval concepts of space from this perspective would
have two serious drawbacks. First of all, it would leave out most of what
later medieval authors had to say about place (which they considered
the relevant term, rather than "space"), subordinating the wide range
of medieval views on place to medieval views related to Newton's
absolute space.

A second drawback to understanding late medieval conceptions of
space in relation to Newton's absolute space is that it would privilege
absolute space as if Einstein's special and general theories of relativity
had not supplanted Newton's absolute space, not to mention the development of such recent ideas as wrinkles in space-time. There have
been other scientific revolutions after the Scientific Revolution of the
seventeenth century.

The primary goal of this paper, then, is to consider the discussions
that took place in the later Middle Ages related to the concept of
space or to the Latin word *spatium*, not in relation to what went on
in the seventeenth century but in their own right. There is a great deal
of relevant evidence. Koyré collected some of it in a 1949 article, "Le
vide et l'espace infini au XIVe siècle," which contains long texts and

1 Alexandre Koyré, *From the Closed World to the Infinite Universe* (Baltimore, MD: Johns Hopkins
   University Press, 1957), 4.
2 Koyré, *From the Closed World*, 169.

translations from the works of Henry of Ghent, Richard of Middleton, Walter Burley, and Thomas Bradwardine. Likewise, in a 1982 book entitled *Tempo e spazio nel medioevo*, Massimo Parodi similarly translates into Italian long primary-source texts concerning time and space by William of Ockham, John Buridan, Nicole Oresme, Nicholas of Autrecourt, John of Ripa, William of Heytesbury, and others.[3]

The most prolific American scholar writing on the topic of space in the Middle Ages is Edward Grant. In a long series of articles, and then in his books *Much Ado about Nothing: Theories of Space and Vacuum from the Middle Ages to the Scientific Revolution* (1981) and *Planets, Stars, and Orbs: The Medieval Cosmos, 1200–1687* (1994), Grant traced ideas of place, void, and space in a huge number of works from the High Middle Ages through Newton's *Principia* (1687). To summarize even the high points of what Grant discusses would be impossible in a single chapter. Also, by carrying both his books through to Newton, Grant inevitably makes Newton's absolute space the end point of the development he traces. In earlier papers on concepts of space, I too discussed Newton, whose thoughts about space in his unpublished papers cast a fascinating light on his efforts to overcome the constrictions concerning possible concepts of space left over from earlier authors.[4] But this is not the subject here.

Instead, choosing depth rather than breadth, I devote a large part of my discussion to the writings of the brilliant fourteenth-century French Aristotelian Nicole Oresme, many of whose relevant works were edited and published in the second half of the twentieth century.

3 Massimo Parodi, *Tempo e spazio nel medioevo*, Storia della Scienza 24 (Turin: Loescher Editore, 1982).

4 Cf. Edith Sylla, "Imaginary Space: John Dumbleton and Isaac Newton," in *Raum und Raumvorstellungen im Mittelalter*, ed. Jan Aertsen and Andreas Speer, Miscellanea Mediaevalia 25 (Berlin: Walter de Gruyter, 1998), 206–25. While the present paper was awaiting publication, I made use of it to prepare a talk for a 2015 conference at the Université de Fribourg (Suisse). A paper based on that talk has already been published as Edith Sylla, "From the Closed World to the Infinite Universe: The Evidence of Nicole Oresme," in *Lieu, espace, mouvement: Physique, métaphysique et cosmologie*, ed. T. Suarez-Nami, O. Ribordy, and A. Petagine, Collection *TEMA*, no. 86 (Rome: FIDEM 2016), 207–28.

These writings encompass most if not all of the topics related to space, as word or concept, discussed by late medieval natural philosophers and mathematicians. Oresme both explicates Aristotelian ideas related to space or place and proposes understandings of space different from those of Aristotle. Every now and then, to avoid excessive narrowness without claiming to be comprehensive, I will discuss especially interesting related work done by earlier thinkers.

In section 2 of what follows, after describing what Aristotle wrote about place in book IV of his *Physics*, I will discuss what Oresme wrote about place in his questions on that section of Aristotle's work. Whereas Aristotle argued that place was best defined as the innermost unmoving surface of the surrounding container, Oresme opined that it might be best to define it as the space intercepted between the sides of the container that would be void if no body were there, thus introducing the word "space" into the definition of place. In section 3, I will discuss what Oresme says about imaginary space outside the cosmos in his commentary in French on Aristotle's *On the Heavens*. In section 4, I will discuss what Oresme did with regard to quantifying or mathematizing the science of motion in relation to *spatium*, which meant at that time not three-dimensional space but distance or interval in one dimension or more rarely in two dimensions. This section will be followed by concluding remarks.

The commentaries on Aristotle's *Physics* preserved in manuscript or print were primarily connected to undergraduate teaching in the university faculties of arts, including preparing students to lead disputations on Aristotle's works once they had become bachelors or masters of arts. Consequently, these works included arguments for and against alternative answers to the questions they raised, and they did not presume to be offering significantly newer and better arguments that might cause a significant shift in the academic consensus on the issues and their resolution. By the mid-fourteenth century in Paris, however, William of Ockham's responses based on ontological minimalism did have a considerable influence on Oresme as well as on other commentators on Aristotle's *Physics*, whether or not these later commentators agreed with Ockham.

2. ARISTOTLE ON PLACE

I start with Aristotle's conception of place since this is background for much of the work discussed here. In book 4 of the *Physics* Aristotle argued—against the atomists' view that the universe consists of atoms and empty space or void—that there is no such thing as empty space or void. He concluded that "place" (*locus* in Latin) should be identified as the innermost unmoving surface of the surrounding body. The place of a fish in a lake is the innermost surface of the water surrounding it, and the place of the terrestrial realm, composed of the elements earth, water, air, and fire, minerals, plants, animals, humans, and so forth, is the innermost surface of the orb or shell of ether that carries the moon around the earth. Here the water, in the case of the fish, and the ether sphere, in the case of the terrestrial realm, are real corporeal substances, limited at surfaces, which provide the places at issue. According to Aristotle's view, if people speak of the empty space within a room, they are overlooking the fact that this supposed empty space is not empty at all but is filled with air. In supposing that the world is filled by atoms and empty space, atomists had based a scientific theory upon this common misperception.

Aristotle had chosen what "place" should mean in relation to five pretheoretical characteristics that place has: (1) it is the first thing containing that of which it is the place; (2) a thing's primary place should not be less than or greater than the object in place; (3) place should be left behind when an object moves; (4) place is everything of which we say it is "above" or "below"; and (5) each body naturally moves to and remains in its proper place.[5] Thus for Aristotle place had many functions beyond simple location.

---

5 Cf. Edith Sylla, "Space and Spirit in the Transition from Aristotelian to Newtonian Science," in *The Dynamics of Aristotelian Natural Philosophy from Antiquity to the Seventeenth Century*, ed. C. H. Leijenhorst, C. H. Luethy, and J. M. M. H. Thijssen (Leiden: Brill, 2002), 253.

After rejecting the possibilities that place might be matter, form, or three-dimensional extension between the extremities of the containing body (since an empty space would not have the fourth and fifth characteristics, it is not a good candidate for the meaning of "place"), Aristotle concluded that a body's place is the innermost immovable boundary of the containing body at which it is in contact with the contained body that is said to be in place (*Physics* 212a5–7). He argued that a vacuum, if it existed, might be defined as an empty space suitable for holding a body that has no body in it, but in fact, according to Aristotle, there are no vacua inside or outside the finite spherical cosmos. Finally Aristotle defined time as "the number of motion in respect to before and after" (220a24–25). This definition of time meant that there cannot be time unless there are bodies or substances in motion and minds to do the numbering of motion. Analogies between time and space might later lead some to conclude that space, like time, may depend upon human thought, so that it does not exist in the external world independent of human conceptions.

When Aristotle's *Physics* became a standard part of the curriculum of medieval universities, most commentators accepted and defended his definition of place, but they also continued to discuss the alternative possibilities that Aristotle had considered. In the most common form of the medieval Christian Aristotelian worldview, all that exists is God and what God has created: the natural world and angels. The natural world is finite and contained within an outermost sphere, inside of which is a material plenum with no vacua, and outside of which is nothing, not even empty space.

2.1. *Some Medieval Modifications of Aristotle's Concept of Place*

From early times, the Aristotelian concept of place was elaborated and modified in order to deal with problems that were intrinsic to it. One immediate problem concerned the place of the entire cosmos. Since the entire cosmos is not surrounded by anything, there is no inner boundary

of the surrounding body to constitute its place. A second problem concerned the place of a body supposed to be at rest within a moving medium. What, for instance, is the place of the towers of the cathedral of
Notre Dame as the wind blows by them, which means that the inner
boundary of the air surrounding them is constantly changing?

Aside from particular problems such as these, there were two sys-
temic and intertwined developments within medieval Aristotelianism
that had an impact upon the acceptance of Aristotle's definition of
place. First, there was an epistemological separation between mathematics and natural philosophy as autonomous demonstrative
disciplines. In his commentaries on Aristotle's *Physics*, Averroes, while
always aiming to explain Aristotle's text, moved away from the claim of
book 6 of the *Physics* that all magnitudes, physical and mathematical,
must be continuous in the same way, to the alternative claim that while
geometrical magnitudes are continuous, physical magnitudes may well
consist of parts that are at most contiguous and not continuous.[6] It
follows that there is an imperfect analogy between mathematics and
the physical bodies and motions that natural philosophy may describe.
Many fourteenth-century philosophers, both in their philosophical
works and in their commentaries on Peter Lombard's *Book of Sentences*
(a theological textbook), mention the relations of mathematics and
physics. The nominalists, Ockhamists, or *moderni* generally agreed
with Averroes that what is true in mathematics need not be true in
physics and vice versa; different scientific disciplines may be based on
different principles.[7]

---

6 Ruth Glasner, *Averroes' Physics: A Turning Point in Medieval Natural Philosophy* (Oxford: Oxford
University Press, 2009). In the fourteenth century, Thomas Bradwardine continued to as-
sert the isomorphism of all continua, mathematical and physical. See Edith Sylla, "Infinity and
Continuity: Bradwardine and His Contemporaries," in preparation for an Oxford University
Press volume edited by Stewart Shapiro on the history of concepts of continuity.

7 Cf. Edith Sylla, "Averroes and Fourteenth-Century Theories of Alteration: Minima Naturalia
and the Distinction between Mathematics and Physics," in *Averroes' Natural Philosophy and Its
Reception in the Latin West*, ed. Paul J. J. M. Bakker (Leuven: Leuven University Press, 2015),
141–92.

For many medieval Christian Aristotelians, then, there was nothing (no thing) within the cosmos that corresponded to the word "space" (*spatium*). The things that exist are *substances*, both material substances such as bodies and immaterial substances such as angels or prime movers. Substances have essential and accidental forms, and there is no substance or substantial or accidental form that corresponds to the definition of "space." Whereas for Aristotle and for thirteenth-century thinkers like Albertus Magnus and Thomas Aquinas (here called as a group *antiqui*), accidental forms include quantitative as well as qualitative forms, for William of Ockham and most of the *moderni*, terms falling into the category of quantity do not correspond to forms in the external world.

Nominalistic notions of place or space were affected by nominalistic conceptions of the distinction between mathematics and natural philosophy, because, according to this view, geometric concepts, such as those of point, line, and surface, do not correspond to really existing things within the natural universe. Rather, they exist within the minds or imaginations of mathematicians or other scientists. Whereas we could suppose that a late medieval philosopher might posit that outside the cosmos there is space as described by Euclidean geometry, nominalist mathematicians would hold that geometric concepts exist in the minds or imaginations of mathematicians, not in reality.[8]

As far as Aristotle's definition of "place" is concerned, then, this nominalistic distinction between mathematics and physics might be taken to mean that the idea of a surface did not belong as part of a definition of something physical like "place." In many different passages of his works William of Ockham changed Aristotle's definition of "place" to refer to the body immediately surrounding a given body in place insofar as it touches the given body, doing away with the notion of

8 See Edith Sylla, "John Buridan and Critical Realism," *Early Science and Medicine* 14 (2009): 211–47. See also David Sepkoski, *Nominalism and Constructivism in Seventeenth-Century Mathematical Philosophy* (London: Routledge, 2013); Edward Grant, *Much Ado about Nothing: Theories of Space and Vacuum from the Middle Ages to the Scientific Revolution* (Cambridge, UK: Cambridge University Press, 1981), 16, 232–34.

its innermost indivisible surface. He claimed, moreover, that Aristotle and Averroes, what they explicitly said notwithstanding, did not really believe that mathematical indivisibles such as points, lines, and surfaces exist in the natural world.[9]

Intertwined with the ontological minimalism of the nominalists, including their denial of the real extramental existence of anything but substances and qualitative forms, was the *logica moderna*, used both by nominalists like William of Ockham and by realists like Walter Burley. From the point of view of the *logica moderna* the truth or falsity of propositions is to be analyzed by examining the reference or "supposition" of the terms in a proposition, where there are categorematic terms with supposition for things in the external world, and syncategorematic terms that affect the supposition of categorematic terms but do not have their own supposition. One might ask, in this context, whether the term "space" occurring in a proposition is a categorematic term and, if so, what things or entities in the physical world it has supposition for. One possibility was to say that space and time are real, but they are not things, neither substances nor qualitative forms inhering in substances. Sometimes the term "mode" was used to characterize such properties of things that are not full-fledged qualitative forms. Another alternative was to say that "place" is a connotative term, referring to relations of many things and not to an individual substance or quality. But the most significant response to make was to say that propositions involving the term "space" should be expounded

---

9 William of Ockham, *Expositio in Libros Physicorum Aristotelis*, in *Opera Philosophica*, vol. 5, ed. R. Wood et al. (Allegany, NY: St. Bonaventure University, 1985), book IV, t. 35, 68. See also *Quaestiones in Libros Physicorum Aristotelis, Opera Philosophica*, vol. VI, Q. 72, Utrum locus sit aliqua res absoluta distincta a corpore locante; Q. 73, Utrum Philosophus posuerit locum distinctum a corpore locante et locato; Q. 74, Utrum locus sit spatium inter latera continentis; Q. 75, Utrum locus sit corpus continens; Q.76, Utrum locus sit in loco; Q. 77, Utrum sit idem locus numero corporis continue quiescentis quando corpus circumstans continue movetur cira illud; Q. 78, Utrum secundum veritatem locus sit immobilis; pp. 597–611. Also *Quodlibeta Septem*, Quodlibet I, Q. 4, Utrum angelus sit in loco per suam substantiam. William of Ockham, *Opera theologica*, vol. 9, ed. R. Wood et al. (Allegany, NY: St. Bonaventure University, 1980), 24.

into other technically exact propositions, making it clear that space is
being used syncategorematically.[10]

Beyond the distinction between the separate disciplines of mathematics and physics and an analysis (to be explained later) of the truth
of propositions by reference to categorematic and syncategorematic
terms and their supposition, fourteenth-century natural philosophy
was affected by regulations at the University of Paris concerning the relations of masters of arts to masters of theology. In the condemnation in
Paris in 1277, the bishop of Paris determined that masters in the faculty
of arts were not to deny that God could, by God's absolute power, do
anything that is not a logical contradiction. This implied—assuming
that the existence of a vacuum is not a logical contradiction—that a
master should not deny that God could cause a vacuum to exist, even if
there are naturally or in fact no vacuums in the cosmos. Even before the
condemnation of 1277, it was established by the Church hierarchy that
God can cause miracles to happen and does so in the transubstantiation of the bread and wine in the mass. In the fourteenth century, the
moderni often dealt with problems of place or space that arose because
of the assumption of God's absolute power.

---

10 Oresme explains how the word "place" is used syncategorematically writing, "Sed alio modo dicitur
'aliquid' valde large, quod non est significabile per nomen nec demonstrabile <per> pronomen
proprie dicendo 'hoc' vel 'illud,' nec complexe nec incomplexe, sed solum syncategorematice
per adverbia, sicut demonstrando 'hic' vel 'ibi.' Secundo sciendum quod veritatibus habendis
licitum est fingere ista esse entia, sicut patet quarto *Metaphysice*, ubi dicitur quod non entia entia
dicimus; similiter dicimus quod ita est sicut negativa vera significat, ut ista: chimera non est, et
tamen nulla res est ita sicut etiam mathematicus fingit lineam. Et ideo talia possunt appellari
nominaliter, dicendo 'locus' 'vacuum' etc.: et minus <im>proprie in obliquo, dicendo 'in loco';
et propriissime adverbialiter dicendo 'hic' vel 'ibi.' Ex hoc sequitur <tertio> quod aliqualiter
bene dictum est quod locus nihil est, quia nulla res est locus, nec substantia nec accidens sed quia
videtur universaliter negari, ideo non bene sonat, quia non est sicut chimera aut hircocervus.
Immo potest syncategorematice significari et assignari et etiam esse in loco vel esse alicubi est
aliqua condicio, et ad hoc movetur res naturaliter, ut *sic* hic vel ibi. Ideo melius est dicere quod
est spatium." Nicole Oresme, *Questiones super Physicam (Books I–VII)*, ed. Stefano Caroti, Jean
Celeyrette, Stefan Kirschner, and Edmond Mazet (Leiden: Brill, 2013), 461–62. See also Stefan
Kirschner, *Nicolaus Oresmes Kommentar zur Physik des Aristoteles*, Sudhoffs Archiv Beihefte 39
(Stuttgart: Franz Steiner Verlag, 1997), 321. This paper was written using the text in Kirschner's
book before the publication of the Brill 2013 edition. I give page references to both texts.

To summarize: There were at least three sets of ideas that might have affected what Oresme and other fourteenth-century philosophers said about Aristotle's definition of place. First of all, there was the idea that there are many autonomous or semi-autonomous scientific disciplines, based on experience but organized on the model of Euclidean geometry, supposing principles and demonstrating conclusions on the basis of those principles. On this understanding, geometers have their geometric principles, which may or may not correspond to bodies in the physical world, and they have concepts that exist in their minds or imaginations, the main requirement of the discipline of geometry being that its theorems follow necessarily from geometric principles. Second, there was the *logica moderna* and its analysis of the truth or falsity of propositions using the supposition of terms for things in the world or in the mind. Under this umbrella, nominalists like William of Ockham assumed that the only things that really exist as separable entities in the external world are substances and qualities. And third, there was the impact of the jostling between philosophy and theology according to which philosophers were supposed to admit that in addition to the actual world that God has created by his ordained power (*de potentia Dei ordinata*), one should also consider what God could have done or could do by his absolute power (*de potentia Dei absoluta*), which was taken to be anything that would not include a logical contradiction. Whereas Aristotle had tried to prove that a vacuum or empty space is impossible (because, for instance, in it a body would move infinitely fast, but infinite velocity is self-contradictory), by the end of the thirteenth century it was widely accepted that God could cause a vacuum to exist, for instance by annihilating everything inside the lunar orb or sphere of the moon, leaving a large spherical vacuum. What, then, would follow?

In his questions on book IV of Aristotle's *Physics* written in the mid-fourteenth century, Oresme's contemporary John Buridan declared that he was compelled by regulations of the arts masters to consider what might happen if God brought about the existence of a vacuum, for instance by annihilating everything that exists inside the orb of the moon.[11] He supposed that if God annihilated everything inside the sphere of the moon, it could happen that there was no dimension at all within the moon's orb, meaning that God could then create many worlds within the lunar orb, there being no limitation of volume.[12] Only if God created immaterial dimensions within the evacuated lunar orb would it be possible for a body to change its position within the orb. Buridan's reasoning on the issue of whether God could cause a vacuum to exist and of what would follow from this assumption recognized that after positing that a vacuum exists, one might be stumped about how the argument should proceed.[13] This feature of discussions of what might happen *de potentia Dei absoluta* is discussed further in what follows.

2.2. Nicole Oresme's Questions on the Physics, Book IV

Oresme was no doubt influenced by Buridan and vice versa. Although Buridan is assumed to have begun teaching in the arts at Paris before Albert of Saxony or Oresme, the most familiar version of his questions, published in Paris in 1509, is called the *ultima lectura* and may have been put in its existing form in the 1350s, whereas the only extant

---

11 Edith Sylla, "'Ideo quasi mendicare oportet intellectum humanum': The Role of Theology in John Buridan's Natural Philosophy," in *The Metaphysics and Natural Philosophy of John Buridan*, ed. J. M. M. H. Thijssen and J. Zupko (Leiden: Brill, 2001), 221–45. Buridan prefaced his discussion of what might happen if God annihilated everything within the sphere of the moon, with a reference to the oath to be taken by masters in the Parisian Arts Faculty at this time, according to which if they dealt with a topic relevant both to the arts and to theology they would resolve it in accordance with orthodox theology and would refute arguments for the other side, which could not be done without describing the issue.

12 Cf. John Buridan, *Quaestiones super octo libros Physicorum Aristotelis (secundum ultimum lecturam): Libri III–IV*, ed. Michiel Streijger and Paul J. M. M. Bakker (Leiden: Brill, 2016), QUESTIO IV.15, 336–42. A similar argument was made by Albert of Saxony in *Quaestiones super quatuor libros Aristotelis de celo et mundo*, in *Quaestiones et decisiones physicales insignium virorum* (George Lokert, 1518), book I, Q. 9, f. 93vb. See Edward Grant, *Planets, Stars, and Orbs: The Medieval Cosmos, 1200–1687* (Cambridge, UK: Cambridge University Press, 1994), 171n7.

13 This is what Buridan expresses when he says that the intellect must beg. See Sylla, "'Ideo.'"

version of Oresme's questions on the *Physics* is dated to the 1340s, thus before Buridan's *ultima lectura* but after Buridan had been teaching the works of Aristotle in Paris probably for some decades.[14] Thus there could be influence in both directions between Buridan and Oresme as well as between those two and Albert of Saxony, and it is not always possible or fruitful to try to award priority among them. In what follows I sometimes discuss what Buridan writes in order to cast light on the ideas of Oresme.

In his extant questions on Aristotle's *Physics*, Oresme devoted considerable attention to Aristotle's treatment of place and vacuum in book 4. Only one manuscript of his questions is known to exist, and that one seems to show evidence of being a work in progress, in that what Oresme says in one section may differ from what he says in another. There are many manuscripts of Buridan's *Questions on the Physics*, some labeled "the third lecture" and some "the last lecture," and it is likely that Oresme too lectured on the *Physics* more than once and that the single extant manuscript we have contains sections originally composed in different years, which would explain its somewhat patchwork quality.

In the existing version of Oresme's questions found in MS Seville, Bibl. Columbina 7-6-30, there are thirteen questions about place and void.[15] To give the flavor of what a question commentary might be like at this time, it may be worth listing the questions:

Qu. IV.1. Whether place is a surface. (*Utrum locus sit superficies.*)
Qu. IV.2. Whether place is equal to the located. (*Utrum locus sit equalis locato.*)

---

14 The extant version of Albert of Saxony's questions on the *Physics* is likewise thought to have preceded Buridan's *ultima lectura*. See Jürgen Sarnowsky, "Natural Philosophy at Oxford and Paris in the Mid-Fourteenth Century," in *From Ockham to Wyclif*, ed. Anne Hudson and Michael Wilks (Oxford: Basil Blackwell, 1987) 125–34; Jürgen Sarnowsky, *Die aristotelisch-scholastische Theorie der Bewegung: Studien zum Kommentar Alberts von Sachsen zur Physik des Aristoteles* (Münster, 1989).

15 Oresme, *Questiones super Physicam*. See also Kirschner, *Nicolaus Oresmes Kommentar zur Physik.*

Qu. IV.3. Whether place is the limit of the containing body. (*Utrum locus sit ultimum corporis continentis.*)

Qu. IV.4. Whether place is a quantity. (*Utrum locus sit quantitas.*)

Qu. IV.5. Whether place is the body containing or locating. (*Utrum locus sit corpus continens sive locans.*)

Qu. IV.6. Whether place is the space intercepted between the sides of the container which would be void if there were no located [body] there. (*Utrum locus sit spatium interceptum inter latera continentis, quod esset vacuum si non esset ibi locatum.*)

Qu. IV.7. Whether there could naturally be a vacuum in this world. (*Utrum naturaliter possit esse vacuum in hoc mundo.*)

Qu. IV.8. Whether if a vacuum existed there would follow a contradiction. (*Utrum ad vacuum esse sequatur contradictio.*)

Qu. IV.9. Whether in local motion of simple heavy and light bodies a medium is required and this on account of succession. (*Utrum in motu locali gravium et levium simplicium requiratur medium et hoc propter successionem.*)

Qu. IV.10. Whether a simple heavy body in moving has resistance in itself. (*Utrum grave simplex in movendo habeat resistentiam in se ipso.*)

Qu. IV.11. Whether a simple heavy or light body [in a vacuum] would move locally successively. (*Utrum grave simplex aut leve <in vacuo> moveretur localiter successive.*)

Qu. IV.12. Whether a mixed body in a vacuum would move locally successively. (*Utrum mixtum in vacuo localiter moveretur successive.*)

Qu. IV.13. Whether it is possible for some mutation to occur suddenly and all together [in]divisibly. (*Utrum*

possibile sit aliquam mutationem fieri subito et tota simul
<in>divisibiliter.)[16]

The titles of most of these questions fit closely with Aristotle's text, asking questions about what Aristotle said in this part of the *Physics*. It takes knowledge of previous commentaries on the *Physics* to know where more recent issues are having an effect.[17] In his replies, Oresme often, but not always, agrees with William of Ockham. In some passages Oresme is obviously reflecting Ockham's views. For instance, as has been mentioned, Ockham denied the real or physical existence of mathematical indivisibles, such as points, lines, and surfaces. According to Ockham, geometers might use terms referring to such indivisibles, but they existed only in the imagination, not in reality. This view appears in Oresme's questions where he asks whether place might be defined in terms of the surrounding body rather than the surrounding surface (Question IV.5). Oresme also reflects Ockham or nominalism in mentioning the possibility that "place" is to be taken as a connotative term.

Rather than being independent from each other, Oresme's answers to his questions on place are connected. In his answer to the first question, he says that in answering such questions one must begin by defining the term at issue, in this case the term *locus*. Then one must suppose some principles commonly conceded by everyone; some may be known by experience, others from the definition, and still others simply from the terms involved. For any demonstration to be probable or plausible

---

16 Oresme, *Questiones super Physicam*, viii–ix; Kirschner, *Nicolaus Oresmes Kommentar zur Physik*, 294–356. (This is relevant because, if there were motion in a vacuum, it might be sudden.)

17 See Cecilia Trifogli, *Liber Quartus Physicorum Aristotelis: Repertorio della Questioni. Commenti Inglesi ca. 1250–1270* (Florence: SISMEL Editioni del Galluzzo, 2007), for a list of questions that had been asked up through 1270 by English commentators. See also Edith Sylla, "Guide to the Text," in John Buridan, *Quaestiones super octo libros Physicorum Aristotelis (secundum ultimum lecturam): Libri III – IV*, ed. Michiel Streiger and Paul J. M. M. Bakker (Leiden: Brill, 2016), cliv–clxxiv.

(*probabilis*), it must not be inconsistent with the suppositions.[18] After setting out the suppositions, Oresme sets out three opinions about the definition of place. The first is that place is the surface of the containing body, which is other than the body. This is the opinion of Aristotle and Averroes, he says.[19] The second opinion is that place is the containing body. This is so because it is a surface, but surface is not other than body.[20] The third and last opinion is that place is the space intercepted between the sides of the container that would be a vacuum if no body were there.[21] Having given the alternative possible definitions of place, Oresme comments that none of the possible choices is demonstrable, nor can any of them be demonstratively refuted. From all of the possible choices there follow some things that seem unreasonable, except perhaps for the last choice.[22] Here it is worth pointing out that the second definition modifies the first definition in order to take account of Ockham's reformulation of Aristotle's definition of place to avoid implying that indivisible surfaces really exist. If the first definition is to be accepted, Oresme says, it must be understood that the term *locus* is being used equivocally and connotatively, i.e., that it does not have supposition for something existing in the external world.

With regard to the heavens, Oresme writes, its place may be said to be the earth at its center (since there is no body outside the heavens to be its place). The place of the world may be said to be the center of the earth, except that (taking account of the argument that a point is nothing) this should be rephrased to say: for the earth to be in its natural place its center of gravity should be equally distant from all parts of the heaven.[23]

---

18 Oresme, *Questiones super Physicam*, 423–24; Kirschner, *Nicolaus Oresmes Kommentar zur Physik*, 294.

19 Oresme, *Questiones super Physicam*, 426; Kirschner, *Nicolaus Oresmes Kommentar zur Physik*, 296.

20 Oresme, *Questiones super Physicam*, 426; Kirschner, *Nicolaus Oresmes Kommentar zur Physik*, 296.

21 Oresme, *Questiones super Physicam*, 426; Kirschner, Nicolaus *Oresmes Kommentar zur Physik*, 296.

22 Oresme, *Questiones super Physicam*, 426; Kirschner, Nicolaus *Oresmes Kommentar zur Physik*, 296.

23 Oresme, *Questiones super Physicam*, 427; Kirschner, Nicolaus *Oresmes Kommentar zur Physik*, 297.

Notable in Oresme's reply to the second question, whether place is
equal to the located body, is his reply to the third principal argument
that in the case of a sphere, the convex surface of the located sphere and
the concave surface of the containing sphere would not be equal if one
posited that place is the containing body (following the Ockhamist
or nominalist denial of indivisible surfaces and changing the definition of place to containing body rather than surface). Oresme replies,
"To the third it is conceded that the two equal spheres would have the
same center and would touch each other in more than one point, as
the Commentator says in this Book IV: 'whatever are contiguous, the
mathematician imagines as one,' and therefore mathematically the concave surface of the containing and the convex surface of the contained
are held to be one."[24] Notable in Oresme's reply to the fifth question is
his explanation that since Aristotle is defining what it means to be in
place, one should not say that place is a body, even though that is true,
because it is not part of the definition of place, and one should reply
with connotative terms expressing the conception of place.[25]

Finally, Oresme arrives at Qu. IV.6, which asks whether place is the
"space intercepted between the sides of the container which would
be void if there were no located [body] there." Both Aristotle and
William of Ockham had discussed but rejected this possibility. In
his reply Oresme again faces issues that arose because of the *logica
moderna*: what would be the supposition of the terms in such a definition in terms of the space intercepted between the boundaries?
After listing some of the many things that could be meant by being
or thing (*ens*), Oresme suggests that in analyzing the truth or falsity
of propositions, it is licit to allow words referring to fictional entities
(*sciendum quod pro veritatibus habendis licitum est fingere ista esse entia,*

24 Oresme, *Questiones super Physicam*, 435; Kirschner, Nicolaus *Oresmes Kommentar zur Physik*, 303.
25 Oresme, *Questiones super Physicam*, 451–52; Kirschner, *Nicolaus Oresmes Kommentar zur
Physik*, 314.

sicut patet IV Metaphysice, ubi dicitur quod non entia dicimus), where "place" or "space" would be such a fictional entity.[26] If this is the case, he says, then, the definition of place as something which is neither a substance nor a quality might be the best choice, although some might find it hard to accept that place is nothing (*locus est nihil*).[27]

To Aristotle's argument that if space or a vacuum had three dimensions then when a body is present, the dimensions would interpenetrate, Oresme replies that there will be interpenetration, but this is not a problem, because an empty space would not have the sort of dimensions that bodies have.[28] Oresme concludes that, if it were not unusual, the definition of place as the space intercepted between the sides of the container which would be void if there were no located (body) there, would perhaps be the most satisfactory one.[29] Thus Oresme's case shows that it was possible, although not common, to embrace a concept of three-dimensional space in the fourteenth century, even within a commentary on a work of Aristotle connected to university teaching. But does Oresme's empty space have intrinsic dimensions?

Some people, seeing Oresme's answer to his sixth question, might immediately classify it as something moving in the direction of Newton's absolute space, but moving in the direction of absolute space may not be what is of greatest significance in what Oresme had to say. First of all,

---

26 Oresme, *Questiones super Physicam*, 461–62; Kirschner, *Nicolaus Oremes Kommentar zur Physik*, 321. In the commentaries examined by Trifogli, *Liber Quartus*, there are no moves similar to the ones Oresme makes here. Here I use the word "fictional" from the past participle of *fingere*, i.e., *fictum*. One could also propose to use the words "constructed" or "hypothetical."

27 Oresme, *Questiones super Physicam*, 461–62; Kirschner, *Nicolaus Oresmes Kommentar zur Physik*, 321, ll. 176–81.

28 Oresme, *Questiones super Physicam*, 460, 463; Kirschner, *Nicolaus Oresmes Kommentar zur Physik*, 321, 323.

29 Oresme, *Questiones super Physicam*, 464; Kirschner, *Nicolaus Orsemes Kommentar zur Physik*, 323, ll. 255–58. Compare William of Ockham, *Expositio*, book IV, cap. 6, §§10–11, 69. Note that the editors of Ockham's *Expositio* identify the *aliqui* whose arguments Ockham discusses as Aegidius Romanus and, in chapter 7, sec. 4, John Duns Scotus. Ockham himself reports the arguments of Averroes.

Oresme was not the first medieval author writing in Latin to conclude, even tentatively, that place is the space that would be intercepted between the sides of the container of the thing in place if there were no body there. Stefan Kirschner, Chris Schabel, Paul J. J. M. Bakker and Sander W. De Boer have written about authors before Oresme who argued for a definition of place as the empty space that would be present between the sides if there were no body there.[30] To the repeated suggestion that if there were a vacuum it would be an empty space, the sticking points were that both a vacuum and an empty space seemed to be nothing. And if there were any empty space, as, for instance might occur if God annihilated everything inside the sphere of the moon, then that empty space might have no dimensions in it; at most its size might be judged by the bodies surrounding it.

In his *Questio de loco*, Gerard of Odo addressed this problem in a way that sounds very like something that Newton later said, arguing that it is not only substances and accidents that exist—space has its own entity: "I say that that space which is in a vacuum is not entirely nothing. And if it were asked whether it is a substance or an accident, I would reply that neither this nor that properly speaking, but it is only a space thing (*ens spatium*), nor can it be resolved into other concepts by which it may be described."[31] So Oresme was not first to opt for a

---

30 Stefan Kirschner, "Nicole Oresme," in *The Stanford Encyclopedia of Philosophy*, ed. Edward Zalta (2009); Chris Schabel, "The Reception of Peter Auriol's Doctrine of Place, with Editions of Quaestions by Landulph Caracciolo and Gerard of Sienna," in *Scrinium Friburgense: Représentations et conceptions de l'espace dans la culture médiévale* (2009), 147–92; Paul J. J. Bakker and Sander W. de Boer, "*Locus est spatium:* On Gerald Odonis," *Quaestio de loco, Vivarium* 47, nos. 2–3 (2009): 294–330.

31 Bakker and de Boer, *Locus est spatium* (note 29), [181] 327, "Dico quod illud spatium quod est in vacuo non est omnino nichil. Et si queratur utrum sit substantia vel accidens, respondeo quod nec hoc nec illud est proprie, sed solum est ens spatium, nec potest resolvi in alios conceptus per quod describatur. Sed experimentum docet, ut multe rationes superius facte tradunt, quod est aliquod tale spatium in quo est totum universum, qualiscumque entitatis sit. Et si non possit reddi proprie quidditas illius, non propter hoc debet negari esse, quia de multis phisicus probat quia sunt. Probat enim quod est aliquis primus motor; ignorat autem quidditatem eius et speciem illius primi motoris. Quare licet non apparet quidditas illius spatii, non tamen propter hoc negari debet ipsum spatium." For Newton, see Sylla, "Imaginary Space," 219: "Perhaps now it may be expected that I should define extension as substance or accident or else nothing at all. But by no means, for

definition of place in terms of empty space, and to propose a "space thing" might seem to Gerald Odonis's readers a pretty weak solution to the problem of what empty space could possibly be. So far no historian has shown that Oresme had a significant following with regard to his choice among Aristotle's definitions of place.

Suppose, however, that we are interested in the transmission and progress of scientific disciplines over time. What were the fourteenth-century authors of questions on Aristotle's *Physics* such as Oresme doing to transmit or contribute to the further development of physics? First of all, of course, they were teaching university students (or in Oresme's case the king of France and his court) both the content of Aristotelian sciences and the methods for evaluating those sciences. In the fourteenth century, the methods of mastering and critiquing sciences were mostly verbal, emphasizing logic, but some Aristotelians were beginning to make more use of mathematics. In the case of physical place or space, a very frequent approach was to test theories by making counterfactual suppositions to see what they might imply. In the case of place/space, one might suppose that God annihilates everything inside of the orb of the moon or that a man attempts to reach outside of the heavens, and then might consider what would transpire.

Oresme's attention seems to have been focused on the feature that in the definition of place as the space intercepted between the sides of a container that would be a vacuum if no body were located there, the condition, namely "if no body were there," is thought to be impossible—there are in fact no places in the cosmos in which there is no body. So if the definition were to be accepted, it might be only because, although it is naturally impossible to have a vacuum, God could by his absolute power cause one to exist, for example by annihilating everything inside the sphere or orb of the moon. This could happen only if an empty space is not self-contradictory. In his discussion

---

it has its own mode of existence which fits neither substances nor accidents." From A. R. Hall and M. B. Hall, *Unpublished Scientific Papers of Isaac Newton*, Cambridge 1962/1978, 131–32.

Oresme distinguishes senses of "impossible." In the sixth century AD John Philoponus had already brilliantly applied counterfactual reasoning to the understanding of place. Since there is no other chapter in this volume dealing withPhiloponus, I will transgress the boundaries of the Middle Ages to see how hejustified counterfactual reasoning.

2.3. John Philoponus, Corollaries on Place and Void

To a modern reader Aristotle's difficulties with empty space may seem hard to understand, but already in the sixth century Philoponus had rejected Aristotle's definition of place and had assumed instead that there could be an extended volume with no body in it. It seems that Philoponus's commentary was not well known in the fourteenth century, perhaps because it had been translated from Greek to Arabic, but not to Latin by that time.[32] Nevertheless, it is worth examining what Philoponus had to say, because he clearly rejected several of Aristotle's arguments against defining place as space.

Philoponus writes in critique of Aristotle's argument (*Physics* IV.4, 211b19–23) that place cannot be a three-dimensional extension. First he argues that it is foolish to think that if place were three-dimensional, it would penetrate and divide the body in place:

To think that place, if it is an extension, penetrates through the whole of the body that comes to be in it, and secondly that it also divides in such a way as to make an actual infinity of parts, and that the place itself is actually divided to infinity—this seems to me quite foolish and not even plausible. For if, when they said place is extended in three dimensions, they meant that it is also a body, even then these absurd consequences would perhaps not follow, although nevertheless the paralogism would have some seductive power. But

---

32 Cf. Stefan Kirschner, "Oresme's Concepts of Place, Space, and Time in His Commentary on Aristotle's *Physics*," *Oriens-Occidens: Cahiers du Centre d'histoire des sciences et de philosophie arabes et médiévales* 3 (2000): 145–79.

since they do not suppose place is a body (for they do not claim that to be extended is the same as to be a body), but bodiless (for by its own definition it is void) what necessity is there either that the void must pass into the body that is placed in it, or that it must automatically and in actuality divide the body if it does so pass through it? When it passed through the void, the body just filled it. Furthermore, if the void passed through the body, what kind of necessity was there that it must at once divide it, since it is bodiless? For something bodiless, passing through a body, makes no division or cut in it. At least, whiteness and heat and all the other qualities passing right through the whole of any body (I mean depth and breadth and length) make no division in it, and this is not because they are qualities but because they are bodiless. Body is not of such a nature to be divided by the bodiless.

If they say, "But the void is an extension, and therefore it will divide," even so I see no necessity in it. For even if it is extended in three dimensions, nevertheless it is totally inert and bodiless and just nothing other than empty space. Now how can what is wholly inert and created without any bodily quality, hardness or softness or resistance of any kind or any other power, make a division in bodies? A surface, applied to a surface, makes no division in it; indeed, even if ten thousand surfaces are applied to each other, they do not bring about any increase, nor divide each other, and similarly, if ten thousand lines are applied to each other, they do not make any division in each other or any increase, but ten thousand are able to be applied to each other in the same place (and this for no other reason than that they are bodiless). Just so, obviously, a three-dimensional extension, being bodiless, applied to a three-dimensional one will produce no division nor any other effect whatever.[33]

---

33 Philoponus, *Corollaries on Place and Void, with Simplicius: Against Philoponus on the Eternity of the World*, trans. David Furley and Christian Wildberg (London: Duckworth, 1991), 15–16.

In contrast to Philoponus's argument, for Aristotle and most medieval Aristotelians extension seems to be inextricably bound to corporeality or even impenetrability. The quantity of a body is taken to be its extension, and there is no clear conception of mass as a quantity of matter different from extension. Prime matter for Aristotle and medieval Aristotelians may have "indeterminate dimensions" (*dimensiones interminatae*) such that the same matter with the form of water may have a given extension but, when it is turned to steam, have ten times that extension. On this picture, heavy water is turned into light air, and so there is no opening to consider the possibility that quantity of matter as weight or heaviness would be conserved in such a transformation.

Philoponus then imagines various cases in which a vacuum (or equivalently an empty space) can be brought about. For example:

> Consider the following. If there is no distinct extension receiving them, over and above the bodies that come to be in it, let us in thought remove the bodies in the middle and see if it is really so. So then, if we think of the bodies within the heaven as not being there—I mean earth, water, air, and fire—what would remain in the middle but an empty extension? For it was plainly possible to extend straight lines from the centre to the circumference everywhere: so what is it through which we draw the lines but empty extension extended in three dimensions?

Here it is notable that Philoponus is making use of geometrical arguments, talking about lines. In the previous passage he had talked about surfaces, leaving it unstated whether these are supposed to be physical or mathematical. But when he removed in thought the bodies within the heavens, was he thinking of the action and of what remains as physical, mathematical, or perhaps supernatural?

> Let no one say that the hypothesis is impossible. (It was not a conclusion from my argument; when a hypothesis has an impossible

consequence, from the impossibility of the consequence we refute the hypothesis.) For we often make impossible hypotheses for the sake of seeing the nature of things in themselves. Aristotle himself, objecting to those who claim that the earth stands unmoved because of the rapid rotation of the heaven, says "If we stop the heavens in theory, where will it [sc. the earth] move to." And again in turn, he studies bodies in and of themselves by separating them from all quality and all form; and we arrive at a conception of matter by separating all form from it and studying it naked, all by itself. It is not absurd to use hypotheses even if they are impossible, for examination of other things; on this ground, since some people explained the stationary position of the earth by the motion of the heaven, Aristotle says that we should stop the heaven in theory, and ask where the earth will go by nature, so as to see whether the movement of the heaven really is the cause of the stationary position of the earth. Plato, too, separating in thought the cause of the order of the universe from the cosmos, asks how the universe would be, all by itself and without God. Each of these cannot possibly come about; all the same, theory separates in thought things naturally conjoined, so as to see how each thing is by itself in its own nature. And so I too, since some will not admit that what receives bodies is an extension distinct from them, but maintain that the only thing extended in three dimensions in the nature of things that exist is body-extension—I too in the same way say: if it is so, grant me in theory that the bodies inside the heaven are not there. So, is no empty extension left in the middle? But I think it is obvious: for if there were nothing between the boundaries of the concave surface of the heaven, the boundaries of the heaven would collapse when the interior bodies were removed in thought. But that is impossible, since it is not because of the interior bodies that the heaven is as it is: it would still be the same, if there were nothing there.[34]

---

34 Philoponus, *Corollaries on Place*, 36–37. It is worth noting that Philoponus, in writing about drawing lines through the evacuated sphere, did not assume, as Oresme would later assume, a distinction between the disciplines of mathematics and physics.

Here Philoponus claims to believe that the only things extended in three dimensions are bodies, but then he assumes that if the concave surface of the empty heavens remains spherical, there must be remaining within it three-dimensional extension. This is an additional supposition. As we know from modern physics, it is possible that if everything were removed from within the heavens—or, more likely, if a great mass was contained in the heavens—what we call a black hole might result, drawing everything into it.

Philoponus then goes on to an earthly example in which collapse is an alternative possibility: he supposes that a bronze sphere is filled with air that is then changed to water or earth, taking up a smaller volume and leaving empty space within the sphere or causing it to collapse. He goes on:

> But even though Nature does not allow this, let it be granted me, in theory, that the bronze does not collapse and the air inside does change to earth, and you will see that there is an extension in the middle distinct from the bodies in it. What is absurd in this, that just as we separate matter in theory from all forms for the purpose of studying its nature, even though it is impossible that this should ever happen, so we also suppose hypothetically that the air trapped in the middle of the bronze sphere changes to earth without the sphere collapsing, so that we may observe the consequence? But what I postulate is not outside nature, but happens daily—I mean the change of air into earth.[35]

What Philoponus is doing here is very like what Oresme and other natural philosophers of the fourteenth century would do: to hypothesize a case, perhaps one that is naturally impossible, in order to see what follows. The *moderni* have two ways in which they introduce a

---

35 Philoponus, *Corollaries on Place*, 37–38.

nonnatural situation. One is to suppose that God does something by
his absolute power, and the other is to propose something imaginary
or in the mind of the mathematician. Often the same result is supposed
to follow in either of these ways.[36] Interestingly, Philoponus reports
a disagreement between his predecessors over the question whether,
in supposing that condensation might bring about a vacuum within
a bronze sphere or else cause the sphere to collapse, the disputant
was begging the question or falling into the logical fallacy called *pe-
titio principii*. Since this is so relevant to the second main topic of this
paper concerning so-called imaginary space outside the last sphere of
the heavens, it is worthwhile to give another sample from Philoponus's
discussion in notes. The original publisher in 1618 is Henry Savile; the
publisher in 1964 is Minerva.

> Themistius was wrong to object to Galen: the latter postulated hypo-
> thetically that no other body flowed in when the water in the jar was
> removed, in order to study the consequence, and he [Themistius]
> objected that he was begging the question. He says: "But let us sup-
> pose that no other body flowed in when the water was removed, so
> there remains a separate extension inside the surface [sc. the inner
> surface of the walls of the jar]. But the hypothesis is irrational, my
> wise and clever Galen: it hypothesizes the very thing we are inquiring
> about. We inquire whether there can be a separated extension—and
> you say 'let us suppose there is a separated extension.' So you invent
> your own extension and draw it just as you want, but you don't dem-
> onstrate what is really there."

So says Themistius; but I believe it is obvious to everyone that his
answer is silly. If it was agreed that the extension exists, but one asked

---

36 In his *De Causa Dei Contra Pelagium*, Thomas Bradwardine set up situations in which infinites
could be compared by saying, for instance, that souls and bodies should be put in parallel rows
"by the omnipotence of God truly or by imagination fictitiously" (*per Dei omnipotentiam vere vel
per imaginationem ficte ita dispositis*). See Thomas Bradwardine, *De Causa Dei Contra Pelagium*
(London, 1618; reprint Frankfurt am Main, 1964), 121C.

whether it can exist by itself, empty of body, as Aristotle does ask in the following passage, and then Galen hypothesized that when the water flows out no other body enters instead, he was indeed begging the question. But since that is not the question now, but whether there is any extension at all, distinct from body-extension, which is the place of bodies, and Galen claims that when the water has departed no other body enters, he does not say, as you claim, Themistius, "Let there be an extension separate from the bodies inside the jar," but "Let no other body enter when the water runs out, and so let us see whether there is anything inside or not." If in general you think that when the water has run out, if we do not hypothesize another body entering, it follows that there is a separated extension inside, you yourself are caught on your own wings: for you say there is another extension inside, but it is never empty of body, as we too agree. For we do not say that this extension ever remains empty of body, but that it is different from all the bodies that come to be in it although it never comes to be empty of body; and for this reason there is interchange of bodies and the force of the void, so that place-extension may never remain empty of body.[37]

If it is physically impossible that the jar ever remain empty of body, then the water will never run out of the jar with nothing replacing it. But what if God can cause it to happen because it is not logically impossible? Then if the jar does not collapse, nothing will be within it. If it seems to the human imagination that there will remain three-dimensional space, then at most it will be imaginary and so will not have a real physical effect. Conundrums like this may explain Oresme's only tentative endorsement of the definition of place in terms of empty space. Given Oresme's wording, it appears that he did not feel under pressure to claim certainty in the matter.

---

37 Philoponus, *Corollaries on Place*, 38–39.

Can we understand Oresme's position more clearly by looking at his Qu. IV.8, which has a short and sharp discussion of the different senses of "impossible"? The question is Qu. IV.8, "Consequently it is asked whether to the existence of a vacuum would follow a contradiction" (*utrum ad vacuum esse sequatur contradictio*). The principal arguments begin:

> It seems that it would, because it follows that the sides will be distant because between them is a vacuum, but they would not be distant, because nothing is between them. Secondly, God could not make a vacuum, therefore its existence implies a contradiction. The inference holds, because it is said that [God] can do whatever does not imply [a contradiction]; and the antecedent is clear, because that vacuum would be useless, since it would not have any nature, nor would anything be posited there; also there would be disorder in the universe, if God did something useless and disordered. Third, in Book IV Aristotle proved that if there were a vacuum, motion would occur in it indivisibly, and then there would be motion and there would not be motion because all motions are measured in time.[38]

Oresme gives an argument for the other side and then sets out distinctions on which he bases his answer:

> The opposite is argued because the ancients posited that a vacuum exists, therefore it is at least possible in imagination, and no such implies a contradiction.... First ... I make some suppositions: First, that no natural force is infinite, as natural is distinguished from voluntary, nor is any voluntary force [infinite] according to the opinion of Aristotle. ... The second supposition is that in truth God is of

---

38 Oresme, *Questiones Physicorum*, IV. Qu8, 472; Kirschner, *Nicolaus Oresmes Kommentar zur Physik*, 329.

infinite power and is a free agent. The third is that it follows that
God can do whatever does not imply a contradiction, since he is of
infinite power and a voluntary agent is not limited.

Then there is a distinction that "impossible" is said in three ways in
this case:

> First simply [impossible] is what cannot happen by any finite or in-
> finite power, and such would imply a contradiction, or to the pos-
> iting of such an impossible there would follow that contradictories
> would be true, such as that the diameter would be commensurable
> with the side.
>
> Secondly, that is said to be impossible, which is infinitely difficult,
> which can be done by no finite power, as to move instantaneously
> with a resistance or with infinite velocity.
>
> Third that is said to be impossible, which is only finitely difficult,
> but there is no natural power which can do it, and in this way it
> would be impossible to move the whole earth from its place, because
> the force that could do this would not be infinite, but nevertheless
> Aristotle says that there is none that could do this. And in truth no
> natural force can do this. This [kind of impossible] is called "false
> impossible" by the Commentator in *On the Heaven*, Book I, and
> in the *Physics*, Book IV, where a "false possible," is, for instance, to
> rarify a medium infinitely.
>
> From this it follows as a corollary that impossible in the first way
> is simply impossible, and the other impossibles are in some respect
> (*secundum quid et in respectu*).
>
> Second, it follows that from the impossible in the first sense,
> follows anything. This is clear because from this there follow two
> contradictories and from a copulative between contradictories can
> be inferred anything. . . .
>
> Third it follows that to the impossible in the second way
> there follows not whatever you wish (*non quodlibet*), because a

contradiction does not follow from such, because it is not simply impossible but difficult to imagine, as motion to be sudden and the like.

Fourth, I say that to the impossible in the third way there does not follow just anything nor something difficult to imagine. And thus such is to be admitted, as the Commentator wishes in *On the Heaven*, Book I, and in the *Physics*, Book IV, and he says that Aristotle often uses such a hypothesis (*positione*).

Then the first conclusion is that for a vacuum to exist is not impossible in the first way [because it does not lead to a self-contradiction], but only in the second way: it is of infinite difficulty to rarefy a body *in infinitum*. From which follows the principal conclusion that it does not imply a contradiction, and also it follows that it can be done by God, which was proved first by the second supposition and is clear from this: because that is only difficult, therefore it is not impossible and from this can be proved that supposition, namely that God could do whatever does not imply, etc.[39]

In this way Oresme unravels a tangled skein of senses in which something may be said to be impossible. He goes on to describe the ways in which God could cause a vacuum to exist. But from this it follows, he says, that if there were a vacuum, it would be a distance, because it is impossible to imagine that the concave surface of the heaven is still concave and void, unless there is a distance within it.[40] This is not because from what is impossible anything follows.[41] A vacuum is impossible *secundum quid* or in the second and third ways. It is not naturally possible, and, moreover, it would be useless (*frustra*), in that there would be no nature in the space and the order of nature would be perturbed. This is a sign that nature does not want to suffer a vacuum and it is proved

39 Ibid. Qu. IV.8., 473-474.
40 Oresme, *Questiones Super Physicam*, Q. IV.8, 474; Kirschner, *Nicolaus Oresmes Kommentar zur Physik*, 330.
41 Oresme, *Questiones Super Physicam*, Q. IV.8, 474; Kirschner, *Nicolaus Oresmes Kommentar zur Physik*, 330.

in experience. Even an infinite natural force could not cause a vacuum to exist because it is infinitely difficult, and thus the force would not exceed the resistance. On the other hand, if God caused a vacuum to exist, then it would be natural for a vacuum to exist, because anything God does is natural. It is more difficult to cause a vacuum to exist than to cause a sudden motion against a resistance. This is clear because an infinite natural force, such as gravity, can move suddenly, and it has already been said that no infinite natural force can cause a vacuum. There are three levels of difficulty: finitely difficult, infinitely difficult, and impossible. The difficult can be done by a finite power, by an infinite natural power, and by God. Even an infinite natural power cannot overcome a difficulty equal to it, such as causing a vacuum (*nec virtus infinita naturalis in difficultatem infinitam*). Even God cannot do the impossible. This can be a beautiful (*pulcra*) consideration, he concludes.[42]

The bottom line here is that God could cause a vacuum to exist because its existence is not a self-contradiction or does not imply a contradiction. Oresme seems to be persuaded that if a vacuum existed it would have intrinsic dimensions. He writes, "From this it follows that, if there were a vacuum it would be a distance, because it is impossible to imagine that the concave surface of the heaven is still concave and void, unless there is a distance within it(Ibid., 474)."

The problem, however, which Oresme does not seem to notice here is that, in this context having three dimensions and being a body were thought to be the same thing. A trace of this can be seen in the custom of talking about plane geometry and solid geometry, the latter meaning three-dimensional geometry.[43] In Buridan's question III.15,

---

42 Oresme, *Questiones super Physicam* Qu. IV. 8, 475; Kirschner, *Nicolaus Oresmes Kommentar zur Physik*, 331. "Hoc posset esse consideratio pulcra."

43 See Charles Davies's preface (1875) in his translation of Legendre's *Elements of Geometry* (1858; New York, 1890) "The term 'solid,' used not only by Legendre, but by many other authors, to denote a limited portion of space, seems calculated to introduce the foreign idea of matter into a science which deals only with the abstract properties and relations of figured space. The term 'volume' has been introduced in its place, under the belief that it corresponds more exactly to the idea intended."

"Whether there is some infinite magnitude," the principal argument is that if there is some space outside the heaven, it is infinite, but then it goes on: "Therefore if it could be shown that there is space there, it ought to be conceded that it is infinite. And that space, since it would have length, width, and depth, would be a body. Therefore it should be conceded that there would be an infinite body."[44] Since this is the principal argument, Buridan is not committed to it. In a long answer to the question, he writes:

> It seems that it should be believed, and I believe, that God could annihilate everything that is below the orb of the moon and within the concavity of the orb of the moon with the orb remaining, and even with the whole heaven remaining in the same magnitude and figure that it now has. This case having been posited, it should be seen what would follow.
>
> I say that if this case is posited, nothing would be in or within the concavity of the orb of the moon, because the whole has been posited to be annihilated. And thus there would not be any space and also there would not be a vacuum within this concavity, because it implies a contradiction that nothing is inside the concavity and that a vacuum or space is within the concavity, because since this proposition "vacuum is within the concavity" or "space is within the concavity" is affirmative, it is necessary, if it is true, that the term "space" or "vacuum" has supposition for something. Therefore this follows: "vacuum is within the concavity, therefore something is within the concavity"; and this is contradictory to the first proposition, which said that nothing was within the concavity (Ibid., 138).

What about the distance between the sides of the evacuated lunar orb? Buridan writes:

---

44 Buridan, *Quaestiones Physicorum* (Leiden, 2015), 133.

I say that in this it is difficult to satisfy the imagination because it always appears to the imagination that there is space there, as it always appears to sense that the sun is not larger than a horse and that it is much smaller than the earth. Nevertheless, in such things the intellect ought to correct such appearances of sense or imagination. I say, therefore, because we are not talking of cases that are naturally possible, but miraculously possible, that God could form there a very big body, that is bigger than this world. And it is true that that body would not be in that small body or place circumscriptively or commensurably. This should be believed, because within the small quantity of the Host and in its small place there is the body of Christ as large as it was at the last supper (*cena*) and as large as it is in paradise, and configured in the same way—indeed in any quantitative part of the Host, however small, there is the whole large body of Christ, optimally configured. But this magnitude of the body of Christ is not in the Host in a way commensurable to the magnitude of the Host. And no less could God make a bigger body in the place and with the magnitude of a millet seed. On account of this I also conclude that within the concavity of the orb of the moon God could also make a body a hundred times larger than the world, not changing the magnitude and figure of the orb of the moon. Indeed if there were a body in a circumscriptive way measurable by the magnitude of the orb, it could not be larger than it now is, because it would be necessary for its diameter to be the third part approximately of the circular line drawn in the concavity of the orb of the moon.[45]

Unlike Oresme, then, Buridan first assumes that if God annihilated everything inside the sphere or orb of the moon, what was left in the center would have no intrinsic dimension and bodies of all sizes could be posited within it, although they would be there definitively rather

45 Ibid., 138.

than circumscriptively. Further on, however, Buridan writes that God
could also, if he chose to, put distances in the vacuum not inhering in
any substance:

> I say therefore, since we could imagine a vacuum in two ways . . . it
> is possible by divine power for a vacuum to exist in two ways. This is
> believed by me and not proved by natural reason; therefore neither
> do I intend to prove it, but only to say the way in which this appears
> possible to me . . . as far as the first way of imagining a vacuum to be
> is concerned, I suppose that God can make an accident without a
> subject and can separate accidents from their subjects and conserve
> them separately. Therefore God can make an accident without any
> substance or any accident distinct from it. Secondly, it seems that
> for God the penetration of dimensions is not impossible. Indeed he
> can make several bodies to be together in the same place without
> their differing from each other in position, that is without one being
> outside the other with regard to position (*situm*). Therefore God
> can make simple dimension or space separate from all natural sub-
> stance, in which or with which, without it receding, natural bodies
> can be received. This will be called the first imagination of vacuum
> previously described. Then about the second way of imagining a
> vacuum, I believe, as previously argued, because God could annihi-
> late this inferior world conserving the heaven and the magnitudes
> and figures just as and as great as they now have. And then the con-
> cave orb of the moon would be evacuated (*vacuum*).[46]

---

46 Streijger and Bakker, *Quaestiones super Physicorum, Libri III–IV*, 268–69. "Dico igitur quod,
cum duplici modo possemus imaginari vacuum, sicut dictum est in alia quaestione, possibile
est utroque modo vacuum esse per potentiam divinam. Et hoc est mihi creditum et non ratione
naturali probatum; ideo nec istud intendo probare, sed solum dicere modum secundum quem hoc
apparet mihi possibile. Primo igitur quantum ad primum modum imaginandi vacuum esse, ego
suppono quod Deus potest facere accidens sine subiecto et potest accidentia separare a subiectis
suis et separatim conservare; ideo potest simplicem dimensionem creare absque hoc quod cum ea
sit aliqua substantia vel etiam aliquod accidens distinctum ab ea. Secundo videtur quod non est
impossibile apud Deum dimensionum penetratio, immo ipse potest plura corpora facere simul

I think it is safe to say that when Oresme and Buridan were writing there were open questions about what would transpire if God annihilated everything inside the sphere of the moon. Would there be intrinsic dimensions or not? For characterizing late medieval concepts of space in relation to the history of concepts of space, one might say that in the middle of the fourteenth century a lot of attention was paid to place as a physical concept and to alternative ways of understanding place. Some of these alternative conceptualizations involved consideration of the possibility that a good definition might be that place is the space intercepted between the sides of the container (of the thing in place) that would be void if there were no located body there. This was problematic because the word "space" in this definition did not supposit for any thing (substance, quality, or quantity) but had a syncategorematic effect, referring to a number of things and their relations. Although this was complicated from a logical point of view, ultimately "space" came to be part of mathematical expressions, as in saying, for instance, that in a uniform motion space traversed equals velocity multiplied by time: $s = vt$. For this outcome, space was understood to mean distance. This will be considered in section 4.

To sum up: In his questions on Aristotle's *Physics*, book 4, Oresme reviewed the arguments for and against the definitions of place as the innermost surface of the surrounding body or as the space between the sides of the place that would be empty if the body were not there. He concluded that, all things considered, the latter definition would probably be best, but he explained how to defend the other proposed definitions, both the definition supported by Aristotle and Averroes, and the modification of this definition made to take account of the

---

esse in eodem loco absque hoc quod differant ab invicem secundum situm, scilicet absque hoc quod unum sit extra alterum secundum situm. Igitur Deus potest facere simplicem dimensionem sive spatium ab omni substantia naturali separatum, in quo vel cum quo absque hoc quod cedat recipi possunt corpora naturalia; et hoc vocabitur vacuum primam imaginationem prius narratam. Deinde de secundo modo imaginandi vacuum credo, sicut prius arguebatur, quia Deus posset annihilare istum mundum inferiorem conservando caelum et magnitudines et figuras quales et quantas nunc habet; et tunc concavum orbis lunae esset vacuum."

nonexistence of indivisible surfaces. Along the way, Oresme described the basic structure of an Aristotelian scientific discipline, in which one presupposes principles, some of which are definitions while others are based on experience, and then demonstrates conclusions that follow from these principles. In the case of place, Aristotle had properly started with commonly accepted truths about place, which he used as criteria in choosing between alternative possible definitions of place. While admitting the nominalistic ontological minimalism shaping the discussion, Oresme allowed that constructed concepts such as space, which do not correspond to things really existing in the external world, can be helpful in streamlining scientific discourse, understanding that such concepts or terms are connotative rather than denotative and syncategorematic rather than categorematic. Space is nothing, but it is a useful term to make use of in scientific discourse, always assuming that propositions including space can be expounded as equivalent to complex syncategorematic propositions.

So much for what Oresme said in his questions on the *Physics* about Aristotle's definition of place, Ockham's modification of it to avoid reference to indivisible surfaces, and about the third definition that defines place by referring to the extension between the sides that would exist if there were no body present, which he thought might be best. Lest one immediately jump to the inference that Oresme has moved at least a tiny bit in the direction of conceiving absolute space à la Newton, it should be kept in mind that at the time of Oresme, the Latin word *spatium* meant in most cases linear distance or more rarely two-dimensional area, so Oresme probably did not have a conception of space as we think of it, that is, as involving no body but having an intrinsic metric in three dimensions. This will be investigated further in the next part, but before that, we might look at the evidence of some others of Oresme's works to confirm that he was not in the habit of thinking of space as three-dimensional.

In his work *On the Causes of Miracles*, Oresme denied that there could be action at a distance through a vacuum or empty space. Against

Avicenna's suggestion that the intellective soul or the imaginative faculty could move bodies at a distance, he wrote:

> I say that [if Avicenna were right] it could happen through a vacuum, since through a vacuum I would imagine and wish in such a way that a certain thing would fall or etc. . . . I say that even through an infinite space [*spatium etiam infinitum*] [it would happen if Avicenna were right], since there could not be imagining and wishing through just so much and not through more, etc. I say that he contradicts himself, [which is evident] if one looks carefully at what he says earlier and at how the soul moves the body, for the mover and the moved are always together in some form of togetherness (see the *Physics*, Book 8).[47]

And in book 1, Question 17 of his commentary on Aristotle's *On Generation and Corruption*, Oresme likewise discusses whether all action and passion occurs by contact such that the agent always touches what suffers the action.[48] He concludes that there is always contact and that no medium can separate the mover and what is moved—neither a plenum nor a vacuum. Some people say that spiritual agents can act with no more than metaphorical touching, such as when the prime movers move the celestial spheres.[49] But no natural agent can act on a distant body except by multiplication of its species, which cannot happen through a vacuum; if it could happen, then its action could extend infinitely since there is no resistance in a vacuum.[50] In this version of the discussion Oresme explicitly uses the word *distantiam* where, in

---

47 Bert Hansen, *Nicole Oresme and the Marvels of Nature: A Study of His* De causis mirabilium *with Critical Edition, Translation, and Commentary* (Toronto: Pontifical Institute of Mediaeval Studies, 1985), 354–55. I have added some words to the phrases in brackets.

48 Nicole Oresme, *Quaestiones super De generatione et corruptione*, ed. Stefano Caroti (Munich: Verlag der Bayerischen Akademie der Wissenschaften, 1996), 142.

49 Oresme, *De generatione*, 144.

50 Oresme, *De generatione*, 144–45.

On the Causes of Miracles, he had used the word *spatium*. In section 4, I will return to the point that "space" as we understand the concept is not a technical term of medieval mathematics or natural philosophy, but before that, I want to look at what Oresme says about space outside the cosmos in his commentary in French on Aristotle's *On the Heaven*.

3. NICOLE ORESME, *LE LIVRE DU CIEL ET DU MONDE*

Oresme's *Livre du ciel et du monde* was written in French for the king and his court rather than for a university audience. In book 1, chapter 24 (by his count), Oresme discusses extracosmic void space in relation to the possibility of multiple worlds.[51] The first Aristotelian text and Oresme's gloss are:

> *Text:* In addition, it is clear that beyond the heavens or beyond our world there exists neither place, nor void, nor time, for in every place there can be a body. And those who say there can be a void say that a void is where there is no body whatsoever and it is possible that a body could be there.

> *Gloss:* Outside the heavens there can be no body. . . . Consequently, outside the heavens there is no place, no plenum, and no void.[52]

So at first Oresme simply explains Aristotle's text. Note that Aristotle and Oresme are writing about place, not space. Further on Oresme says:

> Now we have finished the chapters in which Aristotle undertook to prove that a plurality of worlds is impossible, and it is good to

---

51 Oresme has divided Aristotle's chapter 12 into many chapters.

52 Nicole Oresme, *Le livre du ciel et du monde,* ed. A. D. Menut and A. J. Denomy (Madison: University of Wisconsin Press, 1968), 161; Aristotle, *Physics,* bk. 1, ch. 9, 279a17–18 (only the first part of the text).

consider the truth of this matter without considering the authority of any human but only that of pure reason. I say that, for the present, it seems to me that one can imagine the existence of several worlds in three ways. One is that one world would follow another in succession of time. . . . Such a process will take place in the future an infinite number of times, and it has been thus in the past. But this opinion is not touched upon here and was reproved by Aristotle in several places in his philosophical works. It cannot happen in this way naturally, although God could do it and could have done it in the past by His own omnipotence, or He could annihilate this world and create another thereafter. . . .

Another speculation can be offered which I should like to toy with as a mental exercise. This is the assumption that at one and the same time one world is inside another so that inside and beneath the circumference of this world there was another world similar but smaller. Although this is not in fact the case, nor is it at all likely, nevertheless, it seems to me that it would not be possible to establish the contrary by logical argument.[53]

But it is the third way there could be multiple worlds that is of interest here:

The third manner of speculating about the possibility of several worlds is that one world should be [conceived] entirely outside the other in an imagined space (*en une espasce ymaginee*), as Anaxagoras held. This is the only manner [*cest seulle maniere*] of another world existing that Aristotle refutes here as impossible. But it seems to me that his arguments are not clearly conclusive.[54]

---

53 Oresme, *Le livre du ciel*, 167.
54 Oresme, *Le livre du ciel*, 171.

After giving several arguments against this third possibility, Oresme comes to an argument involving a vacuum or empty space:

> If two worlds existed, one outside the other, there would have to be a vacuum between them for they would be spherical in shape; and it is impossible that anything be void, as Aristotle proves in the fourth book of the *Physics*. It seems to me and I reply that, in the first place, the human mind consents naturally, as it were, to the idea that beyond the heavens and outside the world, which is not infinite, there exists some space whatever it may be (*aucune espace quelle que elle soit*), and we cannot easily conceive the contrary. It seems that this is a reasonable opinion, first of all, because if the farthest heaven on the outer limits of our world were other than spherical in shape and possessed some high elevation on its outer surface similar to an angle or a hump and if it were moved circularly, as it is, this hump would have to pass through space which would be empty—a void—when the hump moved out of it.[55] Now, if we assumed that the outermost heaven was not thus shaped or that nature could not make it thus, nevertheless, it is certainly possible to imagine this and certain that God could bring it about. From the assumption that the sphere of the elements or of all bodies subject to change contained within the arch of the heavens or within the sphere of the moon were destroyed while the heavens remained as they are, it would necessarily follow that in this concavity there would be a distance and empty space (*une distance et une espasce wide*). Such a situation can surely be imagined and is definitely possible although it could not arise from purely natural causes, as Aristotle shows in his arguments in the fourth book of the *Physics*, which [arguments] do

---

55 This case of points sticking out of a rotating heaven is in Aristotle, *De Caelo*, book 2, ch. 4, 287 12–23. See also John Buridan, *Quaestiones super libris quattuor De Caelo et Mundo* (Cambridge, MA: Mediaeval Academy of America, 1942; reprint, New York: Kraus Reprint, 1970), book 1, Q. 20, 92, 94–95; book 2, Q. 6.

not conclude that it is impossible otherwise, as we can easily see by
what has been said (*lesquelles ne concludent pas que ce soit impossible
autrement, si comme il puet apparoir legierement per ce que dit est*).[56]

In this situation it follows that outside the world there is an empty
incorporeal space:

> Then (*donques*), outside the heaven is an empty incorporeal space
> quite different from any full and corporeal space (*une espasce
> wide incorporelle d'autre maniere que n'est quelconque espace pleine
> et corporelle*), just as the extent of this time called eternity is of a
> different sort than temporal duration, even if the latter were per-
> petual, as has been stated earlier in this chapter. Now this space of
> which we are talking is infinite and indivisible, and is the immen-
> sity of God and God Himself, just as the duration of God called
> eternity is infinite, indivisible, and God Himself, as already stated
> above. Also we have already declared in this chapter that, since our
> thinking cannot exist without transmutation, we cannot properly
> comprehend what eternity implies; but, nevertheless, natural reason
> teaches us that it does exist. In this way the Scriptural passage, Job
> 26:[7], which speaks about God can be understood: Who stretchest
> out the north over the empty place (*vacuum*). Likewise, since ap-
> perception of our understanding depends upon our senses, which
> are corporeal, we cannot comprehend nor conceive (*comprendre ne
> proprement entendre*) this incorporeal space which exists beyond the
> heavens. Reason and truth, however, inform us that it exists (*nous
> fait congnoistre que elle est*). Therefore, I conclude that God can and
> could in His omnipotence make another world besides this one and
> several like or unlike it. Nor will Aristotle or anyone else be able

---

56 Oresme, *Le livre du ciel*, 176, ll. 285–307; 177. Here, as elsewhere, I have modified the translation, in particular where I have inserted the French text.

to prove completely the contrary. But, of course, there has never been nor will there be more than one corporeal world, as was stated above.[57]

In this text there seems to be a non sequitur: Oresme first says what *would be the case if* God created more than one spherical world, using the word *donques* to link his statement of what God *could do* to a result, but then he seems to assert that the resulting incorporeal space outside the world *is* the case.

In another passage of *Le livre du ciel et du monde* Oresme repeats this inference from what is possible by God's omnipotence to what is fact in a way that seems intended. In this passage, Oresme again compares the way God is present in time to the way God is present in space:

Text. The Ancients attributed to the gods the heavens and the higher regions as the place which alone is immortal [or imperishable].

Gloss. And Averroes says here that all laws and doctrines agree with one accord that God is in the heavens and is eternal. And the place of the Eternal must be eternal. To aid in understanding this and other matters worthy of consideration, I wish, first of all, to explain how God exists in the heavens or elsewhere and then to discuss the place occupied by other incorporeal things [*choses incorporelles*] and their mode of being. On the first point, the holy doctors have explained how God exists in His creatures through grace or glory or otherwise and how they exist in Him. This is not precisely the proper role for philosophy, but the question how God and immaterial things exist in their place must be considered; for as Averroes has stated, all people say that God is in the heavens and in His proper place. Therefore

---

I say that as God is necessarily present without succession in all past, present, and future time by reason of His indivisible eternity, which contains and exceeds all other time and is its cause ... likewise God in His infinite grandeur without any quantity and absolutely indivisible, which we call immensity, is necessarily all in every extension or space or place which exists or can be imagined. This explains why we say that God is always and everywhere—*semper et ubique*—always through His eternity and everywhere through His immensity. . . . According to the doctors of the church, He is in all places in three ways: by His presence, His power, and His essence (*presence, puissance, essence*). And since God could not cause Himself to cease to be for the space of a day or an hour or since, in improper parlance, He could not not-exist for the space of any time (*par une espace de temps*) whatsoever, just so is it impossible that He should not be in all places according to the three ways just mentioned above; nor would He be able to depart or absent Himself from any place whatever, nor could any place be imagined which would be without the presence of His essence where one could say, "God is not here." This is true not only of the places of this world, but also of imagined infinite and motionless space (*en l'espace infinie ymaginée et immobile*). For, if God made another world or several outside of this world of ours, it would be impossible that He not be in these worlds, and without moving Himself, because God cannot possibly be moved in any way whatsoever. Thus, from what has been said it appears that God is not more in heaven than elsewhere, in accord with the three ways stated above, nor simply when it is a question of Himself. Moreover, it is clear that He is not in the heavens like some object enclosed or comprised within the heavenly spheres, nor like something that does not exist beyond the heavens or earth. . . . [Here Oresme quotes many sources on the glory of the heavens] God does not need the heavens nor any other place for Himself because He is everywhere—both outside and inside the heavens by reason of his infinite and indivisible immensity [*par son immensité infinie et indivisible*], as we have said; and, as for His being, he has no need of anything other than Himself. To say that the heavens are in God who contains all things is more exact than that God is in the heavens, and just as God's eternity is not dependent upon any successive duration, so then neither is His immensity dependent upon any extension, dimension, or local distance [*ne depent de quelcunque extension, dimension ou distance local*], but all depends upon Him since He is the cause of everything by His absolutely free will: He hath done whatsoever he wished.[58]

Here, among much else not quoted, Oresme states explicitly how his reasoning moves from the possibility that God could by his omnipotence create other worlds outside the cosmos to the inference that God is now and always has been in the infinite imaginary space outside the cosmos. Here Oresme takes as given what theologians hold as true about God. If God could create bodies and hence space anywhere outside the cosmos, then God would always be in all such places because, had He created something there, he would be present there; but He would not move there, because God does not move; therefore God must already, eternally be there.[59]

Thus, in Oresme's argument, infinite immobile imagined space exists outside the cosmos, the characteristics of which result from an argument that starts from a naturally impossible premise and then reaches a conclusion held to be true at the time of speaking because of a truth about God, namely that God does not move. As in the case of the definition of place in book 4 of the *Physics*, Oresme thus reaches a conclusion that was not common among his contemporaries, although it was not unprecedented.

---

58 Oresme, *Le livre du ciel*, 277–85, ll. 41–61; 71–87; 158–65 (slight changes to translation).
59 Similar reasoning is found in other authors.

3.1. The Place of Angels

After discussing the presence of God outside the cosmos, Oresme's next topic is the place of angels.[60] He compares the position of angels in space to that of light rays coming in through the window. As immaterial substances, angels are not intrinsically of any corporeal magnitude. Angels can take on different sizes, but not all sizes; an angel cannot have a dimension larger than the diameter of the world, no matter how slender the angel might become in other directions.[61] A great many angels could be in a small volume, as in the Bible a legion of demons was cast out of a man (Mark 5:1–20), but, for Oresme and other fourteenth-century *moderni*, an angel would not be at a point, because points are not real but figments of the mathematical imagination. One might have thought that Oresme would consider that his courtly audience would be accustomed to picturing angels as like humans with wings. Even in depicting the prime movers of the celestial spheres, artists typically showed anthropomorphic angels located at the poles of the spheres turning cranks although in the text mentioned earlier from Oresme's *De generatione*, it was implied that celestial prime movers might not be in place at all.[62] Oresme does not, however, make allowances for his lay readers but assumes that angels are immaterial substances, and hence indivisible or in place definitively.

With regard to the motion of angels, Oresme lists different possibilities, considering some as impossible.[63] The fourth view states:

---

60 For ideas of the place and motion at Paris just before Oresme, see, e.g., Francisci de Marchia, *Reportatio IIA (Quaestiones in secundum librum Sententiarum, QQ. 13–27*, ed. Tiziana Suarez-Nani, William Duba, Emmanuel Babey, and Girard J. Etzkorn (Leuven: Leuven University Press, 2010), 75–106, Q. 16: Utrum angelus per se sit in loco vel tantum per accidens. Art. 1. Utrum et quomodo angelus sit in loco. Art. 2. Utrum angelus sit in loco divisibili vel indivisibili; Art. 3, Utrum plures angeli possint simul esse in eodem loco. Art. 4, Utrum angelus moveatur motu continuo vel instantaneo.Art. 5, Utrum angelus possit moveri in instanti.

61 Oresme, *Le livre du ciel*, 289–93.

62 See note 39.

63 Oresme, *Le livre du ciel*, 293–95.

The fourth way would be for the angel to be moved suddenly from one place to a distant place, passing through all the intermediates or mean space between the two, in which it would remain for a single indivisible moment or instant.

This Oresme rejects:

This, I think, is simply impossible, for to be in a space for such an instant or moment amounts to not being in this space at all, because in any successive or permanent continuum, there is, in reality, no such indivisible measure called an instant or point, as I showed some time ago in my commentary on the *Sentences*. There is no indivisible measure except the eternity and immensity of God, which was mentioned in the preceding chapter and in Chapter Twenty-Four of Book I.[64]

In writing about the motion of angels, Oresme is assuming that if angels are moved it may be from the Empyrean heaven to the earth or from one place to another on or near humans on the earth. If so, the extension of the path of angelic motion is marked by the celestial orbs or by the terrestrial bodies (or media) on or through which the angels move. He says that wherever angels go, even if it is to a less sacred space than the heavens, God is present to them. God does not need the heavens or any other place for himself because he is everywhere inside and outside the heavens by reason of his infinity and indivisible immensity. Thus angels provide another arena in which to reason about place and space.

In the case of Oresme's definition of place in his questions on Aristotle's *Physics*, the problems were, first, that Oresme presupposes a condition (that no body is present between the sides of the space) that is naturally impossible and, second, that an empty space seems to be

64 Oresme, *Le livre du ciel*, 295. No copy of Oresme's commentary on the *Sentences* is known.

nothing. In the case of our understanding what Oresme says about infinite space outside the cosmos, the problem is that the space is said to
be imaginary and that it is said to be infinite. How can we understand
what is meant by "infinite imaginary space"? Would it be better to say
"imagined space"? The meaning of "imaginary space" will be discussed
further later.

In the same decades that Oresme discussed infinite space outside the
heavens, Thomas Bradwardine also argued for imaginary space outside
the existing cosmos. In his *De Causa Dei*, Bradwardine also emphasized
God's relation to imagined space outside the cosmos.[65] Like Oresme,
Bradwardine wrote of God being present throughout an infinite space
in an unextended way:

> Therefore God is necessarily, eternally, and infinitely everywhere in
> an infinite imaginary position (*situ*), whence he can be said to be
> truly omnipresent as he is omnipotent. For a similar reason he can
> be said to be in some way infinite, infinitely large, or of an infinite
> magnitude, and even in some way, although metaphysically and im-
> properly, extensively. For he is inextensibly and undimensionally in-
> finitely extended. He coexists all together wholly with an infinite
> magnitude and imaginary extension and with any of its parts. For
> this reason he may similarly be said to be immense and not meas-
> ured, nor measurable with any measure.[66]

Here attention should be paid to the words "even in some way, although
metaphysically and improperly, extensively"; "he is inextensibly and
undimensionally infinitely extended"; "He coexists all together wholly
with an infinite magnitude and imaginary extension." Is Bradwardine

---

65 He is the main author whom Koyré commends for advancing the concept of absolute space.
66 Bradwardine, *De Causa Dei* Contra Pelagium, 178–79, as translated in Sylla, "Imaginary
Space," 214.

saying that God and/or infinite space has intrinsic dimension? More on this later in the paper.

Not all fourteenth-century philosophers concluded that there is infinite (imaginary or not) space outside the cosmos. In contrast to Oresme and Bradwardine, Oresme's older Parisian contemporary John Buridan concluded that probably there is no space outside the cosmos, because God would create such a space only if He intended to create bodies there, and it is unlikely that he would do such a thing. If God wanted to create more things, why would he not have made the existing cosmos larger rather than creating another world?[67]

This is in the same question of Buridan's *Physics* already discussed, where Buridan asks whether there is an infinite magnitude. The first principal argument that there is an infinite magnitude (which Buridan rejected) was that God could make a space outside the cosmos, and if God makes a finite space, there is no reason why he cannot make larger spaces *ad infinitum*. Buridan responds that God can create just as large a space as he chooses.[68] Just as a vacuum is not possible within the orb of the moon, even if God annihilated everything inside the orb of the moon, so analogously it is not possible outside the existing cosmos. But what of the argument that God by his infinite power can do these things? Buridan answers that although it is not possible to demonstrate that God could not have created an infinite space outside of the cosmos, he (Buridan) is of the opinion that there is no space or magnitude nor another world there, because God would have had no reason to create one there.[69]

---

67 John Buridan, *Quaestiones Physicorum*, book III, Qu. 15 (Leiden 2016), 133; (Paris 1509) f. 57vb. Cf. Sylla, " 'Ideo."

68 Buridan, *Quaestiones Physicorum* (Leiden 2016), 140; (Paris 1508), f. 58rb; Thijssen, *John Burdian's Tractatus de Infinito*, 21.

69 Buridan, *Quaestiones Physicorum* (Brill, 2016), 141; (Paris 1508), f. 58rb; Thijssen, *John Burdian's Tractatus de Infinito*, 16–17.

If God annihilated everything inside the orb of the moon there would be nothing there, not even a vacuum or an empty space. It should be held on faith that God could miraculously create there in the magnitude of a millet seed a huge body, greater than the existing world. That body, however, would not be there circumscriptively, the way bodies are in place, but definitively, in the same way that the life-size body of Christ is in the Eucharist, totally in every part. Meanwhile the orb of the moon would retain its spherical shape. If whatever might subsequently be put within it were in place circumscriptively, its largest dimension could be no more than about one-third of the circumference as is true for any sphere, but this is not the case for things in place determinatively.[70]

Summing up the evidence that has been surveyed up to this point, I conclude that Oresme and his contemporaries were testing and modifying what Aristotle said about place using the tools of the *logica moderna* and especially the method of counterfactual hypotheses. According to Aristotle the cosmos is a finite spherical plenum outside of which there is nothing, not even empty space. If this view is confronted with various truths of Christian theology, such as that there are angels that move, there is transubstantiation of the Eucharist such that there is the appearance of bread inhering in no substance, but especially by the assertion that God by his absolute power can or could have done anything that is not known to include a logical contradiction, what are the implications? One lesson that emerges from examining what Oresme and Buridan argued is that one cannot just change, add or subtract, one premise or principle of a discipline and expect to find the unquestionable implications, because in reasoning additional assumptions are usually called for. Oresme and Buridan were affected not only by the injunction not to deny to God any possible

---

70 Buridan, *Quaestiones Physicorum*, book 3, Q. 15 (Leiden 2016), 135–37; (Paris 1508), f. XXX; Thijssen. *John Buridan's Tractatus de Infinito*, 18.

action that does not imply a logical contradiction, but also by their
acceptance of the distinction between mathematics and physics and by
ontological minimalism. So, for instance, definitions of place should
not involve nonexistent geometrical indivisibles such as surfaces.
Moreover mathematics is seen not only as abstracting quantities from
natural things but also as creatively constructing mathematico-physical
subdisciplines. Space (*spatium*) could be understood as a mathematical concept conceived by mathematicians. This means that mathematical entities need not immediately be conceived of as causal agents in
the outside world. Looking at the uses of the expression "imaginary
space" within this context leads to the conclusion that imaginary space
for Oresme and others is something conceptual within the minds of
mathematicians or other theorists. It is not understood to be something wholly in the real or outside world. Imaginary space nevertheless
has an important function as a part of a mixed mathematical science.
However, this classification of mathematical entities as imaginary may
not apply to things that are three-dimensional! Indivisibles with no
dimensions (points) and indivisibles with one or two dimensions
(lines and planes) are imaginary (think mathematical), but what has
three intrinsic dimensions is a body and is taken to be real and to exist
in the outside world. The irony is that what has three dimensions is also
a body. This leads to the last part of this paper.

4. THE EVOLVING MEDIEVAL MEANING AND USE
OF THE LATIN WORD *SPATIUM*

I want to reemphasize that before the late Middle Ages, the word
spatium was not a technical term of physics or natural philosophy. In
nontechnical use it meant an uncrowded place or a place where motion is possible. In the Vulgate Latin translation of the Bible, one finds,
for instance in the book of Isaiah, 49:20, "angustus est mihi locus,
fac spatium ut habitem" (The place is too small for me. Make space
where I may dwell). Distance in space might be measured by the time

required for a journey from one place to another, as in Genesis 30:20, "Et posuit spatium itineris inter se et generum trium dierum" (Then he put a three-day journey between himself and Jacob).

In fourteenth-century English, the word "space" also had connotations of the ability to move: if you have space, you have room to move easily. In "The Parliament of Fowls," Chaucer wrote of the situation when all the birds gathered on St. Valentine's Day:

> For this was on seynt Valentynys day.
> Whan euery bryd comyth there to chese his make
> Of every knyde that men thynke may,
> And that so heuge a noyse gan they make,
> That erthe & eyr & tre & euery lake
> So ful was, that onethe was there space
> for me to stonde, so ful was al the place.[71]

Here in Chaucer's English, the words "space" and "place" are used in close proximity, but "place" is a rather neutral word connected to location, whereas "space" connotes the possibility of motion as opposed to being hemmed in. One also finds in fourteenth-century English texts "space of time."

What about mathematics? In the Latin Euclid one does not find what we call "Euclidean space." The word "space" (*spatium*) appears only rarely, and when it does appear, it most often means linear distance. For instance, in the Latin translation of the *Elements* ascribed to Robert of Chester, some form of *spatium* appears (in addition to appearances in proofs) in one postulate, one definition, and two enunciations of theorems. In Heath's English translations the Greek words translated into Latin as *spatium* are not translated into English

---

71 Geoffrey Chaucer, *The Parlement of Foulys*, ed. D. S. Brewer (New York: Barnes and Noble, 1960), p. 80, ll. 309–15. *Onethe* or '*uneathe*' is translated "scarcely."

as "space" but as "distance," "complements," or some other word.[72] In none of these cases does *spatium* mean a three-dimensional extension. Something similar can be said about the passages in which the word *spatium* is used in the proofs of the theorems.

In Bradwardine's *Geometria Speculativa*, an original fourteenth-century work modeled on Euclid's *Elements*, the Latin *spatium* likewise means distance, not a three-dimensional extension. Bradwardine's Postulate 2 of book 1 is the same as Euclid's.[73] Concerning lines meeting at angles, Bradwardine adds, "The whole space (*totum spatium*) which in any plane surface surrounds any point is equal to four right angles."[74] Concerning his seventh conclusion of book 1, Bradwardine writes, "A figure is said to be regular which is equiangular and equilateral. To fill place (*locum*) is here said to be to occupy the whole space (*spatium*) that surrounds some point in a plane."[75] Since it is plane angles that are at issue here, *spatium* is clearly not three-dimensional and in fact seems to be angular. Concerning the first conclusion of part 2, Bradwardine

---

72 Four cases: (1). Euclid, bk. 1, pet. 3 [2]; Robert of Chester, *Robert of Chester's Redaction of Euclid's Elements, the So-called Adelard II Version*, ed. Hubert L. L. Busard and Menso Folkerts (Basel: Birkhäuser Verlag, 1992), 115: "Item super centrum quodlibet quantumlibet occupando spacium [διαστήματι] circulum designare"; Euclid, *The Thirteen Books of the Elements*, ed. and trans. Thomas Heath (New York: Dover, 1956), 154, 199: "To describe a circle with any center and distance." (2) Euclid bk 1, proposition 43: Busard, 129, "Omnis paralellogrami spacii eorum que circa diametrum sunt paralellogramorum supplementa equa sibi invicem esse necesse est" (This and the following texts appear somewhat garbled or perhaps mismatched); Euclid, *The Thirteen Books*, 340, "In any paralellogram the complements of the parallelograms about the diameter are equal [in area, *spatium*] to one another." (3) Euclid, bk. 2, def. ii: Busard, 131, "Omnis paralellogrami spacii [χωρίον] ea quidem que diametros per medium secat paralellograma circa eandem diametrum consistere dicuntur. Eorum vero paralellogramorum que circa eandem diametrum consistunt quodlibet unum cum supplementis duobus gnomo nominatur"; Euclid, *The Thirteen Books*, 370, "And in any parallellogramic area let any one whatever of the parallelograms about its diameter with the two complements be called a gnomon." (4) Euclid, VI.23 [24]: Busard, 180: "Si in suo spacio paralellogramum parciale distinctum toti paralellogramo simile atque secundum suum illius esse fuerit, circa eiusdem diametrum consistit"; Euclid, *The Thirteen Books*, 251: "In any parallelogram the parallelograms about the diameter are similar both to the whole and to one another."

73 Thomas Bradwardine, *Geometria Speculativa*, ed. and trans. George Molland (Stuttgart: Franz Steiner Verlag Wiesbaden, 1989), 22–23.

74 Bradwardine, *Geometria Speculativa*, 26–27.

75 Bradwardine, *Geometria Speculativa*, 34–35.

writes, "Circles whose diameters are equal will themselves be equal. . . . And because centre is over centre, so also will circumference be over circumference, and the whole space (*spatium*) over whole space . . . wherefore they are mutually equal."[76] Here *spatium* means "area."

In part 4, Bradwardine comes to the filling of place (*loci*) by regular solids, so there, if anywhere, one might expect *spatium* to be three-dimensional, but Bradwardine uses *spatium* analogously for the plane and solid cases:

> Next it is necessary to see what is said about filling place and which of the regular bodies are fit for filling place. Both mathematicians and natural philosophers are concerned about this, as is evident from Aristotle in the third book of *De coelo* and from his commentator Averroes and through this a more useful skill in the matter is argued. It is necessary to take filling place in solids analogously with filling place in planes, which was spoken about in the chapter on lines in the first part, for just as there to fill place was to occupy the whole space that surrounds a certain point in the plane, which comes about by four right angles in form or value, as was said there, so also here to fill place is to take up one whole corporeal space (*spatium corporale*) that surrounds a point at which three lines mutually intersect at right angles. And Averroes says that the paucity of surfaces filling their places is the cause of the paucity of bodies filling their places . . . on account of which Averroes seems to posit that only the cube and the pyramid among solids fill place, for the cube in corporeal filling corresponds to the square in superficial filling. . . . I say therefore that according to truth the cube fills place, but according to Averroes' opinion the cube and the pyramid.[77]

---

76 Bradwardine, *Geometria Speculativa*, 62–63.

77 Bradwardine, *Geometria Speculativa*, 134–35. In the translation "place" always translates *locus*, and "space" always translates *spatium*.

In the chapter on spheres, in part 4, the word *spatium* again appears:

> Twelve equal circumposed spheres touch a single sphere.... Because
> there is space in every direction (*spatium est* utrobique)against the
> sides of those six spheres arranged in a circuit of the principal sphere,
> it is easily shown that just three spheres can be taken in one space
> and three in the other. And sense indicates this, for, when we make
> thirteen equal little spheres from wax we see that twelve can be ap-
> plied around the thirteenth in such a way that each touches it below
> and together with this touches four of the lateral spheres, so that
> the contact of any of the lateral spheres is according to five points.[78]

Here Bradwardine is clearly imagining a three-dimensional situation,
and yet the word "space" does not have a clear technical sense different
from space in a plane or angular space around a point. Thus in the Latin
translation of Euclid and in Bradwardine's *Geometria Speculativa*, there
is no special linkage of the Latin word *spatium* with three-dimensional
extension. What about Oresme's use of the Latin *spatium*?

In his *Questions on Euclid's Geometry*, Oresme rarely uses the word
spatium, and when he does, it seems to mean distance. In reply to
Question 5, "Whether according to mathematical imagination it
should be conceded that there may be an infinite circle, in the sense
that from this a contradiction does not follow,"[79] Oresme writes:

> Let Socrates be at the center [of the infinite circle] and Plato be on
> point B, and in the first proportional part of the hour let Socrates
> traverse a foot of this radius, and in the second just as much, and so
> forth, and let Plato come in the same way moving toward Socrates,

---

78 Bradwardine, *Geometria Speculativa*, 142–43.

79 Nicole Oresme, *Questiones super geometriam Euclidis*, ed. Hubert L. L. Busard (Stuttgart: Franz
Steiner Verlag, 2010), 113, "Utrum secundum ymaginationem mathematicam debeat concedi,
quod sit aliquis circulus infinitus ita quod ex hoc non sequitur contradictio."

then they will meet in some intrinsic instant of the hour and in any
such instant only a finite space (*spatium finitum*) has been traversed
and the whole radius is traversed by the two together, therefore that
whole is composed of two finite lines, and therefore it is finite. On
the same basis it can be argued that it is impossible for an infinite
space (*spatium infinitum*) to be contained between two limits.[80]

In a similar context of his questions on Aristotle's *Physics*, book 3,
Question 17 (Whether it implies a contradiction for an infinite to be
between two limits), Oresme writes, "Either two lines starting from
points *C* and *B* [on the infinite circle] are parallel, and then by definition they will never meet and so they will not meet before the center,
or they are not parallel, therefore by definition they will meet in a finite
space (*ad spatium finitum*) or before they are extended *in infinitum*."[81]
    In sum the word *spatium* in the mathematics of Oresme's time most
often means linear distance. Sometimes it may refer to an area or surface, but it rarely refers to something three-dimensional, and never
to a three-dimensional "Euclidean space." Interestingly, when, in
fourteenth-century Latin mathematics or physics, the word *spatium*
or *spacium* occurs, modern translators into English tend to translate
spatium as "interval," recognizing that the Latin does not connote
three-dimensional extension, as does the modern English "space."[82] In
quoting English translations of fourteenth-century Latin texts, then,
I have modified the published translations to use the English "space"
where the Latin has *spatium* so that the historical usage is clear.

---

80 Oresme, *Questiones super geometriam*, 114, my translation.
81 Oresme, *Questiones super Physicam*, 419; Kirschner, Nicolaus *Oresmes Kommentar zur Physik*, 291,
   my translation.
82 This is the case, for instance, in the English translation in Thomas Bradwardine, *Tractatus de
   Proportionibus: Its Significance for the Development of Mathematical Physics*, ed. H. L. Crosby
   Jr. (Madison: University of Wisconsin Press, 1966). Where Bradwardine writes "spatium
   superficiale," Crosby translates "area" (128–29), and where Bradwardine writes "spatium lineale"
   Crosby translates "linear interval" (130–31).

4.1 The Word Spatium in Oresme's Mixed Mathematical Works: Commentaries

But if one does not find in the fourteenth century *spatium* meaning three-dimensional space in natural philosophy or geometry, in mixed mathematical works one does find *spatium* in a technical sense meaning one-dimensional (or rarely two-dimensional) extension.

Oresme's commentary on the *Sphere* of Sacrobosco starts with two questions related to whether mathematics (especially geometry) concerns concepts in the minds of mathematicians or things (entities) in the real world (*in rerum natura*). Concerning the first question, "Whether the definition of 'point' is a good one in which it is said that a point is that of which there is no part," Oresme says that there are two defensible (*probabiles*) positions, first, that a point is not something *in rerum natura* but only something feigned by the imagination (*solum fingitur per imaginationem*), or second, that a point is an indivisible accident which is placed in the category of quantity reductively.[83] Oresme first gives twelve arguments in favor of the view that a point is not something *in rerum natura*. Then, for those who want to hold the second position, he argues against those twelve arguments. The question ends by seeming to support Euclid's definition.[84] But at the start of the second question, "Whether the definition of line is a good one, namely that a line is length without width, at the extremes of which are two points," he writes that it has been seen above (i.e., in question 1) how it may be sustained that points, lines, and surfaces are certain accidents distinct from body in the genus of quantity, and that now (in the second question) it will be shown how the other way can be sustained that posits that lines, points, etc. are nothing, but are only

---

83 Garrett Droppers, "The Questiones de Spera of Nicole Oresme: Latin Text with English Translation, Commentary and Variants," PhD dissertation, University of Wisconsin, 1966, 12, 14.

84 Droppers, "The Questiones," 42.

imagined to be.[85] So that this position may be better understood, he argues against it.

To the argument that, if mathematicians imagine things, such as points, lines, and surfaces, that do not exist, then their imaginations are false, Oresme replies that to imagine something is different from believing or having the opinion that it is so. Mathematics is a hypothetical science (*scientia hypothetica*), which asserts, for instance, that if there were a line, it would be a length, etc. As Averroes said in book 2 of the *Physics*, things need not be as they are imagined by the mathematician. Mathematical propositions are not to be taken literally (*de virtute sermonis*). To imagine a line is different from imagining a chimera, however, because by propositions about points and lines in geometry, we can know the measures or proportions (*commensurationes*) of things really existing.[86] From such hypothetical or conditional propositions we can come to know categorical propositions, as is the case in astronomy, and as is true in Aristotle's *De Caelo*, such as that the heaven is not infinite and that it is spherical, and similar propositions. The terms of geometry can be in the category of quantity even though they signify no existing thing; for instance, if there were only a thousand things in the world, nevertheless a number twice as great could be said to be a species of quantity.[87] Things can be imagined which cannot possibly exist; even so, they need not include an internal contradiction because in showing the impossibility of their existence additional assumptions are made. In *De Caelo*, book 1, the Commentator calls such things possible false (*possibile falsum*).[88]

Here Oresme, in pointing to Averroes's commentary on the *Physics*, book 4, comment 72, raises the issue that some things may be impossible even though they are not self-contradictory. This means

85 Droppers, "The Questiones," 44.
86 Droppers, "The Questiones," 46, 48.
87 Droppers, "The Questiones," 48.
88 Droppers, "The Questiones," 50.

that it is more difficult than one might have thought to determine what God could or could not do based on what is logically possible or impossible. Averroes has in mind Aristotle's argument that there cannot be a vacuum because if there were one and one supposes that an elemental body might move in it, then it could be shown that a body would move equally fast in a vacuum and in a plenum, which cannot be, given rules for the speeds of motion. But the proposed case involves noticing how fast the body moves in the vacuum, then taking a motion of the same mobile that occurs in a plenum, then in effect calculating using the rule that velocity is proportional to force divided by resistance, how much rarer the medium would have to be to correspond to the supposed velocity in the vacuum. The flaw in the proposed case is that it would take a medium rarer than fire for the mobile to move as fast as it is supposed to move in the vacuum, but fire is the rarest possible medium. This case thus involves what Averroes calls a false possible.

What about the terms in Sacrobosco's *Sphere* that refer to nonexisting mathematical entities such as the point at the center of the world, or the pole of the earth or heavens? These entities are imagined, not real, Oresme says. As far as Aristotle's definition of place in terms of the innermost surface of the surrounding body is concerned, it should be understood, he says, that place is the surrounding body, of which we imagine the innermost surface (*dico quod corpus locans proprie est locus, sed non locat nisi secundum partem exteriorem in qua nos ymaginamus superficiem et propter hoc superficies dicitur esse locus*).[89] Oresme concludes Question 2 by indicating how someone who takes geometric indivisibles to be accidents can respond to the arguments made, while someone who takes these terms in the second way can easily respond that a line is nothing except in the imagination.[90]

---

89 Droppers, "The Questiones," 54.
90 Droppers, "The Questiones," 60.

4.2. Oresme's Mixed Mathematical Works: Treatises

Beyond commentaries on mixed mathematical works, Oresme writes treatises, such as *On the Configurations of Qualities and Motions,* his *On the Proportions of Proportions,* and his *Treatise on the Commensurability or Incommensurability of the Motions of the Heaven.* Modeled to some extent on Bradwardine's *On the Proportions of Velocities in Motions* (this is especially true of Oresme's *On the Proportions of Proportions*), the works set out principles for measuring motions (including alteration and augmentation and diminution as well as local motion) and then demonstrate conclusions.

In Oresme's *On the Configurations of Qualities and Motions,* similar figures or configurations represent theorems concerning local motion, difform distributions of intensities or qualities in space, and alterations. In Oresme's theorems about local motion, alteration, and illumination, the Latin word *spatium* has multiple uses mostly unrelated to space in Newton's sense. This can be shown by a few quotations:

In local motion that degree of velocity is greater and more intense by means of which more space or distance [*de spatio vel de distantia*] would be traversed.[91]

Now the intensity of the velocity of motion is ... measured by ... the linear space [*attenditur penes spatium lineare*] which would be traversed.[92]

Whence it is said in Isaias: "And the light of the moon shall be as the light of the sun, and the light of the sun shall be sevenfold as the light of seven days," for evidently the light of one day increased

91 Nicole Oresme, *Nicole Oresme and the Medieval Geometry of Qualities and Motions ... Tractatus de configurationibus qualitatum et motuum,* ed. Marshall Clagett (Madison: University of Wisconsin Press, 1968), part 2, ch. 3, 277.

92 Oresme/Clagett, *De configurationibus,* 279.

intensively by sevenfold is as the light which would be extended through a space of seven days [*luci que per septem dierum spatium extenderetur*].[93]

If some mobile would be moved during one day with a certain velocity, and during the second day twice as slowly, and during the third day twice as slowly as during the second day, and so on to infinity, never in eternity would it traverse twice that which it would traverse during the first day. But given any space less than twice that traversed in the first day, it would at some time traverse as great a space [*sed quocunque spatio dato minori quam duplum ad pertransitum prima die tantumdem spatium aliquando pertransiret*].[94]

In three of these texts, "*spatium*" refers to linear distance, and in one it refers to an interval of time.

In his *On the Proportions of Proportions*. Oresme likewise uses *spatium* to mean distance. For instance, "It must be understood that from a ratio of times, and from a ratio of distances [*spatiorum*] traversed or acquired, or any such [quantities], one can arrive at and know a ratio of velocities."[95]

In his *Treatise on the Commensurability or Incommensurability of the Motions of the Heaven*, Oresme likewise uses *spatium* to mean distance,[96] but also the arc of a circle[97] and area.[98] Finally, he refers to an imagined three-dimensional space (actually, a two-dimensional spherical surface on which the path of the Sun's motion is traced):

It follows from all this that *B* describes daily a new spiral in a space imagined as motionless, which it has never before described; and it

93 Oresme/Clagett, *De configurationibus*, part 3, ch. 7, 409.

94 Oresme/Clagett, *De configurationibus*, part 3, ch. 12, 427.

95 Nicole Oresme, *De proportionibus proportionum & Ad pauca respicientes*, ed. Edward Grant (Madison: University of Wisconsin Press, 1966), 287.

96 Oresme/Grant, *De commensurabilitate*, 197–99, 208, 210–11, 286 (quoting Pliny).

97 Oresme/Grant, *De commensurabilitate*, 260.

98 Oresme/Grant, *De commensurabilitate*, 241.

traverses a path which it has never before traversed. And so, by its track, or imagined flow, *B* seems to extend a spiral line that has already become infinite [in length] from the infinite spirals that were described in the past. . . . In accordance with what has been imagined here, the whole celestial space between the two tropics is traced by *B*, leaving behind a web- or net-like figure expanded through the whole of this space.[99]

The "track, or imagined flow" is obviously not any kind of substance or entity existing in the external world. Thus most frequently for Oresme the word *spatium* refers to distances or to surfaces representing mathematical quantities in two dimensions.

The efforts made by Oresme (like those of the so-called Oxford *Calculatores*, such as Thomas Bradwardine and Richard Swineshead) to develop a concrete mathematical discipline in which one may measure motion with respect to cause (*tanquam penes causam*) and with respect to effect (*tanquam penes effectum*) were among the most successful projects that were pursued by Oresme and the other fourteenth-century *moderni*. That the word *spatium* was used in these efforts to mean linear distance rather than a three-dimensional extension does not mean that these efforts were irrelevant to the history of concepts of space. Whereas Aristotle's definition of place as the innermost surface of the surrounding body was not a useful basis for trying to develop a meaningful mathematical science of motion (*scientia de motu*), Oresme and the Oxford *Calculatores* constructed many useful concepts that could be translated into mathematics, not the least of which were the concepts of latitudes and degrees, where latitudes might be understood by analogy to lines or, on the Continent, to triangles.[100]

---

99 Oresme/Grant, *De commensurabilitate*, 276.

100 For some logical works in which *spatium* appears, see Richard Kilvington, *The Sophismata of Richard Kilvington*, Auctores Britannici Medii Aevi, XII, ed. Norman Kretzmann and Barbara Ensign Kretzmann (New York: Oxford University Press for the British Academy, 1990), which includes the sophismata: S12, Socrates pertransivit A spatium; S13 Socrates pertransibit

Oresme's work *On the Configurations of Qualities and Motions* was one of the most influential works in this genre.

The role of the concept of latitude in Oresme's *Quaestiones super De Generatione et corruptione* exemplifies the usefulness of this constructed concept for talking about issues that may be mathematized. A beautiful example is the way Oresme uses *latitudo* in his analysis and answer to his last question, II.15, "Whether any corruptible has a determinate period of its duration," where by "period" is meant a determinate time during which something corruptible lasts as measured by the revolutions of the heaven, and the corruptibles in which he is most interested are living things.[101] The fifth cause of the longer or shorter period of duration of a corruptible, he says, is the magnitude of the latitude of proportion of primary qualities with which the form of such a corruptible can remain, or in other words how much variation in the proportions can occur without causing death. For humans the allowed variation is very narrow, so the lifespan is short, whereas for crows the latitude is broad, so they might live 360 years.[102] This use of the word "latitude" is close to the use originally found in Galen, considering the variation in degrees of health, where the latitude of health is a sort of scale. Even a kind of animal that strongly resists corruption may not last long if there is a small latitude of complexion under which it can exist.[103] Setting aside violent causes of death, Oresme concludes that

---

A spatium; S14, Socrates incipiet pertransire A spatium, et Socrates incipiet pertransivisse A spatium, et non prius incipiet pertransivisse A spatium quam incipiet pertransivisse A spatium; S15, A spatium incipit esse pertransitum. Then later S27. Socrates incipiet posse pertransire A spatium; S28. A spatium incipiet esse pertransitum a Socrate; S29. Socrates movebitur super aliquod spatium quando non habebit potentiam ad movendum super illud spatium. Everywhere in these sophismata where the word *spatium* appears, the Kretzmanns translate it "distance." William Heytesbury, *Regule Solvendi Sophismatum* (Venice, 1494), f. 37v., "Motuum ergo localium uniformis est quo equali velocitate continue in equali parte temporis spacium pertransiretur equale." f. 52r, commentary, "latitudo motus localis habet attendi penes spacium." f. 52v, Commentary of Messinus, "In uniformi itaque motu habet velocitas totius magnitudinis sic mote localiter attendi penes lineam quam describeret punctus velocissime motus."

101 Oresme/Caroti, *Quaestiones de generatione*, 293.
102 Oresme/Caroti, *Quaestiones de generatione*, 298.
103 Oresme/Caroti, *Quaestiones de generatione*, 300.

there is an approximate maximum duration for a given species and that for humans is perhaps more than seventy years.[104] He will define the period for a species and the mean of the latitude between the maximum and minimum lifespan as the period of that species and says that it is a pretty speculation whether the mean should be taken arithmetically or geometrically.[105] Of course a person can live longer than the period for the human species (we would say the life expectancy), as a human can live to fifty years old. Some will live longer or shorter periods depending on their location, diet, and so forth, even if they do not die a violent death.

This is just one example of Oresme's use of an extended or metaphorical sense of space, i.e., a concept of dimension, extension, or interval (the latitude of variation in human complexion) to apply mathematics to natural science. There are many other cases that might be mentioned in which Oresme and the other fourteenth-century *moderni* apply extensions or dimensions in a wider sense to a mathematical science of nature.

As a historian of science, I have been interested in the efforts of Oresme and other fourteenth-century *moderni*, especially the Oxford *Calculatores*, to construct mixed mathematical scientific disciplines. In this, many of them were influenced by Ockhamistic ontological minimalism in combination with the *logica moderna* that analyzed the truth of propositions making use of the reference (the so-called supposition) of terms for things in the real world. While a very simple case of this might be, for instance, to formulate the proposition that the earth is a sphere, where sphericity is a form inhering in the material earth, the most important achievements of the *moderni* involved propositions containing so-called syncategorematic terms. When a proposition containing syncategorematic terms is to be explicated using the idea

---

104 Oresme/Caroti, *Quaestiones de generatione*, 301. Then he adds that the time through which heaven cannot endure is perhaps one thousand years.

105 Oresme/Caroti, *Quaestiones de generatione*, 302.

of reference or supposition (their term), it is almost always explained as being equivalent to two or more propositions in which the terms have simpler types of supposition. Thus one says that the proposition "Socrates begins to run" is equivalent to the two propositions "Socrates is not now running" and "Before any instant after this Socrates will have been running"' these two propositions are appropriate because there is no first instant of any motion.

To mathematize motion, then, the *moderni* did not analyze simple propositions such as "All men are mortal," but instead much more complicated propositions requiring exposition into multiple propositions with varying suppositions of their terms. When Oresme concluded that were it not so unusual, perhaps the best definition of place would be the extension between the sides of a body in place that would remain if the body were not there, he was tentatively endorsing an opinion that required exposition of the proposition into a technically correct form. Thus one should not say that if everything inside of the sphere of the moon were annihilated, there would be a vacuum where the bodies previous were, because there is no such thing as a vacuum. Nothing would be inside of the evacuated sphere. What one should say is that the sphere would be evacuated. Then it is the sphere for which "evacuated" has supposition and the sphere is in fact there.[106]

From the examples of Oresme's questions on Aristotle's *Physics*, his commentary in French on Aristotle's *De Caelo*, and his mixed mathematical works, I have described how what Aristotle had to say, including

---

106 John Buridan, *Metaphysicales Quaestiones breves* (Paris 1518; reprint Frankfurt a.M. 1964), book 4, Q. 14ff. 23vb, 24rb, "Tunc ad propositum videamus descriptiones huius termini 'vacuum' indicantem quid nominis, scilicet locus non repletus corpore: hec oratio significat omnia loca de mundo indifferenter per illum terminum 'locus': et significat etiam omne repletum corpore: sed modo divisivo ... propter quod ista oratio sive mentalis sive vocalis 'locus non repletus corpore' pro nullo supponit nec per consequens illa dictio 'vacuum': quia illa dictio et illa oratio non differunt nisi secundum vocem. . . . Sed tamen ego nego quod hoc nomen 'chimera' significat chimeram. Immo significat omnia composita et omnia impossibilia componi: et etiam hoc nomen vacuum non significat vacuum si impossibile sit vacuum esse. Immo significat omnia loca et omnia repleta corpore, modo tamen diverso qui non habet correspondentiam in re."

its weak points, motivated Oresme to come to the conclusions he came to. What Oresme says was also motivated by the nominalistic or Ockhamistic or Averroistic separation of mathematics and physics, which called in question any positive extension inside the evacuated orb of the moon or outside the cosmos where there was no body. The influence of logic on what Oresme had to say about the possibility of three-dimensional extension without a body was intertwined with the effect of theological doctrines or condemnations particularly because of the effect of the Condemnation of 1277 to require support of the proposition that God can do anything that is not a logical contradiction.

Medieval students, as part of their undergraduate education, repeatedly practiced exercises called "obligations" (*de obligationibus*) involving competition between two speakers. First a proposition was posed (the *positio* or *positum*), which the respondent was obliged to accept as given for the exercise to begin. Then other propositions were posed, which the respondent had to accept or reject in light of the *positum*, always trying to avoid self-contradiction. The *positum* itself could be false in fact or even naturally impossible. What mattered was that correct or valid inferences be drawn from the *positum* together with any later propositions that had been accepted. This led to careful consideration not only of what was possible but of what might be compossible or simultaneously possible.[107] Given consideration of God's absolute power, as well as of God's ordained power, careful distinctions had to be made between what was naturally possible versus what might be logically supernaturally possible. In the passages from Oresme discussed earlier, his reasoning about what might follow if God created multiple worlds draws upon such

---

107 There were alternative sets of rules for disputations *De obligationibus*. In one set of rules, each new proposition put forth had to be compared only to the original *positum*, and not also to the replies that had been given to previous propositions. See Paul Vincent Spade and Mikko Yrjönsuuri, "Medieval Theories of Obligationes," *Stanford Encyclopedia of Philosophy*, ed. Edward N. Zalta, Winter 2017, http://plato.stanford.edu/cgi-bin/encyclopedia/archinfo.cgi?entry =obligationes.

modal logic. Many centuries earlier, as mentioned, John Philoponus
had also proposed drawing inferences from false or even impossible
premises.

Such reasoning can be found in many places in Oresme's work. For
example, with regard to the possible rotation of the earth, in his commentary on book 2 of *Le livre du ciel et du monde*, Oresme describes
the motion of the heavens and says:

> So, it does not follow that because the heavens move in a circle the
> earth or some other body must remain motionless at their center,
> for, supposing that this is so and that the consequent is true, still
> the consequence is not valid because circular motion as such does
> not require that any body rest motionless in the middle of a body so
> moved. It is not absolutely impossible nor does it imply a contradic-
> tion, rather it is possible, to imagine that the earth moves with the
> heavens in their daily motion, just as fire in its sphere and a great part
> of the air participates in this daily motion, according to Aristotle in
> the first book of *Meteors*. Although nature could not move the earth
> thus, it is however possible in the second meaning of *possible* and
> *impossible* in Chapter Thirty of Book I.[108]

5. CONCLUDING REMARKS

This paper on the concept of space in the later Middle Ages might
have been thought to be addressed to an unpromising subject, given
that "space" was not a theoretical term in Aristotelian natural philosophy. I have shown that when the term "space" appears in the works
of Oresme (or other late medieval authors) it rarely means something
similar to Newton's absolute three-dimensional space, and, unless one
considers imaginary space, most frequently it means distance or even

---

108 Oresme, *Le livre du ciel*, 367. He refers to 211–213.

an extent of time. It is not that medieval Aristotelians could not conceive of three-dimensional space; they knew that the ancient Greek atomists had thought the universe was composed of atoms and empty space. But they tended to hold that space, as usually defined, is a self-contradictory concept.

Once it became customary to consider what God might do in his absolute power, most commentators accepted that, even if there were no naturally existing empty spaces, it is possible that God could cause a vacuum or empty space to exist, for instance, by annihilating everything inside of the orb of the moon. But what then? Philoponus had explained in the sixth century that one could posit that something impossible is true as a way to clarify the understanding of reality.[109] Philoponus himself had followed this program to revise or overthrow significant parts of Aristotle's science.[110] For fourteenth-century Aristotelians, physics and cosmology (the doctrines contained in Aristotle's *Physics* and *On the Heavens*) were potentially demonstrative sciences based on principles and demonstrating conclusions. One cannot expect simply to insert an exception into the demonstrative science of physics and then proceed. By the fourteenth century, Aristotelianism was supposed to hold that the world contains substances qualified by accidents depending for their existence on the substances. If a vacuum or empty space was supposed to have a definite measurable extension, this would mean that present in the vacuum was an accident not inhering in any substance. Already, theologians had concluded that in the transubstantiated Eucharist there were accidents not inhering in a substance. Thomas Aquinas and those following him had said that in the transubstantiated Eucharist the quantitative form (i.e., the extension) had been given by God the ability to serve in place of the substance of bread as the basis for inherence of the other

109 Philoponus, *Corollaries on Place*, 36–37. See quotation above at note 33.
110 Richard Sorabji, ed., *Philoponus and the Rejection of Aristotelian Science* (Ithaca, NY: Cornell University Press, 1987).

qualities. On the other hand, Ockham and those following his point of view concluded that there actually are no quantitative forms, so that the qualities of the Eucharist are simply there without inhering in any substance.[111]

Thus, for the fourteenth-century *moderni*, once one has accepted that God could annihilate everything inside the sphere of the moon, before drawing inferences about what would be the case, one would have to admit additional suppositions or principles perhaps from other scientific disciplines as Buridan indicated when he said that it would be necessary, so to speak, for the intellect to borrow (*Ideo quasi mendicare oportet intellectum humanum*).

Place and space were not independent concepts that could be added or subtracted from the other principles of Aristotelian science without disturbing many other concepts, whether defined as terms or as existing entities (*quid nominis* or *quid rei*). What one might think about the concept of empty space was dependent on what was held with regard to prime matter, mathematics, quantity, motion, God, angels, and so forth and so on. This is why one cannot understand the thought of any late medieval scholar on the concept of space without a wide examination of the whole context within which he was reasoning, thinking, or imagining. If, for instance, it is a principle of Aristotelian natural science that all and only corporeal substances have three dimensions, where does that leave an Aristotelian who is asked to reason about the place of an incorporeal substance such as God or an angel in a vacuum or empty space?

Rather than trying to solve such metaphysical problems, the fourteenth-century *moderni* chose to develop a mathematico-physical science of the measurement of motion both with respect to cause

---

111 Edith Sylla, "Autonomous and Handmaiden Science: St. Thomas Aquinas and William of Ockham on the Physics of the Eucharist," in *The Cultural Context of Medieval Learning*, ed. John Emery Murdoch and Edith Dudley Sylla, Boston Studies in the Philosophy of Science, vol. 26 (Dordrecht: Reidel, 1975), 349–96.

(*tanquam penes causam*) and with respect to effect (*tanquam penes effectum*) and covering alteration and augmentation and diminution as well as local motion. As part of this science, they developed new quantitative concepts such as latitudes and degrees of quality, velocity, acceleration, proportion, and so forth and built demonstrative subdisciplines on the basis of these concepts, which they imaginatively and creatively developed. Then they demonstrated sets of conclusions, such as the conclusion that a uniformly accelerated motion will cover as much space in a given time as a uniform motion at its middle degree, which could then be compared to observations to see if they fit.

Believing that mathematics, even concrete mathematics, such as mathematical astronomy, mechanics, dynamics, or kinematics, exists primarily in the minds of mathematicians and not as quantitative forms in external reality, the nominalistic mathematicians could construct mathematical definitions and suppositions and could then demonstrate consequences on the basis of these suppositions. I think that the nominalistic and voluntaristic approach to mathematizing nature was a valid alternative to the Platonic approach, associated by Koyré with Galileo.[112] To repeat: In the nominalistic approach, one sets out principles, often arising from reflection on observation, that are at least physically possible and then derives consequences mathematically. Later on, one may consider whether the entire resulting structure matches physical reality. Typically, it is not things but motions that are of concern. And attention is paid to problems of the structure of the continuum if the places or forms gained or lost in motion are supposed to be continuous (or not).

Although we might think that once pieces of scientific disciplines were developed, they should have been compared to observation

---

112 Alexandre Koyré, "Le vide et l'espace infini au XIVᵉ siècle," *Archives d'histoire doctrinale et littéraire du money âge* 17 (1949): 45–91; Koyré, *From the Closed World.* See also Sepkoski, *Nominalism and Constructivism*; Antoni Malet, "Isaac Barrow on the Mathematization of Nature: Theological Voluntarism and the Rise of Geometrical Optics," *Journal of the History of Ideas* 58 (1997): 265–87.

to see if they fit or not, this is not what we find in the texts, which are most often connected to university teaching. Then the testing of the doctrines or analytical techniques is done in the many genres of disputations engaged in at universities. Abstractly one might suppose that when the analytical techniques were tested against each other one might discover which ones were superior and might drop the inferior ones, but since the disputations took place year after year with different classes of students, there was not really a venue in which competition could lead to theoretical winners and losers. As seen in Edward Grant's *Planets, Stars, and Orbs*, similar activity was still going on through the seventeenth century.

In the kinematics and dynamics developed by Oresme, the Oxford *Calculatores*, and others following them, structures of theorems were developed into small subdisciplines which might sometimes become parts of larger works. Meanwhile, the university students who studied works on proportions and disputed sophisms using mathematical techniques (or analytical languages), such as those using measures of motions or first and last instants, developed habits of critical and mathematical thinking that might continue to be of use in relation to many and varied subject matters.[113]

On this route to the development of mathematico-physical science, space is a concept that derives its meaning from its position within a larger disciplinary structure. Rather than attempting to show empirically or by experiment that space exists, one develops a mathematical description of motion in which space—whether one-, two-, or three-dimensional—has a mathematical role. When a whole system is developed, then the concept of space to be found in that comprehensive

---

113 In the Renaissance, however, the mathematics of ratios was reinterpreted so that the dynamics derived from "Bradwardine's rule" lost their mathematical foundation. See Edith Sylla, "The Origin and Fate of Thomas Bradwardine's *De proportionibus velocitatum in motibus* in Relation to the History of Mathematics," in *Mechanics and Natural Philosophy before the Scientific Revolution*, ed. W. R. Laird and S. Roux, Boston Studies in the Philosophy of Science (Dordrecht: Springer Verlag, 2008), 67–119.

system might be accepted at the same time to refer to something real. Rather than thinking that mathematics is absolutely certain and necessary and rather than trying to discover physical sciences that are equally certain and necessary, the fourteenth-century *moderni* treated mathematics and physical science as equally hypothetical, often well-confirmed and in accordance with experience, but not absolutely known to be true.[114]

Where fourteenth-century Aristotelians were most original within the general range of concepts of space in the sense of dimension was perhaps in conceiving of dimensions other than length, breadth, and width. Then intensity or latitude of heat could be a dimension, as could the intensity of motion or the latitude of velocity be a dimension. Time could be a dimension. There could even be a latitude of proportion within which proportions increased and decreased (which would, in a sense, be a logarithmic scale in our terms). And for all these dimensions one could inquire whether they were continuous and homogeneous or contained discontinuous parts.

---

114 One might say that they took geometry to be empirical, an attitude that was taken up again in the nineteenth century as people began to develop non-Euclidean geometries.

Reflection

SPACE, VISION, AND FAITH

Linear Perspective in Renaissance Art and Architecture

Mari Yoko Hara

> The eye is the window of the human body, through which the soul contemplates and
> enjoys the beauty in the world. For this, the soul is content in its human prison and
> without sight this human prison is its torment.
>
> LEONARDO DA VINCI, *Treatise on Painting*

Was pictorial perspective, a conventional technique in applied
geometry, of practical artistic value?[1] Or was it an idea that
conveyed a worldview and a modern subjectivity—a "revolution
in the history of seeing?"[2] The art historian Erwin Panofsky
advanced both interpretations in his influential 1924 publication,
Perspective as Symbolic Form. To Panofsky, spatial construction in
the pictorial field was ambiguously "as much a consolidation and
systematization of the world as an extension of the domain of the

---

1 The epigraph is from Leonardo da Vinci, *Trattato della Pittura,* capitolo 28, Biblioteca Apostolica
Vaticana, MS.Urb.Lat.1270,http://www.treatiseonpainting.org/cocoon/leonardo/chap_one/vu/
CID28/01#chap_top. "Questo [l'occhio] è finestra de l'human corpo per la quale la sua via specula
e fruisce la bellezza del mondo per questo l'anima si contenta della humana carcere et sanza questo
essa humana carcere è suo tormento."

2 Hans Belting, *Florence and Baghdad: Renaissance Art and Arab Science* (Cambridge, MA: Belknap
Press of Harvard University Press, 2011), 13.

Mari Yoko Hara, *Space, Vision, and Faith* In: *Space.* Edited by: Andrew Janiak, Oxford University Press
(2020). © Oxford University Press.
DOI: 10.1093/oso/9780199914104.003.0007

self."[3] Considering the artists' motives in employing perspective provides a different avenue of inquiry into this question.

In developing techniques such as linear, color, and aerial perspective, painters like Piero della Francesca (c. 1415–1492) and Leonardo da Vinci (1452–1519) surely pursued pictorial verisimilitude pragmatically. But their rules, which were elaborated upon, codified, and widely disseminated by others in numerous treatises throughout the fifteenth and sixteenth centuries as practical instruments of the trade, also allowed the artists much more than the mere transcription of the world's appearance. In the words of the celebrated humanist Cristoforo Landino (1424–1498), "perspective bestows reason to art" because it is "part philosophy, part geometry."[4]

In the representational tradition, space and vision (and therefore sensory perception) were bound together intricately, in part because a virtual space in a perspective image was logically constructed as a single viewer's field of vision, and every object within it was portrayed in geometrical relation to an imaginary perceiving eye.[5] Antonio Averlino, called Filarete (c. 1400–1469), explained the system succinctly in his *Treatise on Architecture*: "The centric point (in a perspective painting) is your eye, on which everything should rest just as the crossbowman always takes his aim on a fixed and given point."[6] (See Figure R3.1.) A perspectival representation embeds the beholder's vision within its own structural constitution and acknowledges the physical presence of

3 Erwin Panofsky and Christopher Wood, *Perspective as Symbolic Form* (New York: Zone books, 1991), 67–68.

4 "Arte *idest* la prospectiva: che di questo assegna la ragione. La prospectiva è parte di philosophia et parte di geometria." Cristoforo Landino, *Comento sopra la Comedia di Dante Alighieri poeta fiorentino* (Commentary to *Purgatorio* canto XV) (Florence, 1481).

5 David Summers, *Real Spaces: World Art History and the Rise of Western Modernism* (London: Phaidon, 2003), 431–89, on virtuality. The issue of the ideal viewpoint is much discussed in the literature on perspective.

6 Antonio Averlino [Filarete], *Filarete's Treatise on Architecture*, trans. John Spencer (New Haven, CT: Yale University Press, 1965), 1:304–5.

FIGURE R3.1. Jan (Hans) Vredeman de Vries (1526–1575), *Perspectiva*, Leiden, 1604, copper plate engraving, plate 30.

the observer before it. This one-to-one rapport with the beholder was arguably what made the technique most appealing to artists. While discoveries of binocular and conic vision by Johannes Kepler (1571–1630) and others allowed seventeenth-century practitioners to simulate sight in their works more convincingly, I would argue that the main appeal of perspective remained in its potential for immediate visual dialogue with a viewer. Renaissance artists played with this concept in their works with great imagination and erudition.

The Florentine architect Filippo Brunelleschi (1377–1446) was one of the first to experiment with systematic spatial representation based on Euclidean geometry, ophthalmology, and optics. He is credited with inventing linear perspective in two famous panel paintings that showed the Florentine baptistery and the palazzo della Signoria (the city council building).[7] While neither of these two paintings survives, Brunelleschi's expertise in perspective is still much evident in his extant architectural projects, such as the Basilica of San Lorenzo in Florence (Figure R3.2). Brunelleschi used projective geometry and a rigorous modular system to articulate the interior of this church, taking the diameter of the column as its basic unit of measurement. The proportional relationships between each part and between each part and the whole are marked directly onto the built fabric—by the lines on the floor, the ceiling coffers, and the corbels along the nave arcade, for instance. With these carefully coordinated visual cues the architect reveals his mathematical design principles. The visual effects of this space as a whole are akin to those of a linear perspective painting, where space is shown to recede regularly and all oblique lines converge at a vanishing point (here set above the high altar).[8] Brunelleschi's proportional system articulates two critical notions: first, that space was measurable; second, that its

7 On Brunelleschi's experiments with linear perspective, from a vast literature, see Martin Kemp, "Science, Non-Science, and Nonsense: The Interpretation of Brunelleschi's Perspective," *Art History* 1, no. 2 (1978): 134–61; David Summers, *Vision, Reflection, and Desire in Western Painting* (Chapel Hill: University of North Carolina Press, 2007), 61–67; Antonio Manetti, *The Life of Brunelleschi* (College Park: Pennsylvania State University Press, 1970); Leon Battista Alberti, *Leon Battista Alberti: On Painting. A New Translation and Critical Edition* (Cambridge, UK: Cambridge University Press, 2011).

8 Rudolf Wittkower, "Brunelleschi and 'Proportion in Perspective,'" *Journal of the Warburg and Courtauld Institutes* 16, nos. 3–4 (1953): 275–91.

FIGURE R3.2.   Filippo Brunelleschi (1377–1446), Basilica of San Lorenzo, Florence
1419–59.

measurability was relational to the viewing subject's eye.[9] With his
linear perspective construction, Brunelleschi blurs the boundaries
between mental space, the space of everyday experience, and the
spiritual realm, representing the harmony of the cosmos as well as
our place within it.

The space that Renaissance visual artists meticulously rendered
in perspective often pertained to the spiritual dimension.
Astonishingly, the mathematical rendering of space served, if
anything, devotional art richly rather than impair its efficacy. In his
graceful San Giobbe altarpiece, for example, the Venetian painter
Giovanni Bellini (c. 1430–1516) enlisted pictorial perspective

9 Manetti, *Life of Brunelleschi*, 42. Manetti saw Brunelleschi's invention as a science that sets down
   "properly and rationally the reductions and enlargements of near and distant objects *as perceived
   by the eye*" (emphasis mine).

fully in the service of devotional practice (Figure R3.3). Heavenly figures—the Madonna and child, saints, and angels—occupy a fictive throne room, depicted to scale as an extension of the architectural chapel space where the beholder would have actually encountered the work. The perspective in the altarpiece helps the painter create a visionary experience for his audience, directing the beholder's devotional gaze toward a celestial apparition, and to a realm that lies beyond what can be seen corporeally in nature.[10] By suggesting direct access to the divine realm, the pictorial representation alters the nature of the real space the viewer occupies as well, transporting him or her to a supernatural place.

In Leonardo Parasole's (1570–1630) woodblock print after Antonio Tempesta (1555–1630) of *Christ Restoring Blind Bartimaeus to Sight* from 1590 (Figure R3.4), two narrative moments are present within a single representation, breaking the normative relationship between spatiality and temporality. Linear perspective is employed to symbolically represent the sense of sight that Bartimaeus miraculously regained.[11] The scene establishes a literal analogy: the spatial rendering technique signifies effective vision. But if vision is synonymous with an orderly perspectival vista here, it is hardly a neutral instrument for the passive processing of sensory data. Rather, it is an exalted form of spiritual seeing, a divine gift that leads mankind to true knowledge and wisdom. It reveals not only the appearance of the universe but also its ordering principles, and, as the open-armed gesture of the awe-struck protagonist suggests, the results of this revelation are

---

10 Paul Barolsky, "Naturalism and the Visionary Art of the Early Renaissance," *Gazette des Beaux-Arts* 129 (1997): 57–64.

11 The blind man's name is given only by Mark (10:46–52) as Bartimaeus, which literally means "son of Timaeus." This could be a reference to Plato's famous dialogue by the same title, where vision is discussed as a means to acquire true knowledge.

FIGURE R3.3. Giovanni Bellini (c. 1430–1516), San Giobbe altarpiece, 1487. Galleria dell'Accademia, Venice.

FIGURE R3.4. Leonardo Parasole (c. 1570–1611) after Antonio Tempesta (1555–1630), *Christ Restoring Blind Bartimaeus to Sight*, 1590–91. Woodblock print, 100mm x 123mm. Copyright, The British Museum, 1868.0612.592.

arresting. Perspective is figured here as an important character in its own right within the narrative, one that articulates our relationship to nature as well as to the divine.

CHAPTER FOUR

Geometry and Visual Space from Antiquity to the Early Moderns

Gary Hatfield

....

The phenomena of sight have been subject to geometrical analysis from antiquity. A core principle in this study has been that we see in straight lines. In looking out through an open window, we see those objects for which a straight line can be drawn from eye to object. These straight lines may be imagined between us and every visible point, that is, all the points (or small areas) that we can see. If we turn to face the objects in the room, straight-line vision again applies. We can notice that those parts of the carpeted floor are visible that are not occluded by the table or by books resting on the carpet. An object can block a line of sight that would otherwise reach what is behind it. There are further regularities. If the eyes change their position, for instance, if we stand up, new portions of the carpet come into view and other portions that were visible before are now occluded by the table. Those

Gary Hatfield, *Geometry and Visual Space from Antiquity to the Early Moderns* In: *Space*. Edited by: Andrew Janiak, Oxford University Press (2020). © Oxford University Press.
DOI: 10.1093/oso/9780199914104.003.0008

portions of the carpet that can be seen lie on imaginary straight (or rectilinear) lines running from face to carpet.[1]

From antiquity, the rectilinearity of vision has been a foundation of optics (considered as the science of vision). The fact of rectilinearity admits of various theoretical explications. Rectilinearity does not of itself reveal its causal basis or the character of any causal interactions between world and eye. Does the eye send out a visual power that touches the objects, as ancient extramission theorists held, or do the objects in the world impress themselves somehow upon the eye, as intromission theorists hold, or do both types of causal process occur? A significant characteristic of medieval theories of vision was the transition, within geometrical optics, from mainly extramission theories to newly dominant intromission theories. We will follow this transition, although it is not our primary focus.

The fundamental insight that vision occurs along straight lines permits the use of geometrical constructions in describing how we see. We can easily understand the occlusion of portions of the carpet by tracking a line from our viewpoint past the edge of the table to the carpet itself. Other aspects of our visual experience can also be modeled by considering the relations between lines of sight. As a friend walks away from us, the angle formed by lines from our viewpoint to her feet and the top of her head gets progressively smaller. Or if our friend is standing next to a young child, so that both are at the same distance, the child takes up a smaller angle.

These simple facts may seem to explain a pervasive aspect of our visual experience: that we perceive things as having different sizes. However, the simple fact that the person walking away takes up a smaller visual angle, or that an adult and a smaller child who stand at the same distance

---

1 Complications arising from that fact that we have two eyes were known from antiquity and are noted as needed; here we might note that, for many purposes, the lines of sight from the two eyes can be treated phenomenologically as having a unified origin at the bridge of the nose. Other subtleties, such as those arising from the diffraction of light at an edge, are not further noted.

take up respectively larger and smaller visual angles, does not explain all aspects of our visual experience of size. Consider this fact. Suppose you are standing on the sidewalk speaking to two neighbors who are of the same height. One is five feet away, the other ten feet. The nearer person subtends a visual angle that is twice that of the more distant neighbor. Yet the nearer person is not experienced as being twice as tall as the farther person. Accordingly, phenomenally experienced sizes do not directly follow visual angles. Or consider the classic moon illusion. Astronomers have long determined that the moon on the horizon and the moon overhead subtend the same visual angle. Yet it has frequently been observed that the moon on the horizon looks larger than the moon overhead. Again, size perception does not simply follow visual angle.

Do these examples entail that geometry cannot be used in describing the perception of size? Indeed not. But they show that the geometry of size perception is more complicated than a direct covariance with visual angle. Moreover, they suggest that size perception does not always track the objective sizes of things. Thus, not only is the sun perceived as a small disk when, in reality, it is many times larger than the earth, but the same heavenly body (sun or moon) may appear a different size on the horizon than when overhead.

This chapter examines the development of a geometrical framework for understanding and explaining spatial aspects of visual perception, which includes the perception of sizes, shapes, and positions of things in the field of view. Within this framework, our narrative thread will be selective, focusing on size perception and bringing in other factors only as needed. This focus allows for a comparative examination of how a single problem was treated geometrically by various theorists, ancient, medieval, and modern.[2]

---

2 Historically minded readers may question the legitimacy of seeking to track "the problem of size perception" across authors some of whom are separated by two millennia. Can there have been common problems and comparable approaches across such a long swath of time? I find no a priori reason why there should not have been. Optics as a science had a continuous textual tradition (later texts referring to, or clearly drawing on, earlier texts—this continuous tradition constituting only a subset of the texts that once existed). Even though optics was placed in differing social and

We have noted that geometrical constructions were applied not only to instances of veridical perception, in which visual experience matches or corresponds with physical sizes, shapes, and positions, but also to cases of illusion or misperception. In the latter cases, the experienced spatial properties do not match the physical objects. These illusory cases might then promote a notion of a spatial experience that does not simply copy the spatial characteristics of objects but includes aspects arising from the subject's manner of perceiving. This in turn might yield the notion that visual experience creates its own *visual space*, whose characteristics can be described and explained using geometrical constructions. This chapter asks whether the notion of a specifically visual space also came to be implicit (or indeed explicit) for veridical perception.

The first section examines the ancient background, focusing on Euclid's and Ptolemy's accounts of a visual pyramid or visual cone formed by visual rays emitted from the eye and on Ptolemy's introduction of additional psychological factors into his explanations. The second section examines the sophisticated intromission theory of the medieval Islamic natural philosopher Ibn al-Haytham. He articulated a coherent body of psychological explanations for visual experiences of spatial properties, which was taken notice of by authors in the Latin West. The subsequent three sections consider the accounts of spatial perception in Kepler, Descartes, and Berkeley.

---

intellectual contexts across this time, theoretical constructions remain comparable. Problems may evolve, but similarities may still obtain between new and old. Further, there is no a priori reason to suggest that, at a gross level of description, phenomenological observations cannot be compared. This is not to assume that phenomenal experience is "the same" in every respect in all sensory and intellectual contexts. The claim for comparability must be sustained by the plausibility of the specific comparative analyses offered.

ANCIENT BACKGROUND

Within ancient science, astronomy and optics pushed the furthest in using geometry to describe natural phenomena. Ancient astronomy recorded the positions of stars according to their place in a presumed celestial sphere, as observed along a line of sight from observer to star. Ancient Greek astronomy adopted the explanatory principle that only uniform circular motions should be used in forming geometrical structures that could explain the observed motions of the sun, moon, stars, and planets. The celestial sphere of stars was thought to rotate once a day about the earth at its center, also yielding a daily rotation of the moon, sun, and planets, with these bodies further changing their positions in relation to the fixed stars in monthly, yearly, or longer periods.

The ancient Greek cosmologist Eratosthenes (c. 235 BCE) sought to determine the size of the Earth using measurements of the lengths of shadows at different latitudes. These efforts took advantage of the rectilinear propagation of light from the sun to the Earth, on the assumption that the sun is at such a great distance that the rays of light reaching the Earth are effectively parallel. Somewhat earlier, Aristarchus had used the same assumption to estimate the ratio between the distance from the Earth to the moon and to the sun. Even earlier, in explaining the location and shape of the rainbow, Aristotle had appealed to the rectilinearity of the lines of sight from observer to water droplets to the sun (or the moon, in rare cases). Although this discussion occurred in his *Meteorology*, in the *Posterior Analytics* he observed that the study of the rainbow is related to optics as the latter is related to geometry—that is, each is "under" the other.[3] By this he meant that some disciplines, including optics, must look to geometry for the principles that govern

---

3 Aristotle, *Meteorology*, trans. E. W. Webster, in *Complete Works of Aristotle*, ed. Jonathan Barnes, 2 vols. (Princeton, NJ: Princeton University Press, 1984), 1:555–625, at 373a22–377a27; Aristotle, *Posterior Analytics*, trans. A. J. Jenkinson, in *Complete Works of Aristotle*, 1:39–166, at 79a10–13. Aristotle's works are cited, as usual, using Bekker numbers.

the geometrical part of their subject matter. As he famously explained in the *Physics*, "While geometry investigates natural lines but not *qua* natural, optics investigates mathematical lines, but *qua* natural, not *qua* mathematical."[4]

From antiquity, the science of optics was unequivocally a science of the principles of vision. As a geometrical science of vision, the ancient Greeks divided it into three compartments: *optics*, or the theory of direct vision (vision in unbroken straight lines relating eye and object); *dioptrics*, or the theory of vision in refracted lines; and *catoptrics*, or the theory of vision in reflected lines.[5] Ancient geometrical optics was *extramissionist*: it posited visual rays emitted from the eye and intercepted by objects in the field of view as the means by which the sense of vision gains contact with and so is able to see those objects. These rays proceed rectilinearly, unless refracted by a change in medium or reflected by a mirror. Nonetheless, ancient optics also examined the rectilinear propagation of light from luminous bodies, such as the sun, the moon, or a candle, not only in the case of cast shadows but also in the concentration of the sun's rays by burning mirrors.[6]

In optics proper, the discussion of extramitted visual rays was related to the phenomenology[7] of visual experience. This can be seen in the

---

4 Aristotle, *Physics*, trans. R. P. Hardie and R. K. Gaye, in *Complete Works of Aristotle*, 1:315–446, at 194b10–11. This passage does not explicitly say that optics is "under" geometry in its treatment of mathematical lines qua natural. Still, Aristotle's statement in the *Posterior Analytics* that optics looks to geometry for the principles governing its geometrical structures is consistent with this quotation from the *Physics*. For a recent discussion of the mathematical sciences in Aristotle, see James Lennox, "'As If We Were Investigating Snubness': Aristotle on the Prospects for a Single Science of Nature," *Oxford Studies in Ancient Philosophy* 35 (2008): 149–86.

5 Hero of Alexander, as quoted in David C. Lindberg, *Theories of Vision from al-Kindi to Kepler* (Chicago: University of Chicago Press, 1976), 14. Another ancient writer, Geminus, omits dioptrics and lists scenography as the third branch of optics, as noted by Abdelhamid I. Sabra, ed. and trans., *The Optics of Ibn al-Haytham: Books I–III, On Direct Vision, Vol. 2: Introduction, Commentary, Glossaries, Concordance, Indices* (London: Warburg Institute, 1989), lvi.

6 Wilbur Knorr, "The Geometry of Burning-Mirrors in Antiquity," *Isis* 74 (1983): 53–73.

7 Here and throughout I used the term "phenomenology" in a broad sense, to mean the description of visual experience. I thus do not intend a specific connection with the phenomenological tradition in philosophy associated with Edmund Husserl and Martin Heidegger. My usage has kinship with the phenomenological tradition of the Gestalt psychologists and their notion of a

first systematic treatise on optics extant, that of Euclid, who lists seven "definitions" or postulates at the start of the work:

1. Let it be assumed that lines drawn directly from the eye pass through a space of great extent;
2. and that the form of the space included within our vision is a cone, with its apex in the eye and its base at the limits of our vision;
3. and that those things upon which the vision falls are seen, and that those things upon which the vision does not fall are not seen;
4. and that those things seen within a larger angle appear larger, and those seen within a smaller angle appear smaller, and those seen within equal angles appear to be of the same size;
5. and that things seen within the higher visual range appear higher, while those within the lower range appear lower;
6. and, similarly, that those seen within the visual range on the right appear on the right, while those within that on the left appear on the left;
7. but that things seen within several angles appear to be more clear.[8]

These postulates suppose that the relation between the eye and things in the field of vision can be adequately described through lines or rays that come from the surface of the eye (or from a point within the eye) and go forth to touch objects. The visual field has a circular character, creating a cone that has its apex at or in the eye and its base on the objects

---

description of "direct experience" or experience as we have it, kept as much as possible apart from theoretical conceptions of what experience ought to be like, on which see Kurt Koffka, *Principles of Gestalt Psychology* (New York: Harcourt, Brace, 1935), 73.

8 Euclid, "The *Optics* of Euclid," trans. Harry Edwin Burton, *Journal of the Optical Society of America* 35 (1945): 357. Work originally written in the fourth c. BCE.

seen.[9] Only those things upon which the rays fall are seen. Perceived size correlates with visual angle. Visual up or down and right or left correlate with rays upward or downward from, and to the right or left of, the center of the visual cone. Things upon which more rays fall are seen more clearly. The many propositions that follow these definitions make clear that Euclid considered the rays to be geometrical lines and to be finite in number, so that as the distance increases, the sizes of the gaps between the rays increase (hence the "angles" of postulate 7).

For our purposes we may focus on postulate 4 and its use in subsequent propositions. Euclid held that perceived size directly varies with visual angle. This has several phenomenally plausible consequences. Thus in proposition 36, having shown that for a circle perpendicular to the line of sight all diameters subtend the same visual angle, but that for a circle oblique to the line of sight some diameters fall under a larger angle, some a smaller one, he concludes, "The wheels of the chariots appear sometimes circular, sometimes distorted," by which he means that they sometimes appear ovoid. He further considers parallel lines going into the distance, such as the parallel ruts made by wagon wheels on a straight dirt road.[10] As seen from E (Figure 4.1), the lines along the ruts can be imagined with transversals (such as KT, LZ, and BG). Visual rays (such as EK, ET) intersect the parallel lines at each transversal, forming visual angles (such as KET and LEZ) that diminish as the transversals become more distant. Accordingly, the transversals are seen as smaller and the wagon ruts appear to converge in the distance.

Euclid's results are phenomenally plausible, because things do look small in the distance, and parallel lines, such as railway tracks going away from the perceiver, do phenomenally converge. But, as our next

9 The terms "field of vision" and "visual field" are here used in a phenomenological sense, to specify the range of directions in front of the perceiver within which things are seen, and outside of which things are not seen, assuming a stable gaze. Later authors, including Ptolemy, noted that things seen toward the edge of the visual cone are seen less clearly (see Lindberg, *Theories of Vision*, 17).

10 My example, which is historically plausible.

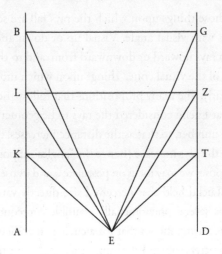

FIGURE 4.1. Lines *AB* and *DG* are parallel. Transversals *KT, LZ*, and *BG* are seen
from *E* under progressively smaller visual angles, and so, in Euclid's account, are seen
with diminishing sizes. Adapted from Euclid, *Optica & Catoptica*, trans. John Pena
(Paris: Wechel, 1557), 8.

theorist,[11] Ptolemy (second century),[12] contended, matters are not that
simple.

Ptolemy was also an extramissionist. Although he differed from
Euclid in holding that the visual pyramid does not have gaps between

11 The source material for ancient optics is severely reduced from what once existed; for discussion,
see A. Mark Smith, "Ptolemy and the Foundations of Ancient Mathematical Optics: A Source
Based Guided Study," *Transactions of the American Philosophical Society* 89 (1999): 11–19. The optical treatises of Euclid and Ptolemy receive the greatest attention from recent interpreters.

12 The extant version of Ptolemy's work is a Latin translation of an unknown Arabic translation
of the unknown Greek original. In the ensuing paragraphs, textual references are inserted into
the body of the text, by book and section. The relevant editions are Claudius Ptolemy, *L'Optique
de Claude Ptolémée: Dans la version latine d'après l'arabe de l'émir Eugène de Sicile*, ed. and
trans. Albert Lejeune (Leiden: Brill, 1989), Latin text with French translation, and *Ptolemy's
Theory of Visual Perception: An English Translation of the Optics*, ed. and trans. A. Mark Smith
(Philadelphia: American Philosophical Society, 1996). The extant work is missing the first book,
covering the properties of light, the extramitted visual flux, and their interaction. Subsequent
books cover the basics of vision itself, vision in plane, convex, and concave mirrors, and vision
involving refraction. The third-hand status of the text and its corrupted state make close readings
perilous.

rays but is continuous, he treated rays as elements within this continuous cone. He held that "luminous compactness" is intrinsically visible
(II.4), a term that refers to a body illuminated by a source of light and
having sufficient density to impede the extramitted visual rays rather
than allowing them to pass through unaffected. The rays are intrinsically sensitive to color, which is a primarily visible attribute; except
luminosity itself, nothing is seen without color (II.5–6). The percep-
tive faculty uses its awareness of color to perceive other attributes, including the length of the ray: "Longitudinal distance is determined by
how far the rays extend outward from the vertex of the cone" (II.26).
Directions (up and down, right and left) are felt in relation to the geometry of the cone. Finally, the perception of size, shape, place, activity,
and rest arises from perceiving illuminated, colored bodies in a direction at a distance and as changing over time. The visual faculty judges
such properties and thereby produces appearances of size, shape, place,
and motion (II.7–8).[13]

Ptolemy's discussions of size and shape perception are difficult to in-
terpret, but several things are sufficiently clear. First, although he held
visual angle to be an important factor in size perception, he did not
equate size perception with visual angle. In particular, he wrote that, in
a case such as Figure 4.2:

> If two magnitudes, *AB* and *GD*, have the same orientation and
> subtend the same angle at *E*, then, since *AB* does not lie the same
> distance as *GD* [from point *E*] but is closer to it, *AB* will never ap-
> pear larger than *GD*, as seems appropriate from its proximity [to

---

13 Sometimes it seems as if Ptolemy invokes judgment in a way that responds to a given appearance
and does not alter the appearance to create a new appearance: of two things that appear to have the
same size, one may be judged to be farther away on other grounds (II.58). In other cases, it seems
as if judgment itself yields an appearance (II.59). For discussion of the relation between judgment
and phenomenality more broadly in the history of visual theory, see Gary Hatfield, "Perception
as Unconscious Inference," in *Perception and the Physical World: Psychological and Philosophical
Issues in Perception*, ed. Dieter Heyer and Rainer Mausfeld (New York: Wiley and Sons, 2002),
115–43.

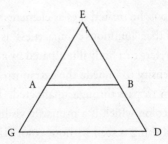

FIGURE 4.2. Perception of size at a distance as analyzed by Ptolemy, c. 160. Adapted from Claudius Ptolemy, *L'Optique de Claude Ptolémée: Dans la version latine d'après l'arabe de l'émir Eugène de Sicile*, ed. and trans. Albert Lejeune (Leiden: Brill, 1989), 40.

E]. Instead, it will either appear smaller (which happens when the distance of one from the other is perceptible), or it will appear equal (which happens when the difference in distance is imperceptible). (II.56)

When objects subtending the same visual angle but lying at different distances are correctly perceived as being at different distances, the one farther away appears larger.[14]

With Figure 4.2 in mind, it is tempting to suppose that Ptolemy has here formulated an early version of the size–distance invariance hypothesis (SDIH), according to which perceived size is a direct function of perceived visual angle and perceived distance.[15] The latter two are combined to yield perceived size according to a precise function, so that perceived size is exact at each perceived distance. When angle and distance are perceived accurately, so is size. In this case, the diagram describes both the objective relations among angle, distance, and size and the perceived relations, which achieve full veridicality.

---

14 Location *E* is the center of rotation of the sphere of the eye, on which, see Albert Lejeune, *Euclide et Ptolémée: Deux stades de l'optique géométrique grecque* (Louvain: Bibliothèque de l'Université, 1948), 54–55.

15 Helen E. Ross and Cornelis Plug, *The Mystery of the Moon Illusion: Exploring Size Perception* (Oxford: Oxford University Press, 2002), 28.

However, although Ptolemy clearly holds that perceived size increases with perceived distance, he does not directly state that it does so with geometrical precision. There are two questions here. First, does he hold perceived size to vary in direct proportion to perceived distance? The diagram suggests that he does, but he is not explicit.[16] Second, does he hold that the appearances that result from combining distance and angle are veridical? The difference in distance between the two lines in Figure 4.2 is said to be "perceptible," which might mean either that the fact that *GD* is farther away than *AB* is perceived qualitatively, or that the exact distance between them is perceived. In fact, for there to be a difference in perceived size, full accuracy is not required. Moreover, in noting the effect of obliquity on perceived size, Ptolemy treats perceptible differences in visual angle, distance, and obliquity as qualitative factors that balance one another in an either/or manner. Thus, in Figure 4.3, a difference in angle (line *AB* falls under a larger angle than *LM*) can be outweighed by the fact that *LM* is farther away than *AB* and also is at a slant, in which case *LM* can be perceived as larger than *AB*. If the difference in distance and obliquity is "outweighed" by the difference in angles, then *LM* will appear smaller than *AB*, and if the differences balance out, the two lines will appear equal. There is no clear statement that the amount of distance and the amount of obliquity enter into a calculation. The factors would appear to "balance" one another so that either (1) the pans of the balance are equal (factors cancel out) or (2) one set of factors makes the pan go down and so wins out.[17]

---

16 Another ancient author, Cleomedes, was explicit that the relations between real and apparent distance and real and apparent size are the same (Ross and Plug, *The Mystery*, 29).

17 There are cases in which Ptolemy's geometrical explanations do seem to indicate a precise perceptual outcome. In examining cases of reflection in the mirror, Ptolemy's diagrams and discussions at least suggest that objects seen in the mirror are seen at a distance that equals the length of the ray. In this discussion, he says that objects in the mirror are seen at the same distance as they would be seen in direct vision (which does not explicitly affirm that the distance is perceived veridically in direct or mirror vision, because direct vision cannot be assumed always to be accurate). But he also says that in both direct and mirror vision, "the farther removed they [the objects] are, the farther away they appear to be from the eye according to the amount by which the visual rays are

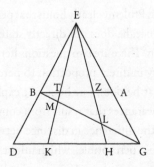

FIGURE 4.3. The effect of visual angle, orientation, and distance on size perception. If the orientation and distance of *BG* are accurately perceived, it appears larger than *AB*. By contrast, if *LM* lies relatively near to *AB*, as in the diagram, it will appear smaller than *AB* even though it is perceived as slanted and as farther away. But if *LM* lies sufficiently beyond *AB* and its distance and orientation are accurately perceived, it appears larger than *AB*. Adapted from Claudius Ptolemy, *L'Optique de Claude Ptolémée: Dans la version latine d'après l'arabe de l'émir Eugène de Sicile*, ed. and trans. Albert Lejeune (Leiden: Brill, 1989), 44.

This qualitative treatment of differences in distance is also found in Ptolemy's treatment of the use of color in painting, which provides the basis for his account of the moon illusion. Ptolemy notes that "mural-painters use weak and tenuous colors to render things that they want to represent as distant" (II.124). As he explains (II.126), for objects that are perceived as having the same visual angle and for which no difference in distance is perceptible by the length of visual ray, bright objects appear closer and hence smaller (as *AB* in Figure 4.2), and darker objects appear farther way and larger (as *GD* in Figure 4.2)—on the assumption that as an object becomes more distant, it affects sight more weakly and hence appears dimmer. These considerations can explain why the moon (or sun) appears smaller when above and larger on the

lengthened" (III.76). If he means absolutely by the amount that the rays are lengthened, then distance is perceived veridically. We know, however, from his other discussions that he doesn't hold that distance is always perceived veridically, so that differences in distance might be perceived to be correctly ordered without being metrically accurate.

horizon: they appear brighter when overhead but dimmer on the horizon (II.120, III.59).[18]

Ptolemy noted other tendencies toward inaccuracy in perception, which he did not evaluate with metric precision. Thus his general statement about shape perception is that "the visual faculty perceives shapes by means of the shapes of the bases upon which the visual rays fall" (II.64). As it turns out, this holds only for the shapes of surfaces that are perpendicular to the axis of vision. Objects that are oblique to the line of sight appear with a distortion: "Squares and circles will appear oblong, because, among equal sides and diameters, those at right angles to the axial ray of the eye subtend a greater angle than those inclined [to that ray]" (II.72). However, if the length of the visual rays were accurately perceived in such cases, one could expect shape to be accurately perceived (the circle perceived as a circle at a slant and the slanted length perceived accurately, as might happen if LM in Figure 4.3 were perceived with metric accuracy). Accordingly, the perception of the circle as oblong must arise from a misperception of the length of its diameters (a misperception of size due to obliquity). Ptolemy doesn't take up the other case from Euclid, of parallels receding into the distance. His remarks on circles and squares, while having some phenomenological plausibility, do not fully articulate and resolve questions about accuracy of perception of the length of the rays or specify geometrical structures that would fully account for the phenomena.

---

18 He may be relying on experience in asserting that the sun and moon appear dimmer on the horizon than overhead. Interpretation of Ptolemy on the moon illusion is vexed; see Abdelhamid I. Sabra, "Psychology versus Mathematics: Ptolemy and Alhazen on the Moon Illusion," in *Mathematics and its Application to Science and Natural Philosophy in the Middle Ages*, ed. Edward Grant and John Murdoch (Cambridge, UK: Cambridge University Press, 1987), 217–47; Ross and Plug, *The Mystery*, 153–54.

Ibn al-Haytham and the Geometry of Sight

Ibn al-Haytham is known in the history of theories of vision as the first author to develop a geometrically convincing *intromission theory*. The ancient atomists proposed an intromission theory in which thin skins of atoms, called *eidola*, are transmitted into the eye. Aristotle spoke of a change in the medium that is transmitted into the eye. Neither of these theories proposed a geometry of sight. Extramission theories were more easily aligned with a rectilinear geometry of visual rays, as we have seen in Euclid and Ptolemy.[19] The reasons for this should become clear as we examine the challenges that Ibn al-Haytham met.

Ibn al-Haytham's contributions to a new intromission theory are many. Two points that he accepted about light are especially important: (1) that light is the direct agent of vision (as opposed to something that merely renders the medium transparent); and (2) that, when light from a source (such as the sun or a candle) falls on an opaque body with a matte surface (so, not a mirror), light is scattered in all directions from each point (small area) on which it lands (I.3.29–98).[20] Accordingly, for an object in the field of vision, light is scattered from each point of the object to all points on the surface of the eye. The various points on the surface of the eye therefore receive light rays from all directions in the visual field. The intromission theorist needs to find a means by which, from this confusion of light rays, the points on the object can be seen each as lying in only one direction, so that, normally, the perceived visual directions align with the physical directions to points on the object.

Ibn al-Haytham met this problem by working backward from the visual pyramid (or visual cone) as phenomenally given. He hypothesizes

---

19 Indeed, Aristotle's discussion of the geometry of the rainbow seems extramissionist (Lindberg, *Theories of Vision*, 217, n39; see ch. 1 for an overview of ancient theories of vision).

20 Ibn al-Haytham, *The Optics of Ibn al-Haytham: Books I–III, On Direct Vision, Vol. 1: Translation*, ed. and trans. Abdelhamid I. Sabra (London: Warburg Institute, 1989), cited by book, chapter, and section. Work originally written c. 1030.

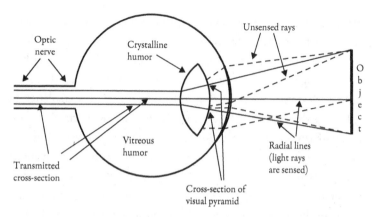

FIGURE 4.4. The geometry of sight according to Ibn al-Haytham. Only light rays that meet the cornea and crystalline humor at right angles are sensed. These light rays follow the geometrically constructed *radial lines*, or *lines of the ray*, of a visual pyramid with its apex at the center of the eye. The light rays are then refracted at the rear of the crystalline humor and convey a cross-section of the visual pyramid into the optic nerve. The rays that touch each end of the object form a visual angle which, together with perceived distance, enters into size perception. Source: author's diagram.

that the eye receives only those rays of light that follow the rectilinear paths of imaginary mathematical rays drawn from the center of the eye to each point on the surface of the object. This imaginary construction exhibits the same geometrical structure as the visual pyramid—albeit with the direction of causation reversed (object to eye vs. eye to object). He posits that the front surfaces of the eye (the cornea) and of the crystalline humor (our "lens") are circular arcs with a common center, and that only those incoming light rays that are perpendicular to the surface of the cornea are received and sensed (Figure 4.4). These incoming light rays fall exactly along the imagined and constructed outgoing lines, which he calls "lines of the ray" or "radial lines" (I.3.62).[21]

---

21 In Ibn al-Haytham's theory, incoming light rays do not actually converge into a single point at the center of the eye. Rather, when leaving the crystalline humor (the rear surface of which they do not intersect perpendicularly), they are refracted so as to enter the tubular optic nerve. The rays preserve the arrangement they had upon entering the eye and so maintain their correspondence with

Having reconstituted the visual pyramid on an intromissive basis, Ibn al-Haytham faced yet other challenges not faced by Ptolemy. Distance is no longer given through an ability to feel the length of the outgoing visual rays, because such rays are now regarded as mere mathematical constructions. Ibn al-Haytham met this challenge by explaining that individuals learn to perceive distance, starting especially with distance along the ground plane running outward from the place they are standing. In interacting with objects by moving about, they come to experience this distance in any of various units, including arm lengths, paces, and arrow flights (II.3.149–55). He develops this part of his theory in great detail, but we must move on to consider how he uses perceived distance in his account of size perception (including aspects of shape perception).

Like Ptolemy, Ibn al-Haytham held that light and color are perceived by "pure sensation" (II.3.25). All other properties, including distance, size, and shape, are perceived by "recognition" or by "judgment and inference" (II.3.25). The judgment and inference in size perception requires perception of the angles of the radial lines. The directions of incoming light rays are (it seems) directly "sensed" by the sentient power (II.3.96), and the "faculty of judgment" then discerns that a corresponding radial line can be extended into the visual field to intersect the surfaces from which the light has come. These directions give the faculty of judgment the visual angles that enclose (touch the outline edges of) an object in the field of view (Figure 4.4).

Ibn al-Haytham explicitly disagrees with those previous mathematicians (which he leaves unnamed) who held that visual angle is sufficient for size perception, agreeing with those who contend that the distance and the orientation of objects must be taken into account in perceiving their sizes (II.3.135–36). Starting from phenomenology, he urges that objects that increase their distance from us by a moderate

directions in the visual field (Lindberg, *Theories of Vision*, 86; Sabra, *Introduction, Commentary*, 76–77).

amount continue to be perceived as being of the same size despite decreasing in visual angle (II.3.136), a phenomenon now known as size constancy. Similarly, if the differing distances to the edges of a square or circle that is oblique to the line of sight are accurately perceived, then those figures are not perceived as oblong or distorted, but the true sizes of the sides of the square or the diameters of the circle are perceived. Ibn al-Haytham maintains that size perception is fully accurate for moderate distances (II.3.135–48).

In contrast with Ptolemy, there is no doubt that Ibn al-Haytham enunciated a version of the SDIH. He describes in some detail a process of learning by which the "faculty of judgement" comes to appreciate the relations among visual angle, distance, and size. Visual angle (proportional to an arc where the visual cone intersects the eye) varies as a single object of constant physical size moves closer to or farther from the eye:

It becomes confirmed in the soul and in the faculty of judgement that as the object recedes from the eye, the place occupied by its form in the eye gets smaller along with the angle subtended by the object at the center of the eye. And when that is confirmed, then it is established in the faculty of judgement that the area where the object's form occurs and the angle subtended by the object at the eye's centre are in accordance with the object's distance from the eye. And when that is established in the soul, then the faculty of judgement, when discerning the object's magnitude, will not take into account the angle alone, but will consider both the angle and the distance because it has been established that the angle varies with the distance. The magnitude of objects is therefore perceived only by judgement and inference. (II.3.143)

Elsewhere, Ibn al-Haytham explains that these judgments and inferences become habitual and occur so rapidly that they go unnoticed (II.4.18–36). They yield an *appearance* of the size of the object (as a subsequent quotation will indicate). Ibn al-Haytham here indeed affirms a direct mathematical relationship among perceived visual angle, perceived distance, and perceived size.

The SDIH by itself does not entail that objects are always, or indeed ever, perceived with their true sizes; it merely says how perceived angle, distance, and size interact, without guaranteeing that any of these elements are accurately perceived. But, as has been noted, Ibn al-Haytham believed that objects are perceived with their true sizes as long as the distance is moderate (and the lighting good, and the object not placed at an immoderate angle, etc.). In such cases, perceived size incorporates both visual angle and perceived distance. To illustrate this point about size constancy (our term, not his), he describes an observer who holds his hand in front of his face and notices how much of a distant wall the hand covers, or how much of the sky. The observer is aware that the hand takes up the same visual angle as the portion of the wall, or the sky, that it covers. But the hand is not seen (visually perceived) to be of the same size as the portion of wall or sky:

> It is, therefore, clear from this experiment that sight perceives the size of an object by means of the magnitude of its distance as well as by estimation by means of the angle, and not by estimation by the angle alone. If the perception of size were dependent on angle alone, two unequally distant objects subtending the same angle at the eye's centre would be seen as equal. But sight never perceives such objects as equal, provided that it perceives their distances and makes certain of the magnitudes of these distances. (II.3.148)

Sight perceives the true magnitudes of objects which are at moderate distances (II.3.160); hence, the SDIH and perceptual constancy obtain for moderate distances.

Ibn al-Haytham also uses the SDIH to explain visual errors. At immoderate distances, objects appear smaller than they are. In such cases, he explains, objects look smaller because both their visual angle and their distance are perceived as smaller than they are (II.7.17)—an explanation that accords with the SDIH. He also considers circles or squares seen at an angle oblique to the line of sight. For moderate distance and obliquity, the shapes of the circle and square are perceived accurately. At immoderate distances, a circle or a square is perceived as if it were facing the perceiver frontally, and so is perceived as oblong or distorted: "When looking at an exceedingly distant object which is oblique to the radial lines and not frontally oriented, sight will perceive the object as if it were in the frontal position and not sense its obliquity. It is for this reason that sight perceives the square or circular surface of a body from an exceedingly great distance to be oblong when these bodies are oblique to the radial lines" (II.7.4). This result is again predicted by the geometry of the visual cone. If the distances along the edge of the square or circle were perceived accurately, one would perceive a square or circle at a slant as a square or circle. But such objects subtend unequal visual angles on their two principal axes. The visual angle is greatest at the axis of rotation and is equal to the angle subtended if the object were frontal. The angle is smallest on the other principal axis, which is perpendicular to the axis of rotation. At excessive distances, the different distances to positions along the rotated edge are not perceived, and so the shape is perceived as frontal and oblong (that is, as an elongated rectangle or an oval). At moderate distances, these differences in visual angles also occur, but the distances are accurately perceived and hence so are the shapes.

We can see here a clear difference between Ibn al-Haytham and both Euclid and Ptolemy. They held that, even close at hand, circles and squares oblique to the line of sight are perceived as oblong. This has some phenomenal plausibility, since the circular opening of a coffee cup (or of a clay pot thrown on a wheel), seen from above and to the side, so that its opening is oblique to the line of sight, subtends different visual angles along the two principal axes of the mouth.

Ibn al-Haytham has theoretical resources that might be brought to bear in explaining what Euclid and Ptolemy say (although I am not aware that he actually made this argument). He might suggest that, in seeing the circular opening of the ceramic object at moderate distance and obliquity, one can perceive the opening as circular while also becoming aware that the visual angles differ along differing axes. He certainly holds that "sight" must ascertain the differing visual angles, as part of its accurate perception of the circular opening. As he explains, this amounts to sight becoming aware of the directions to the various points on the rim of the object. The observer might notice that these directions form a larger visual angle along the horizontal axis, while also perceiving the circularity of the opening. In this way, he could affirm shape constancy at moderate distances while also noting the ability of perceivers to access differences in visual angles along various axes for objects oblique to the line of sight.

To my knowledge, Ibn al-Haytham did not address Euclid's point about parallel lines converging in the distance. Nonetheless, his position that size constancy is complete indicates that, for moderate distances, parallel lines would be seen as fully parallel. This is phenomenologically less plausible than the claim that the circular opening in a ceramic object is perceived as a circle at a slant. Standing on a normal sidewalk, or looking down railway tracks (or wheel ruts), the lines may strike one as phenomenally converging even at moderate distances. Let us keep this problem in mind as we consider early modern theorists, starting with Kepler.[22]

KEPLER REINTERPRETS THE VISUAL PYRAMID

Kepler is credited with working out the optical system of the eye as a set of refractive surfaces (in the cornea and the lens) that project a

---

22 Ibn al-Haytham's optics was much discussed in the Latin West, especially in the writings of Roger Bacon, John Pecham, and Witelo. Space does not permit examining size perception in these authors. For an introduction to their works on vision, see Lindberg, *Theories of Vision*, ch. 6; A. Mark Smith, *From Sight to Light: The Passage from Ancient to Modern Optics* (Chicago: University of Chicago Press, 2015), ch. 6.

true optical image of objects in the field of view onto the retina. Taken one way, his work turned the theory of vision on its head. For Ibn al-Haytham and his Latin followers, the light rays that enter the cornea and lens along the normal line were refracted only at the rear of the lens so as to enter the transparent fluid of the hollow optic nerve while preserving the two-dimensional ordering in which they were received. This establishes a one-to-one correspondence between the points on objects in the field of view and the transmitted "forms" of light and color that enter the optic nerve and affect the sentient power.[23] By contrast, for Kepler the cornea and lens project a true optical image onto the back of the eye (see Figure 4.5). The image is upside down and reversed, relative to the order of things in the field of vision. Kepler accepted, as had Ibn al-Haytham, that from each point on a matte object in the field of view light rays bathe the front surface of the cornea. He treated the rays from each point as forming a pencil of light in relation to the cornea and lens (as in Figure 4.5). In a well-disposed eye, the cornea and lens refract these rays and focus them into a point (or small area) on the retina, and the various points collectively form an image. At the least, this called for a major recasting of the functional anatomy of the eye and its neural processes, topics that Kepler touched upon and elaborated to some extent in his *Paralipomena to Witelo*.[24]

The fact that Kepler developed a mathematical theory of physically projected images is emphasized by those interested in the origins of post-Newtonian physical optics, that is, in optics as the theory of

---

23 There were other accounts of how the forms received in the crystalline (or the *aranea*, considered to be a tunic across the rear of the crystalline) are transmitted, including that the retina receives the stimulation at the edge of the crystalline and transmits it by a nonoptical neurophysiological process. This view is found in Galen, Hunain ibn Ishaq, Averroes (ibn Rushd), and numerous Renaissance anatomists (Lindberg, *Theories of Vision*, 40–41, 53–56, 170–75).

24 References in the text are to Johannes Kepler, *Optics: Paralipomena to Witelo and Optical Part of Astronomy*, ed. and trans. William H. Donahue (Santa Fe, NM: Green Lion Press, 2000), cited by chapter and section or other part, giving a page number as needed. The translation has been emended on occasion. A modern Latin edition is *Ad Vitellionem Paralipomena, quibus Astronomiae Pars Optica Traditur*, in *Gesammelte Werke*, vol. 2 (Munich: Beck, 1939). Work originally published in 1604.

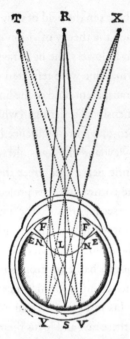

FIGURE 4.5. The eye as a lens and screen system, as theorized by Kepler and Descartes. Pencils of light scatter from *T, R,* and *X* and are focused back into a point at *V, S,* and *Y.* Light scatters in all directions from *T* and the other points, but only those light rays that are refocused into points on the retina are represented in the diagram. It is customary to use diagrams from Descartes's works to illustrate Kepler's discovery (as is done here), since Kepler himself did not provide a suitable image. Produced by Gerard van Gutschoven for the 1664 edition of *L'Homme.* Source: René Descartes, *L'Homme de René Descartes,* ed. Claude Clerselier, 2nd edition (Paris: Theodore Girard, 1677), author's collection.

physical light,[25] but that story is not our focus. Rather, we are interested in how Kepler related his new theory of the retinal image to the extant theories of the geometry of the perceptions of sight, as applied to visual angle, distance, and size.

---

25 For example, Smith, *From Sight to Light.*

Kepler's new account of the retinal image posed a problem for visual theory. On the assumption that the retina is the sensitive surface of the eye (not the crystalline, now reidentified as a lens), and also assuming that the retina and the back of the eye are not translucent, there is needed a new theory of the retinal reception of light and the subsequent neural transmission of the received image into the brain. Kepler was not committed to any one theory of this transmission (ch. 5, sec. 2, 180), leaving that topic to the natural philosophers (as opposed to himself, as a practitioner of the mathematical sciences of optics and astronomy).

Regarding the geometry of sight, Kepler's discussion addresses familiar themes. In the *Paralipomena*, his primary purpose was to provide new foundations for the optical part of astronomy. He is therefore concerned with the refraction of light (as in a telescope) and with the visual image that is experienced as the result of such refraction. Preliminary to this topic, he examines the formation of experienced images from light reflected in a mirror (ch. 3). He contrasts this experienced "image," which exists only in the imagination, with the physical "picture" that is formed on the retina, or indeed on any surface that is behind a suitable lens (ch. 5, definition after prop. 18, 210).[26] The image has four main characteristics: color, position or direction, distance, and quantity (size). As Kepler uses the term, we are to include among "images" only portrayals of those properties at a false location (as happens with a mirror). Nonetheless, he uses the same principles to account for both images and the veridical perception of the properties. Hence, we may attend to what he says in his discussion of mirrors to find his general account of vision. We are particularly interested in direction, distance, and size (quantity).

---

26 Kepler isn't always consistent in his usage of "image" and "picture," but we can accept his distinction for our own purposes, as it distinguishes two fundamentally different concepts within his optics, the purely mental image as experienced and the purely physical picture on the retina.

In his account of direction, he aligns himself with the notions of a visual pyramid (or visual cone) and visual angles within the pyramid. Having noted that the eye is a globe and that the visual field corresponds to a hemisphere, he continues:

> It is therefore fitting that *the ratio of individual objects to the whole hemisphere be estimated by the sense of vision, in the ratio of the entering form to the hemisphere of the eye.* And this is what is commonly called the visual angle, or the vertex of the visual pyramid within the eye, whose base is the object itself. For in any single gaze, the eye becomes the center of the visual hemisphere. . . . Although all the solid angles are in a point, which is the center either of the eye or of a particular one of its coverings, they nonetheless cannot be distinguished in a point: thus, a surface is required, by which the eye may measure the solid angle, as is evident from the geometrical writers. This round shape of the eye is therefore itself sufficient to place among the principles we might know by plain common sense, that *the eye has a sense of the angles set up about it.* (ch. 3, prop. 8, 79)

Kepler in effect adopts the visual pyramid. It is for him, as for Ibn al-Haytham, a geometrical construction that cannot be directly equated with physical light rays, which in Kepler's theory form pencils of light that are refracted by the cornea and lens so as to produce a collection of points on the retina (a "picture"). The visual pyramid has its vertex in the center of the eye, which, Kepler later conjectures, is the center of curvature of the retina (ch. 5, sec. 2, 184). It consists of lines constructed between a point in the visual world, through the center of the eye, to a point on the retina, lines which do not follow the paths of the majority of light rays in a given pencil, since these spread out and then are refracted and refocused.

As regards distance perception, Kepler offered a new means for its accomplishment—a means that was available to pre-Keplerian theorists but (apparently) not developed by them. He explains that

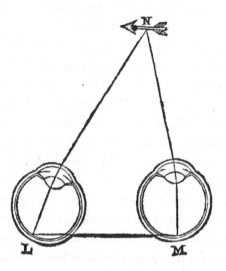

FIGURE 4.6. The triangle of convergence. The converging eyes fixate point *N*. Interocular line segment *LM*, together with the angles of rotation for the eyes in a given fixation, form a specific triangle. Because segments *LN* and *MN* are intended to converge on the focal point of the eyes, the lines should be straight, not broken as in the diagram, and eye *M* should be rotated slightly left. Diagram by van Gutschoven. Source: René Descartes, *L'Homme de René Descartes*, ed. Claude Clerselier, 2nd edition (Paris: Theodore Girard, 1677), author's collection.

the "common sense" becomes acquainted with the distance between the two eyes and then learns to associate distances to the common focal point of the two eyes with particular angles of convergence of the eyes (see Figure 4.6). The same method can be used with one eye, by moving the head from one location to another, mimicking the position of the two eyes.[27] He invoked the geometry of the triangle, which specifies that angles of convergence covary with distance for a given set

27 Kepler also developed a geometrical account of distance with one eye that depends on sensitivity to the angle between the edges of the pupil and the projected image on the retina for a given object. For explanation, see Gary Hatfield, "Natural Geometry in Descartes and Kepler," *Res Philosophica* 92 (2015): 123.

of eyes, and then conjectured that perceivers learn to take account of this covariation (ch. 3, prop. 8; ch. 9, sec. 2).[28]

Finally, in his brief remarks on size perception, Kepler continues the earlier theories in which visual angle and perceived distance come together in the perception of size. He accounts for the "legitimate comprehension of quantity" in the usual way: "It follows upon the comprehension of the angle and of the distance, where the sense of vision, from the sides that come together at the eye and the angle set up between them, makes a judgment about the base of the pyramid, which is the quantity of the object seen" (ch. 3, prop. 15, 83). The "sides" are the lines to the edges of the object, which form the visual angle. If the judgment of the base of the pyramid is accurate, then we have size constancy. Kepler doesn't give us much more on size perception, nor does he examine the perception of oblique circles and squares or discuss the moon illusion.[29]

We may note that although Kepler's theory of the retinal image required a significant change in visual physiology, it did not require any radical change in the geometrical account of size perception, as is indicated by Kepler's own retention of the notion of a visual pyramid. In the seventeenth century, Kepler's new functional anatomy of the eye was swiftly adopted into optical writings and led to further discussions of neural transmission. These also largely continued the geometrical analysis from pre-Keplerian theory.

---

28 François de Aguilón, *Opticorum Libri Sex: Philosophis iuxta ac Mathematicis Utiles* (Antwerp: Plantin, 1613), bk. 3, prop. 4–5, 156–57, although continuing the pre-Keplerian tradition of optics, described triangles of converging optic axes as a means for perceiving distance. If, as August Ziggelaar, *François de Aguilón S.J., 1567–1617: Scientist and Architect* (Rome: Institutum Historicum, 1983), 60–61, contends, Aguilón was not familiar with the *Paralipomena*, then either we have simultaneous discovery or there is a common (but as yet unknown) pre-Keplerian source for the theory that convergence of the optic axes can yield distance perception.

29 Kepler discusses the problem of measuring the objective visual angle of the moon under various conditions (*Paralipomena*, ch. 5, sec. 5, 233; ch. 11, prob. 5), but I haven't found him discussing the moon illusion itself. The problem of determining the objective angle was motivational in his work on pinhole images, leading to his theory of optical "pictures" (Lindberg, *Theories of Vision*, 186–88).

DESCARTES AND THE GEOMETRY OF SIZE PERCEPTION

Descartes provided a comprehensive natural philosophical interpretation of the new physiology of vision, including the physical character of
light and the neural transmission of optical stimulation from the retina
into the brain, topics that he covered in great detail in the *Treatise on
Man* and summarized in the *Dioptrics*.[30] The latter work arose from a
project to theorize lenses for telescopes and to make them, and so it
emphasized refracted light in its title. But it also covered traditional
topics in the theory of visual perception, including accounts of the perception of "light, color, location, distance, size, and shape" (AT 6:130,
O 101) and a brief discussion of mirror vision. Descartes's account of
size and shape perception again continues the themes and principles we
have seen.

Descartes developed a corpuscular theory of light, according to
which light is pressure in an ethereal medium. This pressure acts me-
chanically and follows ray geometry in being scattered from each
point on the surface of an object. Color in light amounts to spin on
the particles of the medium, and surface colors impart one or another spin. The pressure and spin follow ray geometry in that ambient light is focused by the cornea and lens onto the retina, which
consists of fine nerve fibers. These fibers transmit motion from each
eye along the optic nerves into the brain in the point-for-point pattern we have seen before (as a two-dimensional order). The nerve
fibrils influence openings in the brain, also in a point-for-point pattern, causing subtle nervous fluid to flow forth from a gland in the

---

30 References to the *Treatise on Man* are to the Adam and Tannery edition of Descartes's works (AT),
    vol. 11 (with page number), followed by page reference to *Treatise on Man*, ed. and trans. Thomas
    Steele Hall (Cambridge, MA: Harvard University Press, 1972), abbreviated "H." References to
    the *Dioptrics* are to AT, vol. 6 (with page number), followed by page reference to René Descartes,
    Discourse on Method, Optics, Geometry, and Meteorology, trans. Paul J. Olscamp (New York: Bobbs-
    Merrill, 1965), abbreviated "O." Emended translations are marked with an asterisk (*).

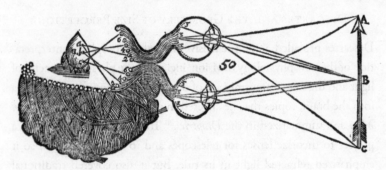

FIGURE 4.7. The visual system as portrayed in Descartes's *Treatise*, showing
pineal physiology and the transmission of the two-dimensional pattern of light
into the brain through a pattern of neural motions. Diagram by van Gutschoven.
Source: René Descartes, *L'Homme de René Descartes*, ed. Claude Clerselier, 2nd edition
(Paris: Theodore Girard, 1677), author's collection.

center of the brain (the pineal gland). This flowing again retains the
point-for-point pattern (see Figure 4.7).[31]

Descartes's accounts of distance, size, and shape perception show
both traditional elements of the visual pyramid (although not so
named by him) as well as innovations. He put forward new ideas particularly about distance perception. The Keplerian anatomy, as Kepler
himself realized, calls for a mechanism in the eye to retain good focus
for near and far vision, a process now known as "accommodation."
Kepler thought that perhaps the eye muscles act to change the shape
of the whole eye (and hence its focal length) so as to achieve accommodation.[32] Descartes mentions this possibility, but appears to favor
a system in which the eye acts to change the shape of the lens (AT

31 Descartes has mechanized the optical anatomy and physiology of the nervous system in a way
   that translates concepts from ancient and medieval optics into a mechanical idiom. An example
   is his reducing the stimulation from the two eyes to a single pattern on the surface of the pineal
   gland, thereby explaining single vision with two eyes. Ibn al-Haytham (II.7.7–10) also posited a
   common form or pattern in the brain to explain single vision. Kepler (*Optics*, 180, ch. 5, sec. 2) as
   well speculates briefly that the conjoining of the optic nerves serves the function of single vision
   (but requires a different physiology of neural transmission than that found in Ibn al-Haytham and
   his follower Witelo).

32 Johannes Kepler, *Dioptrice* (Augsburg: David Franke, 1611; reprint, Cambridge, UK: Heffer,
   1962), prop. 64.

11:155–56, H 56). Kepler did not relate the neural processes that effect this change to distance perception. But Descartes realized that since the brain processes that control accommodation would covary with the distance of objects from the eye, such processes could provide information about distance, allowing the mind to *see* distance (AT 6:137, O 105–6). He also believes that the brain processes controlling the convergence of the eyes covary with distance (AT 11:186–88, H 98–100). In each case, he in effect posits a psychophysiological regularity between the brain processes controlling the muscles that produce accommodation and convergence and the perceptual experience of the distance to the objects of fixation. In addition to these innovative ideas, he invokes traditional means to account for distance perception, such as weak or dulled colors as indicating distance or reduced visual angle for objects of known size.[33]

In the text of the *Dioptrics*, these innovative elements are placed into a framework that is recognizably shaped by the visual pyramid and the SDIH. Descartes begins his account of the perception of spatial properties with location or position, which he describes as "the direction in which each part of the object lies in relation to our body" (AT 6:134, O 104). He compares sensing of direction by the eye with a blind man holding two sticks that cross. (In the *Treatise*, the two sticks touch a single point on an object [AT 11:160, H 62].) The analogy with a blind person is of interest in its own right. But our focus here is on the way it establishes direction as the framework for discussing distance, size, and shape. For, as Descartes proceeds, the directions serve a function similar to the radial lines in Ibn al-Haytham or the visual pyramid in Kepler. The system of directions[34] is in effect the skeleton to which distance is attached to yield the perception of size and shape.

---

33 See Hatfield, "Natural Geometry," for more detail.

34 In the quotation, Descartes specifies the directions in relation to the body, not to the center of the eye. Something similar is hinted at in Ibn al-Haytham (III.2.11–13). Descartes may here be offering a concession to the phenomenology of a single visual world as seen by two eyes, with directions coordinated with the center of the face.

Descartes's account of size perception advances a clear statement of the SDIH and the tendency toward shape constancy. Speaking of objects, Descartes says:

> Their size is estimated according to the awareness, or the opinion, that we have of their distance, compared with the size of the images that they imprint on the back of the eye; and not absolutely by the size of these images, as is obvious enough from this: while the images may be, for example, one hundred times larger when objects are quite close to us than when they are ten times farther away, they do not make us see the objects as one hundred times larger because of this, but as almost equal in size, at least if their distance does not deceive us. (AT 6:140, O 107*)

The size of the image "on the back of the eye" is the retinal extent that Kepler has already treated as equivalent to visual angle (here treated as an area). Descartes denies that perceived size varies with visual angle (see also AT 6:145, O 111). Accordingly, perceived size is a function of visual angle and perceived distance. We "see" the sizes of objects as "almost" the same when they are near and far, which indicates that the combination of angle and distance creates the experience of size and does not merely support a detached judgment about size. This amounts to a claim of nearly perfect size constancy for moderate distances.[35]

Descartes relativizes perceived size to perceived distance, whether the latter is accurate or not, when he remarks that we perceive size accurately if we are not perceptually deceived about distance. In analyzing the moon illusion (or moon and sun illusion), he in effect appeals to the SDIH. We experience the moon and sun as being at most one or two feet in diameter (he claims). The problem is not that

---

35 Descartes's description of *nearly* perfect size constancy suggests that he could accommodate converging parallels (as with wagon ruts) by suggesting that, as things become more distant, distance is slightly underperceived, but he doesn't make the point explicitly.

we cannot phenomenally present them as larger, because we do experience objects larger than one or two feet in diameter. Rather, we are limited in the distance at which we experience them: we experience them as being at most one hundred or two hundred feet away. This distance combines with visual angle to yield the perception of a small disk. The illusion of a larger horizon moon or sun arises because we experience the distance to the horizon as being longer, owing to the many intervening objects, whereas we experience the distance as shorter overhead, where there are no intervening objects (AT 6:144–45, O 111).

Descartes gives an account of shape perception similar to that of Ibn al-Haytham. We perceive shape by perceiving the positions (direction and distance) of the various parts of an object: "Shape is judged by the awareness, or the opinion, that we have of the position of the various parts of the objects, and not by the resemblance of the pictures in the eye; for these pictures usually contain only ovals and diamond shapes, yet they cause us to see circles and squares" (AT 6:140–41, O 107*). The retinal images of circles and squares that are oblique to the line of sight have the shape of ovals and diamonds, in which the diameter of a projected circle is longer on one axis than another. In terms of visual angles, the visual angle from edge to edge is wider along the axis of rotation of the circle, narrower along the diameter perpendicular to that. But we "see" circles and squares. Which is to say that, for moderate distances, we accurately perceive the diameters of the circle as equal and at various distances from our vantage point, as Ibn al-Haytham taught.

Descartes thus continues the geometrical analysis of size and shape perception from the optical tradition, as purveyed by Ibn al-Haytham and his Latin interpreters. He uses the same principles for veridical size perception as for illusory perception. In both cases, visual angle (visual directions) and perceived distance combine to generate an experience of a spatial configuration in the field of vision. He effectively describes a perceptual space of perceived directions, sizes, and shapes, analyzed in accordance with a visual pyramid of phenomenal directions and distances.[36]

BERKELEY'S REJECTION OF A GEOMETRY OF SIGHT

Berkeley framed a theory of vision in which he sought to minimize the appeal to the geometry of sight and to explain the visual perception of distance, objective size, and objective shape through a process of learning, with touch educating vision. In this discussion he makes explicit or implicit use of some findings from geometrical optics while rejecting others, especially as regards the perception of distance by "lines and angles" (§12).[37]

Berkeley's *New Theory of Vision* (*NTV*), published a year before his *Principles of Human Knowledge*,[38] was intended secretly to prepare the way for the immaterialism in the second work. This preparation was to be done in large part by showing that there are no common, geometrically described spatial properties found in the immediate objects of touch and vision. This move was really quite radical, as it rejected the doctrine of "common sensibles," accepted by both Aristotle and Descartes, according to which size, shape, motion, and other spatial properties are sensed by both touch and vision.

Berkeley's claim that visible size and tangible size are of different kinds, sharing no common structure, is counterintuitive. We'll come back to it. More specifically as regards vision, Berkeley posits that originally our visual experiences of size and shape accord with a correlate

36 This conception is affirmed by Jacques Rohault, *System of Natural Philosophy*, trans. Samuel Clarke, 3rd edition, 2 vols. (1671; London: Knapton, 1735), when he describes vision as consisting in the formation of an "immaterial image" (I.32.1) in the mind, which accounts both for our seeing objects as they are (I.32.13) and for illusions (I.32.22–23).

37 References are to section numbers of George Berkeley, *An Essay towards a New Theory of Vision*, 3rd edition (1709; Dublin: Rhames and Papyat, 1732), and (below) *The Theory of Vision Vindicated and Explained* (London: J. Tonson, 1733).

38 George Berkeley, *A Treatise concerning the Principles of Human Knowledge* (Dublin: Rhames and Papyat, 1710).

of the retinal image and not with the objective sizes and shapes of things, as determined by touch. Visual magnitude originally is equated with visual angle, and visual figure with a counterpart of retinal figure. Distance is not originally perceived by sight. Through learning, we come to associate tangible distances, sizes, and shapes with cues found within the original or *immediate* visual experiences. Thus, with the muscular feelings associated with the convergence of the eyes, we associate tangible distances (measured by arm extension or paces). These associated tangible distances become the *mediate* objects of vision, yielding a phenomenal experience of visible objects at a distance. The value for distance, however, is not combined with visible magnitude to yield objective size (as in our previous theorists, from Ptolemy on). Rather, the same visual cues as yield the experience of distance are directly associated with tangible size. A small visual magnitude associated with muscle strain for near convergence yields the perception of a small tangible (objective) size, as the mediate object of vision.

Berkeley wants to deny that the human body, its sense organs, and physical light inhabit a common space, described by geometry (§§149–51). He is eager to reject any necessary connection between tangible distance and visual angle, explicable through the projection of physical light onto the retina. While I do not question this description of Berkeley's motivation, I do find him relying on geometrical arguments. I consider his use of lines and angles in two regards. First, Berkeley writes as if the visible magnitude for a given object covaries with tangible distance. How does he know this? Second, he has a famous argument from the geometry of sight to the conclusion that "distance, of itself and immediately, cannot be seen" (§2) that I wish to analyze.

In the *NTV*, Berkeley remarks that computations with lines and angles can be useful for determining "the apparent magnitude of things" (§78). Apparent magnitude varies with tangible distance to an object of constant tangible size. Here Berkeley uses the lines and angles of optics to describe the tangible path of physical light ("physical" inasmuch as Berkeley treated the tangible world as the world of physics).

By parallel reasoning, the visual figure of a tangible circle oblique to the tangible line of sight would be an oval. In the *Theory of Vision Vindicated and Explained* (*TVV*), Berkeley affirms this conception of how tangible sizes and shapes are correlated with visible sizes and shapes. He imagines the construction of a tangible perspective grid in front of an observer, with lines from the tangible eye to various points in the tangible scene (§§55–57). The places where the lines intersect the plane grid then predict the visible sizes (which track visual angles) and visible shapes.

In this way, Berkeley in effect adopts the geometry of the visual pyramid as applied to lines of sight from eye to scene. He treats a perspective cut on the pyramid as a predictor of the proper objects of sight (original or immediate visual ideas). Note that he denies any causal relation; he does not hold that the tangible magnitudes on the retina *cause* visual sensations exhibiting the various visible properties. Rather, he posits a regular correspondence among the various sensory ideas as established and maintained by "the Author of Nature" (*NTV*, 3rd ed., §147). But how does he know the relation between tangible and visible ideas? According to his own principles (§10), he should claim an immediate phenomenal awareness of visible magnitude and figure. And he does note that things farther away subtend noticeably smaller visual angles (§44). But he doesn't offer a general justification of this sort. Instead, he appeals to the geometry of visual angle or of the visual cone.

The most celebrated passage from the *NTV* is §2: "It is, I think, agreed by all that distance, of itself and immediately, cannot be seen. For distance being a line directed end-wise to the eye, it projects only one point in the fund of the eye, which point remains invariably the same, whether the distance be longer or shorter." Here Berkeley also appeals to a geometrical result, to establish the (alleged) commonplace that distance, being a single line from eye to object, cannot be seen because it projects into a point on the retina (or at the eye).[39] What

---

39 The most likely source for Berkeley's claim is William Molyneux, *Dioptrica Nova*, 2nd edition

line is here equated with distance? Surely not the line taken by light rays as they enter the eye, since those form a pencil that expands and contracts, meaning that some of the rays are bent (refracted). So presumably we have here a line of sight as a geometrical construction in the visual pyramid. That line does not offer information about its own length; rather it depends on a fixed location of the eye and fixed points in the scene for its construction.

However, there is information about distance contained even in the light coming from a single point (small area) in the field of view and projected through refraction as a single point on the retina. For, as noted by Descartes, the eye must adjust itself in order to be in focus for points closer or farther away (within distances of a few feet). Also, as noted by both Kepler and Descartes, the convergence of the two eyes on a single fixation point varies with distance. Berkeley was aware of such explanations and rejected them. His argument characterizes authors such as Kepler and Descartes as holding, in the case of convergence, that the mind calculates the distance by taking account of the rotations of the eyeballs and the distance between them, and then applying an angle-side-angle construction. Berkeley objects that to calculate, one would need to be aware of the rotation of the eyeballs, fixation lines, and interocular distance. But, he claims, manifestly not all perceivers (including children and common people) are aware of these geometrical constructions or are able to perform the needed calculations.

Berkeley's objections are guilty of *ignoratio elenchi*, that is, of refuting an argument not made by his opponents. In the case of accommodation, and plausibly also for convergence, Descartes did not hold that

---

(London: Tooke, 1709). But in the very passage in which Molyneux says "Distance of it self, is not to be perceived; for 'tis a Line (or a Length) presented to our Eye with its End towards us, which must therefore be only a Point, and that is Invisible," he allows that, through convergence, distance can be perceived for objects near at hand: "But as to nigh Objects, to whose Distance the Interval of the Eyes bears a sensible Proportion, their Distance is perceived by the turn of the Eyes, or by the Angle of the Optick Axes" (113). He does not specify a psychology of the operations underlying convergence, but he had available to him both learning and nativist accounts.

the mind calculates. Rather, he posited an innate psychophysiological
mechanism by which the brain states that control accommodation and
convergence through the ocular musculature—brain states that therefore vary with distance as they adjust the muscles—directly cause in the
mind an experience of the appropriate distance by an institution of nature (an innate law of mind-body interaction). It also seems that Kepler
did not explain the perception of distance by convergence as a matter
of calculation but of learning to associate a tangible distance with a
degree of convergence (*Optics*, ch. 9, sec. 2). Even Ibn al-Haytham did
not hold that the mind uses geometrical calculation to become aware
of size, but rather that it learns piecewise the relations between visual
directions and tactually learned distances.

The theories of Ibn al-Haytham, Kepler, and Descartes differ from
that of Berkeley in that the first three conceived of visual and tactual
space as of the same kind and so as comparable to one another (even
in cases of illusion). They therefore could allow tactual learning to directly inform, without translation, the experience of visual distances.
In contrast, Berkeley contended that visual and tactual space are of
completely different kinds. His arguments for the latter point would
need to be convincing if he wanted to dismiss the previous theories
without begging the question.

Be that as it may, it is clear that Berkeley, too, regularly availed
himself of the geometry of the visual pyramid in his theory of vision. Phenomenologically, he would agree with Ibn al-Haytham and
Descartes that oblique squares and circles, at least at near distances,
are experienced as squares and circles (*NTV* §§139–44, *TVV* §59).
For Berkeley, this would happen only in mature perceivers who have
learned to associate tangible sizes and shapes with the—for them now
unnoticed—visible sizes and shapes. He thus describes a phenomenal visual world in which size and shape constancy obtain for near
distances, in which case the SDIH holds as a phenomenological description. He does so in conjunction with applying the visual pyramid,
now allied with a psychology of association. His new psychology gives

independent accounts of distance and size perception and so, as a psychological process, does not accept the direct combination of distance with visual angle according to the SDIH.

THE GEOMETRY OF SPATIAL PERCEPTION

There is a long history of the application of geometrical constructions to spatial vision, including the perception of distance, size, and shape. As a geometrical description of the phenomenology of sight, this application showed development. Thus, whereas Euclid equated visual size with visual angle, Ptolemy and many later authors described perceived size as a function of perceived angle and perceived distance. Berkeley agreed that size constancy obtains, and so he accepted this phenomenological description.

Beyond using geometrical constructions in describing visual experience, Ptolemy, Ibn al-Haytham, Kepler, and Descartes all subscribed to some form of psychological account in which visual angle is combined with perceived distance to yield perceived size. Berkeley rejected this explanation, instead arguing that, although the same cues are used in distance and size perception, they operate independently in the two cases.

Berkeley's argument that touch educates vision was widely accepted in the eighteenth and nineteenth centuries. However, there also arose a nativist theory in opposition to Berkeley, according to which much of spatial vision is due to innate mechanisms that undergo environmental tuning.[40] Beyond the issue of nativism, there is continuing discussion of how best to describe the phenomenology of visual

---

40 This nativism grew especially in the nineteenth century, in the works of Caspar Theobald Tourtual, *Die Sinne des Menschen in den wechselseitigen Beziehungen ihres psychischen und organischen Lebens: Ein Beitrag zur physiologischen Aesthetik* (Münster: Coppenrath, 1827) and Thomas K. Abbot, *Sight and Touch: An Attempt to Disprove the Received (or Berkeleian) Theory of Vision* (London: Longman, Green, 1864). On this controversy in nineteenth-century German physiology and psychology, including the nativism of Ewald Hering as opposed to the empiricism of Hermann von Helmholtz, see Gary Hatfield, *The Natural and the Normative: Theories of Spatial Perception from Kant to Helmholtz* (Cambridge, MA: MIT Press, 1990) and R. Steven Turner,

space.[41] Questions remain open concerning the proper description of the experience of a circle oblique to the line of sight. There is ongoing discussion of how to describe the perception of parallels receding into the distance. The application of geometrical constructions to aspects of phenomenal visual experience continues. And it sustains continuity with a long past of describing visual experience by relying on the phenomenological observation that we see in straight lines. As we saw with Descartes, such geometrical constructions are applied to a visual space of perception, which may or may not accurately present the physical spatial properties of the objects that reflect light to the eyes. The properties and status of this visual space remain topics of research.[42]

In the Eye's Mind: Vision and the Helmholtz–Hering Controversy (Princeton, NJ: Princeton University Press, 1994).

41 For entry into the ongoing discussion, see Mark Wagner, *Geometries of Visual Space* (Mahwah, NJ: Erlbaum, 2006); Gary Hatfield, "Philosophy of Perception and the Phenomenology of Visual Space," *Philosophic Exchange* 42 (2011): 31–66; Gary Hatfield, "Phenomenal and Cognitive Factors in Spatial Perception," in *Visual Experience*, ed. Gary Hatfield and Sarah Allred (Oxford: Oxford University Press, 2012), 35–62; Eric Schwitzgebel, "Do Things Look Flat?," *Philosophy & Phenomenological Research* 72 (2006): 589–99; Walter Hopp, "No Such Look: Problems with the Dual Content Theory," *Phenomenology and Cognitive Science* 12 (2013): 813–33.

42 The members of the workshop on space held at Duke University in 2013 gave initial feedback on the ideas developed herein, for which I thank them. Thanks also to Louise Daoust and Marie Barnett for helpful comments on the penultimate version. This research was supported by NEH grant FA-57881-14.

Reflection

SPACE FOR THOUGHT

Jennifer Groh

How thought is mediated by the activity of neurons in the brain is one of the great mysteries of our time. Over the past sixty years, a succession of new methods has allowed neuroscientists to investigate brain signals with ever-increasing levels of detail. But despite the resulting slew of data, we have much to learn about how biological mechanisms create higher cognitive abilities such as thought and language.

One intriguing theory of brain function suggests that there may be a connection between the brain mechanisms underlying perception and those responsible for cognition. Known variously as grounded or embodied cognition,[1] this theory postulates that thinking involves activating some subset of sensory and motor pathways of the brain connected to the sensory or motor attributes related to your current thoughts.

---

1 For example, L. W. Barsalou, "Grounded Cognition," *Annual Review of Psychology* 59 (2008): 617–45; Rafael Núñez, "On the Science of Embodied Cognition in the 2010s: Research Questions, Appropriate Reductionism, and Testable Explanations," *Journal of the Learning Sciences* 21, no. 2 (2012): 324–36.

Jennifer Groh, *Space for Thought* In: *Space*. Edited by: Andrew Janiak, Oxford University Press (2020). © Oxford University Press.

DOI: 10.1093/oso/9780199914104.003.0009

For example, when you mentally picture sitting on the couch
in your living room drinking a cup of coffee, that thought
might be implemented by partially activating the visual, tactile,
auditory, smell, taste, and motor responses that would occur
if you were actually doing so. Put another way, thought might
involve simulations run via the brain's extensive sensory and
motor infrastructure.

One important implication of this idea is that the way sensory
and motor areas function in their so-called day jobs may impact
how our thought processes unfold. That is, what these brain areas
do in response to sensory events, or how they guide motor actions,
may spill over into how they contribute to thinking, shaping the
nature of these cognitive simulations.

That's where space comes in. The brain deals with space in nearly
every aspect of what it does. When you watch your child playing
in the yard, your visual system monitors the location of your child
relative to the street, particularly as your auditory system warns you
that a car is approaching too fast from around the corner. When
you call out to your child, your brain issues motor commands to
move your tongue and lips to the series of positions needed to
form each phoneme in the speech sounds "Get out of the road!"
Location, whether of the external events or of the relevant parts of
the body, is the overarching theme of what the sensory and motor
areas of the brain must monitor and control in such everyday
scenarios.

Studies of the neural basis of sensory and motor processing have
established two important ways that neurons encode or represent
the spatial aspects of the sensory events or planned movements.[2]

---

2 Jennifer M. Groh, *Making Space: How the Brain Knows Where Things Are* (Cambridge, MA: Harvard University Press, 2014).

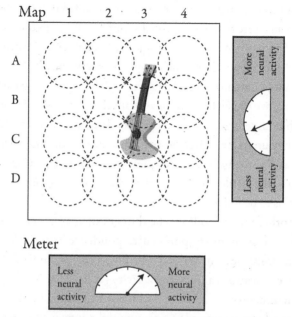

FIGURE R4.1. Brains have two main formats for encoding information: which neurons are active and how active they are. In the visual and tactile systems, individual neurons are sensitive to the locations of stimuli and respond only to stimuli in the right location for that neuron—the receptive field (indicated by the dashed circles). Where a stimulus is located can be inferred from which neurons are activated by that stimulus. This type of code is referred to as a map. The image of the guitar would activate neurons A3, B3, and C3. In other systems, such as the auditory system in the primate brain, the locations of stimuli can be inferred by knowing how active a common population of neurons is. For example, if a guitar is located to the right, "right-preferring" neurons will exhibit a level of activity indicating how far to the right the guitar sound is coming from. Here, level of activity serves as the needle on a dial of "rightness," a type of code known as a meter.

In some instances, information about space is reflected in a kind of neural "map" of location. In such a map, individual neurons are responsive to specific, discrete, and often small regions of space. A visual neuron, for example, might respond only to visual stimuli located within a narrowly circumscribed region, say, an inch or two in diameter.[3] Different neurons respond to different locations, and across an entire population, visual stimuli at all possible locations in space influence the activity of some specific subset of the neurons in the population. Often, such maps are literally map-like: they have a topographical organization in which neighboring neurons are sensitive to neighboring areas of space. Your senses of vision and touch both represent space in this way. The pattern of activity, i.e., which neurons are active, informs other areas of the brain where the visual stimulus (such as the rambunctious child playing in the yard) or the tactile stimulus (such as the mosquito biting your hand) is to be found.

Another type of code can be thought of as a "meter." Instead of involving a point-to-point correspondence between locations and neurons, such meter codes involve a correspondence between locations and neural activity levels. That is, a large swath of neurons might respond for any location, but how vigorously they respond as a group might convey information about where that location is. Movements are the prime example. When you move your arm up, how far it goes depends on how much activity your muscles generate. The same muscles contract for both small and large movements, but they will contract longer or harder to move the arm farther. Sound is similar: how vigorously different left-preferring versus right-preferring groups of neurons respond helps you detect where a sound is to your right or left.[4]

If sensory and motor processing have anything at all to do with thought, then it seems likely that spatial maps and meters play some role. Recruiting these pathways for thought-as-simulation

---

3 Or much less, or much more—it depends on the brain area and how far away the stimuli are.

4 Kristin Kelly Porter and Jennifer M. Groh, "The 'Other' Transformation Required for Visual-Auditory Integration: Representational Format," *Progress in Brain Research* 155 (2006): 313–23.

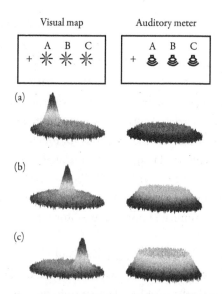

FIGURE R4.2. Sometimes the same population of neurons can serve as a map for one type of stimulus and a meter for another. This schematic depicts the activity patterns observed in the primate superior colliculus in response to visual and auditory stimuli. Visual stimuli at different locations activate different neural populations (illustrated as different colored "hills" of activity in panels A–C, left side). Sounds at those same positions activate neurons throughout the structure, but with a level of activity that depends on the sound's location (A–C, right side). Source: J. Lee and J. M. Groh, "Different Stimuli, Different Spatial Codes: A Visual Map and an Auditory Rate Code for Oculomotor Space in the Primate Superior Colliculus," *PLoS One* 9 (2014): e85017.

might involve activating spatial patterns in the maps, activating graded levels of activity in the meters, or both. Indeed, evidence suggests that the parietal cortex plays a dual role both in encoding the locations of visual and auditory targets and in allowing humans and monkeys to count—a kind of thought that involves systematically ordered relationships between quantities. Mentally manipulating numbers thus seems well suited to being carried out by brain structures that handle quantitative relationships of other types. It is presently a matter of debate whether these mathematical functions of the parietal cortex are handled as a map or as a meter.[5]

Another example involves the brain's map of the body and body-related language. Words related to different parts of the body, such as "kick" and "lick," have been shown to evoke activity in different locations in body-related cortical areas in a fashion roughly resembling the brain's map of the body for touch or movement.[6] In fact, even metaphorical usage of touch-related words, such as "I had a rough day," can evoke activity in the body-related cortex.[7] Such observations support the idea that when understanding language, your brain may simulate sensory and motor activity related to that meaning.

The cognitive linguist George Lakoff and the philosopher Mark Johnson have noticed that spatial terms may be used to denote even nonspatial relationships.[8] For example, we may say we are *close* to someone or that someone is a *distant* relative; that we have *high* regard for someone or that someone has been *lowered* in our estimation. This important insight suggests a way for sensory and motor brain mechanisms to support not only concrete thought, for which the sensory and motor connection may be obvious, but also more abstract thinking.

A critical question that has yet to be answered is how the brain simultaneously processes sensorimotor signals and thought. One possibility is that there are in fact distinct brain circuits for

5 J. D. Roitman, E. M. Brannon, and M. L. Platt, "Monotonic Coding of Numerosity in Macaque Lateral Intraparietal Area," *PLoS Biology* 5 (2007): e208; J. D. Roitman, E. M. Brannon, and M. L. Platt, "Representation of Numerosity in Posterior Parietal Cortex," *Frontiers in Integrated Neuroscience* 6 (2012): 25; A. Nieder and S. Dehaene, "Representation of Number in the Brain," *Annual Review of Neuroscience* 32 (2009): 185–208.

6 O. Hauk, I. Johnsrude, and F. Pulvermuller, "Somatotopic Representation of Action Words in Human Motor and Premotor Cortex," *Neuron* 41 (2004): 301–7.

7 S. Lacey, R. Stilla, and K. Sathian, "Metaphorically Feeling: Comprehending Textural Metaphors Activates Somatosensory Cortex," *Brain Language* 120 (2012): 416–21.

8 George Lakoff and Mark Johnson, *Metaphors We Live By*. Chicago: University of Chicago Press, 1980.

sensation and thought and that the relationship between the two
is therefore one of similarity rather than identity. Thought-related
circuitry might be similar to sensorimotor circuitry because
it may have evolved through a process of duplication of brain
resources, creating extra capacity in brain circuits that could be
used for thought but that would still show the fingerprints of its
evolutionary history. Whether the thought-circuits and perception-
circuits are coextensive or distinct but similar, the paramount
importance of perceiving and moving in space is likely to leave its
distinctive mark.

CHAPTER FIVE

Space in the Seventeenth Century

Andrew Janiak

When the seventeenth century began, the natural world was finite and the human place within it secure; by century's end, nature had been embedded in an infinite space calling humanity's special status into question. In the old picture, one inherited from Aristotelianism, nature's familiarity was well established and nature was amenable to study through familiar philosophical techniques involving little mathematics. After the revolutionary challenges to Aristotelianism by Galileo and Descartes had been absorbed and extended by Leibniz and Newton, natural philosophy underwent a seismic shift: mathematics took center stage in the study of nature, and space's infinity became the "fundamental principle of the new ontology."[1] There is little doubt that

1 See Alexandre Koyré, *From the Closed World to the Infinite Universe* (Baltimore, MD: Johns Hopkins University Press, 1957), 126. As Kuhn writes in his *Copernican Revolution*, published in the same year as Koyré's classic: "From Bruno's death in 1600 to the publication of Descartes's

Andrew Janiak, *Space in the Seventeenth Century*. In: *Space*. Edited by: Andrew Janiak, Oxford University Press (2020). © Oxford University Press.

DOI: 10.1093/oso/9780199914104.003.0010

this shift from the "closed world" to the "infinite universe," in Koyré's famous phrase, represents a profound development of the seventeenth century. It is perhaps as momentous as the transition from a Ptolemaic to a Copernican worldview, with which it was intertwined. [2]

It is tempting to describe the shift captured in Koyré's title by noting that mathematicians, astronomers, and philosophers shifted from thinking of space (or sometimes the world) as finite to thinking of it as infinite. This description of the century's shift is predicated on the idea that the concept of space itself underwent little alteration—the change was in breaking free of old prejudices or assumptions and beginning to think that space might actually be infinite. That is, we hold the concept of space fixed, and then alter our notion of its features. But as it turns out, this is anachronistic: it involves a description of the developments within the seventeenth century from the point of view of the century's end. Briefly put: it specifically involves today's interpreters in employing an attitude toward thinking about space that is widespread at century's end and then imposing that perspective

---

Principles of Philosophy in 1644, no Copernican of any prominence appears to have espoused the infinite universe, at least in public. After Descartes, however, no Copernican seems to have opposed the conception." Thomas Kuhn, *The Copernican Revolution: Planetary Astronomy in the Development of Western Thought* (Cambridge, MA: Harvard University Press, 1957), 289. Thomas Digges in the late sixteenth century might be the exception that proves Kuhn's rule; see Steven Shapin, *The Scientific Revolution* (Chicago: University of Chicago Press, 1996), 22.

2 The two developments were intertwined, but distinct. In an influential early article on Cartesianism, Marjorie Nicholson distinguishes the developments and then boldly pronounces the shift in thinking about space to be more significant: "Few, however, seem to have noticed the effect of the Cartesian idea of indefinite extension upon one of the most significant of all seventeenth-century conceptions: the idea of infinity, the problem of the possibility of an infinite number of worlds, or of a universe infinitely extended. In this conception lies the key to the characteristic form taken in England, at least, by the idea of progress, and to one of the most profound changes which occurred in seventeenth-century thought; for the real change in men's conceptions of themselves and of the universe came less through Copernicanism than through the expansion of the boundaries of thought through the idea of infinity." Marjorie Nicholson, "The Early Stages of Cartesianism in England," *Studies in Philology* 26 (1929): 370. For Nicholson, then, it was not merely the special attention given to the concept of space but the attention to its infinity—to a universe "infinitely extended"—that represented a profound shift in seventeenth-century thought. But the process whereby philosophers began to focus their attention on space itself, rather than on nature or the world, was a complex one, and it took considerable effort before they were willing to accept the idea that space was infinite, in possibility if not in fact.

on mathematicians, astronomers, and philosophers working at the century's beginning. Ironically, this interpretive approach, tempting as it is, and despite its attempt to describe a profound shift in human thinking, dramatically downplays how radical the transitions within these fields in this century really were. The transition was not merely from a finite to an infinite world, from the Scholastic to the modern, but more profoundly, it was a shift in which the concept of space, along with its structure, became a singularly important analytic focus for mathematicians, natural philosophers, and metaphysicians alike.

Even the most revolutionary thinkers working between, say, 1600 and 1650 did not take the concept of space to be of any special philosophical significance, if they contemplated such a concept at all. Concomitantly, they did not analyze the structure or the nature of space itself. Motion, objects, God, persons, even nature itself—these were the objects of their study; not space. For figures working within mathematics, metaphysics, and natural philosophy between 1650 and 1700, however, it had become commonplace to contemplate the concept of space, to consider space's structure, and to ponder the nature of space. Whereas an earlier thinker would analyze Euclid's famous parallel postulate by considering the operations and features of figures and lines, a later thinker would consider what the postulate might tell us about space's structure and about the structure of a space in which the postulate failed to hold.[3] Whereas an earlier thinker would analyze motion by considering what would happen to a body moving rectilinearly under no external constraints, a later thinker would consider what the principle of inertia might tell us about space itself. Whereas an earlier thinker would analyze extension as a crucial attribute of

---

3   See the fascinating work of Vincenzo De Risi, *Leibniz on the Parallel Postulate and the Foundations of Geometry* (Cham, Switzerland: Springer International, 2016), which focuses on Leibniz's understanding of the foundations of geometry in general, and of the parallel postulate in particular, but which also has important implications for our understanding of the focus of geometricians in the century as a whole.

physical substances, a later thinker would ask whether the inherited substance-accident metaphysics could accommodate Euclidean space.

In considering the trends that led to a new philosophical emphasis on space, along with a new focus on the question of its basic structure, the danger of anachronism looms large. It is precisely because figures like Leibniz and Newton are so close to us compared with their medieval predecessors that we are tempted to use *our* basic categories to understand *them*. We are tempted to think about metaphysics or theology, physics or mathematics, in our terms when analyzing Leibniz or Newton; we find no such temptation when we read ancient or medieval sources, for their world is too foreign for such an approach. It seems obvious to us, for instance, that there is an aspect of physics called the theory of motion, which involves such things as the principle of inertia and which has obvious consequences for our understanding of the nature of space. Equally obvious is the idea that geometry is the science of space, which involves the notion that it provides us with information about space's structure. And so on. We then—in a seemingly harmless fashion—look to the great philosophers of the seventeenth century to discover what they thought about the theory of motion and its relation to space or about geometry and its relation. This is tempting, but interpretively dangerous: a great evolution took place during the course of the century, so we must resist the temptation to read the whole century through our eyes, or even through the eyes of someone like Leibniz or Newton at century's end. Numerous philosophers and mathematicians presented theories of motion, along with ideas about what we would call inertia, without believing that such issues had any special consequences for thinking about space, indeed, without necessarily having any particular view about space itself. The concept of space, to the extent that it occurs at all in such thinkers, is decidedly unimportant. Similarly, we now understand that space can be conceived from a variety of perspectives, including non-Euclidean ones, but numerous mathematicians over the centuries analyzed the famous parallel postulate in Euclidean geometry by thinking about what it means for two

lines to be parallel without ever asking questions about the structure
of space itself. This seems odd from our perspective. But there is strong
evidence that near century's end, Leibniz was in fact the first mathematician to consider the parallel postulate by thinking about space's
structure rather than thinking merely about lines and figures.[4] Space
became an object of study in mathematics, metaphysics, and natural
philosophy over the course of the seventeenth century. Perhaps something similar happened to time with the advent of the special theory of
relativity in the early twentieth century.

The seventeenth century ended, and the eighteenth century began,
with a profound and lasting debate between Isaac Newton and his
followers and his great challenger G. W. Leibniz and his followers. In
mathematics, natural philosophy, metaphysics, and other fields, the
co-discoverers of what we now call the integral and differential calculus represented two dramatically opposed camps. Leibniz's famous
and extensive correspondence with Newton's friend and colleague
Samuel Clarke at the beginning of the eighteenth century indicated
that the two camps differed profoundly on the proper understanding
of space and time. Indeed, the debate between the Newtonian "abso-
lutist" conception of space and the Leibnizian "relationalist" conception continued well into the twentieth century.[5] This chapter's focus
enables us to view this familiar philosophical topic from a new perspective: despite their numerous and deep differences, Leibniz and
Newton fundamentally agreed on the importance of the concept of
space for mathematics and philosophy. They agreed not only that
mathematicians and philosophers should ponder the concept of space
and the basic structure of space itself, but also that it was worth placing
these topics at the center of a major international debate that would

---

4 I owe this point to a fascinating talk with Vincenzo De Risi.

5 See, e.g., Larry Sklar, *Space, Time and Spacetime* (Berkeley: University of California Press,
   1974); John Earman, *World Enough and Spacetime* (Cambridge, MA: MIT Press, 1989); and
   more recently, Rob DiSalle, *Understanding Spacetime* (Cambridge, UK: Cambridge University
   Press, 2006).

ensnare numerous thinkers in England and on the Continent. To say the least, it is difficult to imagine a figure such as Bacon, Galileo, or Descartes engaging in a protracted dispute concerning space. Thus, the Leibniz-Clarke correspondence is a telling emblem of the century's shift. Precisely because that correspondence was so influential, Leibniz, Newton, and their followers managed to convince many of their readers that space itself, and its representation, is worthy of special attention in numerous fields.

The dramatic rise in the importance of thinking about space in seventeenth-century mathematics and philosophy had lasting consequences. It continued to serve as a profoundly important object of study throughout the next two centuries, and its status as such remains secure today. Many developments in the relevant fields—including the dominance of Newtonian mechanics in the late eighteenth and into the nineteenth century, the emergence of non-Euclidean geometry in the nineteenth century, and the development of the theory of relativity in the early twentieth century—ensured the continuing importance of space. This fact renders our task difficult. We simply take it for granted today that, e.g., geometry was always considered the science of space; we presume that physics has always been concerned with such things as space and time, matter and motion; we assume that metaphysicians have always had to ponder whether space itself exists or whether it is merely a kind of abstraction or ideal entity. It is therefore difficult for us to imagine a time before all of these assumptions had been made, a time when geometers, natural philosophers, and metaphysicians paid space—and its conceptual representation—little heed. That's the task of history, and of this chapter.

Our contemporary categories can confuse us when we consider early seventeenth-century knowledge. Consider motion. It might seem obvious to a contemporary reader that the motion of a body involves its changing spatial position over time, and that the concept itself is therefore inherently connected to the concept of space, just as it must be inherently connected to the concept of time. But as we will see, many seventeenth-century figures thought about motion by thinking about paths, trajectories, object relations, and a host of other topics, without pondering space itself. Similarly, what we now call the principle of inertia is obviously at the center of seventeenth-century thinking about motion, and Newton provided what became the canonical formulation of the principle with his first law of motion in 1687. For Newton, the laws of motion have important consequences for what space must be like, a point he emphasized in his unpublished anti-Cartesian manuscript, *De Gravitatione*.[6] But this late seventeenth-century fact can provide a misleading lens when we wish to understand the century as a whole, for Newton's predecessors did not share this notion. It is true that some previous thinkers—such as Galileo, Beeckman, and Descartes—held various ideas that are relevant or similar to Newton's law.[7] But for Newton's predecessors, the question is this: To what extent did any philosopher pondering what we would call inertia also consider the potential consequences for the character of space or for our concept of it? By century's end, this question was commonplace, but it was rare before 1650.

Descartes is an important representative of thinking about motion before 1650, and his work was central to developments in both England and on the Continent throughout the rest of the century. His canonical work in natural philosophy, *Principia philosophiae* (1644), presents three laws of motion, the first two of which are linked to the development of the principle of inertia. In part 2 of this work, on the principles of material things, Descartes discusses space in sections 10 through 18, motion in sections 23 through 33, and then the three

---

6 See Isaac Newton, *Philosophical Writings*, ed. Andrew Janiak, 2nd edition (Cambridge, UK: Cambridge University Press, 2014).

7 There is a lively debate about which philosopher—Galileo, Beeckman, Gassendi, Descartes, etc.— first formulated what we would now call the principle of inertia, and also about the related question of whether there is such a thing as that principle before 1687, which saw the publication of Newton's *Principia mathematica*. For an innovative and nuanced account of such issues, see David M. Miller, *Representing Space in the Scientific Revolution* (Cambridge, UK: Cambridge University Press, 2014).

SPACE IN THE SEVENTEENTH CENTURY 237

laws in sections 37 through 42. Hence on the surface, it appears that Descartes is thinking about space, motion, and the laws in tandem, much as a contemporary reader might expect. But when we look at the details of Descartes's analysis of space—and the allied notions of internal place, external place, etc.—we find that our expectation is hampered, for Descartes argues that there is no "real distinction" between space and corporeal substance (section 10). His argument is as follows:

> There is no real distinction between space, or internal place, and the corporeal substance contained in it; the only difference lies in the way in which we are accustomed to conceive of them. For in reality the extension in length, breadth and depth which constitutes a space is exactly the same as that which constitutes a body. The difference arises as follows: in the case of a body, we regard the extension as something particular, and thus think of it as changing whenever there is a new body; but in the case of space, we attribute to the extension only a generic unity, so that when a new body comes to occupy the space, the extension of the space is reckoned not to change but to remain one and the same, so long as it retains the same size and shape and keeps the same position relative to certain external bodies which we use to determine the space in question. (AT VIIIA:45)

We may conceive of (e.g.) a stone's extension as a feature of it, and of the place it used to occupy near a tree as distinct from it, but this distinction arises in our conception of these things; it is not a real distinction. In fact, space itself is nothing but body. In Descartes's natural philosophy, then, the concept of space, and space itself, drops out; we can analyze the natural world using only the concepts of motion and body, along with the laws that govern them, for space is identical to body. Presumably, that is why the concept of space—or of generic extension—plays no role in what Descartes regards as the proper

concept of motion, or the idea of motion in the "strict sense." Motion
in that sense is defined as follows:

> If, on the other hand, we consider what should be understood by
> *motion*, not in common usage but in accordance with the truth of
> the matter, and if our aim is to assign a determinate nature to it, we
> may say that *motion is the transfer of one piece of matter, or one body,
> from the vicinity of the others which immediately touch it, and which
> we consider to be at rest, to the vicinity of others* [*ex vicinia eorum
> corporum, quae illud immediate contingent & tanquam quiescentia
> spectantur, in viciniam aliorum*]. (AT VIII-1:53–54)

The moving body's vicinity is not understood in terms of space or of
positions within space, but in terms of the body's relationship with
other bodies. For Descartes, properly speaking, to move is to change
one's relationship with other bodies. Space itself, to the extent that one
can formulate a clear concept of such a thing, is irrelevant.

Even if the concept of space itself is not relevant for Descartes's understanding of motion and its causes, one might still ask: What does
such a concept consist in, from his point of view? One might expect that the author of the *Géométrie* (1637) would reply that space
is a three-dimensional Euclidean magnitude. Or perhaps it is that
which contains lines and planes and figures of various sorts in various
relationships with one another. Regardless of what Descartes indicates
in his mathematical work, however, he is quite clear in his natural philosophy that "the idea of a space" is rather different. He hints in section
11 of part 2 of *Principia philosophiae* that one can conceive of an empty
space, not in the sense that one can have a representation of a space that
is actually empty of body per se, but rather in the sense that one can
conceive of "something" that is extended in three dimensions without
ipso facto conceiving of that thing as bearing any other features (such
as being red or smelling like a rose). And that, in turn, is "just what is
comprised in the idea of a space," even a space that is called "empty."

For Descartes, then, the idea of a space just is the idea of *something* that is extended in three dimensions. It is identical in content to the idea of a stone when we represent the stone merely as being extended and not as bearing any other features (such as weight or color, etc.). This is the *content* of our idea. Moreover, Descartes analyzes the *reference* of "space" in the next section, contending that the word refers to the size, shape, and position of some body relative to other bodies. Whether we consider meaning or reference in Descartes's terms, space and body are identical.

It might be thought prejudicial to put things in this way. After all, from Descartes's point of view, space does not drop out of his natural philosophy as irrelevant any more than body drops out, for they are one and the same! If you like: if the current president of the United States is crucial to my analysis of contemporary global politics, then Donald Trump is crucial too, and he doesn't drop out as irrelevant just because he *is* the president. Indeed, he is relevant *because* he is the president. Similarly, space is crucial in Descartes's system because body is crucial, and they are one and the same.

But this objection misses a deeper point: when we speak of space in contemporary terms, we do not think of corporeal substance or of extended body; we think of a three-dimensional magnitude with certain features. Thus, we cannot use our term "space," or our contemporary concept, to much effect when studying Descartes; we must use the concept of extended body instead, since that reflects the conceptual structure of Descartes's system. There is nothing like *what we call space* in that system. More important, there is nothing like what Leibniz or Newton calls space in that system, either, as we will see.

What this means, finally, is that when Descartes analyzed motion—and presented the idea that a body moving rectilinearly will continue moving in that way until something impedes it—he did so without thinking about what we call space. Bodies in motion continue in motion. What is motion? It is a change in relation between the moving body and its vicinity, which is constituted by other bodies. Space, spaces, positions, places, etc. are irrelevant. If Descartes had begun part 2 of *Principia philosophiae* by presenting his three laws of motion, then this might not have been clear. But he wisely began by explaining that space is identical to body, and then proceeded to define motion as a change in relations among bodies, and only then presented his three laws. When read in context, the laws tell us nothing about what we call space. To consider that issue is to ponder a non-Cartesian philosophical topic.

Descartes was not alone in this conception. In the first book of *The Elements of Philosophy* (1655), entitled "Concerning Body," Hobbes presents a strikingly similar view. He distinguishes between two conceptions of space: first, *imaginary space*, the "phantasm" or imaginative representation of some body existing without the mind, one in which we represent only the extension of that body; and second, *real space*, the extension of a body, one that is independent of our thought (unlike our representations) and coincident or coextended with some part of space.[8] To illustrate: An apple on my desk has a certain extension (it occupies three spatial dimensions), which Hobbes calls a *real space*. But when I look at my apple and then close my eyes and imagine it, I am dealing with an *imaginary space*. Here is the kicker: since real space is identical to the extension of bodies, there can be no such thing as empty space.[9] Of course, we can *imagine* empty space—that is where we obtain imaginary space—because we can imagine the extension of a body considered independently of that body and its other features ("accidents"), but such a represented empty space is merely a representation. For instance, I can see my apple, imagine it, and then imagine that all its features—its redness, its smell, etc.—other than its extension disappear, and then I am left with the *place* of the apple, which Hobbes identifies with imaginary space.[10] Unlike the apple itself, the

---

8 Thomas Hobbes, *Elements of Philosophy* (London, 1839), II, 8, §4.
9 See Hobbes, *Elements of Philosophy*, II, 7, §2.
10 Hobbes, *Elements of Philosophy*, II, 8, §5.

place of the apple is not part of the world around me; it's just a phantasm or representation. So empty space is not a contradictory notion—it is not logically impossible—but since it is merely something that we can imagine, rather than something that can exist, it is not a feature of nature.[11]

Philosophical treatments of space are an important exception to the general rule that the great "moderns" of the seventeenth century—from Galileo to Hobbes, from Descartes to Cavendish, from Leibniz to Newton—made their names by breaking from Aristotelian and Scholastic approaches. When the topic is natural change, causation more generally, the proper analysis of sensory perception, the structure of human knowledge, etc., the moderns broke with what they took to be the dominant approaches of the medieval period and the Renaissance. Not so with space. For at least the first half of the century, modern thinkers were not more interested than their predecessors in thinking of space and its structure as fundamental philosophical topics of inquiry. Like Descartes, Hobbes is an excellent example of this fact. He was of course one of the most important moderns of his time, a great critic of Aristotelian ideas, and a proponent of the latest thinking about the mechanical philosophy; but he did not take the analysis of space to be of any more significance than Descartes did.[12]

---

11 Nowadays, we would probably say that for Hobbes, empty space is a logical but not a metaphysical possibility, since he considers real space to be identical with the extension of a body: without a body present, we have no extension of that body, and therefore we have no real space that isn't identical to some body's extension.

12 Hobbes's "Epistle Dedicatory" to the first part of his *Elements*, written to the earl of Devonshire, exhibits his status as a modern thinker, proclaiming the motion of the earth (indicated by Copernicus) and the importance of studying motion after the fashion of Galileo. Before Copernicus, Galileo, and Harvey, who discovered the motion of the blood, "there was nothing certain in natural philosophy" (Hobbes, *Elements*, 1:viii). Lest his allegiance to the moderns be in any doubt, he adds a brief history of philosophy, proclaiming that when the thinkers of the early Church began to incorporate ideas from pagan philosophers into their work, they encountered many "foolish and false" ideas from the "physics and metaphysics of Aristotle" (1:x). As he argues in the *Elements*, what the "writers of metaphysics"—by which he obviously means various kinds of Aristotelian philosophy—call formal and final causes are in fact just *efficient* causes (part 2, ch. 10, §7). In a sense, he was even more committed to the mechanical philosophy than one of its principal founders, Descartes, because Hobbes rejected the very idea of immaterial substance, which meant that human beings lacked any aspect that exceeded the reach of mechanistic explanations,

This does not mean, however, that the moderns in the first half of the seventeenth century had nothing to say about space. We have already encountered both Descartes's and Hobbes's views in this area. But what is perhaps most remarkable about their views is that they took the topic of space to be centered on precisely the kinds of question broached by their Scholastic and Aristotelian predecessors and interlocutors. One of the primary questions about space in the medieval period, and perhaps the primary question for someone like Descartes or Hobbes, is the question of the vacuum.[13] Does nature abhor a vacuum, and if so, does that mean that empty space is not possible? Perhaps the best confirmation of this fact is Hobbes's famous debate with the experimental philosopher Robert Boyle in the early 1660s. In that debate, even when Hobbes confronted some of the most important new research in natural philosophy during his lifetime, he decided to focus on the possibility of the vacuum.

Before his debate with Boyle began, Hobbes had already rejected the possibility of a vacuum in his *Elements of Philosophy*. The most significant aspect of his analysis involves a *gedankenexperiment* designed to prove that a vacuum is not actually possible (even if it is logically possible). Hobbes explains: If we take a vessel AB, which has little holes at its bottom, B, and a large hole at its top, A, and if we fill it with water, we find that the water will not flow through the holes at B unless the hole at A is open. This is counterintuitive, says Hobbes, because "the natural motion of the water" as a heavy body would be toward the ground, but my covering the hole at A hinders this motion. Why is that so? Hobbes explains: The water cannot flow through the holes at B unless the air adjacent to them has been displaced, and that displacement cannot happen, in turn, unless the opening of the hole at A allows air to

---

at least in principle. See John Henry, "The Reception of Cartesianism," in *The Oxford Handbook of British Philosophy in the Seventeenth Century*, ed. Peter Anstey (Oxford: Oxford University Press, 2013), 121.

13   Edward Grant, *Much Ado about Nothing: Theories of Space and Vacuum from the Middle Ages to the Scientific Revolution* (Cambridge, UK: Cambridge University Press, 1981).

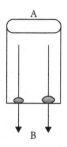

FIGURE 5.1. "An example from Hobbes."

flow into the vessel (see Figure 5.1).[14] Hobbes clearly endorses a plenist view in his causal explanation of this phenomenon. Moreover, he apparently presupposes a mechanist conception of causal relations—one articulated explicitly earlier in the text[15]—when he assumes that the only way that my covering the hole at A, which is spatially separated from the holes at B, could prevent water flowing through those holes is if the air acts as an intermediary by blocking the water flow, for the air adjacent to B is contiguous with air near the middle of the exterior of the vessel, which is contiguous, in turn, with the air adjacent to A. His mechanist view earlier in the text takes this form: there can be no cause of motion in any body except in a contiguous body.[16] Thus, Hobbes's mechanical view of causation would prevent him from endorsing any explanation of this phenomenon that violates his prohibition against noncontiguous bodily causation.

Hobbes's argument can be read as having several basic steps: first, if there were a vacuum adjacent to B, then there would be nothing there to prevent the water from following its "natural motion" through the holes; second, the air adjacent to B prevents the water from flowing; third, the only way that the air at B can be displaced to make room

14 Hobbes, *Elements of Philosophy*, IV, 26, §2.
15 Hobbes, *Elements of Philosophy*, II, 9, §7.
16 Hobbes, *Elements of Philosophy*, II, 9, §7.

for the water to flow is if something contiguous to the air causes it to move; and fourth, an event at A, like removing the cover over the hole, could influence the air at B only if the two phenomena are contiguous to one another, in this case, through the intermediary air surrounding the vessel on all sides. Think of the fourth point roughly as follows: removing the covering at A allows some air particles to push on the water in the vessel; their displacement allows adjacent air particles to take their place; and so on, until there is room for the water at B to take the place of the air particles formerly located there. In a vacuum, the water at B would flow regardless of what is done at A, since the two are spatially separated. Of course, as Hobbes admits, this argument presupposes that the water has a natural motion toward the ground, by which he means at least that our goal is to explain why the water does *not* fall.[17]

In his *New Experiments Physico-Mechanicall* of 1660, Boyle presents forty-three experiments involving what he called his "pneumatical engine," which was designed and operated with Robert Hooke's assistance. He indicates in his note to the reader that his goal is to study "the nature of the air" with his experiments and to further his "grand design of promoting experimental and useful philosophy" with them.[18] Before describing any of the forty-three experiments, Boyle undertakes a long description of the apparatus that Hooke designed, referring in great detail to its various parts as outlined in a figure that opens the work. He then tackles the philosophical heart of the matter at the outset: there may be certain leaks in the glass vessel and the attached air pump, which has an intriguing consequence for a long-standing philosophical question. He writes, "Even at a very small leak there may

---

17 This is complex: as a good anti-Aristotelian, Hobbes explicitly rejects the notion of a natural place on the grounds that it's inconsistent with (what we would call) the principle of inertia and with gravity, which he thinks is due to an attraction of the earth. As for the latter, he indicates that no one has ever explained that attraction. He does not indicate how he conceives of the relation between his mechanist commitments and his endorsement of attraction.

18 Robert Boyle, *The Works of Robert Boyle*, ed. Michael Hunter and Edward Davis (London: Pickering and Chatto, 1999), 1:143.

enough get in, to make the *vacuum* soon loose that name; by which I here declare once for all, that I understand not a space wherein there is no body at all, but such as is either altogether, or almost totally devoid of air."[19] Thus Boyle indicates that he will take the old philosophical (and contested) concept of the vacuum to apply only to some space in which there is no air, or very little, rather than to a space that is empty of body altogether. The reason is clear: Boyle was perfectly well aware that many philosophers, including Descartes and Hobbes, had argued strenuously against the possibility of a vacuum in the latter sense, and so he chose to remain silent on that question. Yet he insisted that although he may never have achieved a vacuum even in his restricted—in what some have called his experimental or operational—sense, nonetheless he came close enough in his experiments to have discovered "hitherto unobserved *Phaenomena* of nature," including of course the "spring" of the air.[20]

Having already committed himself to a plenist and a mechanist conception of nature, Hobbes wrote a lengthy critique of Boyle's *New Experiments Physico-Mechanicall* a year after its publication in a work entitled *Dialogus Physicus*. Hobbes begins his dialogue with a note to the reader indicating his view of what he calls "physics": it is the "science of natural causes." This is no surprise to readers of *The Elements of Philosophy*. From Hobbes's point of view, as the dialogue makes clear, Boyle's experiments with the air pump are aimed at tackling two principal issues: first, the question of whether a vacuum is possible; and second, the "nature" of the air. Hobbes argues that the latter is logically prior to the former: one cannot determine whether a vacuum in nature is genuinely possible unless one first determines the nature

---

19 Boyle, *Works*, 1:163.

20 See Boyle, *Works*, 1:164–65. Boyle thinks that his experiments have enabled him to discover a "hitherto unobserved" feature of ordinary air, its "springiness," which in this period he seems to think is distinct from weight and possibly from pressure. One can "explicate" his experimental results if one postulates this feature of the air, although of course the feature itself remains imperceptible by any direct means.

of the air itself. In particular, an experiment with an air pump cannot determine the possibility of a vacuum until that nature is established. He then argues for the following conception of the air's nature: air is a continuous fluid quantity; it is both infinitely divisible and subtle. That is, if one takes any part of the air—say, the amount of air in a small enclosed space like an ordinary light bulb—one can always conceive of that quantity as being divided by some process. So any quantity of air is divisible into half that quantity; hence the air is infinitely divisible. Hobbes immediately argues for the irrelevance of the air pump on this basis: one can contend that the air pump creates a vacuum when the pump sucks all the air out of an otherwise sealed cylinder, but the experiment can never prove this result, because the air can flow into any space, however small. Thus when the mechanism supposedly sucks air out of the cylinder, in fact, air continues to flow into it through even the smallest pores within the glass cylinder (or another part of the apparatus). If you like, the nature of air prevents Boyle from constructing an airtight apparatus. Clearly, it might appear to ordinary observers as if the air is evacuated, but the subtle nature and infinite divisibility of air means that it cannot be truly airtight. Hence by the end of the fifth page of the dialogue, Hobbes has argued that experiments are irrelevant if one wishes to investigate the possibility of a vacuum.

Typically, contemporary readers take this famous episode in mid-seventeenth-century British natural philosophy to illustrate Hobbes's unfortunate resistance to Boyle's superior experimental methods that generated so many insights in the 1660s (although Shapin and Schaffer vigorously challenged this interpretation with their famous *Leviathan and the Air Pump* in 1985).[21] But what we see here is that although Boyle transforms a topic, viz., the possibility of a vacuum, by using new means to answer an old question, he does now show any interest in

---

21 Steven Shapin and Simon Schaffer, *Leviathan and the Air-Pump* (Princeton, NJ: Princeton University Press, 1985).

space itself beyond the very traditional focus on the vacuum, which had of course been a principal focus of discussions of space for centuries.[22]

The great moderns of the first half of the century—including Descartes, Hobbes, and Boyle—inherited their philosophical questions about space from a much earlier tradition stretching back to the medieval period and the Renaissance. It was not until the second half of the century—especially the 1670s and 1680s—that we see a rupture with this tradition and thinkers such as Leibniz and Newton begin to treat space and its structure as worthy of philosophical analysis in a new way.

One reason the shift in emphasizing the importance of space from the first half of the seventeenth century to the second half is unfamiliar is that later thinkers rarely emphasized the shift in their own philosophical writings. Indeed, in some respects, their construal of developments in the theory of motion earlier in the century, e.g., could serve to obscure the shift. They emphasized continuity rather than rupture. Newton provides a clear instance of this phenomenon in the Scholium following the corollaries to the laws of motion: "The principles I have set forth are accepted by mathematicians and confirmed by experiments of many kinds. By means of the first two laws and the first two corollaries Galileo found that the descent of heavy bodies is in the squared ratio of the time and that the motion of projectiles occurs in a parabola, as experiment confirms, except insofar as these motions are somewhat retarded by the resistance of the air."[23] In this passage, Newton supports his three laws of motion by indicating the experimental evidence in their favor, along with the authority of the mathematicians—he may have had figures such as Wren, Wallis, and Huygens in mind—who have accepted them. Intriguingly, he singles out Galileo by noting that he used (something akin to) the laws to reach his famous results involving free fall and projectile motion. Leaving

---

22 A classic work on this topic is Grant, *Much Ado about Nothing*.

23 Newton, *Philosophical Writings*, 99.

aside the accuracy of this specific attribution to Galileo, it does appear that something is missing from Newton's account. The section entitled "Axiomata, sive leges motus," in which this Scholium to the laws appears, is immediately preceded by the Scholium to the Definitions, and in that section, Newton clarifies his understanding of space, time, and motion. (Indeed, this builds on the ideas about motion already outlined in the Definitions, where we learn what Newton means, e.g., by quantity of motion.) This obviously helps to frame the discussion of motion in the next Scholium; for Newton, the laws of motion and the ideas of space, time, and motion are intimately intertwined. We can clearly say that Galileo did not think about things in that way.

Despite this rare reference to another thinker (Galileo), Newton actually developed his ideas about space, time, and motion by thinking through what he took to be the inadequacies in Descartes's *Principia*. In particular, he noted that problems with the Cartesian theory of motion led him to conclude that he required a new conception of space and of body as well. Although such details are absent from the terse and dense argumentation of the Scholium following the Definitions at *Principia mathematica*'s beginning, they are perfectly clear in Newton's anti-Cartesian, unpublished tract, now known by its first line, *De Gravitatione*. He writes that in his *Principia*, part 2, Descartes takes himself to have demonstrated

that body does not differ at all from extension, abstracting hardness, color, weight, cold, heat, and the remaining qualities which body can lack, so that at last there remains only its extension in length, width, and depth, which therefore alone pertain to its essence. And as this has been taken by many as proved, and is in my view the only reason for having confidence in this opinion, and lest any doubt should remain about the nature of motion, I shall reply to this argument by saying what extension and body are, and how they differ from each other.[24]

---

24 Newton, *Philosophical Writings*, 35.

Thus, with an eye on the proper theory of motion, Newton will undertake to show how space and body differ from one another.

Newton's internal critique of the Cartesian theory of motion is elegant and well known. In essence, his contention is as follows: There is an inherent, if hidden, tension within the Cartesian system, one between its explicitly presented concept of motion (in the "proper" sense) and its three laws of nature, which tell us about the motions of bodies. Specifically, Descartes's "proper" view indicates that motion is a change in relations between the moving body and its vicinity, when the latter is construed as being at rest. Leaving aside potential complications with the notion that the vicinity must be "regarded" as resting, this concept suggests fundamentally that motion involves a change in relations between the moving body and other bodies. This is a perfectly sensible notion. And despite the fact that Descartes carefully distinguishes this notion from what he calls the ordinary ("vulgare") conception, this philosophically appropriate concept actually coheres nicely with common sense. Motion involves changing one's relations—e.g., one's distance—to other things. This is typically how we perceive motion as well. But the laws of nature may not accord with common sense. They indicate that a moving body will continue moving until something impedes it—not exactly an obvious idea, from the perspective of common sense—and that motion per se is rectilinear, which means that bodies moving in a curvilinear path tend to deviate from that trajectory. Yet if motion is actually a change in relations, then it seems, prima facie, that we can alter a body's motion by pushing objects in its vicinity, for that will change its relations with them. More precisely, we could alter a moving body's motion by having it change its relations with its vicinity, which is regarded as being at rest, until suddenly we push its newly acquired vicinity along with it, thereby stopping the body without impeding it. Hence the tension.

If Newton is correct in identifying this tension, what can he do to avoid it in his own system? He makes it clear from the outset, in the often ignored "definitions" that begin *De Gravitatione*, that he will think of motion as "change of place" rather than as a change in object relations. He adds that a place is a part of space that a body fills.[25] Newton is perfectly well aware that this idea involves a rejection not merely of the Cartesian theory of motion—indeed, Descartes takes the ordinary person to regard motion as involving a change of place, which he jettisons on various philosophical grounds—but also of the identification of space and body. For if places are parts of space, and if space is identical to body, then the idea that motion involves a change of place just is the idea that motion involves a change in relations with other bodies. And that is the view that Newton rejects in this essay. That is why he ends up explicitly arguing that space and body are distinct from one another, so that he can preserve the idea that motion is a change of place and not a change in object relations. Indeed, he begins the discussion of what he takes to be the errors of the Cartesians with this admission, which follows his first four definitions: "When I suppose in these definitions that space is distinct from body, and when I determine that motion is with respect to the parts of that space, and not with respect to the position of neighboring bodies, lest this should be taken as being gratuitously contrary to the Cartesians, I shall venture to dispose of his fictions."[26] Perhaps it will not be gratuitous if Newton presents arguments to convince his readers of Descartes's problems. Newton spends the next seven pages criticizing the Cartesian theory of motion.

There are two questions remaining. First, if Newton wishes to adopt a theory of motion that lacks the tension within the Cartesian system, what notion should he adopt? And second, assuming that he can avoid that tension by adopting a theory that coheres with the laws of motion, what view of space is consistent with that adoption? These are two of the questions that drive Newton's discussion of space in the Scholium. As for the first question, one might ask as a corollary: If Newton rejects

25 Newton, *Philosophical Writings*, 13.
26 Newton, *Philosophical Writings*, 28.

the Cartesian view that the proper idea of motion—that motion in the true sense—involves a change in object relations, then how else should he think about what he will call true motion? He will contend that true motion is absolute motion; that is, true motion consists in a change of place, where the latter is understood as a part of space independent of objects and their relations. He thinks that the idea that true motion is absolute motion should cohere with the laws of motion, since they seem to indicate that motion does not involve a change in object relations. But the laws also indicate that there is something special about constant rectilinear motion—the germ of this idea, at least, is already in Gassendi and in Descartes—because it requires no forces. One might say that at least prima facie, this idea sits better within Newton's framework than within Descartes's. The laws do not tell us that we can discover rectilinear motions, nor that there are any in nature. But they do raise the question of what it would mean for there to be such motion. Newton asks this question of Descartes, and in the Cartesian system this is a seemingly difficult issue, because a straight-line motion would have to be understood in terms of the moving body's relations to other bodies, such that those other bodies would have to define some motion as being straight. It might be possible to work out this idea. But on the surface, the Newtonian system seems better adapted to handle this idea: it tells us instead that a motion is straight in virtue of whether it traces a straight line in space itself, independent of objects and their places and relations. The point here is metaphysical rather than epistemic: we may not be able to discover any such motion, and there may in fact be no such motion in all of nature, but at least we lack any difficulty in understanding what such a motion would consist in.

When discussing questions about space, time, matter, forces, and motion in Leibniz and Newton, not to mention their followers, it is of course tempting solely to emphasize their numerous, influential disputes about all of these topics, and much else besides. The famous Leibniz-Clarke debate obviously helped to set much of the agenda of eighteenth-century philosophy. And yet, as with the discovery of what we now call the integral and differential calculus, at a deeper level of analysis, the projects in physics in which Leibniz and Newton were engaged had a crucial commonality. Naturally, each thinker grew up in a post-Cartesian environment, and each decided to try to make his name by balancing a healthy respect for Descartes's philosophical achievements with a critical attitude toward some of his views. From Newton's famous anti-Cartesian tract, *De Gravitatione*, and the details of his Scholium following the Definitions at the opening of *Principia mathematica*, to Leibniz's famous "An Essay on Some Notable Errors of the Cartesians" to his mature articulation of the nature of space and time, we find a plethora of criticisms of Cartesian ideas. Two central criticisms lie in common between the two thinkers: both Leibniz and Newton determine that the Cartesian identification of body and space must be rejected, and both believe in tandem that Descartes does not recognize the significance of inertia (or of Kepler's laws, for that matter) for understanding motion and, in tandem, space.

From Leibniz's mature point of view, Descartes's contention that space and body are identical represents a mistake at the deepest metaphysical level. Bodies in Cartesian physics are *substances* in the specific sense that even if they cannot exist independently of God, they can exist independently of one another, and just as significantly, they are bearers of properties. (The same is true of their various parts.) They are also the focus of Cartesian physics, for they are the items that are subject to the laws of motion. For Leibniz, however, it is a serious mistake to think that space itself is a substance; indeed, that is one of the primary criticisms that he presents to Clarke. Hence he would object to Descartes's view in his *Principia* that the idea of space just is the idea of a *something* with certain features, that is, a bearer of properties. For to conceive of space in that way, of course, just is to conceive of it as a substance (on a common construal of the latter notion). For Leibniz, in contrast, space is not a real thing, a being, or a substance at all; it is merely an ideal thing, an abstraction. For Leibniz, briefly put, space is the network—he often calls it the "order"—of relations among coexisting objects, just as time is the order of the succession of events. What exists in Leibniz's nature are the physical objects (the substances, at the phenomenal level) themselves, and in virtue of these physical objects existing, they bear various relations with one another (e.g., they are a certain distance apart). So the objects and their relations are what constitute space. Indeed, space is nothing over and above these objects and their relations; it is merely an abstract way of characterizing the network of all such objects and relations. An analogy: In the old days, the telephone network consisted of rotary telephones in homes and offices, a bunch of wires connecting them, and some switches in various centralized locations. The telephone network in those days *just was* the phones and the wires and the switches; there was nothing called "the telephone network" above and beyond these items. (One can throw in their relations for good measure.) In that sense, Leibniz rejects the Cartesian view because it confuses something that is a substance, namely physical body, with something that is nothing like a substance, namely the network of relations among physical bodies.[27]

Questions about the identity of space and body intersect with questions about the application of mathematics to nature (all the rage in the seventeenth century, of course). From Leibniz's perspective, Descartes's physics is not sufficiently mathematical; even a cursory glance at the differences in the vortex theories presented by Descartes in his *Principia* in 1644 and Leibniz in his *Tentamen* in 1689 will confirm this point. It is not merely the case that a plenist view of nature might be difficult to square with the application (e.g.) of geometry to questions about the motions of bodies, on the grounds that bodies and their parts are exceedingly complex and prevent any straightforward application of ideas about lines, planes, and the like. It is also the case, at a deeper level, that Leibniz enables the application

---

27 Of course, these points do not ipso facto constitute an argument against the Cartesian identification of space and body. Rather, they indicate how Leibniz conceives of space in a radically anti-Cartesian way and, indeed, partly for the same reason that he rejects the Newtonian view.

of geometrical—and more complex analytical—techniques to motion because he regards space itself as an ideal thing and therefore akin to a mathematical object. For Leibniz believes that space is homogeneous and infinitely divisible, just as geometrical objects like lines or planes are, and unlike any physical object (which would not be perfectly homogeneous). These facts about space's structure indicate to him a conclusion about space's ontology: it is an abstraction just like mathematical objects are abstractions. One problem with the Cartesian view, then, is that the identification of space and body renders it difficult to grasp how geometrical and analytical techniques can be applied to the messy world of physical objects and their various parts. And he might take it as confirmation of this opinion that in fact, parts 2, 3, and 4 of Descartes's *Principia* discuss the laws of nature, the vortex theory of planetary motion, and a host of other related topics in a qualitative fashion, without any extensive use of the very techniques that Descartes himself championed in his own great work, the *Geometrie*. This is not to make any conclusive claim about Leibniz's intentions in criticizing Descartes. But it does seem fair to conclude that he had both metaphysical and physico-mathematical reasons for rejecting Descartes's view of space.[28]

However, from the point of view of the metaphysical tradition of the seventeenth century, Descartes did have one distinct advantage over Leibniz, and even Newton: in contending that space is identical with body, Descartes faced no special questions about the ontology of space. It was really no more mysterious, or difficult to handle conceptually, than a table or a watermelon. Space is a substance, or each part of space is identical with some material substance. Similarly, Descartes held that time is a mode of material substance, and therefore dependent on it. In this way, he was able to maintain the view that both space

---

28 See the illuminating discussion in Lisa Shabel, "Apriority and Application: Philosophy of Mathematics in the Early Modern Period," in *Oxford Handbook of Philosophy of Mathematics and Logic*, ed. Stewart Shapiro (Oxford: Oxford University Press, 2005).

and time fit perfectly well—without remainder—into the general substance/property framework that many philosophers endorsed in the seventeenth century.[29] Thus if Leibniz or Newton denies the Cartesian identification of space and body, he must confront the question: But then what is the ontology of space? Is it itself a substance, independent of body? Is it somehow a property of some other substance? Or is it something else?

One of the intriguing common elements of those philosophers who reject Descartes's theory of space and body is that they do their best to evade these questions. That is, these philosophers insist that space and body are distinct, but they then wish to reject the contention that if this is the case, then space must somehow be construed either as a substance in its own right or as a property (of some kind) of some substance. Instead, they decide to question the entire substance/property framework. In *De Gravitatione*, Newton writes, "Perhaps now it may be expected that I should define extension as substance, or accident, or else nothing at all. But by no means, for it has its own manner of existing which is proper to it and which fits neither substances nor accidents."[30] In presenting this view, Newton was following in the footsteps of a number of philosophers who wished either to reject the substance/property framework in general, or at least to argue specifically that space need not fit into that framework (which could, of course, be taken as a challenge to the framework's generality). These thinkers prominently include Isaac Barrow, Newton's mathematics teacher at Cambridge and his predecessor in the Lucasian Chair there, and Pierre Gassendi, whose ideas circulated widely in England through the work of Walter Charleton (an author Newton read and commented on when he was a young student at Trinity College).[31]

---

29 He analyzed time in part by regarding a body's duration as one of its modes.

30 Newton, *Philosophical Writings*, 21.

31 See the tenth lecture in Isaac Barrow, *The Usefulness of Mathematical Learning* (London: Austen, 1734), 164; and Walter Charleton, *Physiologia Epicuro-Gassendo-Charltoniana* (London, 1654),

Leibniz of course is a special case. He not only accepted the substance/property framework; he made a career out of claiming that the Aristotelian tradition from which that framework ultimately arose had been mistreated by the "moderns" of his era. From his point of view, any being that exists must fit into the substance/property framework in some way, both at the phenomenal level, where we find material objects and their features, and at the more fundamental level of metaphysics, where we find, in his later thinking at least, monads and their intrinsic features. But as should be clear, Leibniz brilliantly evades any problems in his thinking about space and time by denying that either is a *being* of any kind. Neither space nor time, from his point of view, is an entity, which means that neither must fit within the substance/accident framework. To use one of Leibniz's favorite examples: If we want to provide a metaphysical analysis of something like the Prussian Army, with the goal of cataloguing everything that constitutes it, then we would write down a long list of soldiers and tents, horses and swords, and so on. Once we have listed *all* of the things in the Prussian Army, we would be finished; there would be nothing left over, no remainder, called "the army" that would have to be accounted for in some further way. To account for all the items in the army *just is* to account for the army itself. The same is true of space (and of time): to account for all of the things in nature—all the rocks and trees and planets—is to account for space itself, since it is nothing more than the order or network of the relations among these objects. The analogy is more precise than one might think because a proper analysis of the Prussian Army would likely have to include the relations among the things that constitute it as well. We must write down that so-and-so is a lieutenant, and so-and-so a private, and also that a certain horse belongs in the Fifth Company, etc., if we are to capture properly the things within the army. If we do so, we are taking account of the relations among

which Newton read in his youth. See also Antonia LoLordo, *Pierre Gassendi and the Birth of Early Modern Philosophy* (Cambridge, UK: Cambridge University Press, 2007), 106–24.

the items, and not merely the items themselves. So the analogy with Leibniz's view of space is pretty close.

We might take this line of reasoning one step further. If one accepts the basic substance/property framework, then one has a choice: (1) one can follow Descartes and simply identify space with body, thereby evading metaphysical trouble; or (2) one can reject the Cartesian identification, but then one must deny that space is a "something" at all. Similarly, if one wishes to think of space as distinct from body, but one does not wish to follow Leibniz's route for thinking about space, then of course one can reject the assumption that the substance/property framework is correct. In that case, one can attempt to evade metaphysical trouble, or rather one can deny that the analysis of what counts as such trouble should be understood in terms of that framework.

Because of these very considerations, Leibniz's theory of space and time came in for far less critical assessment than Newton's. For unlike Leibniz's relational theory, Newton insisted that space is indeed something above and beyond all of the natural objects and their relations with one another; it is not merely a set of relations. In that sense, it is unlike the Prussian Army. But then, what is it? This is precisely the kind of question that Leibniz posed to Newton and his followers.

From early on in his career, Newton understood the fact that if he were to reject the Cartesian view, he would have to articulate the ontological status of space in some way. Instead of conceding that space is some kind of substance or feature of some substance, he decided instead to proclaim—as we have already seen—that space has "its own manner of existing." What reason did Newton give for presenting such a radical view (even if it was to be found in Barrow and in Gassendi/ Charleton)? In an especially rich passage from *De Gravitatione*, Newton explains that space is not a substance

because it is not among the proper affections that denote substance, namely actions, such as thoughts in the mind and motions in body. For although philosophers do not define substance as an entity that can act upon things, yet everyone tacitly understands this of substances, as follows from the fact that they would readily allow extension to be substance in the manner of body if only it were capable of motion and of sharing in the actions of body. And on the contrary, they would hardly allow that body is substance if it could not move, nor excite any sensation or perception in any mind whatsoever.[32]

But Newton hastens to add that space is *also* not an accident inhering in a substance, for

we can clearly conceive extension existing without any subject, as when we may imagine spaces outside the world or place empty of any body whatsoever, and we believe [extension] to exist wherever we imagine there are no bodies, and we cannot believe that it would perish with the body if God should annihilate a body, it follows that [extension] does not exist as an accident inhering in some subject. And hence it is not an accident. And much less may it be said to be nothing, since it is something more than accident, and approaches more nearly to the nature of substance. There is no idea of nothing, nor has nothing any properties, but we have an exceptionally clear idea of extension by abstracting the dispositions and properties of a body so that there remains only the uniform and unlimited stretching out of space in length, breadth and depth.[33]

The negative view here is this: Space does not fit into either the substance or the accident category, for it lacks the actions definitive of substance (as tacitly assumed by philosophers who employ this

32 Newton, *Philosophical Writings*, 36.
33 Newton, *Philosophical Writings*, 36.

categorization, according to Newton).[34] It also lacks the dependence on another item characteristic of accidents. Yet it is not *nothing*: we have a clear representation of its features, which include uniformity and infinity. So space is *something*, but not a thing that fits into the standard ontology of Newton's day.

In *De Gravitatione*, Newton evidences an awareness of the peculiar status of space, struggling mightily to explain how something that is neither nothing nor a substance nor an accident can be properly understood by philosophers. He relies on various previous philosophical positions—including Henry More's Cambridge Platonist conception of space, which involves the confusing notions of "emanation" and "emanative effects"—that seem only to muddy the waters. It is promising to see Newton struggling to transcend what we might now regard as the limiting constraints of ontological theorizing in his day, but it is perhaps disappointing to see him conclude that space "is an emanative effect of the first existing being."[35] For the latter idea is simply unclear to many of his readers. Fortunately, by the time of the first edition of *Principia mathematica* in 1687, Newton decided to present his conception of space and time without recourse to these notions.

In the Scholium following the Definitions at the beginning of *Principia mathematica*—in the prefatory material, before book 1 begins—Newton does not tackle what we might call the ontological status of space as directly as he had done in *De Gravitatione*, just as he does not directly criticize the Cartesians by name, as he had done

---

34 This view represents another remarkable area of agreement between Leibniz and Newton: see the first paragraph of Leibniz's "Specimen Dynamicum" in *G. W. Leibniz: Philosophical Essays*, ed. Roger Ariew and Daniel Garber (Indianapolis, IN: Hackett, 1989), 118.

35 Much ink has been spilled in trying to grasp this fundamentally complex notion. See the classic debate between McGuire and Carriero: J. E. McGuire, "Predicates of Pure Existence: Newton on God's Space and Time," and John Carriero, "Newton on Space and Time: Comments on J. E. McGuire," both in *Philosophical Perspectives on Newtonian Science*, ed. Phillip Bricker and R. I. G. Hughes (New Haven, CT: Yale University Press, 1990). See also Howard Stein, "Newton's Metaphysics," in *The Cambridge Companion to Newton*, ed. I. B. Cohen and George Smith (Cambridge, UK: Cambridge University Press, 2002) for a nuanced interpretation of the claim about emanation.

earlier. There is little doubt, however, that he presents his view as an alternative to Descartes's conception, and that he presents certain aspects of space that have important consequences for how he thinks it should be regarded in ontological terms. Newton begins with an important proviso: the Scholium is preceded by a series of definitions that introduce "unfamiliar" terms, or concepts, to the reader, including what would then have been the novel notion of mass (importantly distinct from Descartes's own *quantitas materiae*, which is equal to the volume of a body) and that of centripetal force. But space, time, and motion are perfectly familiar terms and ideas, so Newton need not define them. On the other hand, he does indicate that it is common to think about these ideas solely with reference to "sense perception," a tendency he himself wishes to avoid. Hence the introduction of his famous trifold distinction: we must distinguish absolute and relative, true and apparent, mathematical and common, notions of space, time, and motion.

As with many famous philosophical conceptions, Newton's view is shrouded in misconceptions. Foremost among them is the idea that in the Scholium he is trying to "prove" that space is absolute; similarly, it is often said that Newton is arguing that space is absolute *rather than* relative. These ideas are misleading. In such cases, it behooves us to bracket the historically important interpretations of a text and return to its original wording: "Absolute space, of its own nature and without reference to anything external, always remains homogeneous and immovable. Relative space is any movable measure or dimension of this absolute space." This indicates right at the outset that relative space depends on absolute space, since the former is a "dimension" of the latter. Indeed, he adds, "Absolute and relative space are the same in species and in magnitude, but they do not always remain the same numerically."[36] Hence absolute and relative space are the same

---

36 Newton, *Philosophical Writings*, 84, for both quotations.

qualitatively—e.g., each is a three-dimensional magnitude, unlike time—but they may be distinct *numerically*. For instance, the relative space determined by the walls of my office is the same in species as that portion of absolute space with which it coincides, and at an instant it is numerically the same as that portion of absolute space with which it coincides. But as the earth rotates, the space of my office comes to coincide with another portion of absolute space, which means that they are distinct numerically.

Newton develops a conception of absolute space to assist us in understanding motion. If we have reason to believe—as Newton thinks we do, and as he makes clear in his arguments in *De Gravitatione*—that the true motion of body does not consist in a change of relations between the body and other bodies (whether they constitute its "vicinity" or not), then our question becomes: What, then, does it consist in? Newton suggests that true motion is not relative motion but rather absolute motion: a body that is truly moving may or may not alter its relations to any other body, so its motion should be understood instead as involving a change in its place. But since the relative space that a body occupies may itself move, we should not be tempted to conceive of the body's true motion in terms of its *relative* space; instead, we should conceive of it as a change in its *absolute* place. So true motion is absolute motion. And absolute motion, in turn, obviously involves the notion of absolute space. Newton is partly reassuring us here: we need to think of space as absolute to conceive of true motion in the right way, but we needn't worry about that idea because absolute space is the same in species and in magnitude as relative space. It is not a radically different sort of thing, despite its unfamiliarity to readers.

In regarding space as distinct from body, *pace* Descartes and Hobbes, and in considering space to have certain features—such as immovability—independent of anything external to it, Newton was primed also to focus his attention on the structure of space itself, much as he attended to the structure of time. He writes:

Just as the order of the parts of time is unchangeable, so, too, is the order of the parts of space. Let the parts of space move from their places, and they will move (so to speak) from themselves. For times and spaces are, as it were, the places of themselves and of all things. All things are placed in time with reference to order of succession and in space with reference to order of position. It is of the essence of spaces to be places, and for primary places to move is absurd. They are therefore absolute places, and it is only changes of position from these places that are absolute motions.[37]

For readers of Newton's text who are sympathetic to Cartesianism, or perhaps to Hobbes's views, places within space are defined by the objects that occupy them, or perhaps by relations among them (e.g., a place might be defined as lying a certain distance from the surface of some body). Newton's absolute space, in contrast, has a certain inherent structure independent of any objects that occupy it. That structure consists in an infinite series of places that bear essential location: to be a particular place just is to inhabit a certain location within absolute space, and such a place is immovable in the sense that it would not be itself if it were to be located somewhere else. According to this conception, objects are not placed within space in virtue of bearing some relation to other objects—say, being a certain distance from some centrally located object—but rather in virtue of inhabiting a particular locale, which latter is part of the inherent structure of space. We know that space's structure is inherent to it, finally, because space remains homogeneous and immovable independently of everything else, so there is no event involving objects and their relations with one another—causal relations or spatial—that can alter space itself. By 1687, then, space and its structure had become a significant topic of philosophical investigation.

---

37 Newton, *Philosophical Writings*, 86.

Although Newton certainly helped to ensure that space and its structure would remain important topics of philosophical analysis for the foreseeable future, that fact does not entail that his readers and interlocutors were prepared to endorse his distinction between absolute and relative space. More precisely, although some were happy to concede the usefulness of that distinction, many insisted that the very idea of absolute space is problematic. With such a view comes a host of questions, even if we evade common misconceptions. Consider my office again: We do not encounter much trouble in thinking about the things in my office—the books, the desk, the chair, the pens, and so on—nor even when considering the air that fills my office, but the relative space in which all of these things coexist is a bit more difficult to grasp. What sort of thing is it? Newton does not directly tell us; unlike the extensive discussion in *De Gravitatione*, he neither affirms nor denies that the relative space of my office is a substance, an accident, an emanative effect, or anything else. We merely know that whatever it is, it is the same in species and in magnitude as absolute space. But that merely kicks the can down the road, for what sort of thing is absolute space? Newton seems to think: My readers will not have much trouble in understanding what relative space is—he mentions, but does not clarify, such items as "the space of our air"—and so if I indicate that absolute space is the same in species and magnitude, then they will understand what it is, too. Unlike relative spaces, however, absolute space is immovable—since the things in my office which are definitive of the relative space of my office can move, including its walls, so too can the space of my office—and it remains homogeneous. In this sense, we know two of the properties that absolute space has, but Newton decides against any explanation of its ontological status, so we are left wondering whether it is a kind of substance, a property, or something else.

The conjunction of Newton's bold proclamations about absolute space, coupled with his refusal to articulate the proper ontological conception of such space, led to serious objections. Leibniz led the charge.

As we have seen, Leibniz certainly concurred with Newton that space and its structure require substantial analysis—and perhaps that they had been neglected by earlier figures such as Descartes and Hobbes—but he insisted throughout his long career that the Newtonian conception of space led to a series of serious philosophical errors. Leibniz's most extensive debate with the Newtonians concerning space and time would not occur until the very end of his life: his celebrated correspondence with Samuel Clarke, Newton's parish priest, friend, and supporter in London, is his most famous interaction with the Newtonians, occurring right before his death in 1716.[38] Leibniz fomented the correspondence in November 1715 by sending a pithy, provocative letter to Princess Caroline of Wales, one designed to provoke a response from Newton's circle in London.[39] Leibniz's letters to Clarke are methodologically characteristic: he leaves much of his own systematic and complex metaphysical theorizing—including the monadology—in the background, bringing to the fore only those elements that are both necessary for his criticisms of the Newtonians and also likely to garner

---

38 The exchange first appeared as G. W. Leibniz and Samuel Clarke, *A Collection of Papers which passed between the late Learned Mr. Leibnitz, and Dr. Clarke, in the Years 1715 and 1716* (London: Knapton, 1717, and it was reprinted many times in various editions.

39 Why did Clarke respond on Newton's behalf, and what was Newton's actual role in the correspondence? These questions continue to puzzle scholars; see, e.g., I. B. Cohen and Alexandre Koyré, "Newton and the Leibniz-Clarke Correspondence," *Archives Internationales d'Histoire Des Sciences* 15 (1962): 63–126; Domenico Bertoloni Meli, "Caroline, Leibniz and Clarke," *Journal of the History of Ideas* 60 (1999): 469–86. There is no documentary evidence, such as letters, between Clarke and Newton indicating the contours of Newton's role; then again, at this time, since both men lived in London and Clarke was Newton's parish priest, the lack of letters or other papers is unsurprising. That fact alone is intriguing, for the theological differences between the two are salient: since Newton was a committed anti-Trinitarian—a fact known to Locke and others, such as William Whiston, Newton's successor in the Lucasian Professorship at Cambridge (see James Force, *William Whiston: Honest Newtonian* [Cambridge, UK: Cambridge University Press, 1985])—he may have decided that Leibniz's contentions about "natural religion" in England would best be answered by Clarke, a rising star in the Church at that time and clearly a formidable theological thinker. On the other hand, Clarke himself was certainly not an orthodox Anglican thinker—his *Scripture-Doctrine of the Trinity* of 1712 was read by some as showing at least some sympathy for Unitarian ideas—so he was not an unproblematic figure in this regard. Perhaps just as important, Clarke was a serious metaphysician, a more systematic philosopher than Newton, as was evident from his *Demonstration of the Being and Attributes of God* of 1704. He was therefore in a position to engage Leibniz on metaphysical territory, writing in depth about such issues as the principle of sufficient reason, which Newton apparently did not take seriously.

support from Clarke. Thus the key to many of Leibniz's criticisms is the principle of sufficient reason, which he knows Clarke will endorse, although with a distinct conception of its scope. Leibniz asserts, while Clarke denies, that the principle demands that each act of divine willing requires a reason; for Clarke, divine willing itself is reason enough for some physical state of affairs to obtain.

Leibniz argues in particular that absolute space is incompatible with the principle of sufficient reason, if the latter is properly understood:

> I have many demonstrations to confute the fancy of those who take space to be a substance or at least an absolute being. But I shall only use, at present, one demonstration, which the author here gives me occasion to insist upon. I say, then, that if space were an absolute being, something would happen for which it would be impossible that there should be a sufficient reason—which is against my axiom. And I prove it thus: space is something absolutely uniform, and without the things placed in it, one point of space absolutely does not differ in any respect whatsoever from another point of space. Now from this it follows (supposing space to be something in itself, besides the order of bodies among themselves) that it is impossible there should be a reason why God, preserving the same situations of bodies among themselves, should have placed them in space after one certain particular manner and not otherwise—why everything was not placed the quite contrary way, for instance, by changing east into west. But if space is nothing else but this order or relation, and is nothing at all without bodies but the possibility of placing them, then those two states, the one such as it is now, the other supposed to be the quite contrary way, would not at all differ from one another. Their difference therefore is only to be found in our chimerical supposition of the reality of space.[40]

---

40 See Leibniz and Clarke, *A Collection of Papers*, L 3:5.

Leibniz is clever: he eschews the thorny problem of determining whether Newton's idea of absolute space commits him to thinking of space as a substance by presupposing only that Newton thinks of space as existing independently of objects and their relations. If space is indeed independent in this way, then it would seem that God faces a choice: when creating the world, why place the earth in one particular part of space rather than any other? The parts of space, independently of objects and relations, do not differ from one another in any salient respect, so it would seem that one could not even theoretically devise a reason for placing the earth anywhere in particular, as opposed to anywhere else in particular.[41] But since space with all its places exists independently of everything else, then God must have some reason to place the earth in one place rather than another.[42]

More important, just as the structure of space—for instance, the fact that it is constituted by places with inherent locations—is significant for Newton's discussion in the Scholium, it is crucial in Leibniz's argument against the conception of space in that very text. For it is key to Leibniz's case in his third letter to Clarke that independently of the objects that exist, space is uniform throughout. The conjunction of Newton's idea about space's structure with Leibniz's idea can be difficult to grasp. On the one hand, as Newton says, space itself consists of a series of places that differ from one another solely by their locations, which latter must be essential to those places, since they lack other

41 This argument does not depend on our having the capacity to refer to places within empty space.

42 Leibniz avoids this problem by asserting that space is nothing above the objects in the world and all possible relations among them (hence he holds a kind of *modal* relationalist view, in more modern terminology). For him, God faces no problematic choice, since space does not exist prior to the creation of material objects: to create objects with spatial relations is ipso facto to create space. (To create the Prussian Army, one merely needs to create all its horses and soldiers and weapons, etc.) Clarke's reply to this argument is disappointing: he blocks Leibniz's inference by denying that the divine will must have a reason to place the earth in one place rather than another (Leibniz and Clarke, *A Collection of Papers*, C 3:5). The principle of sufficient reason is not violated in this case, according to Clarke's interpretation of it, because it requires only this: if the earth appears in one place rather than another, there must be a reason that it appears there, and the reason in this case is simply the divine will; there is no further question about why the divine being made a particular choice rather than another.

differentiating features. On the other hand, as Leibniz says, since the places within space lack other features, space itself is uniform: there is no substantive difference between one place (over here) and another (over there). But do the sole features that places seem to have—viz., their inherent locations—count as a substantive difference? Leibniz is counting on the fact that they do not. And if he is right, then he can accept Newton's construal of space's structure as philosophically harmless. Similarly, there is presumably no reason for Newton to deny Leibniz's view that space itself is uniform.

It therefore turns out that Leibniz and Newton actually concur on the *structure* of space. Where they differ is on the philosophical implications of space's structure. Leibniz speaks of the Newtonians as endorsing "the reality of space," which he regards as "chimerical." According to Leibniz, whereas ordinary physical objects are discrete, constituted by their parts with internal distinctions among those parts, space and time are continuous and homogeneous. Leaving aside the deeper metaphysical level of monads, as Leibniz does when corresponding with Clarke, he means that it is physical objects that are the real things; space and time are merely "ideal," abstract entities whose continuity and homogeneity signal this special status. For his part, Newton accepts the idea that space is continuous and homogeneous but denies that these facts signal space's special metaphysical status. Space is neither a substance nor an accident, nor does it supervene on material objects and their relations; it has "its own manner of existing." Leibniz and his followers were never prepared to endorse this idea.

The dispute between Leibniz and Newton regarding space helped to determine the fortunes of space in the philosophical eighteenth century. The criticisms of Newton were widespread and nonpartisan: philosophers from Berkeley and Du Châtelet to Kant joined the chorus of critics. The key to understanding these criticisms is to grasp the precise nature of their connection with the substance/property ontology that many philosophers still assumed in this time period. Berkeley, Du Châtelet, Leibniz, and Kant did not reject Newton's view of absolute space because he fails to articulate a conception of how space fits into a substance/property framework; rather, they contended that if Newton were to insist that space is absolute in the sense of being distinct from body, and also distinct from objects and their relations—not to mention distinct from any set of relative spaces—then he would face a special problem, one that his Cartesian predecessors and Leibnizian interlocutors did not face. If space is not a relation, a network of relations, a body, or even something that supervenes on bodies or relations, then it certainly seems as if it must be some kind of being in its own right. But what kind of being is it? Few philosophers were satisfied with the possible answers to that question.

However, it is unfair to Leibniz to portray him as historically and philosophically important solely for his role as Newton's (and especially Clarke's) critic. It is tempting to argue that Newton placed space itself on the philosophical agenda in 1687 with his remarks in the Scholium following the Definitions before book 1 of *Principia mathematica*, and that Leibniz kept space on the agenda through his criticisms of that view in numerous venues, especially his correspondence with Clarke in 1715–16. Tempting, but unfair. It is more accurate to say that Leibniz and Newton each found Cartesian physics to be hampered by its identification of space and body and by its failure to recognize the importance of inertia for understanding motion; to understand motion through the lens of inertia, in turn, requires one to think about space itself in new ways. It is Leibniz's recognition of the shortcomings of the Cartesian approach, as much as his dislike of Newton's specific method for overcoming those shortcomings, that helps to show the importance of philosophical analyses of space to his eighteenth-century readers and followers.

Nonetheless, it is obviously difficult to overstate Newton's importance for these developments. He articulated a conception of space, time, and motion that was extremely fertile for physics, but considered highly problematic within metaphysics. (The story of what happened to that conception in the eighteenth century is told in the chapter in this volume by Michael Friedman.) This combination is more significant than it might seem. Had Newton's conception been useless for further developments in physics, it might have died on the vine. Had it been useful for physics but metaphysically unobjectionable, it might have merited no further debate. As it turned out, however, this conception helped to ensure that the representation of space, its structure, and its status, remained significant topics of philosophical dispute for the rest of the modern period.[43]

43 For very helpful conversations that substantially altered my argument in this paper, I would like to thank Mary Domski, David Marshall Miller, Vincenzo De Risi, and David Sanford. All translations are my own unless otherwise noted.

Reflection

CHEMICAL LABORATORY AND THE COSMIC SPACE

Mi Gyung Kim

The laboratory has become an indispensable site for the
production and legitimation of scientific knowledge. It
symbolizes modern science and our capacity for an artful
manipulation of nature that produces an environment built
with hybrid things—artificial things that are accepted as
natural. The laboratory works as a contact zone between
the natural and the artificial to forge intelligible sciences. Its
historical development in step with the material practice of
early modern chemistry thus merits a serious consideration in
understanding representations of modern science and their
claims to the truth of nature. The architecture of knowledge-
producing space also reflects the changing identities of scientific
fields and their practitioners.[1]

The chemical laboratory was stabilized as a well-demarcated
space with specialized instruments and techniques in the late
sixteenth century. Its emergence as the space designed for a

---

1 Peter Galison and Emily Thompson, eds., *The Architecture of Science* (Cambridge, MA: MIT Press, 1999).

Mi Gyung Kim, *Chemical Laboratory and the Cosmic Space*. In: *Space*. Edited by: Andrew Janiak, Oxford University Press (2020). © Oxford University Press.
DOI: 10.1093/oso/9780199914104.003.0011

systematic interrogation of the material world undermined, however, chemistry's symbolic connection with the cosmic space. While the elite astronomer Tycho Brahe (1546–1601) placed a chemical laboratory in the basement of his observatory (see Figure R5.1) to study the correspondence between celestial and terrestrial signs, the humanistic scholar Andreas Libavius (c. 1555–1616) designed his imagined chemical townhouse as a civic space that would socialize chemistry as public knowledge. Instead of toiling amid furnaces in a private hideaway to discern cosmic signs, the civic chemist had to maintain an upright household, strive for civic virtue, and participate in society as a free man living in "a body politic of strictest piety." He would arrange furnaces and vessels to display the virtues of their products in full light. A "truly liberal art" had to reveal "not their cosmic significance, but their benefits to mankind."[2] Where the laboratory was located and what it produced would shape chemists' social identity and chemistry's cognitive status in ascertaining the truth of nature, even if its symbolic design and internal division privileged alchemical thought and practice.[3] Libavius's *Alchemia* (1597), which sought to rehabilitate Paracelsian chemical medicine as public knowledge, appeared just a year after Johannes Kepler's *Cosmographic Mystery* (1596), which sought to legitimize the Copernican universe, albeit in mystical terms. In other words, chemistry as useful material knowledge had acquired a distinct social status different from that of astronomy by the turn of the seventeenth century.

---

2 Owen Hannaway, "Laboratory Design and the Aim of Science: Andreas Libavius versus Tycho Brahe," *Isis* 77, no. 4 (1986): 585–610. Also see Bruce T. Moran, *Andreas Libavius and the Transformation of Alchemy: Separating Chemical Cultures with Polemical Fire* (Sagamore Beach, MA: Science History Publications, 2007).

3 William R. Newman, "Alchemical Symbolism and Concealment: The Chemical House of Libavius," in *The Architecture of Science*, ed. Peter Galison and Emily Thompson (Cambridge, MA: MIT Press, 1999), 59–77.

FIGURE R5.1 Engraving from Tycho Brahe, *Astronomiae instauratae mechanica* (Wandsbeck, 1598).

The semipublic laboratory developed in tandem with the purpose-built theater in early modern Europe to constitute a new "space-time knot" that reflected the changing sociopolitical environment. As a space of performance, the laboratory conceptualized nature just as the theater theorized society. Their intense locality made far-flung places and esoteric objects interact in a space "shaped by human relationships with the built environment."[4] The laboratory not only helped articulate the ideal of science as useful knowledge but also configured an ideal polity for Francis Bacon (1561–1626), a statesman who wished to be "invested of that *triplicity* . . . ascribed to the ancient Hermes; the power and fortune of a King, the knowledge and illumination of a Priest, and the learning and universality of a Philosopher."[5] His effort to ground matters of policy on natural laws went beyond the observation and contemplation of nature to advocate a material intervention resembling the alchemist's. An ideal union of England and Scotland to form a peaceful Britannia without the possibility of sedition had to be like a chemical *Miltio*, or a perfect union in quality, rather than a physical *Compositio*, or a mere juxtaposition in place.[6] In the context of intensifying British imperial dreams, Bacon envisaged a utopian commonwealth organized as a research laboratory. In *New Atlantis* (1626), all inhabitants of Bensalem devote themselves to improving material knowledge for the benefit of their fellow citizens. The Salomon's House sets up experimental regions on the ground, underneath the surface, and in the air to enlarge "the bounds of Human Empire." An organized yet

---

4 John Shanahan, Ben Jonson's Alchemist and Early Modern Laboratory Space, *Journal for Early Modern Cultural Studies* 8, no. 1 (2008): 35–66.

5 This is how Bacon wished to characterize James I in his *Advancement of Learning* (1605); reprinted in Francis Bacon, *The Major Works*, ed. Brian Vickers (Oxford: Oxford University Press, 1996), 122.

6 Francis Bacon, *A briefe discourse, touching the happie vnion of the kingdomes of England, and Scotland Dedicated in private to his Maiesti* (London, 1603).

secret commerce of light (knowledge) helps manipulate nature
for humanity by collecting the sciences, arts, manufactures, and
inventions of all the world.[7] The ideal commonwealth as an efficient
laboratory lay at the hidden imperial center to organize the entire
globe as a knowledge space that would serve Bacon's lifelong goal of
philanthropia—not mere charity but a project of building an ideal
commonwealth or empire through a fundamental reform of the
knowledge system.[8] The stabilization of the chemical laboratory as
a civic or moral space weakened chemistry's immediate connection
to the cosmic space, then, while rehabilitating its social status in the
emergent civic order.

In the English Restoration context, leading scientists (*avant
la lettre*) such as Robert Boyle and Isaac Newton integrated
chemistry into their experimental or mathematical visions of
natural philosophy to establish a universal foundation of Anglican
theology.[9] Boyle's philosophical chemistry was meant to forge
a "confederacy" between chemists and corpuscularians in order
to dress up sooty chemical practice in the respectable language
of mechanical philosophy and thereby to transform speculative
natural philosophy into a "true" or experimental philosophy. The
laboratory in its capacity to create new phenomena challenged the
traditional space-time configuration of natural philosophy. In order
to curb the metaphysical discussion on the existence of "vacuum"—
the space entirely void of all material substances—Boyle redefined
it operationally (or physiologically) as a space in which no air
existed. The artificial space produced in the laboratory with a

7 Francis Bacon, *New Atlantis* (1626) in *The Major Works*, ed. Brian Vickers (Oxford: Oxford
   University Press, 1996), 457–89.
8 On the notion of knowledge space, see David Turnbull, "Cartography and Science in Early
   Modern Europe: Mapping the Construction of Knowledge Spaces," *Imago Mundi* 48, no. 1
   (1996): 5–24.
9 The term "scientist" was coined only in the 1830s. Thomas Holden, "Robert Boyle on Things above
   Reason," *British Journal for the History of Philosophy* 15, no. 2 (2007): 283–312.

special instrument—the air-pump—lent credence to a cosmic space that contained nothing, or the concept of space as a container, which would have resonated with the atomistic rather than the Cartesian natural philosophy. The Royal Society of London ran an active campaign to forge a vision of new or experimental philosophy that would "increase the powers of all mankind" and free them from "the bondage of errors." The "absolute perfection of the *true philosophy*" would require a path of "slow, and sure *experimenting*" à la Lord Bacon, for which chemists' labor (except for the alchemist's pursuit of the Philosopher's Stone) imparted "the noblest improvements." This rhetorical differentiation between chemistry and alchemy, which muted the perceived political subversion of the latter, allowed for the fellows of the Royal Society to appropriate the laboratory for a "true" philosophical project.[10] An assembly of gentlemen could direct, judge, conjecture, improve, and discourse upon the experiments to produce a consensus on the "matters of fact" and potentially on a parliamentary polity. True philosophy depended less on the speculative ontology of nature than on the epistemic and social practices in the laboratory.[11]

In Isaac Newton's mathematical natural philosophy, the interatomic chemical space became homologous to the cosmic space. While the Newtonian Synthesis in the conventional historiography refers to his mathematical homogenization of the Copernican universe with the notion of gravity,[12] Newton's own vision included experimental sciences to forge an integrated domain of Nature—the absolute space that was God's dominion

10 J. Andrew Mendelsohn, "Alchemy and Politics in England 1649–1665," *Past and Present* 135 (1992): 30–78.

11 Robert Boyle, "Some specimens of an attempt to make chymical experiments useful to illustrate the notions of the corpuscular philosophy," in *The Works of the Honourable Robert Boyle,* new ed., 6 vols. (London, 1772), 1:354–59; Thomas Sprat, *The History of the Royal Society of London, for the Improving of Natural Knowledge,* 2nd ed. (London, 1702); Steven Shapin and Simon Schaffer, *Leviathan and the Air-Pump* (Princeton, NJ: Princeton University Press, 1985).

12 Alexandre Koyré, *From the Closed World to the Infinite Universe* (New York: Harper, 1958).

and governed by uniform mathematical laws. In offering gravity
as the universal cause of all motions in *Principia* (1687), Newton
harbored a wish to "derive the rest of the phenomena of Nature
by the same kind of reasoning from mechanical [mathematical]
principles." He hoped that all actions in nature were governed
by the "attractions"—gravitational, magnetic, electrical, and
chemical—that would follow the same mathematical law. Just as
the long-distance interplanetary actions were governed by gravity,
the midrange interactions of magnetic and electric bodies might
be caused by the attractions that follow similar mathematical
laws. Chemical attractions at the atomic level would complete
this "analogy of nature"—that nature as God's dominion must be
simple and consonant to itself.[13] Newton's infinite universe was
organized by a set of forces that determined the distances between
the bodies, large and small. Their singular mathematical form—an
inverse square law—evinced the unity of God's design, while their
material manifestations regulated complex interactions between
bodies. The uniform law of attractions would guarantee the
homology between the infinite cosmic space and the infinitesimal
chemical space. Establishing the truth of natural religion—one
that would bolster the moral foundation of the British Empire—
required rehabilitating space and time as God's creation. After
a series of Boyle lectures that sought to reconcile Newtonian
philosophy and Anglican theology, the debate between Gottfried
Wilhelm Leibniz and Samuel Clarke took place in the context of
the Hanoverian succession, which raised the specter of Leibnizian
theodicy in the English political scene.[14]

---

13 Newton, *Opticks* (London, 1718), Query 31.

14 G. W. Leibniz and Samuel Clarke, *A Collection of Papers, which passed between the late learned Mr. Leibnitz, and Dr. Clarke, in the years 1715 and 1716* (London: Knapton, 1717); Steven Shapin, "Of Gods and Kings: Natural Philosophy and Politics in the Leibniz-Clarke Dispute," *Isis* 72, no. 2 (1981): 187–215.

Modern chemistry cultivated as useful knowledge (especially for medicine) did not realize Newton's or Leibniz's theological dreams. Instead, it became a science of making new material worlds. How chemists crafted symbolic spaces to represent the products of their labor is a complicated story, one that should alert us to the historicity of the chemical (and perhaps all scientific) bodies that make and remake our built environment and the ever-expanding chemical empire.[15] In Diderot and d'Alembert's *Encyclopédie*, the chemical laboratory was represented by an affinity table that organized the operations of "salts"—acids, alkalis, and their combinations (see Figure R5.2). The project of enlightened civic chemistry depended on chemists' capacity to organize and represent their sooty practice in a rational manner, even if the relationships (*rapports*) between chemical bodies were visualized through the alchemical symbols that offered a shorthand. The downward gaze from the well-lit laboratory that exposed neatly arranged chemical instruments to the table of affinities traced an itinerary of Nature's metamorphosis that produced useful knowledge. Such an orderly representation of chemical labor cultivated a new generation of chemists. Antoine-Laurent Lavoisier's vision of "a revolution in chemistry and physics," now known as the Chemical Revolution, did not simply consolidate a new theoretical structure for chemistry. It also projected a new ideal of the chemical laboratory. A modern science of chemistry would depend on the metric (barometric, thermometric,

15 Mi Gyung Kim, "Labor and Mirage: Writing the History of Chemistry," *Studies in History and Philosophy of Science* 26 (1995): 155–65; Mi Gyung Kim, "Constructing Symbolic Spaces: Chemical Molecules in the Académie des Sciences," *Ambix* 43, no. 1 (1996): 1–31; Mi Gyung Kim, "A Historical Atlas of Objectivity," *Modern Intellectual History* 6, no. 3 (2009): 569–96.

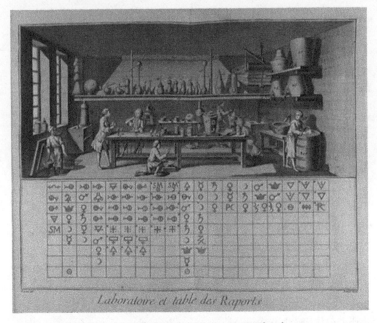

Laboratoire et table des Raports

FIGURE R5.2 Illustration of the laboratory in Diderot's *Encyclopedie*.

gasometric, calorimetric, etc.) measurements that would
produce an algebraic representation of nature. [16] In other words,
chemistry came to partake in the mathematical representation
of nature and, as such, allowed for the pursuit of intellectual
nobility in the laboratory. Jacques-Louis David's portrait of the
Lavoisiers (see Figure R5.3), set in a neoclassical space littered
with shiny brass instruments, was emblematic of chemists' new
social status as masters of the material world, divorced from
their cosmic speculations. Madame Lavoisier stares boldly out
of the canvas to assert her formative presence in crafting the
new chemistry that offered a mathematical representation of

16 Mi Gyung Kim, *Affinity, That Elusive Dream: A Genealogy of the Chemical Revolution* (Cambridge,
MA: MIT Press, 2003).

FIGURE R5.3 Jacques-Louis David, *Antoine-Laurent Lavoisier and Marie-Anne-Pierrette Paulze* (1788).

material actions by traversing between the metric laboratory and the luxurious salon. The material and social triumph of philosophical chemistry irreversibly loosened its connection to cosmographic mystery.

CHAPTER SIX

Space in Kantian Idealism

Michael Friedman

The concept of space is crucially involved in Kant's characteristic form of idealism, which he calls "transcendental" idealism. This doctrine, in the present context, can be thought of as consisting of four interrelated theses. First, the representation of space is a pure or a priori *intuition* belonging to the faculty of sensibility, not a *concept* belonging to the understanding or intellect. Second, the pure intuition of space is the a priori *form* of our perception of outer objects or bodies. Third, this same pure intuition is the primary source of the (synthetic) a priori science of geometry. Fourth, space, together with the outer objects (bodies) perceived within it, has no other reality apart from our pure form of (outer) intuition; neither space nor bodies exist *in themselves* independently of our subjective (characteristically human) form of (outer) perception.[1]

---

1 For Kant there are two forms of (human) sensibility: space and time; the first is the form of what he calls *outer* sense, the second of what he calls *inner* sense. Although the focus of this essay is

Michael Friedman, *Space in Kantian Idealism*. In: *Space*. Edited by: Andrew Janiak, Oxford University Press (2020). © Oxford University Press.
DOI: 10.1093/oso/9780199914104.003.0012

This doctrine, especially the fourth thesis, flies in the face of common sense. What could it possibly mean to say that space—the very same space in which we, along with all other physical bodies, live and move and have our being—has no real existence apart from the subjective constitution of the human mind? The main point of the present essay is that Kant's conception of space (and thus his transcendental idealism) can be properly understood only against the background of what he took to be the central intellectual debate of the eighteenth century between Newton (and his followers) and Leibniz (and his followers). In the *Critique of Pure Reason* (1781/1787) Kant's principal arguments for transcendental idealism—with respect to space, on the one side, and the outer objects (bodies) contained with it, on the other—are found, respectively, in the Transcendental Aesthetic and the (First and Second) Antinomies.[2] Both of these texts, I argue, should be read in relation to Kant's understanding of the debate between Newtonians and Leibnizians.

The Transcendental Aesthetic begins by posing the main question to be addressed:

What now are space and time? Are they actual beings? Are they only determinations or even relations of things, but still such as would also pertain to them in themselves, even if they were not intuited? Or are they such as to attach only to the form of intuition alone, and thus to the subjective constitution of our mind, without which these predicates can be attributed to no things at all? (A23/B37–38)

---

primarily on the former, the relationship between space and time will turn out to be centrally important as well.

2 All references to Kant's writings, except for the *Critique of Pure Reason*, are to volume and page numbers of the Akademie edition of *Kant's gesammelte Schriften* (Berlin: de Gruyter, 1902–); the *Critique of Pure Reason* is cited by the standard A/B pagination of the first and second editions. All translations are my own. The translations of Kant's writings in *The Cambridge Edition of the Works of Immanuel Kant*, under the general editorship of Paul Guyer and Allen W. Wood, use this citation system in the margins.

It seems clear that Kant takes the first alternative to be Newtonian, the second to be Leibnizian, and the third to be his own. Kant takes these alternatives to be exclusive and exhaustive, so that eliminating the first two leaves only the Kantian view still standing.[3]

One of the principal arguments of the Aesthetic appeals to the synthetic a priori status of the science of geometry. Our knowledge of geometry, Kant assumes, is both a priori and nonanalytic. So neither logic nor conceptual analysis can explain the character of this knowledge. Our representation of space, therefore, cannot be a concept, and so, for Kant, it can only be an intuition—which, since the knowledge in question is (assumed to be) a priori, can only be a *pure* intuition pertaining to the form of our outer perception.[4] The clearest presentation of this argument occurs in the Transcendental Exposition of Space added to the Aesthetic in the second (1787) edition:

> Geometry is a science that determines the properties of space synthetically and yet a priori. What must the representation of space then be in order that such a cognition from it may be possible? It must originally be intuition; for no propositions can be inferred from a mere concept that go beyond the concept, which nevertheless takes place in geometry (Introduction V). But this intuition must be found in us a priori, i.e., prior to all perception of an object, and must be pure, not empirical intuition. For geometrical propositions are all apodictic, i.e., bound up with the consciousness of their necessity: e.g., space has only three dimensions; such propositions,

---

3 This reading of the three alternatives (Newtonian, Leibnizian, and Kantian) is not particularly controversial; we shall find strong confirmation for it in what follows.

4 Here Kant is depending on a fundamental distinction between the form and matter of intuition (A20/B34): "I call that in the appearance which corresponds to sensation its *matter*, but that which brings it about that the manifold of appearances can be ordered in certain relations I call the *form* of appearance. Since that within which sensations can alone be ordered and arranged in a certain form cannot itself be sensation in turn, the matter of all appearance, to be sure, is only given to us a posteriori, but its form must already lie ready for it in the mind a priori and can therefore be considered separately from all sensation."

however, cannot be empirical or judgements of experience, nor can
they be inferred from them (Introduction II). (B40–41)

And the obvious conclusion, for Kant, is his own doctrine of transcendental idealism (B41):

> Now how can an outer intuition dwell in the mind that precedes
> the objects themselves and in which the concept of the latter can
> be a priori determined? Obviously not otherwise except in so far as
> it has its seat merely in the subject, as its formal constitution to be
> affected by objects, and thereby to acquire an *immediate representa-*
> *tion*, i.e., *intuition*, of them, and thus only as the form of outer *sense*
> in general.

This conclusion, however, has seemed far from obvious to many
commentators, extending back to Kant's contemporaries. For it seems
that, even if we accept all of Kant's premises, the argument establishes
only the epistemological claim that the primary source of geometrical
knowledge (in both pure and applied geometry) is our pure form of
outer intuition. It does not yet establish the ontological claim that
space just is the pure form of our outer intuition and (together with
the outer objects perceived therein) has no existence in itself independently of this form. There remains a large gap, in other words, between our representation of space and space itself, and it seems that
Kant has simply neglected the alternative that space might be both the
form of our outer intuition and the form of the genuinely real (outer)
objects that exist independently of the human mind.[5] In order fully
to understand why Kant thought that his conclusion followed "obviously" from his premises, we must better appreciate the sense in which

---

5 For discussion of this famous "neglected alternative" objection and its history, see H. E. Allison,
   Kant's Transcendental Idealism: An Interpretation and Defense (New Haven, CT: Yale University
   Press, 1983); revised and enlarged edition (2004), chapter 5, §C.

he took the three alternatives with which he began (A23/B37–38) to be exclusive and exhaustive.[6]

Further light is shed on the transition from epistemological to ontological claims by what Kant says later in the Aesthetic. The crucial passage begins as follows:

> Those who assert the absolute reality of space and time, whether they assume this as subsistent or only as inherent, must be in conflict with the principles of experience themselves. For, if they include themselves within the first (which is commonly the party of the mathematical investigators of nature), then they must assume two eternal and infinite non-things [*Undinge*] subsisting in themselves (space and time), which are there (without there being anything actual), only in order to contain all actuality within themselves. If they choose the second party (that of some metaphysical students of nature), for whom space and time are taken to be relations between appearances (next to or after one another), abstracted from experience, although in the abstraction represented confusedly, then they must contest the a priori validity of mathematical doctrines in relation to actual things (e.g., in space), or at least contest their apodictic certainty, in so far as this can in no way take place a posteriori; and the a priori concepts of space and time, according to their view, are only creatures of the imagination, whose source must actually be sought in experience, from whose abstracted relations the imagination has made something, which indeed contains the generality of [these relations], but which cannot take place without

6 There is a suggestion of these alternatives at the very end of the argument of the Transcendental Exposition (B41): "Thus only our explanation makes the *possibility of geometry* conceivable as a synthetic a priori cognition. Any mode of explanation that does not provide this, even if it may have the appearance of being similar to ours, can therefore be distinguished from ours with the highest degree of certainty." The relevant (possible) explanations, as we shall see, are provided by the Newtonian, Leibnizian, and Kantian alternatives.

the restrictions that nature has connected with them. (A39–40/ B56–57)

We know from Kant's earlier works—especially the *Physical Monadology* (1756) and *Inaugural Dissertation* (1770)—that by "mathematical investigators of nature" he means Newtonians and by "metaphysical students" he means Leibnizians.[7] So the parties in question have now been explicitly identified, along with the two alternatives to Kant's own position described at the beginning of the Aesthetic.[8] Kant's position emerges as the only remaining alternative to the Newtonian and Leibnizian positions in the remainder of our passage:

The first gain this much, that they make the field of appearances free for mathematical assertions. On the other hand, they confuse themselves very much by precisely these conditions when the understanding pretends to extend beyond this field. The latter gain much in the latter respect, namely, the representations of space and time do not get in the way when they wish to judge of objects not as appearances but merely in relation to the understanding; however, they can neither give an account of the possibility of a priori mathematical cognitions (in so far as they lack a true and objectively valid a priori intuition) nor bring empirical propositions into necessary agreement with these [mathematical] assertions. In our theory of the true constitution of these two original forms of sensibility both difficulties are remedied. (A40–41/B57–58)

---

7 For discussion of these earlier works in relation to our passages from the Aesthetic, see Michael Friedman, *Kant's Construction of Nature: A Reading of the Metaphysical Foundations of Natural Science* (Cambridge, UK: Cambridge University Press, 2013), 11–17.

8 Those who assert the "absolute reality" of space and time are just those who deny transcendental idealism. And there are exactly two ways in which such "absolute reality" may be asserted (of space and time): either as "actual beings" (A23/B37), i.e., as "subsistent," or as "determinations or even relations of things" (A23/B37), i.e., as "inherent" (insofar as "determinations or even relations" must inhere in substances).

Kant's position not only explains the special character of our mathematical knowledge; it also overcomes the overwhelming difficulties faced by the only extant alternatives. Yet there are a number of points in this passage that are by no means immediately clear.

It is clear enough why the Newtonians "make the field of appearances free for mathematical assertions" (A40/B57). For their absolute space is in itself pure and entirely empty of appearances (i.e., physical bodies), so that its mathematical properties can in principle be known a priori and with full mathematical precision.[9] But how exactly do they "confuse themselves very much . . . when the understanding pretends to extend beyond this field [of appearances]" (A40/B57)? Kant formulates his point more explicitly in a comment added to the second addition toward the end of the Aesthetic:

> In natural theology, where one thinks an object that is not only no object of sensible intuition for us, but cannot even be an object of sensible intuition for itself, one takes care to remove the conditions of space and time from all of its intuition (for all of its cognition must be intuition and not *thought*, which is always a manifestation of limitations). But with what right can one do this, if one has previously made both into forms of things in themselves—and, indeed, into forms which, as a priori conditions of the existence of things, even remain when one has annihilated the things themselves? (For, as conditions of all existence in general, they must also be conditions for the existence of God.) There is therefore no alternative, if one does not pretend to make them into objective forms of all things, except to make them into subjective forms of our outer and inner mode of intuition. [This kind of intuition] is called sensible, because it is *not original*—i.e., it is not such that the existence of objects of

---

9 In other words, Newtonian absolute space pertains to the *form* rather than the *matter* of the bodies (Kantian outer appearances) contained within it; its structure, therefore, is in principle capable of a priori cognition in Kant's sense (see note 3).

intuition is itself given through it (which, as far as we can comprehend, can only pertain to the primordial being), but it depends on
the existence of the objects, and is thus only possible in so far as the
representative faculty of the subject is affected by them. (B71–72)[10]

Here the primary "confusions" at issue arise from the Newtonian doctrine of divine omnipresence, which is indeed very hard to avoid if one
assumes that space and time are "two eternal and infinite non-things
subsisting in themselves . . . which are there (without there being anything actual), only in order to contain all actuality within themselves"
(A39/B56)—i.e., if one attributes to space and time the attributes of
God's immensity and eternity.[11]

Kant's description of the Leibnizian view, however, is considerably
more puzzling. Are not the fundamental entities, on this view, non-
spatiotemporal simple substances or monads, such that space and time
(as ideal "well-founded phenomena") are then possible as arising from
the purely intellectual relations of coexistence and (internal) causation
holding among these substances and between their own (internal)

---

10 God's knowledge must be intuitive, for Kant, because only this kind of knowledge is *immediate*. Discursive or conceptual thought, by contrast, is always *mediate*, insofar as it depends on
matter given from without (i.e., in intuition) for its content. If space had absolute reality in the
Newtonian sense, therefore, it would be a (transcendentally) objective form of the existence of
all things. But since this leads to absurd consequences (the existence of God in space), only the
Kantian alternative remains. Note that here—and in the related passage earlier in the Aesthetic
(A39–41/B56–58)—Kant does not object to the Newtonian conception on the grounds that if
space were (transcendentally) objective and independent of the human mind a priori cognition of
it would be problematic; he saves this kind of objection instead for the Leibnizian conception.

11 See the General Scholium added to the second edition of the *Principia*, I. Newton, *The
Principia: Mathematical Principles of Natural Philosophy*, ed. and trans. I. Bernard Cohen and
Anne Whitman, assisted by Julia Budenz (Berkeley: University of California Press, 1999): "[The
true God] is not eternity and infinity, but eternal and infinite; he is not duration and space, but
he endures and is present. He endures always and is present everywhere, and by existing always
and everywhere he constitutes duration and space." The Newtonian doctrine of divine omnipresence is a central point of contention in the Leibniz-Clarke correspondence. For an extended discussion of the relationship between Kant's transcendental idealism and this Newtonian doctrine,
see Michael Friedman, "Newton and Kant on Absolute Space: From Theology to Transcendental
Philosophy," in *Constituting Objectivity: Transcendental Perspectives on Modern Physics*, ed. M.
Bitbol, P. Kerszberg, and J. Petitot (Berlin: Springer, 2009), 35–50.

states? And, if so, why should this view be understood as concerned with "relations between *appearances* ... abstracted from experience, although in the abstraction represented confusedly" (A40/B56–57; emphasis added)?[12] Why, accordingly, must the Leibnizians "contest the a priori validity of mathematical doctrines in relation to actual things (e.g., in space), or at least contest their apodictic certainty, in so far as ... the a priori concepts of space and time, according to their view, are only creatures of the imagination, whose source must actually be sought in experience" (A40/B57)?[13]

The specific target of Kant's criticism emerges more clearly in his remark to the antithesis of the Second Antinomy, which concerns the infinite divisibility of matter in space:

> Against this proposition of the infinite division of matter, the ground of proof of which is purely mathematical, the *monadists* have brought forward objections—which, however, already make them objects of suspicion, in that they are not willing to grant that the clearest mathematical proofs are insights into the constitution of space, in so far as it is in fact the formal condition of the possibility of all matter, and they rather view [these proofs] as only inferences from abstract yet arbitrary concepts, which cannot be applied to real things. ... If one listens to [these monadists], then one would have

12 One of the best-known passages in the Leibniz-Clarke correspondence, §47 of Leibniz's Fifth Letter, describes how something like the Newtonian conception of absolute space arises by abstraction from our observation of the relative positions and motions of bodies. What is explained there, however, is not geometrical space but rather space as a dynamical framework for describing the motions and interactions (forces) of bodies; it therefore concerns the relationship between space and time. This is important, as I shall explain later, because it turns out that the most fundamental difference between Leibniz's idealism and Kant's concerns the character of the dynamical framework in question.

13 On the view that space and time arise from the purely intellectual relations of coexistence and causation, holding among ultimate simple substances conceived purely intellectually, the system of relations in question would constitute a formal rather than material element of cognition in Kant's sense. It would therefore be capable, in principle, of a priori cognition. Kant could (and would) object that such a system cannot explain the (assumed) *synthetic* a priori status of our geometrical cognition; it is important to appreciate, however, that he does not make this objection here.

to think, aside from the mathematical point, which is not a part but merely the limit of a space, also physical points, which are indeed also simple, but have the advantage, as parts of the space, of filling it through their mere aggregation. (A439/B467)

These physical points—or physical monads—are thus simple and elementary material substances. As material substances, they are what Kant himself calls *bodies* and thus what Kant himself calls *appearances*. According to precisely the argument of the Second Antinomy, however, all such bodies in the Kantian sense must be infinitely divisible, since they are possible, for Kant, only within our pure intuition of space—which, in turn, is necessarily infinitely divisible in accordance with the "clearest mathematical proofs" (A439/B467).

For the monadists in question, by contrast, the ultimate simple substances or physical points are prior to the space they fill. They are then supposed to *constitute* this space "through their mere aggregation" (A440/B468). Here, however, the monadists that Kant is targeting run squarely into the problem of the composition of the continuum and, more specifically, into Zeno's metrical paradox of extension. According to this paradox, one can never attain an extended region of space by composing any number of unextended simple elements (points), not even an infinite number of such elements. The only way out, therefore, would be to take the elements out of which the space filled by a body is to be composed as merely very small extended regions (rather than unextended points) and, as a consequence, to deny the infinite divisibility of (physical) space. For one would otherwise run into the second horn of Zeno's metrical paradox, according to which an infinite number of extended (finite) elements could never compose a finite extended region (a body). Thus, the monadists that Kant is targeting here not only take the points out of which (physical) space is composed to be what he calls appearances—thereby making our knowledge of space a posteriori. They even go so far as to deny the evident mathematical proposition of infinite divisibility—thereby "contest[ing] the a priori validity of mathematical doctrines in relation to actual things" (A40/B57).[14]

Vincenzo De Risi has argued in detail that the monadists in question in the remark to the antithesis of the Second Antinomy include later representatives of the so-called Leibnizian-Wolffian philosophy, but not Leibniz himself.[15] Indeed, Kant is quite explicit, in the remark to the thesis of the Second Antinomy, that the monadists in question do not include Leibniz:

> I speak here only of the simple, in so far as it is necessarily given in the composite, in that the latter can be resolved into them as its constituents. The proper meaning of the word *Monas* (according to Leibnizean usage) should only extend to that simple which is *immediately* given as simple substance (e.g., in self-consciousness), and not as element of the composite—which one could better call the atom. And, since I want only to prove [the existence of] simple substances in relation to the composite, as its elements, I could call the thesis of the second antinomy transcendental *atomism*. However, because this word has already long been used for the designation of a particular mode of explaining corporeal appearances (molecularum), and therefore presupposes empirical concepts, [the thesis] may be called the dialectical principle of *monadology*. (A440–42/B468–70)[16]

---

14 Zeno's metrical paradox played an important role in eighteenth-century conceptions of space and matter more generally; for an illuminating treatment, including discussions of Kant and his contemporaries, see Thomas Holden, *The Architecture of Matter: Galileo to Kant* (Oxford: Clarendon Press, 2004). Edith Sylla has emphasized that these same problems played a corresponding role in arguments that were developed within the medieval Aristotelian-Scholastic tradition to the effect that the natures of real (physical) things cannot be characterized mathematically.

15 See Vincenzo De Risi, *Geometry and Monadology: Leibniz's Analysis Situs and Philosophy of Space* (Basel: Birkhäuser, 2007), 301–14, which discusses the work of Christian Wolff, Georg Bilfinger, and Alexander Baumgarten in this connection. De Risi is particularly concerned to contrast Leibniz's views on the composition of the continuum with those expounded in Christian Wolff, *Cosmologia generalis methodo scientifica pertractata* (Frankfurt: Renger, 1731); new emended edition, 1737.

16 De Risi considers this passage in the discussion just cited, along with the passages from the *Metaphysical Foundations of Natural Science* that I consider in the following pages.

Kant is clear, therefore, that properly Leibnizian monads are not to be conceived as physical points out of which bodies (together with the space they fill) are supposed to be composed. They are rather mind-like—*and therefore entirely nonspatial*—simple beings, which are given (at least to themselves) in immediate self-consciousness. To be sure, both space and physical bodies in space are in some sense derivative from these beings as ideal well-founded phenomena. In no sense, however, are they composed out of such beings.

It is even more striking, however, that when Kant treats the infinite divisibility of matter and space in the *Metaphysical Foundations of Natural Science* (1786), he not only distinguishes Leibniz from his Leibnizian-Wolffian followers but also explicitly appropriates him on behalf of Kantian idealism. In particular, in the second remark to the fourth proposition (demonstrating the infinite divisibility of material substance) of the Dynamics chapter, Kant appeals to the argument of the Second Antinomy to resolve a conflict concerning infinite divisibility between the "geometer" and the "metaphysician":

One would therefore have to conclude either, in spite of the geometer, that *space is not divisible to infinity*, or, to the annoyance of the metaphysician, that *space is not a property of a thing in itself*, and thus that matter is not a thing in itself, but merely an appearance of our outer senses in general, just as space is the essential form thereof. But here the philosopher is caught between the horns of a dangerous dilemma. To deny the first proposition, that space is divisible to infinity, is an empty undertaking; for nothing can be argued away from mathematics by sophistical hair-splitting. But viewing matter as a thing in itself, and thus space as a property of the thing in itself, amounts to the denial of this proposition. The philosopher therefore finds himself forced to deviate from this last proposition, however common and congenial to the common understanding it may be. (4, 506)

Thus the errors of the "metaphysician" need here to be corrected by
the (transcendental) "philosopher"—i.e., by transcendental idealism.[17]

More interesting, however, Kant proceeds to contrast the "metaphysical" view he is targeting with the views of a (not yet named)
"great man":

A great man, who has contributed perhaps more than anyone else
to preserving the reputation of mathematics in Germany, has frequently rejected the presumptuous metaphysical claims to over-
turn the theorems of geometry concerning the infinite divisibility
of space by the well-grounded reminder *that space belongs only to
the appearance of outer things*; but he has not been understood.
This proposition was taken to be asserting that space appears to us,
though it is otherwise a thing, or relation of things, in itself, but that
the mathematician considers it only as it appears. Instead, it should
have been understood as saying that space is in no way a property
that attaches in itself to any thing whatsoever outside our senses. It
is, rather, only the subjective form of our sensibility, under which
objects of the outer senses—with whose constitution in itself we
are not acquainted—appear to us, and we then call this appearance matter. Through this misunderstanding one went on thinking
of space as a property also attaching to things outside our faculty
of representation, but such that the mathematician thinks it only
in accordance with common concepts, that is, confusedly (for it
is thus that one commonly explicates appearance). And one thus
attributed the mathematical theorem of the infinite divisibility of
matter, a proposition presupposing the highest [degree of] clarity
in the concept of space, to a confused representation of space taken
as basis by the geometer—whereby the metaphysician was then free

17 Note that Kant is perfectly clear that his transcendental idealism runs counter to common sense,
but he takes himself to be "forced" into this position by (among other things) the argument of the
Second Antinomy.

to compose space out of points, and matter out of simple parts, and thus (in his opinion) to bring clarity into this concept. (4, 507)

Thus it is clear, in particular, that the "metaphysician" in question is essentially the same as the representative of the Leibnizian-Wolffian philosophy targeted in the Second Antinomy (A439/B467)—and also, it appears, in the passage contrasting Newtonians and Leibnizians in the Aesthetic (A39–41/B56–58).[18]

In the immediately following discussion Kant goes on to make it clear that the "great man" in question is none other than Leibniz himself:

The ground for this aberration lies in a poorly understood *monadology*, which has nothing at all to do with the explanation of natural appearances, but is rather an intrinsically correct *platonic* concept of the world devised by *Leibniz*, in so far as it is considered, not at all as object of the senses, but as thing in itself, and is merely an object of the understanding—which, however, does indeed underlie the appearances of the senses. . . . Therefore, Leibniz's idea [*Meinung*], so far as I comprehend it, was not to explicate space through the order of simple beings next to one another, it was rather to set this order alongside space as corresponding to it, but as belonging to a merely intelligible world (unknown to us). Thus he asserts nothing but what has been shown elsewhere: namely, that space, together with the matter of which it is the form, does not

---

18 It is clear that the "metaphysicians" targeted here are the same as those targeted in the remark to the antithesis of the Second Antinomy because of the emphasis in both passages on the infinite divisibility of space; moreover, according to the second passage just quoted (4, 507), the "metaphysician" goes on "to compose space out of points, and matter out of simple parts" (4, 507). The connection between the discussion in the *Metaphysical Foundations* and the corresponding discussion in the Aesthetic is that, in both, the space of the "metaphysician" is taken to attach to or be inherent in things in themselves, with the result that the representation of the "mathematician" becomes necessarily confused.

contain the world of things in themselves, but only their appearance, and is itself only the form of our outer sensible intuition. (4, 507–8)

Thus Kant here depicts Leibniz—against the Leibnizian-Wolffian "metaphysician"—as a defender of the Kantian doctrine of transcendental idealism.[19]

There are indeed strong similarities between Leibniz's idealism and Kant's. Leibniz, like Kant, considers two essentially distinct classes of entities: purely intellectual beings or noumena and purely sensible beings or phenomena. Space, for Leibniz, together with the matter or physical bodies that appear within it, is an ideal well-founded phenomenon rather than an ultimate metaphysical reality; moreover, its phenomenal status depends essentially on the perceptual relationships among the mind-like simple substances that constitute ultimate reality, as each such monad mirrors all the others from its own (perceptual) point of view. There is also no doubt that Kant's formulation of transcendental idealism is deeply indebted to his assimilation of Leibniz.[20] It is no wonder, then, that some of the most interesting and sophisticated recent interpretations of Leibniz emphasize the continuities

---

19 Robert DiSalle has suggested that Kant may here be describing his own earlier position in the *Inaugural Dissertation* ("On the Form and Principles of the Sensible and Intelligible [*intelligibilis*] Worlds") of 1770. This makes sense, because Kant both characterizes the realm of simple beings as a "merely intelligible world [*bloß intelligibeln Welt*]" (4, 508) and describes "Leibniz's idea" in terms that he himself can "comprehend" (4, 508). Note, however, that the view of the *Inaugural Dissertation* is quite distinct from Kant's mature or critical transcendental idealism, insofar as he had not yet (in 1770) found a bridge between pure intellectual concepts and our (spatiotemporal) sensibility: the so-called *schematism* of the pure concepts of the understanding. I shall return to this last point later.

20 Kant's assimilation of Leibniz's idealism underwent a long evolution, from the earliest works of his precritical period, such as the *New Exposition of the First Principles of Metaphysical Knowledge* (1755) and *Physical Monadology* (1756), through the *Inaugural Dissertation* (1770), to its culmination in the critical period in the *Critique of Pure Reason* (1781/1787). Fully understanding Kant's relationship to Leibnizian doctrines therefore involves not only distinguishing Kant's attitudes toward Leibniz and his Leibnizian-Wolffian followers, but also distinguishing the stages of Kant's own assimilation of Leibniz at various points in his intellectual development.

between the two thinkers and argue, in particular, for deep continuities between Leibniz's "phenomenalism" and Kant's.[21]

Nevertheless, Kant is very clear in other texts—especially in the Amphiboly of the Concepts of Reflection in the first *Critique*—that the properly Leibnizian conception of space differs quite fundamentally from his own. The most important difference comes under the heading of *matter* and *form*:

> In the concept of the pure understanding matter precedes form, and *Leibniz* consequently first assumed things (monads), together with an inner power of representation, in order afterwards to ground their external relations and the community of their states (namely, their representations) on this. Therefore, space and time were [thereby] possible—the former only through the relation of the substances, the latter through the connection of their determinations among one another as ground and consequence. This in fact is how it would have to be if the pure understanding could be related immediately to objects, and if space and time were determinations of things in themselves. If, however, they are only sensible intuitions, in which we determine all objects simply as appearances, then the form of intuition (as a subjective constitution of sensibility) precedes all matter (the appearances), and therefore space and time precede all appearances and all data of experience, and rather make them possible in the first place. (A267/B323)

Kant is describing the properly Leibnizian view that space and time arise from the purely intellectual relations between and determinations of the mind-like simple substances that constitute ultimate reality: space in terms of relations of coexistence among such substances, time from causal connections between their (individual)

---

21 See especially R. M. Adams, *Leibniz: Determinist, Theist, Idealist* (Oxford: Oxford University Press, 1994), and De Risi, *Geometry*.

determinations or (inner) states.[22] Kant is contrasting this conception of the sense in which space and time are well-founded phenomena with his own conception of them as pure forms of sensible intuition within which alone any substantial real object can be cognized in the first place—as what Kant himself calls an *appearance* (phenomenon) or *object of experience*.

The crucial point, for Kant, is that we can have (theoretical) cognition only of such appearances or objects of experience; (theoretical) cognition of noumena or things in themselves is completely impossible. For, in the absence of an already given spatiotemporal intuition within which to order and thereby determine such objects, the pure understanding on its own is capable of no (theoretical) cognition at all. Whereas I can certainly think objects of the pure understanding—such as God and the soul, for example—independently of spatiotemporal intuition, no such (noumenal) object can be (theoretically) cognized.[23] This is why, for the critical Kant, pure concepts of the understanding such as substance, causality, and community can play their proper role in (theoretical) cognition only if they are associated with what Kant calls spatiotemporal *schemata*: substance with the temporal relation of permanence, causality with the temporal relation of succession, community with the spatiotemporal relation of simultaneous (co)existence.

---

22 Again, this view should be sharply distinguished from the (Leibnizian-Wolffian) view that space is *composed* out of "physical points" (or physical monads) as its parts. De Risi, *Geometry*, is especially concerned to argue that Leibniz's more sophisticated approach to the problem of the composition of the continuum involves moving away from the traditional model of part-whole composition and toward the modern conception of abstract relations between elements in what we now take to be set-theoretic structures.

23 See the important footnote to the (second edition) Preface (Bxxvi): "In order to *cognize* an object it is required that I can prove its possibility (whether in accordance with the testimony of experience from its actuality or a priori through reason). But I can *think* whatever I wish, as long as I do not contradict myself—i.e., if my concept is only a possible thought, even if I cannot guarantee whether or not an object corresponds to it in the sum total of all possibilities." Kant indicates in the remainder of the note that one may be able to cognize such (supersensible) objects through reason from a practical as opposed to purely theoretical point of view—which is why I have inserted the qualifier "theoretically" in parenthesis. I shall return to Kant's conception of practical cognition at the end of this essay.

In the case of the concept of substance, in fact, Kant eventually arrives at an even stronger result. Not only must (phenomenal) substance be temporally extended (as permanent); it must be spatially extended as well—and so, by the argument of the Second Antinomy, it can neither be simple nor consist of ultimately simple (substantial) parts. Kant suggests this conclusion a few pages earlier in the Amphiboly, where he contrasts his own conception of the constitution of matter with Leibniz's monadic conception:

> Only that is internal in an object of pure understanding which has no relation at all (with respect to its existence) to anything different from itself. By contrast, the internal determinations of a *substantia phaenomenon* in space are nothing but relations, and it itself is nothing but a totality of mere relations. We are only acquainted with substance in space through forces that are active in space, either driving others into [this space] (attraction) or stopping their penetration into it (repulsion and impenetrability). We are acquainted with no other properties constituting the concept of a substance which appears in space and which we call matter. As object of the pure understanding, on the other hand, every substance must have internal determinations and powers, which pertain to [its] internal reality. However, what can I entertain as internal accidents except those which my inner sense presents to me—namely, that which is either itself a *thought* or is analogous to it? Therefore, Leibniz, after he had taken away everything that may signify an external relation, and therefore also *composition*, made of all substances, because he represented them as noumena, even the constituents of matter, simple substances with powers of representation—in a word, **monads**. (A265–66/B321–22)

Kant is here alluding to his critical conception of matter (and material substance) as filling the space that it occupies by the interplay of attractive and repulsive forces exerted at every point of the space in question. And it is precisely this conception that underlies the demonstration of infinite divisibility in the Dynamics chapter of the *Metaphysical Foundations*—which is followed, as explained earlier, by a (second) remark rejecting the Leibnizian-Wolffian doctrine of physical monads.[24]

This demonstration of infinite divisibility, moreover, plays an essential role in Kant's demonstration of the permanence of material substance in the second proposition of the following Mechanics chapter—the proposition that the total quantity of matter in the universe is necessarily conserved in all interactions of matter. And the latter proposition, in turn, plays an essential role in Kant's conception of how momentum or what he calls "mechanical moving force" is conserved in all interactions as well. The schematized category of substance is thereby connected to the schematized category of community or interaction, with the result that it is a sufficient condition for the existence of a causal interaction between two material substances that momentum (the product of quantity of matter and velocity) be conserved in the process of action and reaction.[25] Finally, since momentum between two gravitationally interacting bodies is necessarily so conserved, it becomes crystal clear, at this point, that the physics for

---

24 The first remark rejects Kant's own earlier conception in the *Physical Monadology*, according to which matter consists of ultimately simple monads that fill the space they occupy by attractive and repulsive forces exerted at only the central point of the space in question. Kant thereby arrived at a point-center atomism similar to that developed around the same time in Roger Boscovich, *Philosophiae Naturalis Theoria* (Prostat Viennae Austriae: Officina Libreria Kaliwodiana, 1758); trans. (from the first Venetian edition of 1763) J. M. Child (Cambridge MA; MIT Press, 1966). Kant's critical conception of matter, by contrast, is incompatible with the physical monadologies developed by both the Leibnizian-Wolffians and his own earlier self—and, most important in the present connection, with the properly Leibnizian conception of substance as well. For detailed discussion of Kant's earlier physical monadology, in relation to both his critical conception and his evolving divergence from Leibniz, see Friedman, *Kant's Construction*.

25 For further discussion of the interconnections among quantity of matter, mechanical moving force, and momentum in the *Metaphysical Foundations* see Friedman, *Kant's Construction*, chapter 3. Kant reformulates the principle of the permanence of substance in the second edition of the *Critique* as a quantitative conservation law (B224): "In all change of the appearances substance is permanent, and its quantum in nature is neither increased nor diminished." This echoes the corresponding proposition in the *Metaphysical Foundations* (4, 541): "In all changes of corporeal nature the total quantity of matter remains the same, neither increased nor diminished."

which Kant's theory of experience is providing a metaphysical foundation is Newtonian physics—and, indeed, a foundation for this physics
in which gravitational attraction at a distance (and thus causal action
at a distance) is enthusiastically embraced.[26]

We have now reached the heart of the matter. In his lifelong attempt
to find a middle ground between the Leibnizian and Newtonian
positions—between the "metaphysical" and "mathematical"
approaches to nature—Kant always embraced Newtonian rather than
Leibnizian physics. And he gradually came to see, in the critical period, that only *transcendental* idealism, in which "the form of intuition (as a subjective constitution of sensibility) precedes all matter"
(A267/B323), can possibly do justice to the scientific cognition of the
natural world that Newton had in fact achieved. For Newton begins
his argument in the *Principia* by presupposing that (Euclidean) geometry is true of real (physical) space—at least throughout the Solar
System. On the basis of this presupposition and his Axioms or Laws of
Motion, which govern the (physical) concepts of mass, force, and (true
or absolute) motion, Newton is then able to derive the law of universal
gravitation from the initial "Phenomena" described by Kepler's laws
of planetary motion and, at the same time, to establish the center of
mass of the Solar System as the privileged state of rest relative to which
all true motions therein are to be defined. Newton's achievement, for
Kant, is paradigmatic of scientific cognition of nature, and Kant aims,
in the *Metaphysical Foundations*, to give it a metaphysical foundation—
that is, to explain, on the basis of the categories or pure concepts of the
understanding, how this kind of knowledge is possible.[27]

---

26 In sharp contrast to Newton's much more cautious attitude, Kant's understanding of Newtonian
physics involved an enthusiastic embrace of action at a distance throughout his career: see the introduction to Friedman, *Kant's Construction*, and compare Friedman, "Newton and Kant."

27 I discuss Kant's "metaphysical" reinterpretation of Newton's argument for universal gravitation in great detail in Friedman, *Kant's Construction*; see the introduction to Immanuel Kant,
Metaphysical Foundations of Natural Science, ed. and trans. Michael Friedman (Cambridge,
UK: Cambridge University Press, 2004), for a shorter and more accessible account. Kant
reinterprets what he calls "absolute space," in particular, as a limiting idea of reason—as the never
to be arrived at ideal endpoint of a procedure for moving (in accordance with Newton's argument)

Kant's explanation substitutes his own three Laws of Mechanics—
the conservation of the total quantity of matter, inertia, and the
equality of action and reaction—for Newton's Laws of Motion, and
Kant takes these laws to realize or instantiate the three Analogies of
Experience established in the first *Critique*: the principles governing
the categories of substance, causality, and interaction or community. What is most important, as I have emphasized, is that the pure
concepts in question are spatiotemporally schematized here: the quantity of substance is given by the aggregate of movable matter continuously filling a given space; causality pertains to changes in the quantity
of motion (momentum) in a body effected by a second body spatially
external to the first; interaction or community pertains to the relations of coexistence or simultaneity between spatially distant bodies
throughout the whole of (physical) space. So universal gravitation,
as a genuine action at a distance throughout this space, is a paradigmatic realization of the category of community.[28] Similarly, as I have

---

from our parochial perspective here on the surface of the earth to the center of mass of the Solar
System, and from there (in accordance with Kant's own speculative extrapolation) to the center of
mass of the Milky Way galaxy, the center of mass of a rotating system of such galaxies, and so on
ad infinitum. This reinterpretation of absolute space is reflected in an important footnote (A429/
457) to the antithesis of the First Antinomy in the *Critique*, which concerns the extent of the
phenomenal world in space and time. I discuss this footnote, in relation to absolute space in the
Metaphysical Foundations, in Friedman, *Kant's Construction*, 156–59.

28 This is important, not only because Leibnizian physics explicitly rejects such action at a distance
and restricts all physical interaction to impact, but also because of the way in which Leibniz's
own metaphysical foundation for this physics builds an analogous restriction into the more fundamental monadic level. For example, in Gottfried Wilhelm Leibniz, "Specimen Dynamicum,
pro admirandis Naturae legibus circa Corporum vires et mutuas actiones detegendis, et ad causas
revocandis," *Acta Eruditorum, publicata Lipsiae, Calendis Aprilis* (1695): 145–57, translated as
Gottfried Wilhelm Leibniz, "A Specimen of Dynamics," ed. and trans. L. E. Loemker, in *Gottfried
Wilhelm Leibniz: Philosophical Papers and Letters*, 2nd ed. (Dordrecht: Reidel, 1969), 435–52,
Leibniz grounds the phenomenal forces of inertia, *vis motrix* (momentum), and *vis viva* (kinetic
energy)—which together explain interaction by (perfectly elastic) impact—in more fundamental
(passive and active) powers exercised in the realm of non-spatiotemporal noumenal substances
of which the spatiotemporal realm of matter and motion is a well-founded phenomenon. And at
the noumenal or monadic level, more generally, there are no causal interactions among substances
at all, but only a preestablished harmony that coordinates their causally independent unfolding.
Kant discusses the doctrine of preestablished harmony briefly in the Amphiboly, sandwiched between discussions of substance and space and time, under the rubric of the *community of substances*
(A330–31/B274–75).

also emphasized, the category of substance, which is the most fundamental purely intellectual concept for Leibniz, can find nothing at all
ultimately simple and self-subsistent in its application to natural phenomena.[29] As Kant puts it in his Solution of the Second Antinomy,
phenomenal substance—the only kind of substance that can be an object of (theoretical) cognition for us—is merely "a permanent image of
sensibility, and it is nothing but an intuition, in which there is nowhere
anything unconditioned to be found" (A525–26/B553–54).

In sum, Kant's critical conception of transcendental idealism is
based on two fundamental ideas, both of which made perfectly good
sense in his eighteenth-century intellectual context. The first, the argument from geometry, depends on Kant's conviction that geometry is a
synthetic rather than analytic a priori science. Although Leibniz, for
one, did not share this conviction, I believe that Kant's view, all things
considered, was perhaps more reasonable at the time—given the essentially constructive proof-procedure of Euclid's *Elements* together
with the very limited state of eighteenth-century logical theory.[30] And
from Kant's view it does follow, in accordance with the Transcendental
Exposition added to the second edition of the *Critique*, that our representation of space is an (a priori) intuition rather than a concept.
Moreover, given the extant Newtonian and Leibnizian conceptions
of the nature of space and time themselves, it is similarly reasonable
for Kant to conclude that they just are the corresponding intuitive

29 The concept of substance, for the critical Kant, corresponds to nothing truly substantial in inner
sense either, that is, in our self-conscious experience of our own inner states. Here Kant diverges
fundamentally from Leibniz (and Descartes) by arguing that our pure self-consciousness or pure
apperception reveals, by the argument of the Paralogisms of Pure Reason, no actual object that
could be self-subsistent, substantial, or ultimately simple. And by the argument of the Refutation
of Idealism, all substance whatsoever must be realized in space. I discuss these points, in relation
to both the *Metaphysical Foundations* and the *Critique*, in the conclusion of Friedman, *Kant's
Construction*.

30 For my most recent discussion of this issue see Michael Friedman, "Synthetic History
Reconsidered," in *Discourse on a New Method: Reinvigorating the Marriage of History and
Philosophy of Science*, ed. M. Domski and M. Dickson (Chicago: Open Court, 2010), 571–813,
specifically 585–99.

representations—so that intellectually conceived things in themselves (if there are such) are not spatiotemporal at all.

Yet this conclusion by no means amounts to the critical doctrine of transcendental idealism. It was already fully present in the precritical *Inaugural Dissertation* (1770), and it is very close, in any case, to Leibniz's own doctrine of phenomena and noumena, of the sensible and intelligible worlds. In the *Inaugural Dissertation*, however, there was as yet no clear connection between our sensible and intellectual knowledge. There was no basis for concluding that knowledge of purely intellectual noumena is impossible, and, more generally, there was no conception of the necessary schematism of the pure concepts of the understanding in terms of our spatiotemporal intuition—the only kind of intuition of which we human beings are capable. It was only in the *Critique of Pure Reason* (1781/1787) that Kant was able to demonstrate (at least to his own satisfaction) that and how the purely intellectual concepts of substance, causality, community, and so on function as a priori conditions underlying the possibility of all human experience of the sensible world.[31] And an equally important negative conclusion then followed. Such purely intellectual concepts or categories have objective (theoretical) meaning and significance only when applied to objects of our experience in the sensible world; they do not have such meaning and significance when one attempts also to apply them to (putative) supersensible objects such as God and the soul.[32]

---

31 Thus the Transcendental Deduction of the Categories—which was completely rewritten in the second edition—is an essential part of the critical doctrine of transcendental idealism. I discuss aspects of the second edition version, in relation to Kant's conception of space and geometry, in Michael Friedman, "Space and Geometry in the B Deduction," in *Kant's Philosophy of Mathematics, Vol. 1: The Critical Philosophy and Its Background*, ed. C. Posey and O. Rechter (Cambridge, UK: Cambridge University Press, forthcoming).

32 Rae Langton, *Kantian Humility: Our Ignorance of Things in Themselves* (Oxford: Clarendon Press, 1998) interprets Kant's doctrine of "our ignorance of things in themselves" as deriving from a fundamentally Leibnizian conception of substance involving only the *intrinsic* properties of a thing—properties holding independently of a thing's relations to others. She bases this interpretation on a clear and illuminating discussion of Kant's precritical writings, which she then extrapolates into the critical period. For Langton, then, the ignorance in question does not depend on any special features of space and time, but only on the fact that sensibility, for Kant, is receptive—so that it

Nevertheless, it is equally important to Kant that pure intellectual concepts can have objective meaning and reality from a purely
practical point of view. According to the *Critique of Practical
Reason* (1788), in particular, the three principal ideas of pure practical reason—God, Freedom, and Immortality—all acquire such
meaning and reality in relation to our own immediate experience
of the moral law as authoritatively binding on our will. The idea of
Freedom acquires it directly from the immediate experience in question. The other two ideas, God and Immortality, then acquire it indirectly, as necessary presuppositions or postulates for the possibility
of our achieving (or at least continuously approximating) the highest
end of morality: the realization of an ideal moral community of all
human beings (a Kingdom of Ends) here on the surface of the earth.
In the case of these ideas, therefore, although they forever elude our
theoretical cognition, we do have a well-grounded rational faith or
belief in their objective reality—although, once again, only from a
purely practical point of view. It is precisely this that Kant has in
mind in the Preface to the second edition of the *Critique* when he
famously asserts that he had to "deny *knowledge* [*Wissen*] in order to
make room for *faith* [*Glauben*]" (Bxxx).[33]

So it is especially striking, finally, that Kant also finds a purely
practical reinterpretation of the Newtonian doctrine of divine omnipresence throughout all of infinite space. I explained at the beginning of this essay how Kant, in the Aesthetic, rejects the alternative

---

therefore essentially involves an *extrinsic* relation of a thing to us. On the present interpretation,
by contrast, Kant's transcendental idealism is not only based on the radically new conception of
space and time as pure forms of sensible intuition that first emerges in 1770, but also (and most
important) on the distinctively critical doctrine of the schematism of the pure concepts of the understanding that only emerges in 1781.

33 Thus Kant's denial of the possibility of theoretical cognition of the supersensible is precisely what
opens up the possibility for a distinctive kind of practical cognition (Bxxix–xxx): "I can thus not
even *assume* [*annehmen*] God, Freedom and *Immortality* on behalf of the necessary practical use of
my reason, if I do not, at the same time, *deprive* [*benehme*] speculative reason of its pretension to
extravagant insights."

Newtonian conception of space largely because of its commitment to this doctrine. I also suggested (in note 26) that Kant's conception of the extent of the material universe in space in the First Antinomy is closely connected to his reinterpretation of the Newtonian conception of absolute space as a framework for determining true motions. In an important footnote appended to the General Remark to the Third Part of *Religion within the Limits of Reason Alone* (1793) Kant then describes a "sublime analogy" between the (theoretical) community of all matter in space due to universal gravitation and the (purely practical) ideal moral community of all rational (human) beings on the surface of the earth:

> When Newton represents [the universal gravitation of all matter in the world] as, so to speak, divine universal presence in the appearance (*omnipaesentia phenomenon*), this is not an attempt to explain it (for the existence of God in space contains a contradiction), but rather a sublime analogy, in which it is viewed merely as the unification of corporeal beings into a world-whole, in so far as we base this upon an incorporeal cause. The same would happen in the attempt to comprehend the self-sufficient principle of the unification of the rational beings in the world into an ethical state and to explain the latter from the former. We know only the duty that draws us towards this; the possibility of the intended effect, even when we obey this [duty], lies entirely beyond the limits of all our insight. (6, 138–39)

Thus here, once again, Kant's complex and multilayered conception of transcendental idealism has both a positive and a negative aspect within the realm of theoretical cognition. His "metaphysical" explanation of the possibility of Newton's paradigmatic theoretical achievement amounts, at the same time, to a rejection of the doctrine of divine omnipresence—which Kant takes to be Newton's own attempt to achieve "extravagant insight" into the supersensible. Yet Kant also finds, from a purely practical point of view, a legitimate (analogical) use for this same Newtonian doctrine in effectively directing us toward the very highest ends of morality.

Reflection

NON-EUCLIDEAN GEOMETRY

Jeremy Gray

༜

Non-Euclidean geometry grew out of a centuries' long
investigation in many different mathematical cultures of the
grounds for accepting the geometry described in Euclid's
Elements. The *Elements* is not necessarily to be read as a
mathematical description of physical space. It is incompatible
with the Ptolemaic universe, and we have no evidence that it
was intended as anything other than what it is: a largely formal
account of elementary geometry in two or three dimensions,
together with three books on properties of the integers. Some of
it is very sophisticated, and other parts are a confusing mixture of
precise definitions and tacitly assumed beliefs.

The problematic feature that concerns us here is one of Euclid's
assumptions in book 1, that if two lines cross a third and make
angles on the same side of that third line that add up to less than
two right angles, then those lines will meet (on the same side
of the line as the angles have been taken). In the presence of the
other assumptions in the *Elements* many useful results follow; for

Jeremy Gray, *Non-Euclidean Geometry*. In: *Space*. Edited by: Andrew Janiak, Oxford University Press
(2020). © Oxford University Press.
DOI: 10.1093/oso/9780199914104.003.0013

example, if the angles two lines make with a third sum to two right angles, then the two lines never meet—they are said then to be parallel. In particular, the three angles in any triangle sum to two right angles, and the Pythagorean theorem can be proved. Now if this assumption about lines is dropped, none of these results can be proved, and geometers are left with little to say. On the other hand, there is no good reason to believe the assumption, which makes statements about lines meeting indefinitely far away, well beyond what can be checked.

The assumption, generally called the parallel postulate, was made the subject of many investigations that typically hoped to derive it as a theorem from the other assumptions made by Euclid. However, the best analyses succeeded only in showing that some other assumption would do equally well but had no greater claim on anyone than the parallel postulate itself. For example, one might assume that the curve everywhere equidistant to a straight line was itself a straight line, but this too was not self-evidently correct. Or one could assume that the angle sums of triangles were two right angles, or that it was possible to make exact scale copies of figures of different sizes. These assumptions, taken together with the other assumptions of Euclid's *Elements,* do imply the parallel postulate, but they remain assumptions.

Nonetheless, these investigations provoked some profound questions about geometry. What motions are allowed in geometry, for example? Islamic scholars (Ibn al-Haytham and Umar Khayyam) debated whether one may move a figure along a straight line and have it trace out another straight line. Western scholars (Wallis and Lagrange) wondered if the existence of similar figures of different sizes was not a fundamental fact about the universe worthy of being assumed.

The breakthrough came at the start of the nineteenth century,
when, for reasons that are still only imperfectly understood, people
began to believe that a different geometry might be possible,
one in which the angle sums of triangles were always less than
two right angles, and in which two lines that never meet cross
a third and make angles that sum to less than two right angles.
The two men who published accounts of the new geometry were
Nicolai Ivanovich Lobachevskii in Russia and Janos Bolyai in
Hungary. Both men described their results in strikingly similar
terms, although they worked completely independently, and both
men met with such dismal receptions that they died believing
they had failed. Both men could have had much more support
from Carl Friedrich Gauss, who was in a position to influence
others and understood and accepted their work, but that too was
insufficiently given.

Bolyai and Lobachevskii took the view that it was necessary to
describe a three-dimensional geometry if it was to have any chance
of convincing people that it could be a logically valid alternative
description of physical space, a status Euclidean geometry had
attained after the work of Newton. Both took the same novel
definition of the parallel line to a given line in a given plane and
passing through a given point in the plane: it is the line that
separates all the lines that meet the given line from all the lines
that never meet the given line. There are always two such lines, one
in each direction, and these two parallel lines get arbitrarily close
to the given line but never meet it. Both men found a surface in
their three-dimensional space upon which Euclidean geometry
was true, just as in Euclidean geometry we have spheres on which
spherical geometry is true. Both were able to play off these various
geometries until they could express their findings in the language of
trigonometry. Both concluded that it was henceforth an empirical
question as to whether geometry was correctly described by
Euclidean or non-Euclidean geometry.

Many reasons have been put forward to explain why the new geometry was not immediately accepted, among them a supposed stranglehold of Kantian philosophy, and it is almost certainly the case that Kant believed that space had to be considered as Euclid's *Elements* presented it. But the circumstances of the original publications, the lack of support from Gauss, and the profound challenge it presented to centuries of belief and successful practice were also factors. What changed opinions was the posthumous discovery of Gauss's sympathy for the new work and, paradoxically, the discovery by Riemann in Germany and Beltrami in Italy that Gauss's own ideas of geometry could be deepened to provide a much more rigorous and persuasive account than Bolyai and Lobachevskii had themselves been able to present.

The crucial idea that these men seized on independently was that a geometry is a systematic account of such concepts as lengths and angles, straight and curved lines, and lines of shortest length between their points. Gauss had showed that these questions can be posed about a surface without regard for any three-dimensional space in which it may exist. Riemann and Beltrami, in different ways, showed that this approach could be extended to geometries in higher dimensions. In particular, the non-Euclidean geometries of Bolyai and Lobachevskii could be given coherent accounts in this framework, and emerged as geometries in spaces of what is called constant negative curvature. What Riemann, Beltrami, and after them Poincaré did was to describe a geometry by giving a map of it, much as maps of the earth are depicted in an atlas. The consistency of that description was enough to establish the existence of the new geometry.

It is often, and correctly, remarked that the emergence of a new geometry, as plausible as Euclid's but different in its theorems, spelled the end for the idea that Euclidean geometry was the only true geometry and that it could be known a priori. Henceforth, any claim about the nature of space would have to contain a modicum of empirical findings. It is also true that the new geometry marked the end, for a time, of the idea of geometry as an axiomatic subject, and Euclid's *Elements* was subject to a renewed level of criticism that found many gaps and inconsistencies. However, by 1900 Hilbert, as well as several Italian mathematicians, had done much to restore axiomatic systems to geometry. In Hilbert's case, consistency of these systems was provided by giving them arithmetic (coordinate) models and led to deeper questions about the consistency of arithmetic itself. Nonetheless, the framework for geometry provided by Gauss, Riemann, and their successors, known as differential geometry because it grew out of sophisticated applications of the calculus to geometry, changed the way people regarded geometry. Fifty years later the most successful theory of physical space (or rather of space-time), Einstein's general theory of relativity, was written precisely in the language of differential geometry that Riemann had done so much to promote.

Einstein's ideas show, of course, that we are no longer restricted to a straight choice between two accounts of the geometry of space. Nor indeed, in the late nineteenth century, was there ever much doubt that of the two, Euclidean geometry would be the useful one. But the new geometry did dislodge the old one from its unique place and open new questions about what it is for an account of space to be true. Riemann himself was very clear that it had become the business of mathematics to propose many accounts of geometry, and by implication of other topics, to the scientific community, and no longer could mathematics be regarded as a passive description of simple truths. Gradually, and not just because of these geometrical discoveries, the gap widened between true mathematics and proven mathematics, and the view prevailed that all one could ask of a piece of mathematics was that it be self-consistent. This was, for example, Hilbert's view in his disputes with Frege.

What had begun as an inquiry into a possible weakness in
Euclid's *Elements* became the source of two of the fundamental
ideas of modern mathematics: that there are geometries of
spaces other than the one imagined in ancient and even everyday
geometry, and that many mathematical theories, not only in
geometry but in algebra and analysis, can be fully axiomatized.

Reflection

A MATHEMATICAL SCULPTOR'S PERSPECTIVE
ON SPACE

George Hart

❦

Geometrical notions of space provide me, a mathematician-sculptor, with a frame of r]eference for embedded objects. I work with both the physical space that my body and my sculpture inhabit and also the various idealized spaces which are landscapes for the mathematical imagination. My work starts out as visualizations in one of many possible idealized spaces, perhaps a hyperbolic space, a projective space, or a four-dimensional space. One of my methods is to choose objects I feel are worthy of physical existence and *transcribe* them in some way from a space in my mind's eye to a piece of matter that can survive in the space of the physical world.

I use the word "transcribe" as a musician might, thinking here of one of the many commonalities between mathematics and music. A musical piece originally written for one instrument may be transcribed for another instrument or ensemble of instruments. A faithful transcription preserves some essential character of the original while adapting to the tonal and dynamic space of the new instrument. In a deeper sense, I feel the original composer

George Hart, *A Mathematical Sculptor's Perspective on Space*. In: *Space*. Edited by: Andrew Janiak, Oxford University Press (2020). © Oxford University Press.
DOI: 10.1093/oso/9780199914104.003.0014

transcribes musical ideas from a musical space of his or her imagination to a score which embeds the music in the space of some particular instrumentation. In an analogous way, I transcribe ideas from a mathematical space to sculpture in physical space.

Figure R7.1 shows a wood sculpture, *SuperFrabjous*, which originated from a relationship I noticed between the compound of five tetrahedra and the orderly tangle of six pentagons. These exist in ordinary Euclidean three-space, so it is not difficult to make a physical transcription. My artistic choices include the curves I chose, the wood material, and the use of color to distinguish planar surfaces from darker edges. But Euclidean three-space is just one source of inspiration.

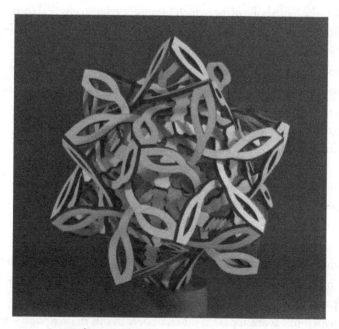

FIGURE R7.1. *SuperFrabjous*, wood, 30 cm.

A major revolution in the history of mathematics developed
from the nineteenth century discoveries of non-Euclidean
and higher-dimensional geometries. Mathematics is no longer
focused on quantitative and geometric properties of the physical
world. Mathematicians now feel their job is to explore any set of
assumptions they wish and develop their logical consequences
into a consistent structure. If the resulting system of ideas is rich,
insightful, and elegant (according to a mathematical aesthetic
which one learns to appreciate in the process of becoming a
mathematician), then the resulting structure is "good" mathematics.
Hyperbolic space is one of the notions which developed in this way
and has entered the repertoire of mathematical culture.

My sculpture *Echinodermania*, shown in Figure R7.2, derives
from uniform tessellations in two-dimensional hyperbolic space,
i.e., the hyperbolic plane, which I transcribed into physical form.
Simply put, hyperbolic space can be intuitively described as having
"a lot more room" than Euclidean space. Four squares exactly fit
together around a point in the Euclidean plane, as one infers by
looking at tiled floors or ceilings. But in the hyperbolic plane, one
can fit five squares around each point, or more. Much more. In a
geometer's imagination, this provides a rich canvas for fantastic
creations.

The Poincaré disk is a standard technique for mapping the
hyperbolic plane to an ordinary, flat circle. But as a sculptor, my
goal in creating *Echinodermania* was to make something nonplanar,
something fundamentally three dimensional. I ended up using a
nonlinear helical mapping of the Poincaré disk to create a 3D form
that I consider visually engaging as a sculpture. The pattern of holes
in Figure R7.2 is subtle, but a mathematical eye will see a regular
pattern to how the holes meet. Holes which are congruent in
hyperbolic space appear as different sizes in this transcription—an
unavoidable consequence of the differences between hyperbolic
and Euclidean space.

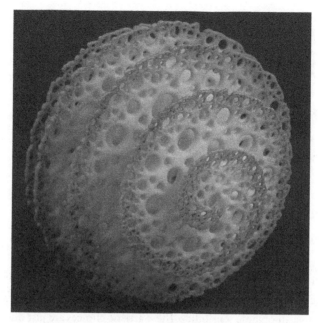

FIGURE R7.2. *Echinodermania,* nylon, 3D printed, dyed, 11 cm.

Figure R7.3 shows a sculpture based on a four-dimensional object
called the *120-cell.* In three-dimensional space there are five regular
convex polyhedra, called the Platonic solids. Euclid's *Elements*
culminates in a proof that there are only five. Plato used them in
a proto-chemistry theory based on conservation of triangles in
which the four classical elements and the universe are associated
with the five solids. But in 1852, Ludwig Schlafli discovered that in
four-dimensional space there are six analogous objects. Subsequent
mathematicians have explored many properties of structures in
higher-dimensional spaces. With practice, one can visualize a great
variety of beautiful higher-dimensional forms. Of the regular
4D polytopes, my favorite is the 120-cell, comprising 120 regular
dodecahedra, three around each edge. Transcribing the 120-cell to
our physical three-dimensional space might be done in many ways.

FIGURE R7.3. *120-Cell* (detail), nylon, 3D printed, dyed, 9 cm.

For the sculpture in Figure R7.3, I used a Schlegel projection of the edges, adjusted the proportions by eye, and smoothed the surface to give an organic sensibility. These artistic choices are just one possibility; I have revisited this form many times.

As a final example, Figure R7.4 shows *Mermaid's Delight*. One aspect of its internal coherence is that all of its surfaces are spherical. I designed it using a process called *central inversion*. This operation effectively turns space inside out, swapping points near the origin with points near infinity. This technique is not commonly used by sculptors, but is natural to mathematicians accustomed to thinking about projective space, in which a well-defined "point at infinity" is available to be swapped with the origin. Again, the mathematician's comfortable habitation of a variety of abstract spaces provides a foundation for transcribing conceptual objects into physical forms.

A separate aspect of my work process is the struggle between coordinate-based and coordinate-free spaces. The space in Euclid's *Elements* has no origin and no preferred axial directions. An object in Euclidean space is not at any specifiable place in that space, and

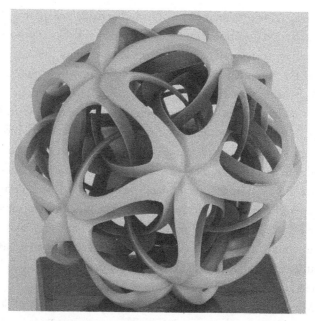

FIGURE R7.4. *Mermaid's Delight,* color 3D printed, 20 cm.

it has no orientation relative to empty space. This is an elegant way to think about objects in space because it minimizes assumptions. Contrast this with Descartes's notion of a coordinate-based space. Each point has coordinates which place it at a specific location in Cartesian space. The axes determine special directions; e.g., a cube randomly placed in Cartesian space is more difficult to visualize than a cube aligned with the axes. That mental baggage is not present when one visualizes a cube in Euclidean space. I generally think of my sculpture as living in an isotropic space with no origin and no preferred directions, but as a practical matter the methods I use to represent objects in computer software are coordinate-based. So while computer software is an essential tool in my work, it also imposes notions of position and orientation that are ultimately artificial from the artistic perspective.

To be more precise, the idea of sculpture living in a space with no preferred directions applies strongly to handheld sculpture that one might turn about to explore from all directions. But larger works are mounted or suspended in some permanent manner, which means they inhabit a space with one special direction. Gravity defines a special *up* direction which the designer (and often the viewer) must understand as central to issues of tension, compression, and support. One should walk around any large sculpture, because a successful work should be interesting from all sides. On a scale of familiar human-size objects, such as sculptures at the surface of the earth, the ambient space is neither isotropic, like Euclidean space, nor fully directionalized, like Cartesian space. I inhabit a special kind of sculptural space, with no standard mathematical equivalent, in which gravity defines a special Z direction but X and Y are not distinguishable.

My sculpting hands are prisoners of this physical space, while my mind is free to explore an infinity of abstract spaces. Enriched by a long history of mathematical creations, I command an inventory of mathematical spaces in which to visualize lovely objects. Via sensitive transcription, I hope to create worthy sculpture in which anyone can see something of the beauty I see in the spaces of my mind's eye.

Bibliography

LITERATURE BEFORE 1900

Abbot, Thomas K. *Sight and Touch: An Attempt to Disprove the Received (or Berkeleian) Theory of Vision.* London: Longman, Green, 1864.

de Aguilón, François. *Opticorum Libri Sex: Philosophis iuxta ac Mathematicis Utiles.* Antwerp: Plantin, 1613.

Albert of Saxony. *Quaestiones super quatuor libros Aristotelis de celo et mundo.* In *Quaestiones et decisiones physicales insignium virorum.* Edited by George Lokert. Vaenundantur in aedibus Iodoci Badii Ascensii & Conradi Resch, 1518.

Alberti, Leon Battista. *Leon Battista Alberti: On Painting. A New Translation and Critical Edition.* Cambridge, UK: Cambridge University Press, 2011.

Aristotle. *Aristotle's Physics: A Revised Text.* Edited by W. D. Ross. Oxford: Clarendon Press, 1936.

Aristotle. *Aristotle's Physics, Books III and IV.* Edited by Edward Hussey. Oxford: Oxford University Press, 1983.

Aristotle. *Complete Works of Aristotle.* Edited by Jonathan Barnes. Princeton, NJ: Princeton University Press, 1984.

Aristotle. *Physikvorlesung*. Translated by Hans Wagner. Berlin: Akademie
    Verlag, 1995.

Bacon, Francis. *A briefe discourse, touching the happie vnion of the kingdomes of
    England, and Scotland Dedicated in private to his Maiesti*. London, 1603.

Bacon, Francis. *The Major Works*. Edited by Brian Vickers. Oxford: Oxford
    University Press, 1996.

Bacon, Roger. *Roger Bacon and the Origins of Perspectiva in the Middle Ages: Bacon's
    Perspectiva*. Edited and translated by David C. Lindberg. Oxford: Clarendon
    Press, 1996.

Barrow, Isaac. *The Usefulness of Mathematical Learning*. London: Austen, 1734.

Berkeley, George. *An Essay towards a New Theory of Vision*. 1709; Dublin: Rhames
    and Papyat, 1732.

Berkeley, George. *Philosophical Works, Including the Works on Vision*. Edited by
    Michael Ayers. London: Dent, 1975.

Berkeley, George. *The Theory of Vision Vindicated and Explained*. London: J.
    Tonson, 1733.

Berkeley, George. *A Treatise Concerning the Principles of Human Knowledge*.
    Dublin: Rhames and Papyat, 1710.

Boscovich, Roger. *Philosophiae Naturalis Theoria*. Prostat Viennae
    Austriae: Officina Libreria Kaliwodiana, 1758.

Boscovich, Roger. *Philosophiae Naturalis Theoria*. Translated by J. M. Child.
    Cambridge, MA: MIT Press, 1966.

Boyle, Robert. "Some specimens of an attempt to make chymical experiments
    useful to illustrate the notions of the corpuscular philosophy." In *The Works of the
    Honourable Robert Boyle*. 6 vols. London, 1772.

Boyle, Robert. *The Works of Robert Boyle*. Edited by Michael Hunter and Edward
    Davis. London: Pickering and Chatto, 1999.

Bradwardine, Thomas. *De Causa Dei Contra Pelagium*. London: Henry Savile, 1618;
    reprint, Frankfurt am Main: Minerva, 1964.

Bradwardine, Thomas. *Tractatus de Proportionibus: its significance for
    the development of mathematical physics*. Edited by H. L. Crosby.
    Madison: University of Wisconsin Press, 1966.

Bradwardine, Thomas. *Geometria Speculativa*. Edited and translated by George
    Molland. Stuttgart: Franz Steiner Verlag Wiesbaden, 1989.

Brahe, Tycho. *Astronomiae instauratae mechanica*. Wandsbeck, 1598.

Buridan, John. *Subtillisimae Quaestiones super octo Physicorum libros Aristoteles*.
    Paris: Petrus le Dru impensis Dionysii Roce, 1509; reprint, Frankfurt am
    Main: Minerva, 1964.

Buridan, John. *Metaphysicales Quaestiones breves*. Paris, Iodicus Badius, 1518; reprint,
    Frankfurt am Main: Minerva, 1964.

Buridan, John. *Quaestiones super libris quattuor De Caelo et Mundo.* Cambridge, MA: Mediaeval Academy of America, 1942; reprint, New York: Kraus Reprint, 1970.

Buridan, John. *Quaestiones super libros Physicorum.* In *John Buridan's Tractatus de Infinito, Quaestiones super libros Physicorum secundum ultimam lecturam, Liber III, Quaestiones 14–19, an edition with an introduction and indexes.* Edited by J. M. M. H. Thijssen. Nijmegen: Ingenium, 1991.

Buridan, John. *Quaestiones super libros Physicorum secundum ultimam lecturam,* Libri III- IV. Edited by Michiel Streiger and Paul J. M. M. Bakker. Leiden: Brill, 2016.

Buridan, John. *Quaestiones super octo physicorum libros Aristotelis.* Paris, 1509; reprint, Frankfurt am Main, 1964.

Buridan, John. *John Buridan's Tractatus de Infinito, Quaestiones super libros Physicorum secundum ultimam lecturam, Liber III, Quaestiones 14 – 19, an edition with an introduction and indexes.* Edited by J. M. M. H. Thijssen. Nijmegen: Ingenium Publishers, 1991.

Charleton, Walter. *Physiologia Epicuro-Gassendo-Charltoniana.* London, 1654.

Chaucer, Geoffrey. *The Parlement of Foulys.* Edited by D.S. Brewer. New York: Barnes and Noble, 1960.

Clarke, Samuel. *A Demonstration of the Being and Attributes of God.* Edited by Ezio Vailati. Cambridge, UK: Cambridge University Press, 1998.

Descartes, René. *Discours de la methode pour bien conduire sa raison, & chercher la verité dans les sciences: Plus la dioptrique, les meteores, et la geometrie, qui sont des essais de cete methode.* Leiden: Maire, 1637.

Descartes, René. *Discourse on Method, Optics, Geometry, and Meteorology.* Translated by Paul J. Olscamp. New York: Bobbs-Merrill, 1965.

Descartes, René. *L'Homme et un traitté de la formation du fœtus du mesme autheur.* Edited by Claude Clerselier. Paris: Charles Angot, 1664; 2nd edition, Paris: Theodore Girard, 1677.

Descartes, René. *Oeuvres de Descartes.* Edited by Charles Adam and Paul Tannery. Paris: Vrin, 1910.

Descartes, René. *Discourse on Method, Optics, Geometry, and Meteorology.* Translated by Paul J. Olscamp. New York: Bobbs-Merrill, 1965.

Descartes, René. *Treatise on Man.* Edited and translated by Thomas Steele Hall. Cambridge, MA: Harvard University Press, 1972.

Diels, Hermann, and Walther Kranz. *Die Fragmente der Vorsokratiker.* 6th edition. Berlin: Weidmannsche Verlagsbuchhandlung, 1951.

Euclid. *Optica & Catoptica.* Translated by John Pena. Paris: Wechel, 1557.

Euclid. "The *Optics* of Euclid." Translated by Harry Edwin Burton. *Journal of the Optical Society of America* 35 (1945): 357–72.

Euclid. *The Thirteen Books of the Elements*. Edited and translated by Thomas Heath. New York: Dover, 1956.

Galilei, Galileo. *Two New Sciences*. Translated by Henry Crew and Alfonso de Salvio. New York: Dover, 1914.

Gerard of Brussels. *Liber de Motu*. In *The* Liber de motu *of Gerard of Brussels*. Edited and translated by Marshall Clagett. In *Archimedes in the Middle Ages*, vol. 5. Philadelphia: American Philosophical Society, 1984.

Hesiod. *The Homeric Hymns and Homerica*. Translated by Hugh Evelyn-White. Loeb Classical Library. Cambridge, MA: Harvard University Press, 1967.

Hesiod. *Theogony, Works and Days, Testimonia*. Edited and translated by Glenn Most. Loeb Classical Library. Cambridge, MA: Harvard University Press, 2018.

Heytesbury, William. *Regule Solvendi Sophismatum*. Venice, 1494.

Hobbes, Thomas. *The Elements of Philosophy, the First Section, Concerning Body*. Edited by William Molesworth. London, 1839.

Hobbes, Thomas. *The English Works of Thomas Hobbes*. London: John Bohn, 1839–45.

Ibn al-Haytham. *The Optics of Ibn Al-Haytham. Books I–III: On Direct Vision*. London: Warburg Institute, University of London, 1989.

Ibn al-Haytham. *Opticae*. In *Opticae Thesaurus: Alhazeni Arabis Libri Septem; De Crepusculis et Nubium Ascensionibus; Vitellonis Thuringopoloni Libri X*. Edited by Friedrich Risner. Basel: Episcopate, 1572; reprint, New York: Johnson, 1972.

Kant, Immanuel. *Kants gesammelte Schriften*. Berlin: de Gruyter, 1902–.

Kant, Immanuel. *Critique of Pure Reason*. Edited and translated by Paul Guyer and Allen Wood. Cambridge, UK: Cambridge University Press, 1998.

Kant, Immanuel. *Metaphysical Foundations of Natural Science*. Edited and translated by Michael Friedman. Cambridge, UK: Cambridge University Press, 2004.

Kepler, Johannes. *Ad Vitellionem Paralipomena, quibus Astronomiae Pars Optica Traditur*. Frankfurt: Claudius Marnius and Ioannes Aubrius, 1604.

Kepler, Johannes. *Ad Vitellionem Paralipomena, quibus Astronomiae Pars Optica Traditur*. In *Gesammelte Werke*, vol. 2. Edited by Franz Hammer. Munich: Beck, 1939.

Kepler, Johannes. *Dioptrice*. Augsburg: David Franke, 1611; reprint, Cambridge, UK: Heffer, 1962.

Kepler, Johannes. *Optics: Paralipomena to Witelo and Optical Part of Astronomy*. Edited and translated by William H. Donahue. Santa Fe, NM: Green Lion Press, 2000.

Kilvington, Richard. *The Sophismata of Richard Kilvington*, Auctores Britannici Medii Aevi, XII. Edited by Norman Kretzmann and Barbara Ensign Kretzmann. New York: Oxford University Press for the British Academy, 1990.

Landino, Cristoforo. *Comento sopra la Comedia di Dante Alighieri poeta fiorentino.* Florence, 1481.

Legendre, Adrien Marie. *Elements of Geometry.* Translated by Charles Davies. New York: American Book Company, 1890.

Leibniz, Gottfried Wilhelm. "Specimen Dynamicum." In *G. W. Leibniz: Philosophical Essays.* Edited and translated by Roger Ariew and Daniel Garber. Indianapolis, IN: Hackett, 1989.

Leibniz, Gottfried Wilhelm. "Specimen Dynamicum, pro admirandis Naturae legibus circa Corporum vires et mutuas actiones detegendis, et ad causas revocandis." *Acta Eruditorum, publicata Lipsiae, Calendis Aprilis* (1695): 145–57.

Leibniz, Gottfried Wilhelm. "A Specimen of Dynamics." Edited and translated by L. E. Loemker. In *Gottfried Wilhelm Leibniz: Philosophical Papers and Letters.* Dordrecht: Reidel, 1969.

Leibniz, G. W., and Samuel Clarke. *A Collection of Papers, which passed between the late learned Mr. Leibnitz, and Dr. Clarke, in the years 1715 and 1716.* London: Knapton, 1717.

Molyneux, William. *Dioptrica Nova.* London: Tooke, 1709.

Newton, Isaac. *Opticks.* London, 1718.

Newton, Isaac. *Philosophiae Naturalis Principia Mathematica.* London: Royal Society, 1687; 2nd edition, 1713; 3rd edition, 1726.

Newton, Isaac. *Unpublished Scientific Writings.* Edited and translated by Marie Boas Hall and Rupert Hall. Cambridge, UK: Cambridge University Press, 1962.

Newton, Isaac. *Philosophical Writings.* Edited by Andrew Janiak. 2nd edition. Cambridge, UK: Cambridge University Press, 2014.

Newton, Isaac. *The Principia: Mathematical Principles of Natural Philosophy.* Edited and translated by I. Bernard Cohen and Anne Whitman, assisted by Julia Budenz. Berkeley: University of California Press, 1999.

Oresme, Nicole. *De proportionibus proportionum & Ad pauca respicientes.* Edited by Edward Grant. Madison: University of Wisconsin Press, 1966.

Oresme, Nicole. *Der Einfluss des Nominalismus auf die Christologie der Spätscholastik nach dem Traktat de Communicatione ideomatum des Nicolaus Oresme.* Edited by Ernst Borchert. Münster: Aschendorffsche Verlagsbuchhandlung, 1940.

Oresme, Nicole. *Le livre du ciel et du monde.* Edited by A. D. Menut and A. J. Denomy. Madison: University of Wisconsin Press, 1968.

Oresme, Nicole. *Nicole Oresme and the Medieval Geometry of Qualities and Motions . . . Tractatus de configurationibus qualitatum et motuum.* Edited by Marshall Clagett. Madison: University of Wisconsin Press, 1968.

Oresme, Nicole. *Tractatus de commensurabilitate vel Incommensurabilitate mottum Coeli (Treatise on the Commensurability or Incommensurability of the Motions of the Heavens)*. Edited and translated by Edward Grant. Madison: University of Wisconsin Press, 1971.

Oresme, Nicole. *Quaestiones super De generatione et corruptione*. Edited by Stefano Caroti. Munich: Verlag der Bayerischen Akademie der Wissenschaften, 1996.

Oresme, Nicole. *Questiones super geometriam Euclidis*. Edited by Hubert L. L. Busard. Stuttgart: Franz Steiner Verlag, 2010.

Oresme, Nicole. *Questiones super Physicam (Books I–VII)*. Edited by Stefano Caroti, Jean Celeyrette, Stefan Kirschner, and Edmond Mazet. Leiden: Brill, 2013.

Pecham, John. *John Pecham and the Science of Optics: Perspectiva Communis*. Edited and translated by David C. Lindberg. Madison: University of Wisconsin Press, 1970.

Peter of Auvergne. *Questions on Aristotle's De Caelo*. Edited and translated by Griet Galle. Leuven: Leuven University Press, 2003.

Philoponus. *Corollaries on Place and Void, with Simplicius: Against Philoponus on the Eternity of the World*. Translated by David Furley and Christian Wildberg. London: Duckworth, 1991.

Plato. *Complete Works*. Edited and translated by John Cooper. Indianapolis, IN: Hackett, 1997.

Proclus. *Commentary on Plato's Timaeus, Volume III—Book 3, Part 1: Proclus on the World's Body*. Edited and translated by D. Baltzly. Cambridge, UK: Cambridge University Press, 2007.

Proclus. *Commentary on Plato's Timaeus, Volume IV—Book 3, Part 2: Proclus on the World Soul*. Edited and translated by D. Baltzly. Cambridge, UK: Cambridge University Press, 2009.

Ptolemy, Claudius. *L'Optique de Claude Ptolémée: Dans la version latine d'après l'arabe de l'émir Eugène de Sicile*. Edited by Albert Lejeune. Leiden: Brill, 1989.

Ptolemy, Claudius. *Ptolemy's Theory of Visual Perception: An English Translation of the Optics*. Edited and translated by Mark A. Smith. Philadelphia: American Philosophical Society, 1996.

Robert of Chester. *Robert of Chester's Redaction of Euclid's Elements, the so-called Adelard II version*. Edited by Hubert L. L. Busard and Menso Folkerts. Basel: Birkhäuser Verlag, 1992.

Rohault, Jacques. *System of Natural Philosophy*. Translated by Samuel Clarke. 1671; London: Knapton, 1735.

Sextus Empiricus. *Against the Physicists*. Edited and translated by Richard Bett. Cambridge, UK: Cambridge University Press, 2012.

Sextus Empiricus. *Sexti Empirici Opera*. Volume Two. Edited by Hermann
Mutschmann. Teubner: Leipzig, 1914.

Simplicius. *Corollaries on Place and Time*. Translated by J. O. Urmson. Ancient
Commentators on Aristotle. London: Duckworth, 1992.

Sprat, Thomas. *The History of the Royal Society of London, for the Improving of
Natural Knowledge*. London, 1702.

Tourtual, Caspar Theobald. *Die Sinne des Menschen in den wechselseitigen
Beziehungen ihres psychischen und organischen Lebens: Ein Beitrag zur
physiologischen Aesthetick*. Münster: Coppenrath, 1827.

William of Ockham. *Expositio in Libros Physicorum Aristotelis*. In *Opera
Philosophica*. Vol. 5. Edited by R. Wood et al. Allegany, NY: St. Bonaventure
University, 1985.

William of Ockham. *Opera theologica*. Vol. 9. Edited by R. Wood et al. Allegany,
NY: St. Bonaventure University, 1980.

William of Ockham. *Expositio in Libros Physicorum Aristotelis*. In *Opera
Philosophica*, volume 5. Edited by R. Wood et al. Allegany, NY: St. Bonaventure
University Press, 1985.

Witelo. *Perspectiva*. In *Opticae thesaurus: Alhazeni Arabis libri septem; De
Crepusculis et nubium ascensionibus; Vitellonis Thuringopoloni libri X*. Edited
by Friedrich Risner. Basel: Episcopate, 1572; reprint, New York: Johnson
Reprint, 1972.

Witelo. *Witelonis perspectivae liber primus, or Book I of Witelo's Perspectiva*. Edited
and translated by Sabetai Unguru. Wroclaw: Ossolineum, 1977.

Witelo. *Witelonis perspectivae liber secundus et liber tertius, or Books II and
III of Witelo's Perspectiva*. Edited and translated by Sabetai Unguru.
Wroclaw: Ossolineum, 1991.

Wolff, Christian. *Cosmologia generalis methodo scientifica pertractata*.
Frankfurt: Renger, 1731. Emended edition, 1737.

LITERATURE AFTER 1900

Abu-Lughod, Lila. "Do Muslim Women Really Need Saving? Anthropological
Reflections on Cultural Relativism and Its Others." *American Anthropologist* 104,
no. 3 (2002): 783–90.

Adams, R. M. *Leibniz: Determinist, Theist, Idealist*. Oxford: Oxford University
Press, 1994.

Algra, Keimpe. "Concepts of Space in Classical and Hellenistic Greek Philosophy."
PhD dissertation, University of Utrecht, 1988.

Algra, Keimpe. *Concepts of Space in Greek Thought*. Leiden: Brill, 1994.

Allison, H. E. *Kant's Transcendental Idealism: An Interpretation and Defense.* New Haven, CT: Yale University Press, 1983. Revised edition, 2004.

Alloula, Malek. *The Colonial Harem.* Minneapolis: University of Minnesota Press, 1986.

Arana, Andrew, and Paolo Mancosu. "On the Relationship between Plane and Solid Geometry." *Review of Symbolic Logic* 5, no. 2 (2012): 294–353.

Arnzen, R. "Wie Mißt Man den Göttlichen Kreis? Phantasievermögen, Raumvorstellung und Geometrischer Gegenstand in Den Mathematischen Theorien Proclus', Al-Fārābīs und Ibn Al-Haythams." In *Imagination—Fiktion—Kreation: Das Kulturschaffende Vermögen Der Phantasie.* Munich: Saur Verlag, 2003.

Arthur, Linda B. *Religion, Dress and the Body.* Oxford: Berg, 1999.

Atherton, Margaret. *Berkeley's Revolution in Vision.* Ithaca, NY: Cornell University Press, 1990.

Averlino, Antonio [Filarete]. *Filarete's Treatise on Architecture.* Translated by John Spencer. New Haven, CT: Yale University Press, 1965.

Bakker, Paul. "Aristotelian Metaphysics and Eucharistic Theology: John Buridan and Marsilius of Inghen on the Ontological Status of Accidental Being." In *The Metaphysics and Natural Philosophy of John Buridan.* Edited by J. M. M. H. Thijssen and J. Zupko. Leiden: Brill, 2001.

Bakker, Paul J.M.M., and Sander W. De Boer. "Locus est Spatium: On Gerald Odonis, "Quaestio de loco," *Vivarium* 47, nos. 2-3 (2000): 294–330.

Barnes, Jonathan. *The Presocratic Philosophers.* London: Routledge, 1982.

Barolsky, Paul. "Naturalism and the Visionary Art of the Early Renaissance." *Gazette des Beaux-Arts* 129 (1997): 57–64.

Barsalou, L. W. "Grounded Cognition." *Annual Review of Psycholgy* 59 (2008): 617–45.

Belting, Hans. *Florence and Baghdad: Renaissance Art and Arab Science.* Cambridge, MA: Belknap Press of Harvard University Press, 2011.

Bergmann, Ulrich. *Studie zum Aristotelischen Ort.* Unpublished manuscript. Fassung Minden, 2004.

Bertoloni Meli, Domenico. "Caroline, Leibniz and Clarke." *Journal of the History of Ideas* 60 (1999): 469–86.

Bouriau, C. "L'imagination Productrice: Descartes entre Proclus et Kant." *Littératures Classiques* 45 (2002): 47–62.

Burnyeat, Myles. "The Sceptic in His Place and Time." In *Philosophy in History.* Edited by Richard Rorty, J. B. Schneewind, and Quentin Skinner. Cambridge, UK: Cambridge University Press, 1984.

Buroker, Jill van. *Space and Incongruence.* Dordrecht: Reidel, 1981.

Burton, Harry Edwin. "The Optics of Euclid." *Journal of the Optical Society of America* 35, no. 5 (1945): 357–72.

Callard, Felicity J. "The Body in Theory." *Environment and Planning D: Society and Space* 16, no. 4 (1998): 387–400.

Carnap, Rudolf. *Der Raum: Ein Beitrag zur Wissenschaftslehre*, Kant-Studien Ergänzungshefte 56 (Berlin: Reuther and Reichard, 1922).

Carnap, Rudolf. *Space: a Contribution to the Theory of Science*. In *The Collected Works of Rudolf Carnap: Volume I: Early Writings*. Edited by Richard Creath. Oxford: Oxford University Press, 2019.

Carriero, John. "Newton on Space and Time: Comments on J. E. McGuire." In *Philosophical Perspectives on Newtonian Science*. Edited by Phillip Bricker and R. I. G. Hughes. New Haven, CT: Yale University Press, 1990.

Chlup, R. *Proclus: An Introduction*. Cambridge, UK: Cambridge University Press, 2012.

Claessens, G. "Proclus: Imagination as a Symptom." *Ancient Philosophy* 32, no. 2 (2012): 393–406.

Clagett, Marshall. *The Science of Mechanics in the Middle Ages*. Madison: University of Wisconsin Press, 1961.

Clay, Diskin. "The World of Hesiod." *Ramus* 21, no. 2 (1992): 131–55.

Cohen, I. B., and Alexandre Koyré. "Newton and the Leibniz-Clarke Correspondence." *Archives Internationales d'Histoire Des Sciences* 15 (1962): 63–126.

Cushing, James. *Philosophical Concepts in Physics*. Cambridge, UK: Cambridge University Press, 1998.

De Risi, Vincenzo. *Geometry and Monadology: Leibniz's Analysis Situs and Philosophy of Space*. Basel: Birkhäuser, 2007.

De Risi, Vincenzo. *Leibniz on the Parallel Postulate and the Foundations of Geometry*. Cham, Switzerland: Springer International, 2016.

DiSalle, Robert. *Understanding Spacetime*. Cambridge, UK: Cambridge University Press, 2006.

Domski, Mary. "Newton and Proclus: Geometry, Imagination, and Knowing Space." *Southern Journal of Philosophy* 50, no. 3 (2012): 389–413.

Dörrie, H., and M Baltes. *Der Platonismus in Der Antike: Grundlagen—System— Entwicklung. Band VIa Die Philosophische Lehre Des Platonismus: Von Der "Seele" Als Der Ursache Aller Sinvollen Abläufe*. Stuttgart: Frommann-Holzboog, 2002.

Droppers, Garrett. "The Questiones de Spera of Nicole Oresme. Latin Text with English Translation, Commentary and Variants." PhD dissertation, University of Wisconsin, 1966.

Duhem, Pierre. *Etudes sur Leonard de Vinci: Ceux qu'il a lus et ceux qui l'ont lu*. Vol. 2. Reprint. Paris: F. De Nobele, 1955.

Duhem, Pierre. *Le système du monde: Histoire des doctrines cosmologiques de Platon à Copernic*. Vol. 1. Paris: Hermann, 1959.

Earman, John. *World Enough and Spacetime*. Cambridge, MA: MIT Press, 1989.

Edgerton, Samuel. *The Renaissance Rediscovery of Linear Perspective.* New York: Basic Books, 1978.

Ferretti, Gabriel. "Pictures, Action Properties and Motor Related Effects." *Synthese* 193, no. 12 (2016): 3787–817.

Finamore, J. F. *Iamblichus and the Theory of the Vehicle of the Soul*. Chico, CA: Scholar's Press, 1985.

Finamore, J. F. "Iamblichus on Light and the Transparent." In *The Divine Iamblichus: Philosopher and Man of Gods*. Edited by Hans Blumenthal and E. G. Clark. Bristol, UK: Bristol Classical Press, 1993.

Finamore, J. F., and E. Kutash. "Proclus on the Psychè: World Soul and the Individual Soul." In *All from One: A Guide to Proclus*. Edited by Pieter d'Hoine and Marije Martijn. Oxford: Oxford University Press, 2016.

Force, James. *William Whiston: Honest Newtonian*. Cambridge, UK: Cambridge University Press, 1985.

Van Fraasen, Bas. *An Introduction to the Philosophy of Time and Space.* New York: Random House, 1970.

Friedman, Michael. *Foundations of Space-time Theories*. Princeton, NJ: Princeton University Press, 1983.

Friedman, Michael. *Kant's Construction of Nature: A Reading of the Metaphysical Foundations of Natural Science*. Cambridge, UK: Cambridge University Press, 2013.

Friedman, Michael. "Newton and Kant on Absolute Space: From Theology to Transcendental Philosophy." In *Constituting Objectivity: Transcendental Perspectives on Modern Physics*. Edited by M. Bitbol, P. Kerszberg, and J. Petitot. Berlin: Springer, 2009.

Friedman, Michael. "Space and Geometry in the B Deduction." In *Kant's Philosophy of Mathematics. Vol. 1: The Critical Philosophy and Its Background*. Edited by C. Posey and O. Rechter. Cambridge, UK: Cambridge University Press, forthcoming.

Friedman, Michael. "Synthetic History Reconsidered." In *Discourse on a New Method: Reinvigorating the Marriage of History and Philosophy of Science*. Edited by M. Domski and M. Dickson. Chicago: Open Court, 2010.

Galison, Peter, and Emily Ann Thompson, eds. *The Architecture of Science.* Cambridge, MA: MIT Press, 1999.

Gallese, Vittorio, and George Lakoff. "The Brain's Concepts: The Role of the Sensory-Motor System in Conceptual Knowledge." *Cognitive Neuropsychology* 22, nos. 3–4 (2005): 455–79.

Gelber, Hester Goodenough. *It Could Have Been Otherwise: Contingency and Necessity in Dominican Theology at Oxford, 1300–1350*. Leiden: Brill, 2004.

Glasner, Ruth. *Averroes' Physics: A Turning Point in Medieval Natural Philosophy.* Oxford: Oxford University Press, 2009.

Gökarıksel, Banu. "Beyond the Official Sacred: Religion, Secularism and the Body in the Production of Subjectivity." *Social and Cultural Geography* 10 (2009): 657–74.

Gökarıksel, Banu. "The Intimate Politics of Secularism and the Headscarf: The Mall, the Neighborhood, and the Public Square in Istanbul." *Gender, Place and Culture* 19 (2012): 1–20.

Gökarıksel, Banu, and Anna Secor. "'Even I Was Tempted': The Moral Ambivalence and Ethical Practice of Veiling-Fashion in Turkey." *Annals of the Association of American Geographers* 102, no. 4 (2012): 847–62.

Gökarıksel, Banu, and Anna Secor. "The Veil, Desire, and the Gaze: Turning the Inside Out." *Signs: Journal of Women in Culture and Society* 40, no. 1 (2014): 177–200.

Gordon, Deborah M. *Ant Encounters: Interaction Networks and Colony Behavior.* Princeton, NJ: Princeton University Press, 2010.

Grant, Edward. "Medieval and Seventeenth-Century Conceptions of an Infinite Void Space beyond the Cosmos." *Isis* 60, no. 1 (1969): 39–60.

Grant, Edward. *Much Ado about Nothing: Theories of Space and Vacuum from the Middle Ages to the Scientific Revolution.* Cambridge, UK: Cambridge University Press, 1981.

Grant, Edward. *Planets, Stars, and Orbs: The Medieval Cosmos, 1200–1687.* Cambridge, UK: Cambridge University Press, 1994.

Griffin, M. "Proclus on Place as the Luminous Vehicle of the Soul." *Dionysius* 30 (2012): 161–86.

Groh, Jennifer M. *Making Space: How the Brain Knows Where Things Are.* Cambridge, MA: Harvard University Press, 2014.

Grünabum, Adolf. *Philosophical Problems of Space and Time.* New York: Knopf, 1963.

Haas, F. A. J. De. *John Philoponus' New Definition of Prime Matter: Aspects of Its Background in Neoplatonism and the Ancient Commentary Tradition.* Leiden: Brill, 1997.

Hannaway, Owen. "Laboratory Design and the Aim of Science: Andreas Libavius versus Tycho Brahe." *Isis* 77, no. 4 (1986): 585–610.

Hansen, Bert. *Nicole Oresme and the Marvels of Nature: A Study of His De causis mirabilium with Critical Edition, Translation, and Commentary.* Toronto: Pontifical Institute of Mediaeval Studies, 1985.

Harari, O. "Methexis and Geometrical Reasoning in Proclus' Commentary on Euclid's Elements." *Oxford Studies in Ancient Philosophy* 30 (2006): 361–89.

Harari, O. "Proclus' Account of Explanatory Demonstrations in Mathematics and Its Context." *Archiv für Geschichte der Philosophie* 90, no. 2 (2008): 137–64.

Hatfield, Gary. "The Cognitive Faculties." In *Cambridge History of Seventeenth Century Philosophy*. Edited by Michael Ayers and Daniel Garber. Cambridge, UK: Cambridge University Press, 1998.

Hatfield, Gary. *The Natural and the Normative: Theories of Spatial Perception from Kant to Helmholtz*. Cambridge, MA: MIT Press, 1990.

Hatfield, Gary. "Natural Geometry in Descartes and Kepler." *Res Philosophica* 92 (2015): 117–48.

Hatfield, Gary. "Perception as Unconscious Inference." In *Perception and the Physical World: Psychological and Philosophical Issues in Perception*. Edited by Dieter Heyer and Rainer Mausfeld. New York: John Wiley and Sons, 2002.

Hatfield, Gary. "Phenomenal and Cognitive Factors in Spatial Perception." In *Visual Experience*. Edited by Gary Hatfield and Sarah Allred. Oxford: Oxford University Press, 2012.

Hatfield, Gary. "Philosophy of Perception and the Phenomenology of Visual Space." *Philosophic Exchange* 42 (2011): 31–66.

Hatfield, Gary, and William Epstein. "The Sensory Core and the Medieval Foundations of Early Modern Perceptual Theory." *Isis* 70 (1979): 363–84.

Hauk, O., I. Johnsrude, and F. Pulvermuller. "Somatotopic Representation of Action Words in Human Motor and Premotor Cortex." *Neuron* 41 (2004): 301–7.

Helmig, Christoph. "Aristotle's Notion of Intelligible Matter." *Quaestio* 7 (2007): 53–78.

Helmig, Christoph. *Forms and Concepts: Concept Formation in the Platonic Tradition*. Berlin: De Gruyter, 2012.

Henry, John. "The Reception of Cartesianism." In *The Oxford Handbook of British Philosophy in the Seventeenth Century*. Edited by Peter Anstey. Oxford: Oxford University Press, 2013.

Holden, Thomas. *The Architecture of Matter: Galileo to Kant*. Oxford: Clarendon Press, 2004.

Holden, Thomas. "Robert Boyle on Things above Reason." *British Journal for the History of Philosophy* 15, no. 2 (2007): 283–312.

Holloway, Julian. "Make-believe: Spiritual Practice, Embodiment, and Sacred Space." *Environment and Planning A* 35, no. 11 (2003): 1961–74.

Holloway, Julian, and Oliver Valins. "Placing Religion and Spirituality in Geography." *Social & Cultural Geography* 3, no. 1 (2002): 5–9.

Hopp, Walter. "No Such Look: Problems with the Dual Content Theory." *Phenomenology and Cognitive Science* 12 (2013): 813–33.

Huffman, C. A. *Philolaus of Croton: Pythagorean and Presocratic. A Commentary on the Fragments and Testimonia with Interpretive Essays*. Cambridge, UK: Cambridge University Press, 1993.

Inwood, Brad. "The Origin of Epicurus' Concept of Void." *Classical Philology* 76 (1981): 273–85.

Jammer, Max. *Concepts of Space: The History of Theories of Space in Physics.* North Chelmsford, MA: Courier, 2013. Reprint.

Johansen, T. K. *The Intellect and the Limits of Naturalism.* Oxford: Oxford University Press, 2012.

Kahn, Charles. *Anaximander and the Origins of Greek Cosmology.* New York: Columbia University Press, 1960.

Kemp, Martin. "Science, Non-Science, and Nonsense: The Interpretation of Brunelleschi's Perspective." *Art History* 1, no. 2 (1978): 134–61.

Kiefer, Markus, and Friedemann Pulvermüller. "Conceptual Representations in Mind and Brain: Theoretical Developments, Current Evidence and Future Directions." *Cortex* 48, no. 7 (2012): 805–25.

Kim, Mi Gyung. *Affinity, That Elusive Dream: A Genealogy of the Chemical Revolution.* Cambridge, MA: MIT Press, 2003.

Kim, Mi Gyung. "Constructing Symbolic Spaces: Chemical Molecules in the Académie des Sciences." *Ambix* 43, no. 1 (1996): 1–31.

Kim, Mi Gyung. "A Historical Atlas of Objectivity." *Modern Intellectual History* 6, no. 3 (2009): 569–96.

Kim, Mi Gyung. "Labor and Mirage: Writing the History of Chemistry." *Studies in History and Philosophy of Science* 26, no. 1 (1995): 155–65.

Kirk, Geoffrey Stephen, John Earle Raven, and Malcolm Schofield, eds. *The Presocratic Philosophers: A Critical History with a Selection of Texts.* Cambridge, UK: Cambridge University Press, 1983.

Kirschner, Stefan. *Nicolaus Orsemes Kommentar zur Physik des Aristoteles.* Contains Oresme's *Questiones Super Physicam* Book III, Qu. 1-17; Qu. IV.1-21, and Qu. V.6-9. Sudhoffs Archiv Beihefte 39. Stuttgart: Franz Steiner Verlag, 1997.

Kirschner, Stefan. "Oresme's Concepts of Place, Space and Time in his Commentary on Aristotle's *Physics*." *Oriens-Occidens: Cahiers du Centre d'Histoire des sciences et de philosophie arabes et médiévales* 3 (2000): 145–79.

Kirschner, Stefan. "Nicole Oresme." *The Stanford Encyclopedia of Philosophy.* Edited by Edward Zalta. 2009.

Knorr, Wilbur. "The Geometry of Burning-Mirrors in Antiquity." *Isis* 74, no. 1 (1983): 53–73.

Knuuttila, Simo. "Positio impossibilis in Medieval Discussions of the Trinity." In *Vestigia, imagines, verba: Semiotics and Logic in Medieval Theological Texts (XIIth.–XIVth. Century).* Edited by Costantino Marmo and Jean Jolivet. Turnhout: Brepols, 1997.

Koffka, Kurt. *Principles of Gestalt Psychology.* New York: Harcourt Brace, 1935.

Koyré, Alexandre. *From the Closed World to the Infinite Universe*. Baltimore, MD: Johns Hopkins University Press, 1957.

Koyré, Alexandre. "Le vide et l'espace infini au XIVᵉ siècle." *Archives d'histoire doctrinale et littéraire du moyen âge* 17 (1949): 45–91.

Kuhn, Thomas. *The Copernican Revolution: Planetary Astronomy in the Development of Western Thought*. Cambridge, MA: Harvard University Press, 1957.

Lacey, S., R. Stilla, and K. Sathian. "Metaphorically Feeling: Comprehending Textural Metaphors Activates Somatosensory Cortex." *Brain Language* 120 (2012): 416–21.

Lakoff, George, and Mark Johnson. "Conceptual Metaphor in Everyday Language." *Journal of Philosophy* 77, no. 8 (1980): 453–86.

Lakoff, George, and Mark Johnson. *Metaphors We Live By*. Chicago: University of Chicago Press, 1980.

Langton, Rae. *Kantian Humility: Our Ignorance of Things in Themselves*. Oxford: Clarendon Press, 1998.

Lautner, P. "The Distinction between Phantasia and Doxa in Proclus' *In Timaeum*." *Classical Quarterly* 52 (2002): 257–69.

Lee, J., and J. M. Groh. "Different Stimuli, Different Spatial Codes: A Visual Map and an Auditory Rate Code for Oculomotor Space in the Primate Superior Colliculus." *PLoS One* 9 (2014): e85017.

Lejeune, Albert. *Euclide et Ptolémée: Deux stades de l'optique géométrique grecque*. Louvain: Bibliothèque de l'Université, 1948.

Lennox, James G. "'As If We Were Investigating Snubness': Aristotle on the Prospects for a Single Science of Nature." *Oxford Studies in Ancient Philosophy* 35 (2008): 149–86.

Lernould, A. "Imagination and Psychic Body: Apparitions of the Divine and Geometric Imagination according to Proclus." In *Gnosticism, Platonism and the Late Ancient World. Essays in Honour of John D. Turner*, edited by Kevin Corrigan et al. Leiden: Brill, 2013.

Lindberg, David C. *Theories of Vision from al-Kindi to Kepler*. Chicago: University of Chicago Press, 1976.

LoLordo, Antonia. *Pierre Gassendi and the Birth of Early Modern Philosophy*. Cambridge, UK: Cambridge University Press, 2007.

Longhurst, Robyn. "The Body and Geography." *Gender, Place & Culture* 2, no. 1 (1995): 97–106.

Longhurst, Robyn. *Bodies: Exploring Fluid Boundaries*. London: Routledge, 2001.

Longhurst, Robyn. "(Dis)embodied Geographies." *Progress in Human Geography* 21, no. 4 (1997): 486–501.

MacIsaac, D. G. "Phantasia between Soul and Body in Proclus' Euclid Commentary." *Dionysius* 19 (2001): 125–36.

Malet, Antoni. "Isaac Barrow on the Mathematization of Nature: Theological Voluntarism and the Rise of Geometrical Optics." *Journal of the History of Ideas* 58 (1997): 265–87.

Manetti, Antonio. *The Life of Brunelleschi.* College Park: Pennsylvania State University Press, 1970.

Marchia, Francisci de. *Reportatio IIA: Quaestiones in secundum librum Sententiarum, QQ. 13–27.* Edited by Tiziana Suarez-Nani, William Duba, Emmanuel Babey, and Girard J. Etzkorn. Leuven: Leuven University Press, 2010.

Marston, Sallie A. "The Social Construction of Scale." *Progress in Human Geography* 24, no. 2 (2000): 219–42.

Marston, Sallie A., John Paul Jones, and Keith Woodward. "Human Geography without Scale." *Transactions of the Institute of British Geographers* 30, no. 4 (2005): 416–32.

Martijn, M. *Proclus on Nature: Philosophy of Nature and Its Methods in Proclus' Commentary on Plato's Timaeus.* Leiden: Brill, 2010.

Martin, J. Christopher. "Impossible *positio* as the Foundation of Metaphysics, or, Logic on the Scotist Plan?" In *Vestigia, Imagines, Verba: Semiotics and Locis in Medieval Theological Texts (XIIth–XIVth century).* Edited by Costantino Marmo. Turnhout: Brepols, 1997.

Martin, Christopher J. "Non-reductive Arguments from Impossible Hypotheses in Boethius and Philoponus." *Oxford Studies in Ancient Philosophy* 17 (1999): 279–302.

Massey, Doreen. *For Space.* London: Sage, 2005.

Massey, Doreen. *Space, Place, and Gender.* London: John Wiley & Sons, 2013.

Maull, Nancy. "Cartesian Optics and the Geometrization of Nature." In *Descartes: Philosophy, Mathematics and Physics.* Edited by Stephen Gaukroger. Totowa, N.J.: Barnes and Noble Books, 1980.

McGuire, J. E. "Predicates of Pure Existence: Newton on God's Space and Time." In *Philosophical Perspectives on Newtonian Science.* Edited by Phillip Bricker and R. I. G. Hughes. New Haven, CT: Yale University Press, 1990.

Mendell, Henry. "Topoi on Topos: The Development of Aristotle's Concept of Place." *Phronesis* 32 (1987): 206–31.

Mendell, Henry. "What's Location Got to Do with It? Place, Space, and the Infinite in Classical Greek Mathematics." In *Mathematizing Space: The Objects of Geometry from Antiquity to the Early Modern Age.* Edited by Vincenzo De Risi. Basel: Birkhäuser, 2015.

Mendelsohn, J. Andrew. "Alchemy and Politics in England 1649–1665." *Past & Present* 135 (1992): 30–78.

Miller, David M. *Representing Space in the Scientific Revolution*. Cambridge, UK: Cambridge University Press, 2014.

Mitrović, B. 2015. "Leon Battista Alberti, Mental Rotation, and the Origins of Three-Dimensional Computer Modeling." *Journal of the Society of Architectural Historians* 74, no. 3 (2015): 312–22.

Mueller-Jourdan, P. *Gloses et Commentaire Du Livre XI Du Contra Proclum de Jean Philopon: Autour de La Matière Première Du Monde*. Philosophia Antiqua 125. Leiden: Brill, 2011.

Moran, Bruce T. *Andreas Libavius and the Transformation of Alchemy: Separating Chemical Cultures with Polemical Fire*. Sagamore Beach, MA: Science History Publications, 2007.

Morison, Benjamin. *On Location: Aristotle's Concept of Place*. Oxford: Oxford University Press, 2002.

Morrow, G. R. *Proclus: A Commentary on the First Book of Euclid's Elements, Translated with Introduction and Notes*. 2nd edition. Princeton, NJ: Princeton University Press, 1992.

Newman, William R. "Alchemical Symbolism and Concealment: The Chemical House of Libavius." In *The Architecture of Science*. Edited by Peter Galison and Emily Thompson. Cambridge, MA: MIT Press, 1999.

Nicholson, Marjorie. "The Early Stages of Cartesianism in England." *Studies in Philology* 26 (1929): 356-74.

Nieder, A., and S. Dehaene. "Representation of Number in the Brain." *Annual Review of Neuroscience* 32 (2009): 185–208.

Nikulin, D. *Matter, Imagination and Geometry: Ontology, Natural Philosophy and Mathematics in Plotinus, Proclus and Descartes*. Ashgate, 2002.

Nikulin, D. "Imagination and Mathematics in Proclus." *Ancient Philosophy* 28, no. 1 (2008): 153–72.

Núñez, Rafael. "On the Science of Embodied Cognition in the 2010s: Research Questions, Appropriate Reductionism, and Testable Explanations." *Journal of the Learning Sciences* 21, no. 2 (2012): 324–36.

O'Meara, D. J. *Pythagoras Revived*. Oxford: Clarendon Press, 1989.

Opsomer, J. "The Integration of Aristotelian Physics in a Neoplatonic Context: Proclus on Movers and Indivisibility." In *Physics and Philosophy of Nature in Greek Neoplatonism*. Edited by Riccardo Chiaradonna and Franco Trabattoni. Leiden: Brill, 2009.

Panofsky, Erwin, and Christopher Wood. *Perspective as Symbolic Form*. New York: Zone Books, 1991.

Papanek, Hanna. "Purdah in Pakistan: Seclusion and Modern Occupations for Women." *Separate Worlds*. Edited by Hanna Papanek and Gail Minault. Columbia, MO: South Asia Books, 1982.

Parodi, Massimo. *Tempo e spazio nel medioevo*. Storia della scienza 24. Turin: Loescher Editore, 1982.

Porter, Kristin Kelly, and Jennifer M. Groh. "The 'Other' Transformation Required for Visual-Auditory Integration: Representational Format." *Progress in Brain Research* 155 (2006): 313–23.

Powell, A. "Review of Markus Schmitz, *Euklids Geometrie und Ihre Mathematiktheoretische Grundlegung in Der Neuplatonischen Philosophie Des Proklos*, Würzburg: Konighausen & Neumann, 1997." *Philosophia Mathematica* 8 (2000): 339–45.

Rabouin, D. "Proclus' Conception of Geometric Space and Its Actuality." In *Mathematizing Space: The Objects of Geometry from Antiquity to the Early Modern Age*. Edited by Vincenzo DeRisi. Basel: Birkhäuser, 2015.

Reichenbach, Hans. *Relativitätstheorie und Erkenntnis apriori*. Berlin: Springer, 1920.

Reichenbach, Hans. *Philosophie der Raum-Zeit-Lehre*. Berlin: De Gruyter, 1928.

Reichenbach, Hans. *The Philosophy of Space and Time*. Translated by Maria Reichenbach and J. Freund. New York: Dover, 1957.

Reichenbach, Hans. *The Theory of Relativity and a priori Knowledge*. Translated by Maria Reichenbach. Berkeley: University of California Press, 1960.

Riel, G. Van. "Proclus on Matter and Physical Necessity." In *Physics and Philosophy of Nature in Greek Neoplatonism*. Edited by Riccardo Chiaradonna and Franco Trabattoni. Leiden: Brill, 2009.

Robert of Chester. *Robert of Chester's Redaction of Euclid's Elements, the So-called Adelard II Version*. Edited by Hubert L. L. Busard and Menso Folkerts. Basel: Birkhäuser Verlag, 1992.

Roitman, J. D., E. M. Brannon, and M. L. Platt. "Monotonic Coding of Numerosity in Macaque Lateral Intraparietal Area." *PLoS Biology* 5 (2007): e208.

Roitman, J. D., E. M. Brannon, and M. L. Platt. "Representation of Numerosity in Posterior Parietal Cortex." *Frontiers in Integrated Neuroscience* 6 (2012): 25.

Rose, Gillian. "Geography and Gender, Cartographies and Corporealities." *Progress in Human Geography* 19, no. 4 (1995): 544–48.

Ross, Helen, and Cornelis Plug. *The Mystery of the Moon Illusion: Exploring Size Perception*. Oxford: Oxford University Press, 2002.

Russell, Jeffrey Burton. *Inventing the Flat Earth: Columbus and Modern Historians*. New York: Praeger, 1991.

Russi, C. "Causality and Sensible Objects: A Comparison between Plotinus and Proclus." In *Physics and Philosophy of Nature in Greek Neoplatonism*. Edited by Riccardo Chiaradonna and Franco Trabattoni. Leiden: Brill, 2009.

Sabra, Abdelhamid I., ed. and trans. *The Optics of Ibn al-Haytham: Books I–III. On Direct Vision, Vol. 2, Introduction, Commentary, Glossaries, Concordance, Indices*. London: Warburg Institute, 1989.

Sabra, Abdelhamid I. "Psychology versus Mathematics: Ptolemy and Alhazen on the Moon Illusion." In *Mathematics and Its Application to Science and Natural Philosophy in the Middle Ages*. Edited by Edward Grant and John Murdoch. Cambridge, UK: Cambridge University Press, 1987.

Sabra, Abdelhamid I. "Sensation and Inference in Alhazen's Theory of Visual Perception." In *Studies in Perception*. Edited by Peter Machamer and Robert Turnbull. Columbus: Ohio State University Press, 1978.

Sambursky, S. *The Concept of Place in Late Neoplatonism*. Jerusalem: Israel Academy, 1982.

Sambursky, S. "Place and Space in Late Neoplatonism." *Studies in History and Philosophy of Science* 8 (1977): 173–87.

Sarnowsky, Jürgen. *Die aristotelisch-scholastische Theorie der Bewegung: Studien zum Kommentar Alberts von Sachsen zur Physik des Aristoteles*. Münster: Aschendorff, 1989.

Sarnowsky, Jürgen. "Natural Philosophy at Oxford and Paris in the Mid-Fourteenth Century." In *From Ockham to Wyclif*. Edited by Anne Hudson and Michael Wilks. Oxford: Basil Blackwell, 1987.

Sattler, Barbara. *Space in Ancient Greek Thought*, monograph manuscript, in preparation for Cambridge University Press series "Key Themes in Ancient Philosophy."

Sattler, Barbara. "Aristotle's Measurement Dilemma." *Oxford Studies in Ancient Philosophy* 52 (2017): 257–301.

Sattler, Barbara. "A Likely Account of Necessity: Plato's Receptacle as a Physical and Metaphysical Foundation for Space." *Journal of the History of Philosophy* 50 (2012): 159–95.

Sattler, Barbara. *The Concept of Motion in Ancient Greek Thought: foundations in logic, method, and mathematics*. Cambridge: Cambridge University Press, 2020, forthcoming.

Sattler, Barbara. "Space, Place and Zeno." Unpublished manuscript.

Schabel, Chris. "The Reception of Peter Auriol's Doctrine of Place with editions of Questions by Landulph Caracciolo and Gerard of Sienna." In *Representations et conceptions de l'espace dans la culture médiévale*. Edited by T. Suarez-Nani and M. Rohde. Berlin: de Gruyter, 2011.

Schlick, Moritz. *Raum and Zeit in der gegenwärtigen Physik*. Berlin: Springer, 1917.

Schlick, Moritz. *Space and time in contemporary physics*. Translated by Henry Brose. New York: Dover, 1963.

Schrenk, L. P. "Proclus on Corporeal Space." *Archiv für Geschichte der Philosophie* 76 (1994): 151–67.

Schrenk, L. P. "Proclus on Space as Light." *Ancient Philosophy* 9, no. 1 (1989): 87–94.

Schwartz, Robert. *Vision: Variations on Some Berkeleian Themes*. Oxford: Basil Blackwell, 1994.

Schwitzgebel, Eric. "Do Things Look Flat?" *Philosophy & Phenomenological Research* 72 (2006): 589–99.

Secor, Anna J. "The Veil and Urban Space in Istanbul: Women's Dress, Mobility and Islamic Knowledge." *Gender, Place and Culture: A Journal of Feminist Geography* 9, no. 1 (2002): 5–22.

Sedley, David. "Philoponus' Conception of Space." In *Philoponus and the Rejection of Aristotelian Science*. Edited by Richard Sorabji. Ithaca, NY: Cornell University Press, 1987.

Sedley, David. "Two Conceptions of Vacuum." *Phronesis* 27 (1982): 175–93.

Senger, Hans Gerhard. "'Wanderer am Weltenrand'—ein Raumforscher um 1530? Überlegunen zu einer *peregrinatio inventiva*." In *Raum und Raumvorstellungen im Mittelalter*. Edited by Jan Aertsen and Andreas Speer. Berlin: Walter de Gruyter, 1998.

Sepkoski, David. *Nominalism and Constructivism in Seventeenth-Century Mathematical Philosophy*. London: Routledge, 2013.

Shabel, Lisa. "Apriority and Application: Philosophy of Mathematics in the Early Modern Period." In *Oxford Handbook of Philosophy of Mathematics and Logic*. Edited by Stewart Shapiro. Oxford: Oxford University Press, 2005.

Shanahan, John. "Ben Jonson's Alchemist and Early Modern Laboratory Space." *Journal for Early Modern Cultural Studies* 8, no. 1 (2008): 35–66.

Shapin, Steven. "Of Gods and Kings: Natural Philosophy and Politics in the Leibniz-Clarke Disputes." *Isis* 72, no. 2 (1981): 187–215.

Shapin, Steven. *The Scientific Revolution*. Chicago: University of Chicago Press, 1996.

Shapin, Steven, and Simon Schaffer. *Leviathan and the Air-Pump*. Princeton, NJ: Princeton University Press, 1985.

Shea, William R. *The Magic of Numbers and Motion: The Scientific Career of René Descartes*. Nantucket, MA: Science History Publications, 1991.

Sheppard, A. "The Mirror of Imagination: The Influence of Timaeus 70e ff." In *Ancient Approaches to Plato's Timaeus*. Edited by R. W. Sharples and A. Sheppard. London: Institute of Classical Studies, 2003.

Sheppard, A. *The Poetics of Phantasia: Imagination in Ancient Aesthetics*. London: Bloomsbury Academic, 2014.

Simmons, Alison. "Spatial Perception from a Cartesian Point of View." *Philosophical Topics* 31 (2003): 395–423.

Simon, Gérard. *Le Regard, l'être et l'apparence dans l'optique de l'antiquité*. Paris: Seuil, 1988.

Siorvanes, L. *Proclus: Neo-Platonic Philosophy and Science*. Edinburgh: Edinburgh
   University Press, 1996.

Sklar, Larry. *Space, Time and Spacetime*. Berkeley: University of California Press, 1974.

Smet, D. De, M. Sebti, and G. De Callataÿ. *Miroir et Savoir: La Transmission D'un
   Thème Platonicien, Des Alexandrins À La Philosophie Arabo-Musulmane. Actes
   Du Colloque International Tenu À Leuven et Louvain-La-Neuve, Les 17 et 18
   November 2005*. Leuven: Leuven University Press, 2008.

Smith, A. Mark. *From Sight to Light: The Passage from Ancient to Modern Optics*.
   Chicago: University of Chicago Press, 2015.

Smith, A. Mark. "Getting the Big Picture in Perspectivist Optics." *Isis* 72
   (1981): 568–89.

Smith, A. Mark. "Ptolemy and the Foundations of Ancient Mathematical Optics: A
   Source Based Guided Study." *Transactions of the American Philosophical Society*
   89, no. 3 (1999): 1–172.

Solmsen, Friedrich. *Aristotle's System of the Physical World*. Ithaca, NY: Cornell
   University Press, 1960.

Sorabji, Richard. *Matter, Space and Motion*. London: Duckworth, 1988.

Sorabji, Richard, ed. *Philoponus and the Rejection of Aristotelian Science*. Ithaca,
   NY: Cornell University Press, 1987.

Sorabji, Richard. *The Philosophy of the Commentators 200–600 AD: A Sourcebook.
   Volume 2: Physics*. London: Duckworth, 2004.

Spade, Paul Vincent, and Mikko Yrjönsuuri. "Medieval Theories of
   Obligationes." *Stanford Encyclopedia of Philosophy*. Edited by Edward N. Zalta.
   Winter 2017. http://plato.stanford.edu/cgi-bin/encyclopedia/archinfo.
   cgi?entry=obligationes.

Stein, Howard. "Newtonian Space-time." *Texas Quarterly* 10 (1967): 174–200.

Stein, Howard. "Newton's Metaphysics." In *The Cambridge Companion to Newton*.
   Edited by I. B. Cohen and George Smith. Cambridge, UK: Cambridge
   University Press, 2002.

Summers, David. *Real Spaces: World Art History and the Rise of Western Modernism*.
   London: Phaidon, 2003.

Summers, David. *Vision, Reflection, and Desire in Western Painting*. Chapel
   Hill: University of North Carolina Press, 2007.

Sylla, Edith. "Autonomous and Handmaiden Science: St. Thomas Aquinas and
   William of Ockham on the Physics of the Eucharist." In *The Cultural Context of
   Medieval Learning*. Edited by John Murdoch and Edith Dudley Sylla. Boston
   Studies in the Philosophy of Science, vol. 26. Dordrecht: Reidel, 1975.

Sylla, Edith. "From the Closed World to the Infinite Universe: The Evidence
   of Nicole Oresme." In *Lieu, espace, mouvement: Physique, métaphysique et*

cosmologie. Edited by T. Suarez-Nami, O. Ribordy, and A. Petagine. Collection *TEMA*, no. 86. Rome: FIDEM, 2016.

Sylla, Edith. "Guide to the Text." In John Buridan, *Quaestiones super octo libros Physicorum Aristotelis (secundum ultimum lecturam): Libri III–IV*. Edited by Michiel Streiger and Paul J. M. M. Bakker. Leiden: Brill, 2016.

Sylla, Edith. "'Ideo quasi mendicare oportet intellectum humanum': The Role of Theology in John Buridan's Natural Philosophy." In *The Metaphysics and Natural Philosophy of John Buridan*. Edited by J. M. M. H. Thijssen and J. Zupko. Leiden: Brill, 2001.

Sylla, Edith. "Imaginary Space: John Dumbleton and Isaac Newton." In *Raum und Raumvorstellungen im Mittelalter*. Edited by Jan Aertsen and Andreas Speer. Miscellanea Mediaevalia 25. Berlin: Walter de Gruyter, 1998.

Sylla, Edith. "John Buridan and Critical Realism," *Early Science and Medicine* 14 (2009): 211–47.

Sylla, Edith. "The Origin and Fate of Thomas Bradwardine's *De proportionibus velocitatum in motibus* in Relation to the History of Mathematics." In *Mechanics and Natural Philosophy before the Scientific Revolution*. Edited by W. R. Laird and S. Roux. Boston Studies in the Philosophy of Science. Dordrecht: Springer Verlag, 2008.

Sylla, Edith. "The Oxford Calculators' Middle Degree Theorem in Context." *Early Science and Medicine* 15 (2010): 338–70.

Sylla, Edith. "Space and Spirit in the Transition from Aristotelian to Newtonian Science." In *The Dynamics of Aristotelian Natural Philosophy from Antiquity to the Seventeenth Century*. Edited by C. H. Leijenhorst, C. H. Luethy, and J. M. M. H. Thijssen. Leiden: Brill, 2002.

Sylla, Edith. "Swester Katrei and Gregory of Rimini: Angels, God, and Mathematics in the Fourteenth Century." In *Mathematics and the Divine*. Edited by Teun Koetsier and Luc Bergmans. Amsterdam: Elsevier, 2005.

Sylla, Edith. "Averroes and Fourteenth-century Theories of Alteration: Minima Naturalia and the Distinction Between Mathematics and Physics." In *Averroes' Natural Philosophy and its Reception in the West*. Edited by Paul J. M. M. Bakker. Leuven: Leuven University Press, 2015.

Tachau, Katherine H. *Vision and Certitude in the Age of Ockham*. Leiden: Brill, 1988.

Taylor, C. C. W. *The Atomists: Leucippus and Democritus. Fragments: A Text and Translation with a Commentary*. Toronto: University of Toronto Press, 1999.

Torretti, Roberto. *The Philosophy of Physics*. Cambridge, UK: Cambridge University Press, 1999.

Trifogli, Cecilia. *Liber Quartus Physicorum Aristotelis: Repertorio della Questioni. Commenti Inglesi ca. 1250–1270*. Florence: SISMEL Edizioni del Galluzzo, 2007.

Tuan, Yi-Fu. "Humanistic Geography." *Annals of the Association of American Geographers* 66, no. 2 (1976): 266–76.

Turnbull, David. "Cartography and Science in Early Modern Europe: Mapping the Construction of Knowledge Spaces." *Imago Mundi* 48, no. 1 (1996): 5–24.

Turner, R. Steven. *In the Eye's Mind: Vision and the Helmholtz–Hering Controversy.* Princeton, NJ: Princeton University Press, 1994.

Vlastos, Gregory. "A Note on Zeno's Arrow." In *Studies in Presocratic Philosophy. Vol. 2: The Eleatics and Pluralists.* Edited by R. E. Allen and David J. Furley. London: Routledge, 1975.

Wagner, Mark. *Geometries of Visual Space.* Mahwah, NJ: Erlbaum, 2006.

Walker, Matt. "Earth News: Ant Mega-colony Takes Over World." BBC. July 1, 2009. http://news.bbc.co.uk/earth/hi/earth_news/newsid_8127000/8127519.stm.

Watson, G. *Phantasia in Classical Thought.* Galway: Galway University Press, 1988.

Weber, Bruno. "*Ubi Caelum terrae se soniungit:* Ein altertümlicher Aufriss des Weltgebäudes von Camille Flammarion." *Gutenberg Jahrbuch* 48 (1973): 381–408.

West, Martin Litchfield, ed. *Theogony: Edited with Prolegomena and Commentary.* Oxford: Clarendon Press, 1966.

Wiens, John A. "Spatial Scaling in Ecology." *Functional Ecology* 3, no. 4 (1989): 385–97.

Wilson, Margaret D. "Descartes on the Perception of Primary Qualities." In *Essays on the Science and Philosophy of René Descartes.* Edited by Stephen Voss. New York: Oxford University Press, 1993.

Winnington-Ingram, R. P. "Note Du Professeur Winnington-Ingram Sûr 251.29 Ss." In *Proclus Commentaire Sûr Le Timée.* Vol. 5. Paris: Vrin, 1968.

Wittkower, Rudolf. "Brunelleschi and 'Proportion in Perspective.'" *Journal of the Warburg and Courtauld Institutes* 16, nos. 3–4 (1953): 275–91.

Wolf-Devine, Celia. *Descartes on Seeing: Epistemology and Visual Perception.* Carbondale: Southern Illinois University Press, 1993.

Wolf-Devine, Celia. "Descartes' Theory of Visual Spatial Perception." In *Descartes' Natural Philosophy.* Edited by Stephen Gaukroger, John Schuster, and John Sutton. London: Routledge, 2000.

Woodward, Keith, John Paul Jones, and Sallie A. Marston. "Of Eagles and Flies: Orientations toward the Site." *Area* 42, no. 3 (2010): 271–80.

Ziggelaar, August. *François de Aguilón S.J., 1567–1617: Scientist and Architect.* Rome: Institutum Historicum, 1983.

Index

For the benefit of digital users, indexed terms that span two pages (e.g., 52–53) may, on occasion, appear on only one of those pages.

Figures are indicated by *f* following the page number

Philoponus and, 125–31
  Pythagorean notion of, 24
Vredeman de Vries, J., 178*f*

water, as basic principle, 22–23
Wiens, J., 99
Woodward, K., 53–54
World Soul, 87n.84, 88n.86

description of, 86–88
projection by, 88–91
space as vehicle of, 91–95

Zeno, 25–28
  metrical paradox, 289–90, 290n.14
  runner paradox, 26, 27n.35
  topos paradox, 25